SAFEGUARDING CHILDREN'S RIGHTS IN IMMIGRATION LAW

SAFEGUARDING CHILDREN'S RIGHTS IN IMMIGRATION LAW

Edited by
Mark KLAASSEN
Stephanie RAP
Peter RODRIGUES
Ton LIEFAARD

intersentia
Cambridge – Antwerp – Chicago

Intersentia Ltd
8 Wellington Mews
Wellington Street | Cambridge
CB1 1HW | United Kingdom
Tel.: +44 1223 736 170
Email: mail@intersentia.co.uk
www.intersentia.com | www.intersentia.co.uk

Distribution for the UK and Ireland:
NBN International
Airport Business Centre, 10 Thornbury Road
Plymouth, PL6 7PP
United Kingdom
Tel.: +44 1752 202 301 | Fax: +44 1752 202 331
Email: orders@nbninternational.com

Distribution for Europe and all other countries:
Intersentia Publishing nv
Groenstraat 31
2640 Mortsel
Belgium
Tel.: +32 3 680 15 50 | Fax: +32 3 658 71 21
Email: mail@intersentia.be

Distribution for the USA and Canada:
Independent Publishers Group
Order Department
814 North Franklin Street
Chicago, IL 60610
USA
Tel.: +1 800 888 4741 (toll free) | Fax: +1 312 337 5985
Email: orders@ipgbook.com

Safeguarding Children's Rights in Immigration Law

Artwork on cover: Aleksandar Mijatovic – Shutterstock

ISBN 978-1-78068-949-4
D/2020/7849/11
NUR 828

British Library Cataloguing in Publication Data. A catalogue record for this book is available from the British Library.

PREFACE

Children on the Move are Children in the First Place

Ton LIEFAARD*

1. 30 YEARS OF THE UN CONVENTION ON THE RIGHTS OF THE CHILD

With the adoption of the UN Convention on the Rights of the Child (UNCRC), on 20 November 1989, and its almost universal ratification 30 years later, the international community sends out a clear message to the world, which has fundamentally challenged – and continues to challenge – the way children are looked at in legal systems across the globe: each child must, first and foremost, be recognised as a human being with human rights and fundamental freedoms. This message has had far-reaching implications for domestic legal systems and the way children are treated, in theory and practice. It has resulted in the development of new legislation or the adjustment of existing law and practices, also under the influence of an emerging body of case law, internationally and nationally.[1] A growing number of studies, more general and specific ones, confirm that the UNCRC and related international and regional standards have had a significant impact on legislation, jurisprudence and policy at the domestic level.[2] The UNCRC has also generated additional standard-setting in different regions in the world, which has contributed to the development of a comprehensive, multi-level, dynamic and also complex legal framework.[3]

---

* Vice-dean of Leiden Law School and holds the UNICEF Chair in Children's Rights at Leiden University, the Netherlands.

1 Karin Arts, 'Twenty-Five Years of the United Nations Convention on the Rights of the Child: Achievements and Challenges' (2014) 61 Netherlands International Law Review 267; Ton Liefaard and Julia Sloth-Nielsen (eds.), *The United Nations Convention on the Rights of the Child: Taking Stock after 25 Years and Looking Ahead* (Brill 2017).

2 See e.g. Laura Lundy, Ursula Kilkelly and Bronagh Byrne, 'Incorporation of the United Nations Convention on the Rights of the Child in Law: A Comparative Review' (2013) 21 International Journal of Children's Rights 442.

3 Ursula Kilkelly and Ton Liefaard, 'International Children's Rights: Reflections on a Complex, Dynamic, and Relatively Young Area of Law' in Ursula Kilkelly and Ton Liefaard (eds.), *International Human Rights of Children* (Springer 2019).

Over the past 30 years, there have been serious efforts made to further develop and tailor the children's rights framework to *specific contexts* in which children live and develop, such as child protection, juvenile justice, health & biomedicine and migration; to *specific themes*, including violence against children, sexual exploitation and trafficking of children, children in armed conflict and children and digital technologies; and to *specific groups of children*, including children in conflict with the law, children as victims and witnesses and children in alternative care. As part of these efforts, the UNCRC's core notions have been upheld and elaborated upon. This is particularly true for the principle that the best interests of the child have to be a primary consideration '[i]n all actions concerning children' (Art. 3(1) UNCRC), which in the view of the UN Committee on the Rights of the Child means that these interests have 'high priority'[4] and assumes an unconditional respect for children's rights and freedoms as a baseline.[5] Other fundamental notions are the right of the child to be recognised as a member of her or his family and to be cared for by her or his parents (see the UNCRC Preamble, arts. 7, 9 and 18 UNCRC), respect for children's evolving capacities and emerging autonomy (Art. 5 UNCRC) and the right to be heard (Art. 12 UNCRC), which has developed into broader concepts such as participation and child-friendly justice.[6] A more recent development revolves around children's access to justice, which, fuelled, among others, by the adoption and entry into force of the Third Optional Protocol to the UNCRC on a communication procedure, underscores the importance of children's access to effective remedies in case of rights violations, without which children's rights have little meaning.[7] Access to justice for children can also be seen as a means to develop more just, inclusive and sustainable societies, also in light of the 2030 Sustainable Development Goals, in which children are taken seriously as actors and citizens.

Yet, persistent challenges remain,[8] one of which revolves around the (lack of) recognition that 'each child' (Art. 2(1) UNCRC) must be acknowledged as rights

---

4 UN Committee on the Rights of the Child, 'General Comment No. 14 on the right of the child to have his or her best interests taken as a primary consideration (art. 3, para. 1)' (2013) UN Doc CRC/C/GC/14, para. 39.

5 Michael Freeman, 'Article 3. The Best Interests of the Child' in André Alen and others (eds.), *A Commentary on the United Nations Convention on the Rights of the Child* (Nijhoff Publishers 2007).

6 See e.g. Aoife Daly and Stephanie Rap, 'Children's Participation in the Justice System' in Ursula Kilkelly and Ton Liefaard (eds.), *International Human Rights of Children* (Springer 2019).

7 Ton Liefaard, 'Access to Justice for Children: Towards a Specific Research and Implementation Agenda' (2019) 27 International Journal of Children's Rights 195; UN Committee on the Rights of the Child, 'General Comment No. 5: General measures of implementation of the Convention on the Rights of the Child (arts. 4, 42 and 44, para. 6)' (2003) UN Doc CRC/GC/2003/5.

8 See e.g Karin Arts, 'Twenty-Five Years of the United Nations Convention on the Rights of the Child: Achievements and Challenges' (2014) 61 Netherlands International Law Review 267.

holder under the international human rights framework and that states should not unlawfully or arbitrarily limit the legal protection children are entitled to under international law. In this regard, it must be acknowledged that many children suffer from this lack of recognition. One could think of girls, children living in street situations, children deprived of liberty, children with (mental) disabilities, children belonging to indigenous communities, among many others. These children belong to the most stigmatised groups of children in societies across the globe, and they may be subjected to rights violations, because of their low status or lack of visibility in society, including the lack of protection against violence and exploitation, international protection, statelessness, denial of access to basic services, education and health care, and unlawful or arbitrary deprivation of liberty. Children on the move constitute such a group as well and also run the risk of being disregarded and denied adequate rights protection, despite the wealth of international instruments targeted at this protection, at the costs of their right to be regarded as children with human rights in the first place.[9]

2. CHILDREN ON THE MOVE

Today, millions of children are on the move worldwide and, although this is not a new phenomenon, its scale is without precedent.[10] Children are fleeing conflicts and wars. They move with or without their parents to attain a better future. Throughout the migration process, children find themselves in a particularly vulnerable position. Children may find themselves and their family without lawful residence in the state they reside in. As a result of unlawful

---

9 See UN Committee on the Protection of the Rights of All Migrant Workers and Members of their Families and Committee on the Rights of the Child, 'Joint General Comment No. 3 of the Committee on the Protection of the Rights of All Migrant Workers and Members of their Families and No. 22 of the Committee on the Rights of the Child on the general principles regarding the human rights of children in the context of international migration' (2017) UN Doc CMW/C/GC/3-CRC/C/GC/22; UN Committee on the Protection of the Rights of All Migrant Workers and Members of their Families and Committee on the Rights of the Child, 'Joint General Comment No. 4 of the Committee on the Protection of the Rights of All Migrant Workers and Members of their Families and No. 23 of the Committee on the Rights of the Child on State obligations regarding the human rights of children in the context of international migration in countries of origin, transit, destination and return' (2017) UN Doc CMW/C/GC/4-CRC/C/GC/23; see also UN Committee on the Rights of the Child, 'General Comment No. 6: Treatment of Unaccompanied and Separated Children Outside their Country of Origin' (2005) Un Doc CRC/GC/2005/6; see also the various contributions in this book.

10 Ciara Smyth, 'Migration, Refugees, and Children's Rights' in Ursula Kilkelly and Ton Liefaard (eds.), *International Human Rights of Children* (Springer 2019), 422 with reference to UNICEF, *Uprooted: The growing crisis for refugee and migrant children* (UNICEF 2016); UNHCR, *Global Trends: Forced Displacement in 2018* (UNHCR 2018).

residence, children are often deprived of or restricted in their liberty.[11] Unaccompanied or separated children, who are dependent on (legal) guardians, are vulnerable to human trafficking and exploitation; sometimes even with involvement of their family.[12] Another significant issue relating to the legal protection of children in immigration law is the prevention of statelessness and the protection of the human rights of stateless children.[13] Recent data of the United Nations High Commissioner for Refugees (UNHCR) suggest that in 2018 111,000 unaccompanied and separated child refugees were reported and that around 27,600 unaccompanied and separated children sought asylum on an individual basis.[14] The UNHCR warns, however, that these numbers are likely to be significant underestimates. Children formed about half of the refugee population in 2018. In its 2016 report on refugee and migrant children, UNICEF reported that '[a]round the world, almost 50 million children have migrated across borders or been forcibly displaced', again a conservative estimate;[15] 28 million boys and girls have fled from violence and insecurity. As UNICEF points out '[t]he story of child migrants and refugees is a global story, not one confined to a single region'.[16]

Despite the proliferation of children's rights worldwide and the growing acceptance of the idea of children's entitlement to special protection, also within immigration law, the focus of migration control often lies heavily on safety and security, often at the cost of adequate human rights protection and the best interests of the child serving as a primary consideration for governments, policy makers and judiciaries.[17] Given the significant numbers of migrant or refugee

---

11 See e.g. Human Rights Watch, 'Children at Risk in US Border Jails: Congress Should End Abusive Conditions' (Human Rights Watch, 20 June 2019) <http://www.hrw.org/news/2019/06/20/children-risk-us-border-jails>.

12 UN Committee on the Rights of the Child, 'General Comment No. 6: Treatment of Unaccompanied and Separated Children Outside their Country of Origin' (2005) UN Doc CRC/GC/2005/6.

13 See e.g UN Committee on the Protection of the Rights of All Migrant Workers and Members of their Families and Committee on the Rights of the Child, 'Joint General Comment No. 4 of the Committee on the Protection of the Rights of All Migrant Workers and Members of their Families and No. 23 of the Committee on the Rights of the Child on State obligations regarding the human rights of children in the context of international migration in countries of origin, transit, destination and return' (2017) UN Doc CMW/C/GC/4-CRC/C/GC/23, para. 20ff and 23ff.

14 UNHCR, *Guidelines on Assessing and Determining the Best Interests of the Child* (UNHCR 2018).

15 UNICEF, *Uprooted: The growing crisis for refugee and migrant children* (UNICEF 2016).

16 Ibid, para. 6.

17 UN Committee on the Protection of the Rights of All Migrant Workers and Members of their Families and Committee on the Rights of the Child, 'Joint General Comment No. 3 of the Committee on the Protection of the Rights of All Migrant Workers and Members of their Families and No. 22 of the Committee on the Rights of the Child on the general principles regarding the human rights of children in the context of international migration' (2017) UN Doc CMW/C/GC/3-CRC/C/GC/22.

children globally and the particular vulnerability of children on the move, this can be considered as seriously problematic.

3. ACADEMIA AND CHILDREN'S RIGHTS IN THE CONTEXT OF MIGRATION

The realities and tensions inherently related to the position of children in immigration has fuelled the development of specific policy documents, standards and case law around the protection of children who are migrating with or without their parents. In Europe, for example, the Council of Europe as well as the European Union have developed special action plans, resolutions, recommendations, communications and strategies around the protection of refugee and migrant children.[18] Regional human rights tribunals and domestic courts are increasingly asked to decide on migration-related matters affecting children.[19] Internationally, the position of migrant children has become the subject of many communications under the Third Optional Protocol to the UNCRC and the first views that have been adopted by the CRC Committee deal with migration-related issues, including the first case which dealt with the deportation of a girl from Denmark to Somalia, where she would face an alleged risk of being forcefully subjected to female genital mutilation.[20] In addition, a growing body of jurisprudence at the international, regional and national level can be identified. In addition, there is a growing body of research on specific elements of asylum and immigration proceedings, including on the exploration of the meaning of children's rights in the context of these proceedings, conducted by academics, international and national governmental and non-governmental organisations and monitoring mechanisms.[21]

This book, which brings together a selection of scientific papers presented at the conference 'Safeguarding Children's Rights in Immigration Law', organised by the Institute of Immigration Law and the Department of Child Law at Leiden

---

18 See e.g. Council of Europe, *Council of Europe Action Plan on Protecting Refugee and Migrant Children in Europe (2017–2019)* (Council of Europe 2017); Council of Europe, *Council of Europe Strategy for the Rights of the Child (2016–2021)* (Council of Europe 2016); European Commission, 'Communication from the Commission to the European Parliament and the Council: The protection of children in migration' COM(2017) 211 final; and the many resolutions and recommendations of the Parliamentary Assembly of the Council of Europe on this matter.

19 See the different contributions to this book.

20 See Julia Sloth-Nielsen, 'Case Note 2018/1. Communication 3/2016: I.A.M. on behalf of K.Y.M. v Denmark' [2018] Leiden Children's Rights Observatory; Mark Klaassen and Peter Rodrigues, 'The Committee on the Rights of the Child on Female Genital Mutilation and Non-Refoulement' [2018] Leiden Law Blog.

21 See e.g. Ciara Smyth, 'Towards a Complete Prohibition on the Immigration Detention of Children' (2019) 19 Human Rights Law Review 1; UNHCR, *Guidelines on Assessing and Determining the Best Interests of the Child* (UNHCR 2018); and the contributions in this book.

University in November 2018, reflects the growing concern for children in immigration. It also shows the diversity of issues related to immigration and children, including family reunification, detention, participation, human trafficking and the rights of siblings in the context of migration, as well as the significance of regional legal systems and infrastructures for the protection of children in migration. While this book includes many contributions from Europe, it is important to point to the developments in other parts of the world, including Africa, South and South-East Asia and the Americas.[22] It is furthermore apparent that much of the scholarship around migration and children focuses on detention.[23] This could be explained by a genuine concern, around the world, of civil society organisations, international and domestic monitoring mechanisms, academia and also intergovernmental agencies about the widespread use of deprivation of liberty of children, and families, in reception, transit, relocation or other migration-related centres. It is fair to say that on this particular matter efforts are made to push for a higher standard than the one laid down in Article 37(b) UNCRC and proclaiming, as suggested by the Committee on the Rights of the Child and the Committee on the Protection of the Rights of All Migrant Workers and Members of their Families that 'child and family immigration detention should be prohibited by law and its abolishment ensured in policy and practice'.[24] As pointed out in scientific literature,[25] this position is not yet supported by international law, but as argued by the committees in their joint general comment

> 'the possibility of detaining children as a measure of last resort, which may apply in other contexts such as juvenile criminal justice, is not applicable in immigration

22 See e.g. Bina D'Costa, 'Of Responsibilities, Protection, and Rights: Children's Lives in Conflict Zones' (2018) 10 Global Responsibility to Protect 261; UNHCR, *Children on the Run* (UNHCR 2014).

23 See also the various contributions on this.

24 UN Committee on the Protection of the Rights of All Migrant Workers and Members of their Families and Committee on the Rights of the Child, 'Joint General Comment No. 4 of the Committee on the Protection of the Rights of All Migrant Workers and Members of their Families and No. 23 of the Committee on the Rights of the Child on State obligations regarding the human rights of children in the context of international migration in countries of origin, transit, destination and return' (2017) UN Doc CMW/C/GC/4-CRC/C/GC/23, para. 12; cf earlier UN Committee on the Rights of the Child, 'General Comment No. 6: Treatment of Unaccompanied and Separated Children Outside their Country of Origin' (2005) Un Doc CRC/GC/2005/6, para. 61; see further Ton Liefaard, 'Deprivation of Liberty of Children' in Ursula Kilkelly and Ton Liefaard (eds.), *International Human Rights of Children* (Springer 2019) and Ciara Smyth, 'Migration, Refugees, and Children's Rights' in Ursula Kilkelly and Ton Liefaard (eds.), *International Human Rights of Children* (Springer 2019).

25 Ton Liefaard, 'Deprivation of Liberty of Children' in Ursula Kilkelly and Ton Liefaard (eds.), *International Human Rights of Children* (Springer 2019) and Ciara Smyth, 'Migration, Refugees, and Children's Rights' in Ursula Kilkelly and Ton Liefaard (eds.), *International Human Rights of Children* (Springer 2019); FRA, *European legal and policy framework on immigration detention of children* (European Union Agency for Fundamental Rights 2017) 30–31.

proceedings as it would conflict with the principle of the best interests of the child and the right to development'.[26]

It remains to be seen how this will develop in the near future, also in light of the findings of the United Nations Global Study on Children Deprived of Liberty, which after its publication in November 2019, is likely to further shape the global agenda on this matter and may push for a higher children's rights standard, specifically in the context of immigration.[27]

4. FINAL REMARKS: CHILDREN ON THE MOVE ARE CHILDREN IN THE FIRST PLACE

One cannot be sure about what the next 30 years of children's rights will bring for children, in general and specifically for children on the move. It can be assumed, however, that children will not stop migrating and that their position therefore requires continuous attention. It can also be assumed that scholarship, on children's rights and on migration (law), has an important role to play in assessing the theoretical and practical meaning of international and regional instruments safeguarding children's human rights and fundamental freedoms and underscoring that *all* children ought to be recognised as children in the first place. The comprehensive, multi-layered, dynamic and complex framework of international law requires academics' constant focus. This book, which includes contributions of different generations of scholars and is also meant for the education of future researchers and professionals, aims to make a contribution in this regard.

---

26 UN Committee on the Protection of the Rights of All Migrant Workers and Members of their Families and Committee on the Rights of the Child, 'Joint General Comment No. 4 of the Committee on the Protection of the Rights of All Migrant Workers and Members of their Families and No. 23 of the Committee on the Rights of the Child on State obligations regarding the human rights of children in the context of international migration in countries of origin, transit, destination and return' (2017) UN Doc CMW/C/GC/4-CRC/C/GC/23, para. 10.

27 Manfred Nowak, The United Nations Global Study on Children Deprived of Liberty, Omnibook 2019; UN GA A/74/136, 11 July 2019; see also Ciara Smyth, 'Towards a Complete Prohibition on the Immigration Detention of Children' (2019) 19 Human Rights Law Review 1.

CONTENTS

LIST OF CASES

HUMAN RIGHTS COMMITTEE

COMMITTEE ON THE RIGHTS OF THE CHILD

INTER-AMERICAN COURT OF HUMAN RIGHTS

EUROPEAN COURT OF HUMAN RIGHTS

EUROPEAN COMMITTEE OF SOCIAL RIGHTS

COURT OF JUSTICE OF THE EUROPEAN UNION

NATIONAL COURTS

BELGIUM

BOTSWANA

NETHERLANDS

UNITED KINGDOM

LIST OF AUTHORS

Marit Buddenbaum
Doctoral candidate at the Department of Private Law at VU Amsterdam, the Netherlands.

Ellen Desmet
Assistant professor of migration law and member of the Migration Law Research Group/Human Rights Centre/CESSMIR at Ghent University, Belgium.

Mark Klaassen
Assistant professor of immigration law at the Institute of Immigration Law, Leiden University, the Netherlands.

Ton Liefaard
Vice-dean of Leiden Law School and holds the UNICEF Chair in Children's Rights at Leiden University, the Netherlands.

Gerrie Lodder
Researcher and lecturer at the Institute of Immigration Law, Leiden University, the Netherlands.

Elizabeth Macharia-Mokobi
Senior lecturer at the University of Botswana Department of Law.

Ioannis Papadopoulos
Doctoral candidate at the Institute of Criminal Justice Studies, University of Portsmouth, United Kingdom

Charis Pasiourtidou
Lawyer at the Research and Documentation Directorate, Court of Justice of the European Union, Luxembourg.

Audrey Plan
Doctoral candidate and research assistant at the Department of Political Science, Trinity College Dublin, Ireland.

Dagmara Rajska
Postdoctoral researcher at the UCERF, Molengraaff Institute for Private Law, Utrecht University, the Netherlands (2018–2019).

Stephanie Rap
Assistant professor in children's rights at the Department of Child Law, Leiden Law School, Leiden University, the Netherlands.

Peter Rodrigues
Professor of immigration law and head of the Institute of Immigration Law at Leiden Law School, Leiden University, the Netherlands.

Domenico Rosani
Research and teaching associate at the Department of Italian Law, University of Innsbruck, Austria, and former trainee at the EU Agency for Fundamental Rights.

Julia Sloth-Nielsen
Professor of law at the Faculty of Law, University of the Western Cape, South Africa, and the Department of Child Law, Leiden Law School, Leiden University, the Netherlands.

Alice Thornton
Family paralegal at TV Edwards Solicitors LLP, United Kingdom.

Adriana Tidona
Migration researcher at Amnesty International, European Regional Office, United Kingdom.

PROTECTION OF MINORS IN EUROPEAN MIGRATION LAW

Peter RODRIGUES*

1. INTRODUCTION

> 'As children in migration are exposed to high risks of violence, trafficking or exploitation along migration routes or may go missing, or become separated from their families, they require a specific protection. Children have the right to be protected, in line with relevant provisions of EU law, including the EU Charter of Fundamental Rights, and with international law on the rights of the child. The child's best interests must be the primary consideration in all actions or decisions concerning children.'

This is a statement of the European Commission in the press release of its communication on the protection of children in migration in April 2017.[1] Swift protection upon arrival and adequate reception conditions for children are proposed along with alternatives to administrative detention and speeding up family tracing and reunification procedures. Similar targets are formulated in the Council of Europe Action Plan on Protecting Refugee and Migrant Children in Europe, which runs from 2017 to 2019.[2] It proposes concrete support to

* Professor of immigration law and head of the Institute of Immigration Law at Leiden Law School, Leiden University, the Netherlands.

1 Communication of the EC, *The protection of children in migration*, COM (2017) 211 final.

2 https://www.coe.int/en/web/special-representative-secretary-general-migration-refugees/action-plan.

Member States at all stages of the migration process, with a special focus on unaccompanied children. Nevertheless, the UNHCR reported that hundreds of unaccompanied girls and boys, newborn babies and pregnant women were particularly at risk due to the extremely poor reception conditions at the hotspots on the Greek islands.[3] EU Member States return unaccompanied minors to Afghanistan even though children's rights organisations have reported that this country is not safe, especially for minors.[4] The Fundamental Rights Agency (FRA) published a report on the immigration detention of children which concludes that detaining children for migration management or asylum reasons is difficult to justify, practically very challenging to implement in line with fundamental rights and clearly not in the child's best interests.[5] However, it is still common practice in most Member States. The content of the Communication of the EC and the Action Plan of the Council of Europe are positive but demonstrate that progress in changes to immigration policy is slow.

This contribution will analyse the protection of minors in European migration law and will contradict the opinion that strong immigration policy considerations would in principle militate in favour of identifying children with the conduct of their parents. Children are rights holders according to the UN Convention on the Rights of the Child (UNCRC) and should not be accountable for the behaviour of their parents. EU Member States are afraid that minor migrants will claim residence permits not only for themselves, but also for their family members. The prevention of abuse of migration law is a legitimate aim, but not in itself an objective justification for keeping children accountable for the conduct of their parents.

2. EUROPEAN LEGAL FRAMEWORK OF CHILDREN'S RIGHTS

According to Article 6 of the Treaty on European Union (TEU), the European Convention on Human Rights (ECHR) and constitutional traditions of Member States are a source of the general principles of EU law.[6] Whenever needed, the Court of Justice of the European Union (ECJ) may refer to these principles to

---

3 http://www.unhcr.org/news/briefing/2018/8/5b88f5c34/unhcr-urges-greece-address-overcrowded-reception-centres-aegean-islands.html.

4 Save the Children, *Afghanistan Country Annual Report 2017*.

5 *European legal and policy framework on immigration detention of children*, FRA (Vienna, June 2017).

6 This section is partly based on section 2 of my publication 'Human Rights and the Best Interests of the Child in European Family Reunification Law' in *Fundamental Rights and Best Interests of the Child in Transnational Families*, E. Bergamini and C. Ragni (eds.), Intersentia (Antwerp 2019) pp. 55–73.

supplement the fundamental rights protected in the Charter of Fundamental Rights of the European Union (Charter). EU courts have generally not directly applied human rights treaties such as the UNCRC, but they do so indirectly, using them as a source of inspiration for EU fundamental rights and general principles of EU law. International human rights law is often a source of inspiration for the ECJ in developing its case law. Fundamental rights form an integral part of the general principles of law, and the ECJ ensures its observance.[7] In Article 3(3) TEU an important target of the EU is formulated; it shall combat social exclusion and discrimination, and shall promote social justice and protection, equality between women and men, solidarity between generations and protection of the rights of the child.

This becomes more concrete in Article 24(2) Charter: 'In all actions relating to children, whether taken by public authorities or private institutions, the child's best interests must be a primary consideration.' This article is based on Article 3 UNCRC, but the text is more succinct than in the UNCRC. The Explanation to the Charter states that Article 24 is based on the UNCRC, particularly Articles 3 (best interests), 9 (unity of the family), 12 (own view) and 13 (freedom of expression) thereof.[8] Similar to Article 3 UNCRC, Article 24 Charter should be read in conjunction with the other rights of the Charter. The codification of the best interests concept in the Charter is to be a shift towards seeing children as independent right holders within the EU, rather than objects of EU law.[9] The best interests concept is also reflected in European migration law and most of the recent Regulations and Directives; the preamble or specific articles refer to the best interests of the child.[10] Preamble 33 of the Procedural Directive 2013/32 reads as follows:

> 'The best interests of the child should be a primary consideration of Member States when applying this Directive, in accordance with the Charter of Fundamental Rights of the European Union (the Charter) and the 1989 United Nations Convention on the Rights of the Child. In assessing the best interest of the child, Member States should in particular take due account of the minor's well-being and social development, including his or her background.'

In this recast Directive a reference has been made to the UNCRC as well as to the Charter. Sometimes the Directive only refers to the UNCRC[11] or just to

---

7 Case C-540/03, *Parliament v. Council*, ECLI:EU:C:2006:429.

8 Explanations relating to the Charter of Fundamental Rights, *OJ* 2007/C 303/25.

9 S. Peers, T. Hervey, J. Kennerer and A. Ward (eds.) *The EU Charter of Fundamental Rights, A Commentary*, Hart (Oxford and Portland 2014) p. 687.

10 See among others Preamble 18 Qualification Directive 2011/95, Preamble 33 Procedures Directive 2013/32, Art. 23 Reception Directive 2013/33, Preamble 16 Dublin III 604/2013, Preamble 22 Return Directive 2008/115 and Article 5(5) Family Reunification Directive 2003/86.

11 Preamble 18 Qualification Directive 2011/95 and Preamble 22 Return Directive 2008/115.

the principle of the best interests of the child.[12] The circumstances that should be taken into account are most extensively formulated in Preamble 18 of the Qualification Directive: the principle of family unity, the minor's well-being and social development, safety and security considerations and the views of the minor in accordance with his or her age and maturity.

Article 24 Charter highlights two additional children's rights. Paragraph 1 states that children have the right to the protection and care that is necessary for their well-being and have the right to have their views taken into consideration. Article 24(3) establishes that every child has the right to maintain a personal relationship and direct contact with their parents on a regular basis. Usually the bodies who handle human rights treaties take into account that Member States should have a certain margin of appreciation on how to implement these rights in their local situation and domestic law.

With the entry into force of the Lisbon Treaty on 1 December 2009, the Charter of Fundamental Rights of the EU acquired the status of primary EU law. It should be mentioned that the scope of the Charter is limited. Article 51(1) Charter states that the provisions of the Charter are addressed to the institutions, bodies, offices and agencies of the EU and to Member States when they are implementing EU law. In *Åkerberg Fransson*, the ECJ clarified that Article 51(1) Charter is applicable in all situations where national legislation falls within the scope of EU law.[13] In order to determine whether a national measure falls within the scope of EU law, it must be determined whether a direct link exists between the impugned national measure and an EU obligation.[14] Looking at the wide scope of European migration law, most national migration laws of the Member States will be related to EU law. Article 51(2) Charter prescribes that none of its provisions extend the field of application of EU law or have the ability to establish new powers or tasks for it. Most of the Charter provisions are almost similar to a provision from the ECHR, and in so far as this is the case, must be interpreted in line with the corresponding provision and case law of the European Court of Human Rights (ECtHR).[15] In the ECHR a special provision on children's rights is missing, but in the last decade the ECtHR included the best interests principle in its jurisprudence on migration and in these cases makes reference to Article 3 UNCRC.[16] Finally, Article 52(3) Charter shall not prevent Union law providing more extensive protection.

First the relevant migration case law of ECtHR will be discussed (section 3) followed by the jurisprudence of the ECJ (section 4).

---

12 Art. 23 Reception Directive 2013/33 and Preamble 16 Dublin III 604/2013.

13 Case C-617/10, *Åkerberg Fransson*, ECLI:EU:C:2013:105, 18.

14 Ibid., *Åkerberg Fransson*, paras. 28–29.

15 Art. 52(3) Charter.

16 Not explicit in *Rodrigues da Silva and Hoogkamer v. the Netherlands*, No. 50435/99, ECHR 2006, para. 44, and explicit in *Nunez v. Norway*, No. 55597/09, ECHR 2011, para. 84.

3. CASE LAW OF THE EUROPEAN COURT OF HUMAN RIGHTS

In the *Nunez* case, the ECtHR referred to Article 3 UNCRC for the first time in an Article 8 ECHR expulsion procedure.[17] According to the Court, there was no doubt the deportation of the applicant was legitimate because of her identity fraud and criminal convictions. Nevertheless, the Court found that the best interests of the child of Article 8 ECHR must be read in conjunction with Article 3 UNCRC and concluded that it was not in the interest of the young children to be separated from their mother:[18]

> '(…) the Court is not convinced in the concrete and exceptional circumstances of the case that sufficient weight was attached to the best interests of the children for the purposes of Article 8 of the Convention. Reference is made in this context also to Article 3 of the UN Convention on the Rights of the Child, according to which the best interests of the child shall be a primary consideration in all actions taken by public authorities concerning children.'[19]

Only in case of exceptional circumstances would removal of the family member be incompatible with Article 8 ECHR. In *Nunez*, the most important exceptional circumstances were the very young age of the children, the children's long-lasting and close bond to their mother, the decision that the father has custody, the disruption and stress that the children had already experienced and the long period that had elapsed before the immigration authorities took their decision to order the applicant's expulsion with a re-entry ban.

In the following case *Butt*, the mother had provided incorrect information to the police and other institutions, and for that reason the removal of the children would be incompatible with Article 8 ECHR only in exceptional circumstances.[20] In *Butt*, the ECtHR, saw no reason to disagree with the general approach of the Borgarting High Court

> 'that strong immigration policy considerations would in principle militate in favour of identifying children with the conduct of their parents, failing which there would be a great risk that parents exploited the situation of their children in order to secure a residence permit for themselves and for the children'.[21]

However, their mother could not exploit the situation of her children, because she had been expelled to Pakistan in 2005 and died in 2007, while her children

17 Ibid., *Nunez v. Norway*.
18 Ibid., para. 84.
19 Ibid.
20 ECtHR 4 December 2012 (*Butt v. Norway*) 47017/09.
21 *Butt*, para. 79.

were living in Norway. According to the ECtHR, the expulsion of the children would be in breach of Article 8 ECHR. The consideration concerning exploitation was repeated in the case of *Kaplan*[22] and corresponds with the observation that the ECtHR has repeatedly observed that as a matter of well-established international law and subject to its treaty obligations, a state has the right to control the entry of non-nationals into its territory.[23]

The balance of interests was at stake in the case of *El Ghatet*.[24] The facts of the case concern an Egyptian national, who applied for asylum in Switzerland leaving his son behind in Egypt.[25] While his asylum application was rejected, the father obtained a residence permit and afterwards Swiss nationality having married a Swiss national. The couple had a daughter and eventually divorced. The father's first request for family reunification with his son was accepted in 2003 but eventually his son returned to Egypt. The father's second request for family reunification in 2006 was rejected. Based on these facts, the Court found that no clear conclusion could be drawn on whether or not the applicants' interest in family reunification outweighed the public interest of the respondent state in controlling the entry of foreigners into its territory.[26] However, the Court noted that domestic courts had examined the best interests in a brief manner and had put forward a rather summary reasoning in that regard. It considered that it did not place the best interests sufficiently at the centre of its balancing exercise and its reasoning, contrary to the requirements under the ECHR, the UNCRC as well as the Constitution of the Swiss Confederation. The Court therefore found a violation of Article 8 ECHR.

The ECtHR has held that there is a broad consensus, including in international law, to support the idea that in all decisions concerning children, their best interests must be paramount.[27] For that purpose, in cases regarding Article 8 ECHR particular attention should be paid to the circumstances of the minor children concerned, especially their age, the situation in their country of origin and the extent to which they are dependent on their parents. However, in the case of *I.A.A.* the ECtHR held that although the best interests of the child was a 'paramount' consideration, it cannot be a 'trump card' which requires the admission of all children who would be better off living in a Contracting State.[28] This statement goes without saying, because the best interests of the child does not mean that the child should always be entitled to a residence permit or that his third-country parent can never be expelled.

22 ECtHR 24 July 2014 (*Kaplan v. Norway*) 32504/11, para. 86.
23 ECtHR 28 May 1985 (*Abdulaziz*) 9214/80, 9473/81 and 9474/81.
24 ECtHR 8 November 2016 (*El Ghatet v. Switzerland*) 56971/10.
25 http://www.asylumlawdatabase.eu/en/content/el-ghatet-v-switzerland-no-5697110-article-8-8-november-2016.
26 *El Ghatet*, para. 52.
27 See *Neulinger and Shuruk v. Switzerland*, 41615/07, ECHR 2010, para. 135.
28 ECtHR 8 March 2016 (*I.A.A. v. United Kingdom*) 25960/13, para. 41.

On the other hand, this statement does seem to also be a warning that the principle of the best interests is not a *carte blanche* and should be made concrete based on the personal circumstances and facts of the case.

4. CASE LAW OF THE EUROPEAN COURT OF JUSTICE

Since the entry into force of the Charter in December 2009, the jurisprudence of the ECJ related to migration and minors has been connected to Article 24 Charter.[29] Nevertheless, Court decisions in which explicit reference is made to the best interests of the child are rare. An exception is the case *O., S. & L.* concerning the family reunification of the partner of a third-country national lawfully residing in Finland, but where the sponsor did not comply with the income requirement.[30] Although the Family Reunification Directive (2003/86) allows these requirements,[31] the ECJ has emphasised that Member States may not apply the implementation of an instrument of EU law in such a way that it disregards fundamental rights such as the right to respect for family life and the best interests of the child. Even when the Directive allows requirements, the administration or domestic courts should always take the personal circumstances of the case into account and must be aware of the best interests of the child. This is in conformity with the guidelines of the European Commission (EC) on the interpretation of the Family Reunification Directive.[32]

In the case of family reunion of the parents of an unaccompanied minor who has received international protection, the preliminary question is: what is the relevant moment in time at which the unaccompanied minor must be deemed a minor to be eligible for family reunion? The ECJ established that the right to family reunification of unaccompanied children may not be made dependent on the moment at which the Member States adopt the decision to recognise the applicant as a refugee.[33] According to the ECJ this would call into question the effectiveness of the relevant provision and would go against the aim of the Directive, which is to promote family reunification and to grant in that regard specific protection to refugees, in particular unaccompanied minors.[34]

---

29 See M.A.K. Klaassen and P.R. Rodrigues, 'The Best Interests of the Child in EU Family Reunification Law: A Plea for More Guidance on the Role of Article 24(2) Charter' (2017) *European Journal of Migration and Law* 19, pp. 191–218.

30 Cases C-356/11 and C-357/11, *O. S. & L.*, ECLI:EU:C:2012:776, para. 76.

31 Art. 7(1)(c).

32 COM(2014)210 final, Communication from the Commission to the European Parliament and the Council on guidance for application of Directive 2003/86/EC on the right to family reunification.

33 See also M.A.K. Klaassen, 'Unaccompanied children becoming young adults and the right to family reunion', Leiden Law Blog, 24 April 2018.

34 Case C-550/16, *A. and S. v. the Netherlands*, ECLI:EU:C:2018:248.

Reference is made to Article 24(2) Charter and Article 5(5) Family Reunification Directive. Both prescribe that the best interests of the child must be a primary consideration for Member States in the application of the Directive. The result of the balancing of interests by the Court is that the relevant moment in time to decide whether an unaccompanied asylum-seeking child is eligible for family reunification, is the moment when the child had applied for international protection.

Article 6(1) Dublin III (Regulation 604/2013) states that the best interests of the child shall be a primary consideration for Member States with respect to all procedures provided for in this Regulation. The Dublin system normally places responsibility for the asylum claim on the Member State of first application. A different approach is demonstrated by the case of *MA* of the ECJ.[35] The main proceedings concerned three unaccompanied minors who had applied for asylum in the United Kingdom after having previously lodged asylum applications in the Netherlands and Italy. None of them had family members legally present in the territory of those states. Considering the vulnerable position of such children, their procedure should not be prolonged more than strictly necessary which means that they should not be subject to a Dublin transfer to another Member State. Because the best interests of a child must be a primary consideration in all decisions adopted by Member States, Article 6(2) should be interpreted as designating the responsible Member State in which the minor is present after having lodged an asylum application. The ECJ based its judgment on Article 24(2) Charter and concluded that the three unaccompanied minors should not be transferred to another Member State.

In 2014, the EC introduced a proposal to revise Article 8(4) of the Dublin Regulation to adjust the Dublin III Regulation in accordance with the *MA* case.[36] A new paragraph 4(a) would render responsible the Member State where a minor asylum seeker is present and has lodged an application for international protection, provided that this is in his or her best interests.[37] Unfortunately, the proposal was not adopted. The Member States fear forum shopping and are not able to take notice of (first) asylum applications in a foreign language. The consequence of this debate is that the text of Article 6(2) Dublin III has been transferred to the draft of Dublin IV in a very restrictive way.[38] It is precisely

---

35 Case C-648/11, *M.A. & Others v. UK*, ECLI:EU:C:2013:367.

36 Proposal for amending Regulation (EU) No 604/2013 as regards determining the Member State responsible for examining the application for international protection of unaccompanied minors with no family member, sibling or relative legally present in a Member State, COM/2014/0382 final.

37 L. van Zelm, 'Dublin IV: Violating Unaccompanied Minor's Best Interests in the Allocation of Responsibility', Leiden Law Blog, 22 May 2018.

38 Proposal for a Regulation establishing the criteria and mechanisms for determining the Member State responsible for examining an application for international protection lodged

the other way around than the ECJ had concluded in *MA*. The proposed text of Article 8(4) Dublin IV holds that the Member State responsible shall be that where the unaccompanied minor first lodged an application for international protection, unless it is demonstrated that this is not in the best interests of the minor. This provision ignores the considerations of the ECJ on the best interests of the child and demonstrates the impact of political pressure by the Member States. It is hard to avoid the impression that this text is partly motivated by the possibility that unaccompanied minors will eventually apply for family reunification with their parents, while the Member States would prefer to retain as much migration control as possible. Migration control is a legitimate aim, but one which should be balanced with the best interests of the child. According to Preamble 18 of the Qualification Directive the indicators for the best interests are the principle of family unity, the minor's well-being and social development, safety and security considerations and the views of the minor in accordance with his or her age and maturity.

In 2017, the ECJ delivered its ruling in *Chavez-Vilchez*.[39] This case considered eight different families and the preliminary question raised was whether the third-country national mother of a minor child with EU citizenship must be allowed to remain in the EU, if the denial of the parent's residence would force the child to leave EU territory with this parent. The Court has held that Article 20 Treaty of Functioning of the EU (TFEU) precludes national measures, including decisions refusing a right of residence to the family members of a Union citizen, which have the effect of depriving Union citizens of the genuine enjoyment of the substance of the rights conferred by virtue of their status.[40] One of these rights is to reside freely on the territory of the EU Member States. All eight families consisted of one or more children with EU citizenship, one third-country national mother and an EU citizen father. The fathers did not take real parental responsibility for their children. Due to the fact that the application for a residence permit of the mothers was rejected, the Dutch authorities had refused to grant the mothers social assistance and child benefit. The claim of the mothers was that their EU citizen children would be forced to leave the territory of the EU, even though they have a father who is a Dutch citizen. According to the ECJ, when considering whether a child would be forced to leave an EU territory if a derived right of residence were to be denied to a third-country national parent, it should be determined whether that parent is the actual caregiver to the child, and to what extent the child is dependent on that parent. It is therefore important to determine which parent is the primary caretaker of the child and whether the child factually depends on the

in one of the Member States by a third-country national or a stateless person (recast), COM/2016/0270 final. 9 January 2018 (15991/17).

39 Case C-133/15, *Chavez Vilchez*, ECLI:EU:C:2017:354.

40 Case C-34/09, *Ruiz Zambrano*, ECLI:EU:C:2011:124.

third-country national parent. The ECJ stressed that the authorities of the Member State must take into account the right to respect for family life (Article 7 Charter) in conjunction with the best interests of the child (Article 24(2) Charter).[41]

The determination process is not only to establish whether the child could live with the parent who is an EU citizen, but also to take individual factors into account. The ECJ mentions the age of the child, the physical and emotional development of the child, the strength of the affective bond between the child and both of its parents, and the risks to the development and well-being of the child if it is separated from the third-country national parent. Next to that, the national authorities must find out where the Union citizen parent lives and whether that parent is actually able and willing to assume sole responsibility for the daily care of the child.[42] In *K.A. and Others*, a case involving the expulsion of a third-country national parent, the ECJ considered that account must be taken of the best interests of the child concerned, of all the specific circumstances, including the age of the child, the child's physical and emotional development, the extent of his emotional ties both to the Union citizen parent and to the third-country national parent, and the risks which separation from the latter might entail for that child's equilibrium.[43]

An interesting pending case is *Tjebbes and Others* on Dutch nationality law.[44] The preliminary question in this case is in the event that parents lose their Dutch nationality, because they have been living for more than ten years outside of the Netherlands and have already acquired a second nationality, will their minor children also automatically lose their Dutch nationality? According to the Dutch nationality law this would indeed be the case, but the consequence of this is that the children then also lose their EU citizenship. Is this in conformity with EU law? Not according to Advocate General Mengozzi, who concluded in this case that the automatic loss of nationality of the parents' minor children is in breach of Article 20 TFEU and Article 24(2) Charter.

5. ARTICLE 2(2) UNCRC REVISITED

Considering the jurisprudence of the ECtHR, the question remains under which circumstances the general approach could be invoked that strong immigration policy considerations would in principle militate in favour of identifying children

41 *Chavez Vilchez*, para. 70.

42 M.A.K. Klaassen, 'The right of residence for non-EU parents of EU citizen children: the Chavez-Vilchez case', Leiden Law Blog, 12 May 2017.

43 Case C-82/16, *K.A. and Others*, ECLI:EU:C:2018:308, para. 72.

44 Case C-221/17.

with the conduct of their parents? Based on the wording of the ECtHR, it seems to me that there should be a substantial risk that parents had exploited the situation of their children in order to secure a residence permit for themselves, which also includes a permit for their children. Looking at the semantic interpretation of 'exploit', it is arguable that there must be at least a slight form of abuse of migration law, because claiming a right should not be qualified as 'exploit'.

The conclusion seems justified that in Article 8 ECHR cases the ECtHR carries out a weighing of interests between migration control on the one hand, and the best interests of the child on the other. This seems a reasonable balance, but the writer disagrees with the statement that children could be identified with the conduct of their parents in relation to exploiting migration law. The UNCRC is a right-based human rights treaty and children should be seen as right holders and not as the family members of their parents. Moreover 'the identifying rule' seems to me to be in conflict with Article 2(2) UNCRC which prohibits the unequal treatment of children because of the activities or behaviour of their parents:

> 'States Parties shall take all appropriate measures to ensure that the child is protected against all forms of discrimination or punishment on the basis of the status, activities, expressed opinions, or beliefs of the child's parents, legal guardians, or family members.'

If the ECtHR refers to Article 3 UNCRC, like in *Nunez*, this article should be read in conjunction with the other rights of the Convention, so also the prohibition of discrimination of Article 2. In the case *Berisha*, two judges delivered a dissenting opinion and stated that children cannot be held responsible or suffer for their parents' incorrect or even illegal behaviour. This would be against the best interests of the children, a principle which is very well developed and is always stressed in the case law of the ECtHR.[45] It is also in breach of Article 2(2) UNCRC.

The role of the ECJ differs from that of the ECtHR, because the Luxembourg Court has to explain concepts of EU law and the domestic courts should adopt this interpretation. Article 24 Charter can play an important role in the interpretation of children's rights in migration cases. However, decisions of the ECJ in which explicit reference is made to the best interests of Article 24 Charter are rare. The case of *MA* demonstrates that a child-friendly interpretation of European migration law is not always accepted by the Member States and this could be a barrier to new child-friendly rules. A new approach that comes close to Article 2(2) UNCRC is the opinion of Advocate General Mengozzi in the

---

45 ECtHR 30 July 2013 (*Berisha v. Switzerland*) 948/12.

case *Tjebbes and Others*, who concludes in relation to loss of EU citizenship that children should not be identified with the conduct of their parents.

Article 2 UNCRC is a *lex specialis* of the prohibition of discrimination in other human rights treaties, such as Article 26 International Covenant on Civil and Political Rights, Article 2(2) International Covenant on Economic, Social and Cultural Rights and Article 14 ECHR. It belongs to the general principles of the UNCRC and the Contracting States are duty holders. While Article 2(1) applies only to those rights guaranteed in the Convention, this is not the case for Article 2(2) which applies to all cases of discrimination of a child on the base of his or her parents' activities or status.[46] This is an additional child-specific form of discrimination, which focuses on the fact that it happens to children who are held responsible or suffer for their parents' incorrect or illegal behaviour. For example, the law makes children suffer because they are born out of wedlock.[47] It should be noted that not all differences in treatment are discriminatory, only those which lack an objective justification. To meet the objective justification test, a legitimate aim should be achieved and the means to do so must be proportionate and necessary. In case the view of the Contracting State is to identify children with the conduct of their parents and refuse them residence, the state must pass the objective justification test. Of course, meeting the standard of proportionality includes taking into account the principle of the best interests of the child. The means of the proportionality test 'must be apt to attain the aim sought, be necessary means to do so and be the least restrictive means to reach that aim'.[48] In my opinion, the value of Article 2(2) to protect the interests of children in migration cases is underestimated.

6. ABUSE OF MIGRATION LAW

In light of the increased number of migrant children arriving in Europe and the growing pressure on national migration management and child protection systems, in 2017 the EC published the aforementioned Communication on the protection of children in migration.[49] It sets out a series of actions which should now either be taken or be better implemented by the EU and its Member States,

46 S. Besson, 'The Principle of Non-Discrimination in the Convention on the Rights of the Child' (2005) 13 *International Journal of Children's Rights* 433–461, p. 447.

47 B. Abramson, *A Commentary on the United Nations Convention on the Rights of the Child, Article 2, The Right of Non-Discrimination*, Martinus Nijhoff Publishers (Leiden/Boston 2008) p. 129. See ECtHR 11 October 2011 (*Genovese v. Malta*) 53124/09.

48 Besson, 'The Principle of Non-Discrimination in the Convention on the Rights of the Child' (n. 46 above) p. 436.

49 Communication of the EC, *The protection of children in migration*, COM (2017) 211 final.

supported by the relevant EU agencies.[50] According to the Communication the best interests principle could be improved:[51]

> 'The child's best interests must be assessed and taken into account as the primary consideration in all actions or decisions that concern him or her. However, at present, the legislation of most Member States does not set out a process for identifying and implementing this requirement, including with regard to durable solutions for unaccompanied children based on an individual and multidisciplinary assessment.'

The Dutch Minister of Foreign Affairs welcomed and supported the Communication, but also made some critical remarks. These remarks concern not only the concept of best interests, but also the lack of attention to the abuse of migration law by children, their family members and people who pretend to be minors.[52] Also according to other Member States, the Communication should address the need to prevent abuse of the asylum procedure. This fear of abuse serves as a reminder of the *Butt* case and the statement that strong immigration policy considerations would in principle militate in favour of identifying children with the conduct of their parents, failing which there would be a great risk that parents exploited the situation of their children in order to secure a residence permit for themselves and for the children. What are the EU law criteria concerning abuse of law?

In EU law the concept of abuse of law has been dealt with from as early as 1974, when it was introduced in the *Binsbergen* case of the ECJ.[53] Since then it has been further discussed in other cases, mainly in relation to areas like tax law. In 2017, the ECJ stated in the case *Edward Cussens* that the principle that abusive practices are prohibited is applied to the rights and advantages provided for by EU law irrespective of whether those rights and advantages have their basis in the Treaties, in a Regulation or in a Directive.[54] According to the ECJ, the principle of abuse of law displays the general, comprehensive character which is naturally inherent in general principles of EU law. This principle is also laid down in Article 54 Charter.

Although no clear definition has emerged so far, a two-element test was prescribed in the *Emsland-Stärke* case.[55] The first element refers to the need to establish 'a combination of objective circumstances in which, despite formal observance of the conditions laid down by the Community rules, the purpose

50 European Border and Coast Guard Agency, European Asylum Support Office (EASO) and the European Union Agency for Fundamental Rights (FRA).

51 Communication of the EC (n. 49 above) p. 14.

52 Parliamentary notes, second chamber, 2016/17, 22 112, 2352, p. 5.

53 Case C-33/74, *Binsbergen*, ECLI:EU:C:1974:131.

54 Case C-251/16, *Edward Cussens*, ECLI:EU:C:2017:881.

55 Case C-110/99, *Emsland-Stärke*, ECLI:EU:C:2000:695.

of those rules has not been achieved'.[56] Here, one should identify the purpose of the relevant provisions, for example by looking at the preparatory documents, and compare this to the purpose and results achieved by the activity at issue. The second element concerns 'a subjective element consisting in the intention to obtain an advantage from the Community rules by creating artificially the conditions laid down for obtaining it (...)'.[57] Establishing this is dependent on the circumstances of the case and might be difficult considering its subjectivity. These criteria for establishing abuse can also be used in other cases than those involving tax law. This follows from the *O and B* case, where a Union citizen returned to his Member State after short periods of residence spent in another Member State to qualify for family reunification with a third-country national.[58] The Free Movement Directive (2004/38) includes a provision against abuse of law, Article 35:

> 'Member States may adopt the necessary measures to refuse, terminate or withdraw any right conferred by this Directive in the case of abuse of rights or fraud, such as marriages of convenience. Any such measure shall be proportionate and subject to the procedural safeguards provided for in Articles 30 and 31.'

A difference should be made between fraud and abuse. According to the Guidelines of the EC to the Free Movement Directive, fraud is likely to be limited to forgery of documents or false representation of a material fact concerning the conditions attached to the right of residence.[59] Abuse can be defined as artificial conduct entered into solely with the purpose of obtaining the right of free movement and residence under Community law which, albeit formally observing the conditions laid down by Community rules, does not comply with the purpose of those rules. Recital 28 of the Free Movement Directive defines marriages of convenience as being marriages contracted for the sole purpose of enjoying the right of free movement and residence under the Directive that a person would not have otherwise. The Guidelines explain that a marriage cannot be considered as a marriage of convenience simply because it brings with it an immigration advantage.[60] The definition of Recital 28 can be extended by analogy to other forms of relationships contracted for the sole purpose of enjoying the right of free movement and residence, such as (registered) partnership of convenience, fake adoption or where an EU citizen

---

56 *Emsland-Stärke*, para. 52.

57 Ibid., para. 53.

58 Case C-456/12, *O and B*, ECLI:EU:C:2014:135, see para. 58.

59 Communication of the EC on guidance for better transposition and application of Directive 2004/38/EC on the right of citizens of the Union and their family members to move and reside freely within the territory of the Member States, p. 15.

60 B. de Hart, 'Europeanization of Love. The Marriage of Convenience in European Migration Law' (2017) *European Journal of Migration and Law* 19, pp. 281–306.

declares himself to be a father of a third-country child to convey nationality and a right of residence on the child and its mother, knowing that he is not its father and not willing to assume parental responsibilities. Also, the anti-abuse clause of the Family Reunification Directive refers to acts with the exclusive goal of obtaining family reunification.[61] To conclude, in EU migration law artificial conduct can only be qualified as abuse if its sole purpose is to obtain residence rights even though, formally speaking, the person concerned does not comply with the migration rules. Jurisprudence of the ECJ demonstrates that this standard is not easy to meet.[62]

7. CONCLUDING REMARKS

Policy instruments like the EC Communication on the protection of children in migration and the Council of Europe Action Plan on Protecting Refugee and Migrant Children in Europe are important instruments to improve the protection of minors in migration. However, it seems to be easier to formulate targets in policy documents than to change the practice of migration control in the Member States. The reality is that minors are seen as a risk of uncontrolled migration; if they have a residence permit, not only their parents, but also their whole family, will have a permit too.

The principle of the best interests in Article 24(2) Charter is hard EU law and implies a clear obligation for the Member States. Looking at the jurisprudence of both European courts, the ECtHR and ECJ, the conclusion can only be that this principle is still under development. The ECtHR agrees that it should be the primary consideration, but also repeats that as a matter of well-established international law and subject to its treaty obligations, a state has the right to control the entry of non-nationals into its territory. This is illustrated by agreeing that strong immigration policy considerations would in principle militate in favour of identifying children with the conduct of their parents. On the other hand, the ECtHR requires that the best interests should be placed sufficiently at the centre of the balancing exercise and its reasoning in the domestic courts. This principle is no 'trump card', but requires the serious balancing of conflicting interests; being better off in the host country is not a strong argument.

In only a few migration cases does the ECJ make an explicit reference to the best interests concept. Recent cases like *Chavez-Vilchez* and *K.A. and Others* give the impression that the court is gradually placing more significance on

61 Art. 16(2)b Family Reunification Directive.

62 J. ten Berg, 'Waar ligt de grens tussen gebruik en misbruik van het recht op vrij verkeer?' (2018) *Asiel & Migrantenrecht* 6–7, pp. 314–321.

the principle. What is really worrying, however, is that where the ECJ explains a provision of Dublin III based on Article 24(2) Charter, Member States refuse to incorporate this explanation in the draft for new EU Migration law (Dublin IV). One reason seems to be that unaccompanied minors are viewed too often as having a hidden agenda aimed at family reunification.

It goes without saying that migration control is a legitimate interest of the Member States. On the other hand, the best interests of the child should be the 'paramount' consideration. Article 2(2) UNCRC prohibits the unequal treatment of minors based on the conduct of their parents or guardians. Thus, to conclude, in the case of migrant minors the balancing of interests cannot be negatively affected merely because of the actions or behaviour of their parents.

PARTICIPATION OF CHILDREN IN ASYLUM PROCEDURES

Stephanie Rap*

1. INTRODUCTION

It can be argued that refugee and migrant children[1] are one of the most vulnerable groups in society, having experienced a dangerous journey, traumatic events in their home country and on the road and often lacking access to essential necessities, such as food, shelter, medical aid and a healthy and stimulating environment for growing up.[2] Once having arrived in the host country, children are often not recognised and respected as individual rights holders and as active

* Assistant professor in children's rights at the Department of Child Law, Leiden Law School, Leiden University, the Netherlands.

1 In this contribution, the term 'refugee and migrant children' is used for all children, below the age of 18, applying for asylum in a host country.

2 UNICEF, *Uprooted. The growing crisis for refugee and migrant children* (UNICEF 2016a); UNICEF, *Danger every step of the way. A harrowing journey to Europe for refugee and migrant*

agents in the asylum application process.[3] Thorburn Stern notes, however, that these children are mostly first considered as migrants, who pose risks to society, rather than vulnerable children who are exposed to risks themselves.[4] Therefore, the vulnerability and precarious situation of refugee and migrant children calls for a strong legal position in asylum procedures. Effective participation in asylum procedures – based on child-friendly and age-appropriate communication and adapted procedures – can strengthen the legal position of refugee children.

Within the larger group of refugee and migrant children, subgroups can be identified of unaccompanied, separated and accompanied children. The UN Committee on the Rights of the Child (CRC Committee) has defined unaccompanied children as 'children, as defined in article 1 of the Convention, who have been separated from both parents and other relatives and are not being cared for by an adult who, by law or custom, is responsible for doing so'.[5] The CRC Committee defines separated children as: 'children, as defined in article 1 of the Convention, who have been separated from both parents, or from their previous legal or customary primary caregiver, but not necessarily from other relatives. These may, therefore, include children accompanied by other adult family members.'[6] The third group of refugee children arrives with their parent(s) or primary caregiver(s). In this contribution both unaccompanied and separated as well as accompanied children are part of the analysis. First, the right to participation will be regarded from an international legal perspective, discussing this right first for children in general and second specifically relating to refugee and migrant children. Three related rights will be highlighted, i.e. the right to be heard, the right to information and the right to (legal) representation.

---

children (UNICEF 2016b); Council of Europe, *Council of Europe Strategy for the Rights of the Child (2016–2021)* (Council of Europe 2016).

3 Wouter Vandenhole, 'Kinderrechten op het scherpst van de snede' (2016) Tijdschrift voor Jeugd- en Kinderrechten 1; Mehek Muftee, 'Children's agency in resettlement: A study of Swedish cultural orientation programs in Kenya and Sudan' (2015) 13 Children's Geographies 131; Ulrika Wernesjö, 'Unaccompanied asylum-seeking children: Whose perspective?' (2011) 19 Childhood 495; Naomi Bushin, 'Researching family migration: A children-in-families approach' (2009) 15 Population, Space and Place 429; Ravi K.S. Kohli, 'The sound of silence: Listening to what unaccompanied asylum-seeking children say and do not say' (2006) 36 British Journal of Social Work 707; Mary E. Crock, 'Justice for the Migrant Child: The Protective Force of the Convention on the Rights of the Child' in Said Mahmoudi, Pernilla Leviner, Anna Kaldal and Katrin Lainpelto (eds.), *Child-friendly Justice: A Quarter of a Century of the UN Convention on the Rights of the Child* (Brill Nijhoff 2015).

4 Rebecca Thorburn Stern, 'Unaccompanied and Separated Asylum-seeking Minors: implementing a Rights-based Approach in the asylum Process' in Mahmoudi, Leviner, Kaldal and Lainpelto (eds.), *Child-friendly Justice* (n. 3 above); see also Jacqueline Bhabha, 'Arendt's Children: Do Today's Migrant Children Have the Right to Have Rights?' (2009) 31 Human Rights Quarterly 410.

5 UN Committee on the Rights of the Child, *Treatment of unaccompanied and separated children outside their country of origin*, General Comment No. 6, CRC/GC/2005/6, para. 7.

6 Ibid., para. 8.

Second, the right to participation will be regarded from a socio-empirical perspective, focusing first in general on research outcomes concerning the participation of children in legal proceedings and second on children involved in asylum proceedings. This contribution closes with concluding remarks.

2. THE CHILD'S RIGHT TO PARTICIPATION

Both at the international and the European level there is growing attention for the participation of children in legal proceedings. In Europe, the adoption of the Council of Europe *Guidelines on Child-friendly justice* has had a catalyst effect on this development.[7] The Guidelines depart from the point of view that children are bearers of rights and that children should be enabled to participate effectively in justice proceedings.[8] The Guidelines contain the principles necessary to ensure that 'all rights of children' are fully respected in judicial proceedings[9] and provide practical guidance for the 47 Council of Europe's Member States to 'give a place and voice to the child in justice at all stages of the procedures.'[10] Specifically, it is noted that '[s]pecific protection and assistance may need to be granted to more vulnerable children, such as migrant children, refugee and asylum seeking children, unaccompanied children, children with disabilities, homeless and street children, Roma children, and children in residential institutions'.[11] On a policy level, the European Commission identified making the justice systems in Europe more child-friendly as a key priority in its 2011 *EU Agenda for the Rights of the Child*.[12] Also, the Council of Europe names participation of all children and child-friendly justice for all children as two of its priority areas in the *Strategy for the Rights of the Child (2016–2021)*.[13] Specifically with regard to refugee children, both intergovernmental organisations have issued policy documents in which a clear link is drawn between the protection of refugee children and promoting child-friendly procedures and practices. In 2017, the European Commission stated in a Communication to the European Parliament and the Council on the protection of children in migration, that appropriate safeguards

---

7 Guidelines of the Committee of Ministers of the Council of Europe on child-friendly justice, adopted by the Committee of Ministers on 17 November 2010 at the 1098th meeting of the Ministers' Deputies.

8 Ton Liefaard and Ursula Kilkelly, 'Child-friendly justice: past, present and future' in Barry Goldson (ed.), *Juvenile justice in Europe: Past, present and future* (Routledge 2018).

9 Council of Europe, Guidelines on child-friendly justice, I, para. 3.

10 Ibid., explanatory memorandum, para. 16.

11 Ibid., III, D, 2.

12 Communication from the Commission to the European Parliament, the Council, the European Economic and Social Committee and the Committee of the Regions, *An EU Agenda for the Rights of the Child*, COM(2011) 60 final.

13 Council of Europe, *Strategy for the Rights of the Child (2016–2021)* (n. 2 above).

must be applied to all children in all stages of the asylum procedure. Access to information, legal representation and guardianship, the right to be heard and the right to an effective remedy are named as key protection measures.[14] Moreover, it is recommended that children need to be informed – in a child-sensitive and age- and context-appropriate manner – on their rights, on procedures and on services available for their protection.[15] The Council of Europe has issued the *Action on Plan on Protecting Refugee and Migrant Children in Europe* in which it highlights the importance of access to rights, access to information and child-friendly procedures.[16] In the following sections, first the right to be heard for children in legal proceedings in general will be explained and second, this right will be further clarified in light of asylum procedures.

2.1. THE RIGHT TO BE HEARD

With the adoption and almost universal ratification of the UN Convention on the Rights of the Child (UNCRC)[17] children are increasingly acknowledged as rights holders; entitled to specific substantive rights and procedural rights and safeguards. Children are no longer seen as vulnerable subjects in need of protection only, but they are enabled to exercise and claim their human rights.[18] At the same time the special position and needs of children are recognised in that they are also entitled to protection and support when needed.[19] The participatory rights[20] are specifically important for children to exercise their

---

14 European Commission, *Communication from the commission to the European Parliament and Council. The protection of children in migration*, COM(2017) 211 final, 9.

15 Ibid., 14.

16 Committee of Ministers, *Council of Europe Action Plan on Protecting Refugee and Migrant Children in Europe*, CM(2017) 54-final, 1–2.

17 UNGA Res 44/25 (CRC) (20 November 1989, entered into force 2 September 1990).

18 Jaap E. Doek, 'The eighteenth birthday of the Convention on the Rights of the Child: Achievements and challenges' (2007) 41 University of Michigan Journal of Law Reform 61; Michael Freeman, 'Taking children's rights more seriously' (1992) 6 International Journal of Law and the Family 52; Ton Liefaard, 'Child-friendly justice: protection and participation of children in the justice system' (2016) 88 Temple Law Review 905; Gerison Lansdown, *The evolving capacities of the child* (UNICEF Innocenti Research Centre 2005); Marie-Françoise Lücker-Babel, 'The right of the child to express views and to be heard: An attempt to interpret Article 12 of the UN Convention on the Rights of the Child' (1995) 3 International Journal of Children's Rights 391; Thorburn Stern, 'Unaccompanied and Separated Asylum-seeking Minors' (n. 4 above); Crock, 'Justice for the Migrant Child' (n. 3 above); Ciara Smyth, *European Asylum Law and the Rights of the Child* (Routledge 2014).

19 Annemarieke Beijer and Ton Liefaard, 'A Bermuda Triangle? Balancing protection, participation and proof in criminal proceedings affecting child victims and witnesses' (2011) 7 Utrecht Law Review 70; Doek, 'The eighteenth birthday of the Convention on the Rights of the Child' (n. 18 above).

20 The right to be heard can be found in several provisions of the UNCRC; more generally participation is provided for in Arts. 13 (freedom of expression), 14 (freedom of thought,

(substantive) rights and the UNCRC is the first international and legally binding instrument that enshrined these participatory rights of children.[21] This also shows the holistic nature of the UNCRC: all the rights are interdependent and interrelated and every right must be acknowledged when dealing with children in specific situations.[22] The meaning of individual rights should be understood by reading and interpreting the other rights of the UNCRC.[23] The holistic approach can for example be seen with regard to the 'general principles', as distinguished by the CRC Committee.[24] These four general principles form 'the value system on which the Convention is based':[25] the non-discrimination principle (Art. 2 UNCRC); the best interests of the child principle (Art. 3(1) UNCRC); the right to life and development (Art. 6 UNCRC), and the right to be heard (Art. 12 UNCRC). The acknowledgement of the right to be heard shows the growing recognition of the international community for the child as a rights holder and an autonomous and active human being, rather than a silent and passive child that only needs protection from adults.[26]

The right to be heard, as it is laid down in Article 12 UNCRC, can be seen as part of the broader umbrella term 'participation'.[27] It implies that children, who are capable of forming their views, have the right to express those views freely in any legal procedure (Art. 12 UNCRC). The CRC Committee has clarified that '[l]istening to children should not be seen as an end in itself, but

conscience and religion) and 15 (freedom of association) and specifically regarding different contexts in Arts. 9(2) (separation from the parents), 21(a) (adoption), 23(1) (children with disabilities), 31(1) (cultural activities), 37(d) (deprivation of liberty), 40(2)(b)(iv) (juvenile justice).

21 Nigel Cantwell, 'The origins, development and significance of the United Nations Convention on the Rights of the Child' in Sharon Detrick (ed.), *The United Nations Convention on the Rights of the Child. A guide to the 'Travaux préparatoires'* (Martinus Nijhoff Publishers 1992).

22 Katrien Herbots and Johan Put, 'The Participation Disc: A Concept Analysis of (a) Child ('s Right to) Participation' (2015) 23 *International Journal of Children's Rights* 154, 169; Julia Sloth-Nielsen, 'Ratification of the Convention on the Rights of the Child: Some implications for South African Law' (1995) 11 South African Journal of Human Rights 401; Thomas Hammarberg, 'Children' in Asbjorn Eide, Catharina Krause and Allan Rosas (eds.), *Economic, social and cultural rights. A textbook* (2nd ed. Martinus Nijhoff Publishers 2001).

23 Laura Lundy, '"Voice" is not enough: Conceptualising article 12 of the United Nations Convention on the Rights of the Child' (2007) 33 British Educational Research Journal 927.

24 UN Committee on the Rights of the Child, *General guidelines regarding the form and content of initial reports to be submitted by States Parties under article 44, paragraph 1(a), of the Convention*, CRC/C/5, 27 November 2003, para. 12.

25 Sloth-Nielsen, 'Ratification of the Convention on the Rights of the Child' (n. 22 above) 408.

26 Liefaard, 'Child-friendly justice' (n. 18 above); Karl Hanson 'Children's participation and agency when they don't "do the right thing"' (2016) 23 Childhood 471; Doek, 'The eighteenth birthday of the Convention on the Rights of the Child' (n. 18 above); Lansdown, *The evolving capacities of the child* (n. 18 above); Lücker-Babel, 'The right of the child to express views and to be heard' (n. 18 above); Freeman, 'Taking children's rights more seriously' (n. 18 above).

27 See Lundy, '"Voice" is not enough' (n. 23 above).

rather as a means by which states make their interactions with children and their actions on behalf of children ever more sensitive to the implementation of children's rights'.[28] This right applies both to proceedings which are initiated by the child, such as applying for asylum or a complaints procedure, as well as to those initiated by others which affect the child, such as family law procedures or an asylum determination procedure.[29] The views and opinion of the child should be taken into account giving due weight to the age and maturity of the child (Art. 12(1) UNCRC). Article 5 UNCRC gives further guidelines by stating that children's growing capacities should be taken into account in the exercise of their rights. This implies that a balance must be sought between treating children as active agents, who have the right and capacity to exercise their own rights and providing children with protection, because of their ongoing development and immaturity.[30] Moreover, the CRC Committee recommends states parties to the UNCRC to not establish fixed age limits with regard to the implementation of this right.[31] Moreover, every child also has the right *not* to exercise their right to be heard – it is a choice and not an obligation.[32] When a child is heard, this should take place in a setting that contributes to being able to give his[33] opinion freely. This means that the environment may not be intimidating, hostile or otherwise inappropriate to the age of the child.[34] Specifically, the CRC Committee recommends that children are heard behind closed doors in court, also in order to protect the child's privacy, and that adjustments are made to the design of the courtroom, the clothing of judges and lawyers and the waiting areas for children.[35] An important implication of the right to be heard is that the child's opinion must be taken seriously[36] and that the child must be informed about how his opinion was taken into account in the decision-making process.[37] This feedback must ensure that the child has

---

[28] UN Committee on the Rights of the Child, *General guidelines regarding the form and content of initial reports to be submitted by States Parties under article 44, paragraph 1(a), of the Convention*, CRC/C/5, 27 November 2003, para. 12.

[29] UN Committee on the Rights of the Child, *The right of the child to be heard*, General Comment No. 12, CRC/C/GC/12, 20 July 2009, para. 33.

[30] Gerison Lansdown, Shane R. Jimerson and Reza Shahroozi, 'Children's rights and school psychology: Children's right to participation' (2014) 52 Journal of School Psychology 3; Beijer and Liefaard, 'A Bermuda Triangle?' (n. 19 above).

[31] UN Committee on the Rights of the Child, *The right of the child to be heard*, General Comment No. 12, CRC/C/GC/12, 20 July 2009, para. 21.

[32] Ibid., para. 16.

[33] For practical reasons, in this article it is referred to children and adults in the masculine form. Feminine children and adults are to be considered included in the references as well.

[34] UN Committee on the Rights of the Child, *The right of the child to be heard*, General Comment No. 12, CRC/C/GC/12, 20 July 2009, paras. 23, 34, 60; Council of Europe, Guidelines on child-friendly justice, IV, D, paras. 54–63.

[35] Ibid., para. 34; ibid., IV, D, paras. 54–63; Explanatory memorandum IV, D, para. 112.

[36] Ibid., para. 28.

[37] Ibid., paras. 45; 134(i); ibid., IV, A, para. 1(g); Explanatory memorandum IV, A, para. 55; Lundy, '"Voice" is not enough' (n. 23 above).

not only been heard by way of formality, but that his opinion has been seriously considered by the decision-making authority.[38] This is even more important when decisions are taken that go against the wishes of the child.[39]

2.2. THE RIGHT TO PARTICIPATION FOR CHILDREN IN ASYLUM PROCEDURES

The CRC Committee holds the opinion that states should provide children with access to the asylum procedure in a child-sensitive and age-appropriate manner.[40] Moreover, children have the right to express their views on all aspects of the immigration and asylum proceedings (including any decision on care, shelter or migration status).[41] In the case of an asylum claim, the child must have the opportunity to present his reasons that lead to the asylum application.[42] The CRC Committee holds the opinion that '[c]hildren should be heard independently of their parents, and their individual circumstances should be included in the consideration of the family's cases'.[43] The Committee stresses that

> '[s]tates parties should take all appropriate measures aimed at ensuring children's right to be heard in the immigration procedures concerning their parents, in particular where the decision could affect the children's rights, such as the right to not be separated from their parents'.[44]

---

38 Ibid., para. 45. See also UN Committee on the Rights of the Child, *General Comment No. 14 (2013) on the right of the child to have his or her best interests taken as a primary consideration (art. 3, para. 1)*, CRC/C/GC/14, 29 May 2013.

39 Pernilla Leviner, 'Child participation in the Swedish child protection system' (2018) 26 International Journal of Children's Rights 136; See also Floor A.M. Minkhorst, Cilia L.M. Witteman, A. Carien Koopmans, Nickie Lohman and Erik J. Knorth, 'Decision making in Dutch Child Welfare: Child's Wishes about Reunification after Out-of-Home Placement' (2016) British Journal of Social Work 46.

40 UN Committee on the Rights of the Child, Joint General Comment No. 3 (2017) of the Committee on the Protection of the Rights of All Migrant Workers and Members of their Families and No. 22 (2017) of the Committee on the Rights of the Child on the general principles regarding the human rights of children in the context of international migration, CMW/C/GC/3-CRC/C/GC/22, 16 November 2017, para. 35.

41 Ibid., para. 37; see Art. 12(2) UNCRC.

42 UN Committee on the Rights of the Child, *The right of the child to be heard*, General Comment No. 12, CRC/C/GC/12, 20 July 2009, para. 123.

43 UN Committee on the Rights of the Child, Joint General Comment No. 3 (2017) of the Committee on the Protection of the Rights of All Migrant Workers and Members of their Families and No. 22 (2017) of the Committee on the Rights of the Child on the general principles regarding the human rights of children in the context of international migration, CMW/C/GC/3-CRC/C/GC/22, 16 November 2017, para. 37.

44 Ibid., para. 38. See also Crock, 'Justice for the Migrant Child' (n. 3 above).

This means that next to unaccompanied children,[45] accompanied children should be able to exercise the right to be heard, although parents might be the main asylum applicants and children will be able to receive derived status, when the family's asylum application is accepted. The CRC Committee also notes that '[s]pecific best-interests assessments should be carried out in those procedures, and the child's specific reasons for the migration should be taken into account'.[46] This implies that child-specific forms of persecution should be taken into account by the authorities and could lead to granting the child refugee status, independent from his parents.[47] No further guidance is given by the CRC Committee on the age from which accompanied children should be heard. Also, the negative consequences of hearing accompanied children are not acknowledged by the Committee, for example when the story of the child contradicts the parents' story, ultimately resulting in a rejection of the asylum claim. In the European Union, children have the right to present their asylum claim to the authorities. On the basis of the age and maturity of the child, it should be decided whether he can be interviewed. Moreover, the extent to which interviewing the child could be harmful or otherwise inappropriate should also be taken into account. In the latter case authorities can decide to not hear the child.[48] The UNHCR recommends that appropriate communication methods need to be applied, taking into account the age, gender, cultural background and maturity of the child, as well as the circumstances of the flight and mode of arrival. Non-verbal methods that can be applied include drawing, role-playing, storytelling, singing and playing.[49] The UNHCR acknowledges that children are different from adults. Therefore, it is stated that during the interview children might omit vital information or are unable to differentiate reality from fantasy. Moreover, in case of a lack of clarity about the facts of a case or about the credibility of parts of the claim, the benefit of the doubt should be applied liberally.[50] In any case, interviews need to take place in friendly,

---

45 UN Committee on the Rights of the Child, *Treatment of unaccompanied and separated children outside their country of origin*, General Comment No. 6, CRC/GC/2005/6, para. 25.

46 UN Committee on the Rights of the Child, Joint General Comment No. 3 (2017) of the Committee on the Protection of the Rights of All Migrant Workers and Members of their Families and No. 22 (2017) of the Committee on the Rights of the Child on the general principles regarding the human rights of children in the context of international migration, CMW/C/GC/3-CRC/C/GC/22, 16 November 2017, para. 37.

47 See Jason Pobjoy, *The Child in International Refugee Law* (Cambridge University Press 2017) 66.

48 Marcelle A. Reneman, *EU asylum procedures and the right to an effective remedy* (Hart Publishing 2014).

49 UNHCR, *Guidelines on international protection: Child Asylum claims under Articles 1 (A) and 1 (F) of the 1951 Convention and/or 1967 Protocol relating to the Statutes of Refugees*, HCR/GIP/09/08, 22 December 2009, para. 71.

50 Ibid., para. 73.

accessible settings in order to make children feel safe[51] and they need to be conducted by a professional trained in communicating with children.[52]

2.2.1. *The Right to Information*

The right to be heard has close connections with the right to information. The CRC Committee states that the right to information is essential, 'because it is the precondition of the child's clarified decisions'[53] and that 'children should be provided with full accessible, diversity-sensitive and age-appropriate information about their right to express their views feely'.[54] Moreover, information should be of a child-friendly nature and adapted to the child's age and capacities.[55] To receive adequate information is seen as a precondition for the child to be able to give his informed views and make clarified decisions.[56] Specifically in relation to refugee and migrant children, the CRC Committee has recommended that children should be provided with all relevant information, concerning for example the asylum application process, to allow them to express their well-informed views and wishes. The information should be adapted to the level of maturity and understanding of the child.[57] Specifically, refugee and migrant children should be provided with all relevant information 'concerning, for example, their entitlements, services available including means of communication, the asylum process, family tracing and the situation in their country of origin'[58] in an age-appropriate manner.[59] Moreover, the CRC Committee explains that states parties have to ensure that the child receives all necessary information and advice to make a decision in favour of his best interests.[60] The UNHCR Guidelines on International Protection indicate that

---

51 Ibid., para. 72.

52 Joint General Comment No. 4 (2017) of the Committee on the Protection of the Rights of All Migrant Workers and Members of their Families and No. 23 (2017) of the Committee on the Rights of the Child on State obligations regarding the human rights of children in the context of international migration in countries of origin, transit, destination and return, CMW/C/GC/4-CRC/C/GC/23, 16 November 2017, para. 17(c).

53 UN Committee on the Rights of the Child, *The right of the child to be heard*, General Comment No. 12, CRC/C/GC/12, 20 July 2009, para. 25.

54 Ibid., para. 134(a).

55 Ibid., paras. 34, 82. This applies to information, for example, relating to their rights, any proceedings affecting them, national legislation, regulations and policies, local services, and appeals and complaints procedures.

56 UN Committee on the Rights of the Child, *The right of the child to be heard*, General Comment No. 12, CRC/C/GC/12, 20 July 2009, paras. 25, 80.

57 UN Committee on the Rights of the Child, *Treatment of unaccompanied and separated children outside their country of origin*, General Comment No. 6, CRC/GC/2005/6, para. 25.

58 Ibid.

59 Ibid., para. 124.

60 UN Committee on the Rights of the Child, *The right of the child to be heard*, General Comment No. 12, CRC/C/GC/12, 20 July 2009, para. 16; UN Committee on the Rights of the

children should be given 'all necessary information in a language and manner they understand about the possible existing options and the consequences arising from them',[61] among others on the right to privacy and confidentiality and the age assessment procedure.[62] Moreover, children must understand the procedure and its consequences, have access to age-sensitive information about reception, registration, refugee or statelessness status determination and other procedures and services, and decisions should be communicated to children in a language and manner they understand.[63] Finally, children should be informed about the decisions that are taken 'in person, in the presence of their guardian, legal representative, and/or other support person, in a supportive and non-threatening environment'.[64] In case of a negative decision, particular care should be taken in communicating the message and explaining what the next steps are that can be taken in the procedure.[65]

2.2.2. The Right to (Legal) Representation

An important starting point concerns the fact that the right to be heard implies a choice for the child and not an obligation.[66] If a child decides to give his opinion to the relevant authority in a certain (legal) procedure, he then has the choice to do this himself or through a representative (Art. 12(2) UNCRC). The representative of the child can be a parent, but also a lawyer, a guardian (*ad litem*) or a social worker.[67] The child should preferably be heard personally[68] and when this takes place through the intervention of an adult, this person must have sufficient knowledge and understanding of the procedure and have experience in working with children.[69] The CRC Committee acknowledges that a conflict of

Child, Joint General Comment No. 3 (2017) of the Committee on the Protection of the Rights of All Migrant Workers and Members of their Families and No. 22 (2017) of the Committee on the Rights of the Child on the general principles regarding the human rights of children in the context of international migration, CMW/C/GC/3-CRC/C/GC/22, 16 November 2017, para. 35.

61 UNHCR, *Guidelines on international protection: Child Asylum claims under Articles 1 (A) and 1 (F) of the 1951 Convention and/or 1967 Protocol relating to the Statutes of Refugees*, HCR/GIP/09/08, 22 December 2009, para. 70.

62 Ibid., paras. 70, 75.

63 UNHCR, *A Framework for the Protection of Children* (UNHCR 2012).

64 UNHCR, *Guidelines on international protection: Child Asylum claims under Articles 1 (A) and 1 (F) of the 1951 Convention and/or 1967 Protocol relating to the Statutes of Refugees*, HCR/GIP/09/08, 22 December 2009, para. 77.

65 Ibid., para. 77.

66 UN Committee on the Rights of the Child, *The right of the child to be heard*, General Comment No. 12, CRC/C/GC/12, 20 July 2009, paras. 16, 58.

67 Ibid., para. 36.

68 Ibid., para. 35.

69 Ibid., para. 36.

interests can exist between the child and his parents and the representative must bring forward the views of the child correctly to the decision-maker.[70] Moreover,

> 'representatives must have sufficient knowledge and understanding of the various aspects of the decision-making process and experience in working with children. The representative must be aware that he or she represents exclusively the interests of the child and not the interests of other persons (parent(s))...'[71]

It is of importance to distinguish here between the guardian, who is appointed to safeguard the best interests and general well-being of the unaccompanied or separated child, and the legal representative (i.e. a lawyer). The guardian acts as a statutory representative of the child in all proceedings in the same way a parent represents his/her child and complements the limited legal capacity of the child. The guardian must be accessible to unaccompanied children at all stages of the asylum procedure.[72] The CRC Committee notes that unaccompanied children should only be referred to asylum or other administrative or judicial procedures when they have been appointed both a guardian *and* a legal representative free of charge.[73] The guardian should be appointed as soon as the child has been identified and until the child has either reached the age of majority or has permanently left the country.[74] For unaccompanied and separated children, the presence of a guardian or legal representative is required in all planning and decision-making processes, including interviews conducted by the refugee determination authority and any appeal hearings.[75] Moreover, the CRC Committee has specified that all children, including those with parents/in parental care, should be appointed a legal representative to provide representation at all stages in the proceedings and with whom they can communicate freely.[76]

In the EU Asylum Procedures Directive,[77] it is acknowledged that children can have the legal capacity to make an asylum application on their own behalf,

---

70 Ibid., para. 36.

71 Ibid., paras. 36–37.

72 European Union Agency for Fundamental Rights (FRA), *Guardianship systems for children deprived of parental care in the European Union* (Publications Office of the European Union 2015).

73 UN Committee on the Rights of the Child, *Treatment of unaccompanied and separated children outside their country of origin*, General Comment No. 6, CRC/GC/2005/6, paras. 21, 36, 69.

74 Ibid., para. 33.

75 Ibid., paras. 33, 69 and 72.

76 Joint General Comment No. 4 (2017) of the Committee on the Protection of the Rights of All Migrant Workers and Members of their Families and No. 23 (2017) of the Committee on the Rights of the Child on State obligations regarding the human rights of children in the context of international migration in countries of origin, transit, destination and return, CMW/C/GC/4-CRC/C/GC/23, 16 November 2017, para. 17(f).

77 Directive 2013/32/EU of the European Parliament and of the Council of 26 June 2013 on common procedures for granting and withdrawing international protection (recast) [2013] OJ/L 180/60.

but also that this can be done through their parents, adult family members, an adult responsible for them or through a representative.[78] Under the Asylum Procedures Directive states must assure that unaccompanied minors are appointed a representative who can assist them in benefitting from the rights under the Directive and to comply with its obligations.[79] A representative should assist and represent the unaccompanied child, ensure the best interests of the child in the procedure and exercise legal capacity when necessary.[80] In the context of this Directive the term 'guardian' is not used, but the role of the representative can be seen as equalling the role of the guardian as identified by the CRC Committee. During all phases of a formal asylum procedure, a qualified representative should be available free of charge.[81] The child should be informed immediately of the appointment of a representative. States must ensure that the representative is given the opportunity to inform the unaccompanied child about the meaning and possible consequences of the personal interview and how to prepare him or herself for the interview. The representative must also be able to attend the interview and to ask questions or make comments. Even if the representative is present, states may still require the presence of the child.[82] Unaccompanied children and their representatives must be provided, free of charge, with legal and procedural information.[83] States may also provide asylum applicants with free legal assistance in the procedures at first instance.[84] As a minimum applicants have to be provided with free legal assistance and representation in appeals procedures.[85]

3. PARTICIPATION FROM A SOCIO-EMPIRICAL PERSPECTIVE

As stated above, participation is often used as an umbrella term under which different rights and concepts are placed. Krappmann describes participation as 'that what results from expressing views, listening and giving due weight to the views, interests and goals of the child'.[86] Thomas notes that participation can be seen as an activity involving decision-making, being a process or an outcome and

---

[78] Ibid., Art. 7(3). See also Domenico Rosani in this volume.
[79] Ibid., Art. 25(1)(a).
[80] Ibid., Art. 2(n).
[81] Ibid., Arts. 7(3), 19, 20 and 21.
[82] Ibid., Art. 25(1)(a)–(b).
[83] Ibid., Art. 25(3)(b) in the procedures at first instance (in accordance with Art. 19(1)).
[84] Ibid., Art. 20(2), in which case Art. 19(1) does not apply.
[85] Ibid, Art. 20(1).
[86] Lothar Krappmann, 'The weight of the child's view (Article 12 of the Convention on the Rights of the Child)' (2010) 18 International Journal of Children's Rights 501, 502.

involving collective decision-making or decisions about individual children.[87] Herbots and Put see participation both as an end in itself as well as a means to achieve other goals; '[t]hey are rather two ends of a continuum between which lies a grey area'.[88] Sinclair argues that active participation means that children are enabled to influence decision-making and to bring about change. Several other purposes of participation can be identified though: to uphold children's rights, to fulfil legal responsibilities, to improve decision-making, to promote children's protection, to enhance children's skills, to empower children and to enhance their self-esteem.[89] These different definitions of child participation attribute different meanings, goals and importance to participation. From a legal perspective, it can be seen as a fundamental right of the child that should be upheld by states, because children are individual rights holders entitled to the rights as enshrined in the UNCRC. From a socio-empirical perspective it can be argued that participation can have important benefits for the development and well-being of children as well. In this section, first the theoretical underpinnings of the concept of participation will be explained. Second, the results of empirical studies concerning the participation of children in legal proceedings are presented and third the attention is drawn to how children participate in asylum procedures in practice.

3.1. TYPOLOGIES OF PARTICIPATION

One of the earliest conceptualisations of the child's right to participation was made by Roger Hart in his essay written for UNICEF titled *Children's Participation. From tokenism to citizenship*.[90] Hart states that participation is a fundamental right of citizenship and an important element of democratic decision-making. However, children's competencies are underestimated and often they are not listened to, in families and in the wider community. Hart has developed the *ladder of participation*; a typology of children's participation in social movements and projects concerning children. The ladder consists of eight rungs, the lowest three of those referring to levels of non-participation; i.e. manipulation, decoration and tokenism. *Manipulation* refers to the situation where adults use children's participation to make their own point, but where children do not understand the event and their involvement in it. Hart gives the example of 'pre-school children carrying political placards concerning the

87 Nigel Thomas, 'Towards a theory of children's participation' (2007) 15 International Journal of Children's Rights 199.

88 Herbots and Put, 'The Participation Disc' (n. 22 above).

89 Ruth Sinclair, 'Participation in practice: Making it meaningful, effective and sustainable' (2004) 18 Children and Society 106.

90 Roger A. Hart, *Children's Participation. From tokenism to citizenship* (UNICEF 1992).

impact of social policies on children'.[91] This is also the case when children are consulted, but are not provided with any feedback on the extent to which their views had any impact. *Decoration* means that children are present at an event, but they do not know why or what the cause is of the event. Their presence, however, is not orchestrated by adults to show that children support the cause and is therefore placed one rung higher than manipulation. *Tokenism* refers to 'those instances in which children are apparently given a voice, but in fact have little or no choice about the subject or the style of communicating it, and little or no opportunity to formulate their own opinions'.[92] The upper five rungs refer to increasingly effective and genuine forms of participation; i.e. assigned but informed, consulted and informed, adult-initiated shared decisions with children, child-initiated and directed, and child-initiated shared decisions with adults. These rungs refer to actual levels of child participation, running from assigned but informed participation – meaning that children at least know where they participate voluntary in and have a meaningful role – to child-initiated shared decisions with adults. This typology has had an enormous influence on how practitioners and policy-makers look at children's participation.[93] However, several scholars have made adaptations to this model, such as removing the lower rungs and/or the hierarchical order, shifting rungs and adding new ones.[94]

More recently, Lundy has also developed a model to conceptualise the child's right to participation and to provide guidance to decision-makers on how to implement this right. She departs from the point of view that the child's right to be heard runs counter to the instinct and interests of adults, who are ultimately responsible for securing this right. Therefore, conditions should be created which make it impossible for adults who hear the views of children to ignore those views in the decision they take. Therefore, Lundy distinguishes four elements: space, voice, audience and influence. First, safe *spaces* must be created for children to give their views. Second, children must be given information and must be facilitated in giving their views (i.e. *voice*). Third, the views must be listened to by someone (i.e. *audience*) and fourth, the views must be taken seriously and acted upon (i.e. *influence*).[95] Lundy has also further clarified the concept of *tokenism* in stating that it is unacceptable to state that participation should be denied completely, when it is considered tokenistic to involve children: '[i]f it cannot be achieved meaningfully, then it appears to be considered legitimate to not do it at all'.[96] This would be unthinkable in the implementation

91 Ibid., 9.

92 Ibid.

93 Thomas, 'Towards a theory of children's participation' (n. 87 above); Laura Lundy, 'In defence of tokenism? Children's right to participate in collective decision-making' (2018) 25 Childhood 340.

94 See Thomas, 'Towards a theory of children's participation' (n. 87 above).

95 Lundy, '"Voice" is not enough' (n. 23 above).

96 Lundy, 'In defence of tokenism?' (n. 93 above).

of other human rights. In response to this, Lundy states that dialogue between adults and children, feedback to children on their views and giving due weight to their views are important elements of participation and these should be encouraged by decision-makers and authorities, to prevent participation from becoming tokenistic. It is concluded that tokenistic ways of participating can sometimes be a start and is better than not involving children at all.[97]

3.2. PARTICIPATION IN LEGAL PROCEEDINGS

In the past decades, a vast body of research has emerged on the topic of child participation. This concerns participation in different life domains of the child, such as education, health care, policy implementation and reform, political and public decision-making and legal proceedings.[98] In this section, research outcomes on the participation of individual children in legal proceedings will be discussed. Most research to date focuses on the participation of children in civil law proceedings, therefore the outcomes presented below mainly relate to children involved in child protection or custody proceedings. These proceedings are generally initiated by adults, but affect the lives of children as well. The research outcomes presented below provide a starting point for looking at participation of children in asylum procedures, which will be discussed in the final paragraph of this section.

When asking children about their participation in decisions that are taken in their lives, in general, they indicate that they value being heard.[99] Children specifically find it important to be heard personally by a judge (or other decision-maker), because through a personal conversation they are able

97 Ibid.

98 Lundy, '"Voice" is not enough' (n. 23 above); Micha de Winter, *Socialization and civil society. How parents, teachers and others could foster a democratic way of life* (Sense Publishers 2012); Thomas, 'Towards a theory of children's participation' (n. 87 above); Mark Henaghan, 'Article 12 of the UN Convention on the Rights of Children. Where Have We Come from, Where Are We Now and Where to from Here?' (2017) 25 International Journal of Children's Rights 537; E. Kay M. Tisdall, John Davies and Michael Gallagher, 'Reflecting on children and young people's participation in the UK' (2008) 16 International Journal of Children's Rights 343; Mary Donnelly and Ursula Kilkelly, 'Participation in healthcare: the views and experiences of children and young people' (2011) 19 International Journal of Children's Rights 107; Katherine Curtis, Kristin Liabo, Helen Roberts and Maggie Barker, 'Consulted but not heard: a qualitative study of young people's views of their local health service' (2004) 7 Health Expectations 149; Meda Couzens, 'Child Participation in Local Governance' in Martin D. Ruck, Michele Peterson-Badali and Michael Freeman (eds.), *Handbook of Children's Rights* (Routledge 2017).

99 Judy Cashmore and Patrick Parkinson, 'What responsibilities do courts have to hear children's voices?' (2007) 15 International Journal of Children's Rights 43; Ursula Kilkelly, *Listening to children about justice: Report of the Council of Europe consultation with children on child-friendly justice* (Council of Europe, 2010).

to provide their own version of events and not through a mediator (such as a lawyer or guardian).[100] Several studies indicate that participation in decision-making processes may help children understand and accept the final decision, because the reasons for taking the decision are explained and consequently better understood by the child.[101] Research in the field of health care shows that treatment outcomes are probably better when children are involved in decisions from the start of the medical procedure, because it increases their knowledge and understanding of the disease and the role they can play in it.[102] Participation can also aid the personal development of children: it can have a positive influence on developing self-confidence, self-esteem, autonomy[103] and 'open parent–child communication about family conflict, clarify issues rather than leaving them to children's fears and imaginations, make children more aware of the difficulties their families face, and help children feel valued as the subject of a contest'.[104] Moreover, children perceive their own input as more important, feel that they are treated more fairly and respect the decision more quickly, when participating in the decision-making process.[105]

Despite the positive effects that are attributed to participation of children in legal decision-making, children do not always feel sufficiently enabled to participate in legal proceedings. First, children do not always believe that they

100 Ibid.; Karen Saywitz, Lorinda B. Camparo and Anna Romanoff, 'Interviewing children in custody cases: Implications of research and policy for practice' (2010) 28 Behavioral Sciences and the Law 542, 545; Kim van Hoorde et al., *Bouncing Back. The wellbeing of children in international child abduction cases* (European Union funded research project Enhancing the Well-being of Children in Cases of International Child Abduction (eWELL) 2018).

101 Ibid; Tara M. Collins, 'A child's right to participate: Implications for international child protection' (2017) 21 The International Journal of Human Rights 14; Gillian Schofield, 'The voice of the child in family placement decision-making: A developmental model' (2005) 29 Adoption and Fostering 29; Ganna G. van Bijleveld, Christine W.M. Dedding and Joske F.G. Bunders-Aelen, 'Children's and young people's participation within child welfare and child protection services: a state-of-the-art review' (2015) 20 Child and Family Social Work 129.

102 Mary Donnelly and Ursula Kilkelly, 'Participation in healthcare: the views and experiences of children and young people' (2011) 19 International Journal of Children's Rights 107; Svein A. Vis, Astrid Strandbu, Amy Holtan and Nigel Thomas, 'Participation and health–research review of child participation in planning and decision-making' (2011) 16 Child and Family Social Work 325.

103 Lundy, 'In defence of tokenism?' (n. 93 above); Collins, 'A child's right to participate' (n. 101 above); Saywitz, Camparo and Romanoff, 'Interviewing children in custody cases' (n. 100 above) 545; Lansdown, *The evolving capacities of the child* (n. 18 above); Robyn Fitzgerald, Anne Graham, Anne Smith and Nicola Taylor, 'Children's participation as a struggle over recognition' in Barry Percy-Smith and Nigel Thomas (eds.), *A handbook of children and young people's participation. Perspectives from theory and practice* (Routledge 2009).

104 Saywitz, Camparo and Romanoff, 'Interviewing children in custody cases' (n. 100 above) 545.

105 European Union Agency for Fundamental Rights, *Child-friendly justice. Perspectives and experiences of children involved in judicial proceedings as victims, witnesses or parties in nine EU Member States* (Publications Office of the European Union 2017); Judy Cashmore, 'Promoting the participation of children and young people in care' (2002) 26 *Child Abuse and Neglect* 845.

receive sufficient child-friendly information, that would enable their participation and understanding of their rights and the procedures.[106] Moreover, children do not always feel sufficiently protected, stating about experiencing unfriendly and disrespectful behaviour by professionals, such as defence lawyers, judges or police officers.[107] Participation in legal proceedings also carries with it the danger for children to be pressured by their parents to say certain things or to choose sides (e.g. in parental separation or custody cases).[108] Adult decision-makers play an important role in facilitating meaningful participation of the child.[109] Some studies indicate that professionals can have paternalistic views on children's participation, believing that children do not have the skills and competences to be able to participate, but that they should be protected against participation[110] or that the wishes and opinions of the child are only brought forward when they correspond with those of the authorities.[111] Daly notes that 'systems struggle with cases where children have preferences which incline against the prevailing orthodoxy', such as wishing or, on the contrary, not wishing to have contact with one of either parents.[112] Moreover, when the views of the child have been asked, informing the child on how his opinion has influenced the final decision is often lacking.[113] This is even more of importance when the decision goes against the wishes of the child. Overall, it can be stated that there is a lack of clarity on how the views of children should be weighed, in order to give those views 'due weight'.[114] This proves to be especially complex in certain situations, such as when a very young child is involved or when the child's wishes go against the prevailing opinion of parents and/or the

106 Kilkelly, *Listening to children about justice* (n. 99); van Hoorde et al., *Bouncing Back* (n. 100 above).

107 European Union Agency for Fundamental Rights (FRA), *Child-friendly justice* (n. 105 above).

108 van Hoorde et al., *Bouncing Back* (n. 100 above).

109 Danielle Kennan, Bernadine Brady and Cormac Forkan, 'Supporting Children's Participation in Decision Making: A Systematic Literature Review Exploring the Effectiveness of Participatory Process' (2018) British Journal of Social Work 1; Jeanette Cossar, Marian Brandon and Peter Jordan, *Don't make assumptions': Children and young people's views of the child protection system and messages for change* (The Office of the Children's Commissioner 2011); E. McCarthy, 'Young People in Residential Care, their Participation and the Influencing Factors' (2016) 22 Child Care in Practice 368; van Bijleveld, Dedding and Bunders-Aelen, 'Children's and young people's participation within child welfare and child protection services' (n. 101 above).

110 van Bijleveld, Dedding and Bunders-Aelen, 'Children's and young people's participation within child welfare and child protection services' (n. 101 above).

111 Leviner, 'Child participation in the Swedish child protection system' (n. 39 above).

112 Aoife Daly and Stephanie Rap, 'Children's Participation in Youth Justice and Civil Court Proceedings' in Ton Liefaard and Ursula Kilkelly (eds.), *The International Human Rights of Children* (Springer 2018) 15.

113 Collins, 'A child's right to participate' (n. 101 above); Hoorde et al., *Bouncing Back* (n. 100 above); Kilkelly, *Listening to children about justice* (n. 99).

114 Daly and Rap, 'Children's Participation in Youth Justice and Civil Court Proceedings' (n. 112 above).

decision-maker (for example when a child prefers not to have contact with one of the parents). Providing children with an explanation of the decision taken and the weight attached to the child's views could be a safeguard in this case, however, these explanations are often lacking.[115]

3.3. PARTICIPATION IN ASYLUM PROCEDURES

The participation of children in asylum procedures is still an underdeveloped field of research. As explained above, it is acknowledged in international standards that the right to be heard should be upheld for these children; however, little sound academic research has been conducted on the implementation of this right in asylum procedures.[116] The limited research that has been conducted indicates that refugee and migrant children are not sufficiently enabled to participate in predominantly adult-oriented asylum procedures.[117] Asylum application procedures can even be perceived as traumatic events in themselves.[118] It has also been shown, however, that informing people and having them to participate in the process of integration empowers them and helps them to regain control over their life.[119]

When having a closer look at the position of children in asylum procedures, the distinction between unaccompanied and separated on the one hand and accompanied children on the other hand is of importance. Thorburn Stern explains that for both groups of children it is important to be recognised as a rights holder. For unaccompanied and separated children, who lack protection from a parent or caretaker, it is important to be provided with protection against

---

115 Ibid.; Aoife Daly, *Children, autonomy and the courts: Beyond the right to be heard* (Brill Nijhoff 2017).

116 Carla van Os, Margrite Kalverboer, Elianne Zijlstra, W.J. Post and E.J. Knorth, 'Knowledge of the unknown child: A systematic review on the elements of the Best Interests of the Child Assessment for recently arrived refugee children' (2016) 19 *Clinical Child and Family Psychology Review* 185; Helen Stalford, 'David and Goliath: Due Weight, the State and Determining Unaccompanied Children's Fate' (2018) 32 Immigration, Asylum and Nationality Law 258.

117 Smyth, *European Asylum Law and the Rights of the Child* (n. 18 above); Katie Mannion, *Child Migration Matters. Children and young people's experiences of migration* (Immigrant Council of Ireland 2016); Naomi Kennan and Ursula Kilkelly, *Children's involvement in criminal, civil and administrative judicial proceedings in the 28 Member States of the EU* (Publications Office of the European Union 2015); Stalford, 'David and Goliath' (n. 116 above).

118 Leila Darmanaki Farahani and Graham L. Bradley, 'The Role of Psychosocial Resources in the Adjustment of Migrant Adolescents' (2018) 12 Journal of the Pacific Rim Psychology 1; Elaine Chase, 'Security and subjective wellbeing: the experiences of unaccompanied young people seeking asylum in the UK' (2013) 35 Sociology of Health and Illness 858.

119 Marko Valenta and Berit Berg, 'User involvement and empowerment among asylum seekers in Norwegian reception centres' (2010) 13 European Journal of Social Work 483; Chase, 'Security and subjective wellbeing' (n. 118 above).

inter alia discrimination, abuse, violence and exploitation. Furthermore, unaccompanied and separated children file their own asylum claim or a representative files the claim on behalf of them in the receiving country (see section 2.2 of this contribution).[120] For accompanied children it is important to recognise that they can have a specific claim for protection, apart from the family's or have been subjected to child-specific forms of persecution.[121] This difference between both groups of children means that unaccompanied children provide the main source of information about their situation and that they should be heard directly in the asylum procedure by the authorities, if their age and maturity permits this.[122] Accompanied children usually depend on their parents' asylum claim and therefore, in practice, they are not automatically heard in the asylum procedure, although the international standards recommend hearing these children individually as well.[123]

3.3.1. Unaccompanied and Separated Children

In general, it can be stated that children experience a serious lack of information before and during their journey to the host country, regarding the journey itself, the authorities, procedures and access to rights and services.[124] Also, children indicate that upon arrival they are overwhelmed and are not able to process information or are not given adequate information at all. Exchanges and communication with peers are seen as a reliable way of getting access to information, from those they trust.[125]

Despite the fact that unaccompanied and separated children should be heard in the asylum application process, they do not always find it easy to disclose their story to adults.[126] Chase shows in her study among unaccompanied children in the UK that they selectively share information with adults and peers 'to maintain a sense of agency and control over their lives'.[127] These young people displayed a sense of distrust towards social workers or others representing the asylum system, but also protected themselves from getting upset by memories of the

---

120 See also Rosani in this volume.

121 Thorburn Stern, 'Unaccompanied and Separated Asylum-seeking Minors: implementing a Rights-based Approach in the asylum Process' (n. 4 above).

122 UNHCR/UNICEF, *Safe and Sound. What states can do to ensure respect for the best interests of unaccompanied and separated children in Europe* UNHCR/UNICEF 2014) 31.

123 Reneman, *EU asylum procedures and the right to an effective remedy* (n. 48 above).

124 See e.g. K. Kloosterboer, *Kind in het centrum. Kinderrechten in asielzoekerscentra* (UNICEF 2009).

125 Council of Europe, *Child-friendly information for children in migration. What do children think?* (Council of Europe 2018); see also Elaine Chase, 'Agency and silence: Young people seeking asylum alone in the UK' (2010) 40 *British Journal of Social Work* 2050.

126 Kohli, 'The sound of silence' (n. 3 above).

127 Chase, 'Agency and silence: Young people seeking asylum alone in the UK' (n. 125 above) 2065.

past. Uncertainty about their immigration status posed a great degree of burden and feelings of concern on them.[128] Research conducted in the Netherlands shows that unaccompanied children living in foster care are more positive about their life and have more people to turn to for help, compared to unaccompanied children living in reception facilities. The latter group of children experiences a lack of care, love, support and supervision from adults and feels neglected, lonely and sad. Family members and peers are most often named as people they trust and could talk to.[129]

Kohli explains that unaccompanied children may have been instructed by parents or smugglers to present a certain story to the authorities. These are called 'thin stories' which are 'purposefully constructed as an acceptable amalgam in compliance with international conventions related to the status of refugees' and which are perceived as the key to entering or staying in the host country.[130] Stalford sketches a rather grim picture of the current state of affairs concerning the participation of unaccompanied children in immigration procedures in the UK. Although unaccompanied children are generally heard by the immigration authorities, the manner in which they are heard is very worrisome. Children experience hostile interrogation techniques, feel attacked and intimidated, suggesting that questions are asked to expose inconsistencies and to question the credibility of the child's story. The adversarial nature of asylum procedures and the importance attached to the child's testimony and evidence to be provided to substantiate the asylum application are named as causes of the non-implementation of the right to be heard for children.[131] Stalford explains that asylum procedures

> 'perform a rather different function than that envisaged by art 12(1) [CRC], which is less about giving the child the opportunity to have a say in how different aspects of their claim might be disposed of, and more about defending their right to make such a claim in the first place'.[132]

3.3.2. *Accompanied Children*

Concerning the (much larger) group of accompanied children the question arises to what extent they are able to participate in the asylum procedure

128 Kohli, 'The sound of silence' (n. 3 above).

129 Margrite Kalverboer, Elianne Zijlstra, Carla van Os, Danielle Zevulun, Mijntje ten Brummelaar and Daan Beltman, 'Unaccompanied minors in the Netherlands and the care facility in which they flourish best' (2016) Child and Family Social Work 1.

130 Kohli, 'The sound of silence' (n. 3 above) 711.

131 See also Lisa Shamseldin, 'Implementation of the United Nations Convention on the Rights of the Child 1989 in the Care and Protection of Unaccompanied Asylum Seeking Children: Findings from Empirical Research in England, Ireland and Sweden' (2012) 20 International Journal of Children's Rights 90.

132 Stalford, 'David and Goliath' (n. 116 above) 266.

independently or separately from their parents? Several studies indicate that the position of accompanied children receives far less attention compared to unaccompanied and separated children and they are not always provided with the same rights and safeguards.[133] When children are accompanied by parents it is often assumed that it is sufficient if the adult is informed and heard within the asylum procedure and authorities assume that being in the care of a parent excludes them from being in need of assistance, protection or attention of the state.[134] 'Children are included as "accompanying family" or as "dependents" in applications made by adults and their faith is generally tied to those adults.'[135] This implies that the status of the child automatically follows from the refugee status granted to parents. This means that the child receiving derivative protection status from the parent(s) is entitled to the same level of protection as children who are recognised as refugees in their own right.[136] However, as noted above from the international standards it can be derived that child-specific forms of persecution should also be considered in the asylum procedure. Reneman notes that parents may not be aware of independent asylum motives of the child or are unwilling to disclose these to the authorities.[137] Moreover, the development and possible problems that children have to deal with do not weigh in the decision made by the immigration authorities, because oftentimes the authorities are not aware of these problems. Parents are unable to adequately represent the interests of their children, no best interests assessment is carried out by the authorities and sometimes children are not heard separately (e.g. children below the age of 15 in the Netherlands).[138] Recently, in the Netherlands it was ruled in an appeal case that a minor had its own legal interests in an asylum application procedure, because when a minor is granted an independent resident right this is considered more in favour of his interests, compared to receiving a derived resident right from his mother.[139] This judgment shows the increased

133 Suzy Duivenvoorde, 'Het participatierecht van minderjarige vreemdelingen in de Nederlandse asielprocedure' (2018) 3(19) Journaal Vreemdelingenrecht 1–7; Hilde Lidén and Hilde Rusten, 'Asylum, Participation, and the Best Interests of the Child: New Lessons from Norway' (2007) 21 Children and Society 273.

134 ENOC Taskforce children on the move, *Safety and fundamental rights at stake for children on the move* (De Kinderombudsman/Barnombudsmannen 2016) 29; Ann-Christin Cederborg, 'Children's Right to be Heard from their Unique Perspectives' (n. 3 above); Crock, 'Justice for the Migrant Child' (n. 3 above); Lansdown, *The evolving capacities of the child* (n. 18 above); Lisa Ottosson and Anna Lundberg, 'People Out of Place: Advocates' Negotiations on Children's Participation in the Asylum Application Process in Sweden' (2013) 27 International Journal of Law Policy and the Family 266.

135 Crock, 'Justice for the Migrant Child' (n. 3 above) 238.

136 Pobjoy, *The Child in International Refugee Law* (n. 47 above).

137 Reneman, *EU asylum procedures and the right to an effective remedy* (n. 48 above).

138 Margrite Kalverboer and Elianne Zijlstra, *Kinderen uit asielzoekersgezinnen en het recht op ontwikkeling. Het belang van het kind in het Vreemdelingenrecht* (Uitgeverij SWP 2006).

139 ECLI:NL:RVS:2018:3171.

recognition for and importance of the independent rights of accompanied children in immigration law.[140]

Pobjoy goes as far as to argue that in case of a rejection of the asylum application, and where no individual status determination of the child has been carried out, this results in a violation of the duty of non-refoulement and the right to be heard (Art. 12 UNCRC).[141] States, therefore, have implemented status determination procedures for accompanied children; however, this does not automatically mean that the child is heard or that this process takes place rigorously.[142] This also implies that a best interests assessment might not take place in the case of accompanied children. This can be problematic when a separate claim for protection of the child could be considered, that could benefit both the child and his family.[143] A study conducted in Sweden shows that when the views of accompanied children are heard 'their stories are often used strategically to strengthen their parents' asylum claims rather than being assessed and valued on their own terms'.[144] The opposite can also happen, however, where the story of the child contradicts the parents' flight story, which will question the credibility of the story presented to the immigration authority. In Norway, the conversations with accompanied children have been characterised as being tokenistic and professionals need to be trained to a larger degree in conducting interviews with children and in identifying child-specific forms of persecution.[145] Moreover, countries apply different age limits to hearing accompanied children. For example, in the Netherlands accompanied children are heard by the immigration authorities from age 15, whereas in Norway children from the age of seven are heard by the immigration authorities.[146]

3.3.3. *Giving due Weight to the Views of the Child*

As explained above, giving due weight to the views of children is a complex exercise and this is even more so the case in asylum procedures. Smyth argues that:

> 'it is submitted that giving "due weight" to the views of the child in accordance with age and maturity – in the above sense of attributing the proper quality, substance

---

140 Peter Rodrigues, 'Minderjarig kind heeft zelfstandig belang bij zijn beroep, omdat hij mogelijk een sterker verblijfsrecht kan verkrijgen dan het verblijf dat hem bij zijn moeder is vergund' (2019) AB 2019/132, 988.

141 Pobjoy, *The Child in International Refugee Law* (n. 47 above) 62.

142 Ibid.

143 Crock, 'Justice for the Migrant Child' (n. 3 above).

144 Ottosson and Lundberg, 'People Out of Place' (n. 134 above) 284.

145 Lidén and Rusten, 'Asylum, Participation, and the Best Interests of the Child' (n. 133 above) 273; see also Pobjoy, *The Child in International Refugee Law* (n. 47 above) 101–156.

146 Ibid., Liden and Rusten (n. 133 above).

> or credence to the child's views – is simply not possible if the weight to be given to testimony has been pre-determined by rules establishing negative credibility inferences. This is particularly the case when such rules are founded on assumptions about how *adults* conduct themselves credibly (or incredibly) – assumptions that do not hold for children.'[147]

Smyth pinpoints the inherent difficult of hearing the views of children – in light of Article 12 UNCRC – in asylum procedures. She further poses the question: *views on what should be heard?* It is argued that from an evidential point of view it is highly relevant to hear the views of children, to investigate the reasons for the flight, the conditions in the home country and the risks involved in a possible return. However, hearing the opinion of the child on whether he prefers to stay or go back to his home country is irrelevant in the procedure. An analogy can be drawn here with other legal proceedings, such as in juvenile justice, where hearing the child's views on his preferred outcome of the case is of irrelevance to the process, according to Smyth.[148] This merits the question how participation of children in asylum procedures should take shape and whether true participation is possible at all. A related issue is the age from which children should be heard. Giving due weight to the views of a child is tied to the capacities of the child in articulating his views and overseeing the consequences of his involvement in and contribution to the procedure.[149] First, this implies that hearing the child should have added value to the assessment of the asylum application. This can be questioned for example in the case of very young children, who hardly know in which country they are and how their travels have been arranged. Second, the question can be posed to what extent accompanied children should be protected against participating in asylum procedures that are aimed at assessing the credibility of the asylum motives of the family, because of the negative consequences their involvement can have for themselves and/or the family applying for asylum. It should be noted, however, that due weight implies that the extent to which the views of the child are taken into account in the decision-making depends on the capacities and maturity of the child and lies in the hands of the decision-maker. As a consequence, this principle should also apply in asylum procedures and influence how principles such as 'benefit of the doubt' and 'credibility' are applied in practice.

4. CONCLUDING REMARKS

The right to participation is a fundamental right of the child. Its conceptualisation in law and its implementation in practice is a manifestation of the growing

147 Smyth, *European Asylum Law and the Rights of the Child* (n. 18 above) 133.
148 Ibid., 131.
149 Art. 5 UNCRC.

recognition of children as rights holders, whose views and opinions should be taken seriously. Involvement in legal proceedings helps children to understand and accept the decisions that are taken. Also, it gives them a sense of agency and control over their lives and the decisions that have a profound impact on them.

In the context of asylum application proceedings, the participation of children has a distinct dynamic. The available research in this area shows a lack of attention towards adopting a child-friendly approach in involving children in the asylum procedure. Children experience a gap in knowledge and understanding and hearing their views takes place in procedures developed for adults. Moreover, the distinction between unaccompanied and accompanied children is of particular relevance; i.e. the proceedings are either initiated by children themselves or by their parents. The first means that unaccompanied children have to substantiate and explain their asylum motives, the latter means that parents are the main asylum applicants and are central in the procedure. The focus in the asylum procedure lies on evidence gathering and in the case of accompanied children the prevailing rationale is that children will receive derived status from their parent(s). Recently, some more acknowledgement appears to be developing for the notion that children can have asylum motives of their own, that child-specific forms of persecution can be identified and that accompanied children should be recognised as refugees in their own right. However, how to give due weight to the views of children in the asylum procedure and how this relates to assessing credibility and giving children the benefit of the doubt is an area that is largely undeveloped in research and in practice.

Although child participation might have gained common ground in some areas of law, this cannot be concluded yet for the field of immigration law. It can be concluded from this contribution that true participation – as envisaged in Article 12 UNCRC – might not be possible in the context of the current implementation of asylum procedures. However, it is of importance to sensitise professionals of the significance and potential benefits of engaging with children in a child-friendly and age-appropriate manner. Children will benefit self-evidently from this approach, but also authorities might be able to come to a better assessment of the asylum motives and specific forms of persecution that a child or family asks to be protected against. Training of professionals working with children in the asylum procedure is therefore essential.[150]

---

150 See also Smyth, *European Asylum Law and the Rights of the Child* (n. 18 above).

UNACCOMPANIED ASYLUM-SEEKING CHILDREN AS RIGHTS HOLDERS

Theory and Reality in the EU Legal System

Domenico ROSANI*

* Research and teaching associate at the Department of Italian Law, University of Innsbruck, Austria, and former trainee at the EU Agency for Fundamental Rights. The author would like to thank all the friends and colleagues who contributed to this chapter with important insights. In particular, Grigorios Tsioukas, who offered precious suggestions on an earlier version of it; while Katharina Heymann provided excellent assistance in reviewing it from a linguistic point of view. Any errors are mine alone. The views expressed in this chapter are the author's opinions and cannot be referred to the EU Agency for Fundamental Rights.

1. INTRODUCTION

In the past, the understanding of children being 'rights holders' has been widely criticised. The recognition that children have rights on their own, and that they should have the opportunity to – at least, partially – exercise them, was far from obvious. Indeed, children have long been treated as objects of protection rather than as subjects of rights.[1] In the meantime, the idea of children as rights holders has been incorporated into the European legal order, following the example[2] of the 1989 United Nations Convention on the Rights of the Child (UNCRC). Especially the right to be heard is one of the pivotal components of the idea of the child as a rights holder.

However, the practical implementation of this principle is open to criticism. Children are frequently not asked for their views or their consent in the performance of crucial acts and the taking of fundamental decisions affecting their lives. Migrant children – especially if unaccompanied – are particularly affected in this regard. To illustrate this by means of examples: in almost half of the Member States of the European Union medical examinations for age assessment may be carried out without asking the child to consent.[3] Moreover, 14 states do not allow children to lodge an asylum application in their own right, requesting the child's legal representative[4] to provide for it. However, legal representatives are often not appointed in a timely manner, while important deadlines are linked to the moment of the lodging of the asylum application. As a result, the child's access to crucial services such as the education system is gravely postponed.

This contribution deals with the practical implementation of the principle of children as rights holders in the field of migration. It will especially draw on the two mentioned aspects: the child's consent in the framework of medical tests for age assessment, as well as the subject(s) in charge of lodging the asylum

---

1 See e.g. European Commission for Democracy Through Law (Venice Commission), *Report on the Protection of Children's Rights: International Standards and Domestic Contributions* (2014) para. 145. On this topic the scholarship is endless. Cf, amongst others, Michael D.A. Freeman, 'Introduction: rights, ideology and children' in Michael D.A. Freeman and Philip E. Veerman (eds.), *The Ideologies of Children's Rights* (Nijhoff 1992) 5; Simone van der Hof, 'I Agree, or Do I: A Rights-Based Analysis of the Law on Children's Consent in the Digital World' (2016) 34 Wisconsin International Law Review 425. On the development of children's rights throughout the twentieth century cf Jaap E. Doek, 'The Human Rights of Children: An Introduction' in Ursula Kilkelly and Ton Liefaard (eds.), *International Human Rights of Children* (Springer 2019) 3, and also Ton Liefaard, *Deprivation of Liberty of Children in Light of International Human Rights Law and Standards* (Intersentia 2008) 13.

2 Explanations relating to the Charter of Fundamental Rights, OJ C 303/02 [2007], Explanation on Article 24.

3 See section 5.2.

4 Art. 25(1)(a) Asylum Procedures Directive defines the 'representative' as the subject which '*represents and assists* the unaccompanied minor' (emphasis added).

application. While both topics are of critical relevance for most child applicants, the European *acquis* leaves a certain margin of appreciation to the Member States in this regard. After a brief exposition of the legal framework in which the principle of children as rights holders is enshrined (section 2) and of the relevant EU provisions affecting child migrants in this connection (section 3), this chapter will take a closer look at the migrant child's right to be heard (section 4). Successively, the analysis will concern the need to collect children's consent for medical assessment of their age (section 5), and unaccompanied children's possibility to apply for international protection on their own, as well as the risk of postponing children's access to services such as the education system (section 6). In this regard, comparative data on the implementation of the relevant EU provisions in the national legal systems will be provided. The concluding section (7) will assess the current situation and provide some inputs to the ongoing reform of the Common European Asylum System (CEAS).

Pre-eminently, the chapter will discuss the situation of unaccompanied asylum-seeking children. The chapter adopts a legal perspective and will not take policy instruments into consideration, unless they are relevant for the implementation of the legal provisions.[5]

2. GENERAL EU LEGAL FRAMEWORK AS REGARDS CHILDREN

2.1. THE DEFINITION OF 'CHILD' OR 'MINOR'

The European *acquis* does not explicitly provide for a consistently applicable definition of 'child'. Several pieces of legislation arrange for own age thresholds. For its purposes, the Free Movement Directive[6] refers to the 'direct descendants who are under the age of 21'. In the field of labour law, the Young Workers Directive[7] differentiates between 'young person' under 18 years and 'adolescents' for people aged from 15 to 18, and defines 'child' as 'any young person of less than 15 years of age or who is still subject to compulsory full-time schooling under national law'.

However, the UNCRC lays down in Article 1 that '[...] a child means every human being below the age of eighteen years unless, under the law applicable

5 For a list of policy documents on the rights of the child, see European Commission, *'EU acquis and policy documents on the rights of the child'* (last update March 2019) <https://ec.europa.eu/info/sites/info/files/eu_acquis_and_policy_documnets_rights_of_the_child_march_2019.pdf>.

6 Directive 2004/38/EC on the right of citizens of the Union and their family members to move and reside freely within the territory of the Member States [2004] OJ L 158/77, Art. 2.

7 Directive 94/33/EC on the protection of young people at work [1994] OJ L 216/12, Art. 3.

to the child, majority[8] is attained earlier'. The Convention is binding for the Member States, for all of them have signed it, as well as for the EU as general principle of the Union's law.[9]

Indeed, most of the Directives regarding migration and asylum (Qualification Directive,[10] Asylum Procedures Directive,[11] Reception Conditions Directive,[12] Anti-Trafficking Directive,[13] Family Reunification Directive[14]) and the Dublin Regulation[15] consistently refer to the 'minor'[16] as a person below the age of 18 years. Conversely, the Return Directive[17] and the Eurodac Regulation[18] do not provide for an explicit definition of 'minor' or 'child'. In the proposals by the European Commission for a new Common European Asylum System, the Qualification Regulation – repealing the current Qualification Directive – will

8 The age of majority is 18 years in all EU Member States. However, in Scotland children have full legal capacity to enter into any transaction from the age of 16 years. See the Age of Legal Capacity (Scotland) Act 1991 (c. 50), s. 1(1)(b), and the exceptions listed in s. 2.

9 On this topic, cf section 2.3.

10 Directive 2011/95/EU of the European Parliament and of the Council of 13 December 2011 on standards for the qualification of third-country nationals or stateless persons as beneficiaries of international protection, for a uniform status for refugees or for persons eligible for subsidiary protection, and for the content of the protection granted [2011] OJ L 337/9, Art. 2(k).

11 Directive 2013/32/EU of the European Parliament and of the Council of 26 June 2013 on common procedures for granting and withdrawing international protection [2013] OJ L 180/60, Art. 2(l).

12 Directive 2013/33/EU of the European Parliament and of the Council of 26 June 2013 laying down standards for the reception of applicants for international protection [2013] OJ L 180/96, Art. 2(d).

13 Directive 2011/36/EU on preventing and combating trafficking in human beings and protecting its victims, and replacing Council Framework Decision 2002/629/JHA [2011] OJ L 101/1, Art. 2(6).

14 Council Directive 2003/86/EC of 22 September 2003 on the right to family reunification [2003] OJ L 251/12, Art. 2(f).

15 Regulation (EU) No. 604/2013 of the European Parliament and of the Council of 26 June 2013 establishing the criteria and mechanisms for determining the Member State responsible for examining an application for international protection lodged in one of the Member States by a third-country national or a stateless person [2013] OJ L 180/31, Art. 2(i).

16 The Anti-Trafficking Directive uses the term 'child'. In this contribution, the author will mainly refer to minors as 'children', following the wording of the UN Convention on the Rights of the Child and of the EU Charter of Fundamental Rights.

17 Directive 2008/115/EC on common standards and procedures in Member States for returning illegally staying third-country nationals (Return Directive) [2008] OJ L 348/98.

18 Regulation (EU) No. 603/2013 on the establishment of 'Eurodac' for the comparison of fingerprints for the effective application of Regulation (EU) No 604/2013 establishing the criteria and mechanisms for determining the Member State responsible for examining an application for international protection lodged in one of the Member States by a third-country national or a stateless person and on requests for the comparison with Eurodac data by Member States' law enforcement authorities and Europol for law enforcement purposes, and amending Regulation (EU) No 1077/2011 establishing a European Agency for the operational management of large-scale IT systems in the area of freedom, security and justice (Eurodac Regulation) [2013] OJ L 180/1.

contain in Article 2(10) a definition of 'minor' as 'a third-country national or stateless person below the age of 18 years'. References to this definition are provided in the proposals for an Asylum Procedures Regulation[19] and for a Reception Conditions Directive.[20]

2.2. RELEVANT PROVISIONS OF EU PRIMARY LAW

Since children are rights holders, they enjoy all the rights generally enshrined at EU primary level for 'everyone'. Particularly relevant for child migrants are several provisions of the Charter of Fundamental Rights (Charter), which together with the Treaties found the EU primary law. The Union is bound by the Charter, as well as the Member States when implementing Union law (Article 51).[21] They shall therefore respect the rights, observe the principles and promote the Charter's application; in the case of EU institutions, even when they act outside the EU legal framework.[22] Consequently, national acts transposing a Directive, as well as the implementation in practice of the European *acquis*, shall fully respect the rights and freedoms enshrined in the Charter.

To mention only the most important provisions,[23] the Charter commences by reaffirming the value of human dignity, which shall be respected and protected (Art. 1). A right to personal integrity, defined as physical and mental integrity, is laid down in Article 3. In the context of migration and asylum, Article 18 of the Charter acknowledges a right to asylum with respect for the Geneva Convention and the Protocol of 31 January 1967 relating to the status of refugees and in accordance with the Treaties. Article 19 prohibits collective expulsions and limits the possibility to remove, expel or extradite a person. According to Article 21, any discrimination based on grounds as, amongst

19 European Commission, Proposal for a Regulation of the European Parliament and of the Council establishing a common procedure for international protection in the Union and repealing Directive 2013/32/EU, COM(2016) 467 final (2016), Art. 4(1).

20 European Commission, Proposal for a Directive of the European Parliament and of the Council laying down standards for the reception of applicants for international protection (recast), COM(2016) 465 final (2016), Art. 2(4).

21 On the Charter's application by practitioners, cf EU Agency for Fundamental Rights (FRA), *Applying the Charter of Fundamental Rights of the European Union in law and policymaking at national level* (Publications Office 2018).

22 Case C-8/15 *Ledra Advertising Ltd and Others v. European Commission and European Central Bank* [2016] ECLI:EU:C:2016:701, para. 67.

23 Other provisions may also be particularly relevant for children: the respect for private and family life (Art. 7); the right to freedom of expression (Art. 11); the right to education and to have access to vocational and continuing training (Art. 14); or Art. 47, laying down a right to an effective remedy and fair trial. At the same time, the Treaty on European Union (TEU) after Lisbon lists the 'protection of the rights of the child' among the general objectives of the Union (Art. 3, third para.), as well as among the aims of the Union's action in the wider world (fourth para.).

others, ethnic or social origin, language and age,[24] is forbidden. Article 24 is devoted to 'the rights of the child', calling for protection and care and providing that the child's best interests 'must be a primary consideration'.[25] Moreover, this provision explicitly allows children to express their views freely, which have to be 'taken into consideration on matters which concern them' according to their age and maturity. Finally, Article 41 provides for a right to good administration, including the right to be heard in case of individual measures. From several of these provisions derives a general right to be heard for child migrants, which will be analysed in some detail below (section 4).

2.3. RELEVANT PROVISIONS OF INTERNATIONAL LAW AND THEIR RELEVANCE FOR THE EU

Regarding international law, the UNCRC defines 'children' as people under the age of 18 unless majority is attained earlier, as seen. It excludes any discrimination of children on ground of 'national, ethnic or social origin' (Art. 2). In all actions concerning children, 'the best interests of the child shall be a primary consideration' and they have to be provided with 'such protection and care as is necessary' (Art. 3). For the purposes of this contribution, Article 12 is of particular interest as it lays down a crucial provision:

> 'States Parties shall assure to the child who is capable of forming his or her own views the right to express those views freely in all matters affecting the child, the views of the child being given due weight in accordance with the age and maturity of the child.'

Article 6(2) recognises a right to life, survival and development, which the states have to ensure to the maximum extent possible. Article 22 concerns the case of child refugees, laying down that the states shall provide protection

24 Arts. 10 and 19 of the Treaty on the Functioning of the European Union (TFEU) also concern the principle of non-discrimination, although their scope is limited to sex, racial or ethnic origin, religion or belief, disability, age or sexual orientation. The Charter additionally refers to colour, social origin, genetic features, language, political or any other opinion, membership of a national minority, property, and birth. Art. 18 TFEU forbids discrimination on grounds of nationality among European countries.

25 Interestingly, this expression has found misleading translations into some official languages. In Italian, the Charter lays down that 'l'interesse superiore del minore deve essere considerato preminente', therefore providing for the 'superior interest' of the child to be 'considered preeminent'. The adjective 'best' is rendered with an adjective ('*superiore*'), which may be understood as to prioritise the child's interests towards any other position at stake. At the same time, 'a primary consideration' loses the undetermined article and becomes, essentially, 'the' interest having absolute priority. Conversely, the English, German, and French versions define the best interests of the child as 'a' primary consideration.

and humanitarian assistance in the enjoyment of applicable rights as set forth in the Convention, irrespective of whether the child is 'accompanied or unaccompanied'. Articles 28 and 29 recognise the child's right to education, which may be at risk if the access of unaccompanied asylum-seeking children to the education system is postponed due to the delayed appointment of a representative. The Committee on the Rights of the Child has identified the provisions on non-discrimination, the best interests of the child, the right to life, survival and development and the right to express one's views as the four general principles of the Convention.[26]

In contrast to that, the 1950 European Convention for the Protection of Human Rights and Fundamental Freedoms (ECHR) expressly refers to children only in a limited way. Article 5(1)(d) concerns the detention of a 'minor', while Article 6(1) allows the exclusion of the press and public from the passing of judgments where in the interest of 'juveniles'. Article 5 of Protocol No. 7[27] refers to children in the context of equality between spouses. Despite this, several provisions of the ECHR do concern children, even though they are not expressly mentioned. Indeed, the European Court of Human Rights (ECtHR) has developed over the years quite an extensive case law on children's rights.[28] Article 8 in particular acknowledges a right to respect for private and family life to everyone, which is of crucial importance for children, for the ECtHR case law on family unity of migrants is mostly based on it. Particularly relevant for migrant children are also Articles 6 (right to a fair trial), 13 (right to an effective remedy) and 14 (prohibition of discrimination).[29] Albeit the last provision does not expressly mention age as a prohibited ground of discrimination, its list is not exhaustive; the Court has therefore included age within the concept of 'other status'.[30] Moreover, a prohibition of discrimination on the ground of age may arise in the context of several other provisions.[31]

---

26 UN Committee on the Rights of the Child (CRC), *General Comment No. 5 (2003): General measures of implementation of the Convention on the Rights of the Child* [2003] 3 ff.

27 Protocol No. 7 has not been ratified by all EU Member States yet; Germany and the Netherlands have only signed it, while the United Kingdom has not even signed it. All the other Member States of the Council of Europe have ratified the Protocol. Cf Council of Europe, 'Chart of signatures and ratifications of Treaty 117' <http://www.coe.int/en/web/conventions/full-list/-/conventions/treaty/117/signatures?p_auth=lh41BWhg>.

28 EU Agency for Fundamental Rights (FRA) and Council of Europe, *Handbook on European law relating to the rights of the child* (Publications Office 2015) 23.

29 On discrimination, cf also Protocol No. 12, signed in Rome in 2000, which does not explicitly mention age as a ground of discrimination; cf below in this section.

30 *Schwizgebel v. Switzerland* (2010) App no. 25762/07 (ECtHR, 10 June 2010).

31 *D.G. v. Ireland* (2002) App no. 39474/98 (ECtHR, 16 May 2002) and *Bouamar v. Belgium* (1988) App no. 9106/80 (ECtHR, 29 February 1988), regarding Art. 5 of the ECHR; *T. v. the United Kingdom* [1999] App no. 24724/94 (ECtHR, GC, 16 December 1999) and *V. v. the United Kingdom* [1999] App no. 24888/94 (ECtHR, GC, 16 December 1999), both of them concerning Art. 6 of the ECHR, whereas the Court did not consider it necessary to examine the complaint from the perspective of Art. 14.

All the Member States of the EU have signed the UNCRC[32] and the ECHR[33] (not including the latest Optional Protocol to the UNCRC on a communications procedure,[34] nor the protocols of the ECHR, many of which are not signed by all EU Member States). Both documents therefore apply not only to the respective national legal system according to the corresponding constitutional provisions, but they are relevant for the Union as well. While the EU has neither acceded to the ECHR as of yet (although Article 6(2) and Protocol No. 8 TEU oblige it in this regard),[35] nor can it be part of the UNCRC (which is expressly open only to 'States Parties'),[36] the Union is, nonetheless, indirectly bound by both these conventions. Article 6(3) TEU defines as 'general principles of the Union's law' the 'fundamental rights [...] as they result from the constitutional traditions common to the Member States'. Additionally, the Charter's Preamble reaffirms 'the rights as they result, in particular, from the constitutional traditions *and international obligations* common to the Member States [...]' (emphasis added). The fact that all the Member States are parties to both the UNCRC and the ECHR calls on the EU to adhere to their principles and accordingly interpret European and national provisions.[37]

Under this perspective, other international conventions may be relevant for migrant children, too. The European Social Charter[38] has been ratified in its 1961 version[39] by all the Member States. Article 7 ('the right of children and young persons to protection') provides for some regulation as regards young workers and is therefore not directly relevant for child migrants. However, it clearly recognises children as rights holders. Conversely, the scope of application of Article 17 of the revised Charter from 1996[40] is vaster. It is generally devoted

32 United Nations, 'Treaty Collection, Status Convention on the Rights of the Child' <http://treaties.un.org/pages/ViewDetails.aspx?src=IND&mtdsg_no=IV-11&chapter=4&lang=en>.

33 Council of Europe, 'Chart of signatures and ratifications of Treaty 005' <http://www.coe.int/en/web/conventions/full-list/-/conventions/treaty/005/signatures?p_auth=lh41BWhg>.

34 Optional Protocol to the UN CRC on a communications procedure, General Assembly Resolution 66/138 (19 December 2011).

35 On this topic, cf CJEU, *Opinion 2/13 of 18 December 2014*; European Parliament, European Parliamentary Research Service, and Academy of European Law (ERA), *The EU's accession to the ECHR: Selected publications & case law* (2017) <http://www.europarl.europa.eu/RegData/etudes/OTH/2017/607299/EPRS_DIV(2017)607299_EN.pdf>; Vicky Kosta/Nikos Skoutaris/Vassilis P. Tzevelekos (eds.), *The EU accession to the ECHR* (Hart 2014).

36 Cf Preamble of the Convention and Art. 48.

37 Case C-540/03 *Parliament v. Council* [2006] ECR I-5769, para. 37; cf Marcelle Reneman, 'Speedy Asylum Procedures in the EU: Striking a Fair Balance Between the Need to Process Asylum Cases Efficiently and the Asylum Applicant's EU Right to an Effective Remedy' (2013) 25(4) International Journal of Refugee Law 726; EU Agency for Fundamental Rights (FRA) and Council of Europe, *Handbook on European law relating to the rights of the child* (n. 28 above) 27.

38 European Social Charter, ETS no. 035 (18 October 1961).

39 Council of Europe, 'Chart of signatures and ratifications of Treaty 035' <http:/www.coe.int/en/web/conventions/full-list/-/conventions/treaty/035/signatures?p_auth=1ou5SDlo>.

40 European Social Charter (revised), ETS no. 163 (3 May 1996).

to children's rights to social, legal and economic protection and obliges the states to protect children against negligence, violence or exploitation – especially if deprived of their family's support – and to provide for education arrangements. The revised Charter 1996, however, has not been ratified by all the EU's countries.[41]

Other international sources of inspiration in interpreting EU law could be the International Covenant on Civil and Political Rights and the International Covenant on Economic, Social and Cultural Rights, to which all the EU countries are party.[42] Although they have not been ratified by all Member States,[43] the Council of Europe's Convention on the Exercise of Children's Rights,[44] Article 4 of Protocol 4[45] to the ECHR on collective expulsions of aliens and Protocol 12[46] on non-discrimination might also be relevant in this regard.

As previously mentioned, the Geneva Convention of 28 July 1951[47] and the Protocol of 31 January 1967[48] relating to the status of refugees are expressly mentioned in the Charter and have been ratified by all EU Member States.[49]

---

41 Council of Europe, 'Chart of signatures and ratifications of Treaty 163' <http://www.coe.int/en/web/conventions/full-list/-/conventions/treaty/163/signatures>.

42 As regards the first Convention, Art. 24 is entirely devoted to children. Other relevant provisions may be found in Arts. 2, 4, 13, and 18 to 19: International Covenant on Civil and Political Rights, General Assembly Resolution 21/2200 (16 December 1966). Concerning the second Convention, cf especially its Arts. 10 to 13: International Covenant on Economic, Social and Cultural Rights, General Assembly Resolution 21/2200 (16 December 1966). Cf Case 374/87 *Orkem v. Commission* [1989] ECR I-3283, para. 31; Joined Cases C-297/88 and C-197/89 *Dzodzi* [1990] ECR I-3763, para. 68; Case C-249/96 *Grant* [1998] ECR I-621, para. 44; Case C-540/03 *Parliament v. Council* [2006] ECR I-5769, para. 37.

43 Council of Europe, 'Chart of signatures and ratifications of Treaty 160' <http://www.coe.int/en/web/conventions/full-list/-/conventions/treaty/160/signatures?p_auth=1ou5SDlo>. For Protocol 4: Council of Europe, 'Chart of signatures and ratifications of Treaty 046' <https://www.coe.int/en/web/conventions/full-list/-/conventions/treaty/046/signatures>. For Protocol 12: Council of Europe, 'Chart of signatures and ratifications of Treaty 177' <http://www.coe.int/en/web/conventions/full-list/-/conventions/treaty/177/signatures?p_auth=wa9qldta>.

44 The Convention particularly emphasises children's right to be heard and the relevance of having a representative in proceedings before a court; cf especially its Arts. 3 to 6 and 9 to 10: Convention on the Exercise of Children's Rights, ETS no. 160 (25 January 1996).

45 Protocol No. 4 to the Convention for the Protection of Human Rights and Fundamental Freedoms securing certain rights and freedoms other than those already included in the Convention and in the first Protocol thereto, as amended by Protocol No. 11, ETS no. 46 (16 September 1963).

46 Protocol No. 12 to the Convention for the Protection of Human Rights and Fundamental Freedoms, ETS no. 177 (4 November 2000).

47 United Nations Convention relating to the Status of Refugees, General Assembly Resolution 5/429 (14 December 1950).

48 Protocol relating to the Status of Refugees, General Assembly Resolution 21/2198 (16 December 1966).

49 Cf United Nations, 'Status of Treaties – Convention relating to the Status of Refugees' <https://treaties.un.org/Pages/ViewDetailsII.aspx?src=TREATY&mtdsg_no=V-2&chapter=5&Temp=mtdsg2&clang=_en>; United Nations, 'Status of Treaties – Protocol relating to the Status of Refugees' <https://treaties.un.org/Pages/ViewDetails.aspx?src=TREATY&mtdsg_no=V-5&chapter=5&clang=_en>.

Finally, both the EU and its Member States have ratified the Convention on the Rights of Persons with Disabilities.[50] It devotes its Article 7 to children with disabilities, while Article 11 is concerned with the protection and safety of persons with disabilities in situations of risks and humanitarian emergencies.

3. THE CHILD IN ASYLUM PROCEDURES

The European Union has extensive competence in the field of migration and asylum. This is grounded predominantly on Chapter 2 ('Policies on Border Checks, Asylum and Immigration') of Title V ('Area of Freedom, Security and Justice') of the Treaty on the Functioning of the European Union (TFEU). Article 78 TFEU requires the Union to develop a common policy on asylum, subsidiary protection and temporary protection in accordance with the Geneva Convention of 28 July 1951 and the Protocol of 31 January 1967, and other relevant treaties. According to Article 79, the Union shall develop a common immigration policy for the efficient management of migration flows, the fair treatment of third-country nationals residing legally in Member States, and the prevention of and the fight against illegal immigration and trafficking in human beings.

Important pieces of legislation on asylum have been consequently enacted by the European legislator. The most relevant acts for the present analysis have been already mentioned: the Qualification Directive, the Asylum Procedures Directive, the Reception Conditions Directive and the Dublin Regulation. With most of them being Directives, they leave to the Member States a certain scope for decision-making on how to reach their goals.

As regards children, a first crucial difference has to be drawn between accompanied and unaccompanied children. An 'unaccompanied child' is, according to the definition consistently provided by EU legislation,

> 'a minor who arrives on the territory of the Member States unaccompanied by an adult responsible for him or her [...] and for as long as he or she is not effectively taken into the care of such an adult; it includes a minor who is left unaccompanied after he or she has entered the territory of Member States'.[51]

By contrast, an 'accompanied child' is a child travelling with an adult responsible for them. Lacking a protective and supportive family environment, unaccompanied children need advanced protection.[52]

---

50 United Nations Convention on the Rights of Person with Disabilities, General Assembly Resolution 61/106 (13 December 2006); cf United Nations, 'Status of Treaties – Convention on the Rights of Person with Disabilities' <https://treaties.un.org/Pages/ViewDetails.aspx?src=TREATY&mtdsg_no=IV-15&chapter=4&clang=_en#4>.

51 Cf e.g. Art. 2(j) Dublin Regulation.

52 Some of the considerations expressed in this contribution as regards the advanced need of protection of unaccompanied children may be referred to separated children, as well.

Especially in the case of unaccompanied children the question arises, how to appropriately balance the needs of protection and the recognition of the child's autonomy. A protective framework is required to ensure the well-being of particularly vulnerable persons, as unaccompanied children are. Considering their limited experience and the absence of a responsible person, they could get involved in dangerous pathways.[53] At the same time, their need for protection should not lead to neglecting the fact that they are autonomous human beings, and are endowed with participative rights, such as the right to be heard.

During minority, the parents generally are the persons concerned with the child's legal representation and care. In the case of children lacking a family environment, these duties are usually devolved to a legal guardian, often a lawyer. This is also the case for unaccompanied migrant children, whereas the terms used for this person in EU law swing between 'guardian and/or representative',[54] 'representative'[55] and 'legal guardian'.[56] The adoption of the one or the other terminology may theoretically implicate important consequences in defining the role of this person: only complementing the limited legal capacity of the child ('representative') or including also the care of the child's well-being ('guardian'). However, the use of such terminology is frequently inconsistent.[57] The Asylum Procedures Directive, for instance, terms it 'representative' but specifies in Article 25(1)(a) that such a subject 'represents *and assists* the unaccompanied minor' (emphasis added). It has to be nominated 'as soon as possible', although legislation does not provide for its appointment

---

A 'separated child' has been defined as a child who has been separated from both parents, or from their previous legal or customary primary caregiver, but not necessarily from other relatives. A separated child may, therefore, be accompanied by other adult family members: UN Committee on the Rights of the Child (CRC), *General Comment No. 6 (2005): Treatment of unaccompanied and separated children outside their country of origin* [2005] 5.

53 As an example, people-smugglers seeking to recruit children into prostitution tell them to declare themselves as being above the age of majority to prevent being subjected to the protective measures provided for unaccompanied children: International Organization for Migration (IOM), *Human trafficking through the central Mediterranean route: Data, stories and information collected by the International Organisation for Migration* (2017) 19; EU Agency for Fundamental Rights (FRA), *Age assessment and fingerprinting of children in asylum procedures – Minimum age requirements concerning children's rights in the EU* (Publications Office 2018) 10. Cf section 5 below on medical tests for age assessment.

54 Art. 31(2) of the Qualification Directive; Directive 2011/36/EU on preventing and combating trafficking in human beings and protecting its victims (Anti-Trafficking Directive) [2011] OJ L 101/1, Recitals 23 and 24 and Art. 14(2).

55 Arts. 2(j) and 24 Reception Conditions Directive; Arts. 2(n), 7 and 25 Asylum Procedures Directive; Arts. 2(k) and 6(2) Dublin Regulation; Art. 15 Anti-Trafficking Directive.

56 Art. 31(1) Qualification Directive.

57 EU Agency for Fundamental Rights (FRA) and European Commission, *Guardianship for children deprived of parental care* (Publications Office 2014) 14.

from the very first moment an unaccompanied child is identified as such.[58] The representative has to assist the child during important steps of the asylum procedure. On the contrary, the Qualification Directive in Article 31 provides for the appointment of a legal guardian 'as soon as possible *after* the granting of international protection' (emphasis added).

Among the proposals for a new Common European Asylum System, the new Dublin Regulation[59] would still use the term 'representative' (Art. 2). Conversely, the Asylum Procedures Regulation[60] in Article 4(2), the Qualification Regulation[61] in Article 2(19) and the Reception Conditions Directive[62] in Article 2(12) would call this person 'guardian'. The latter would request Member States to appoint it 'as soon as possible and no later than five working days from the moment when an unaccompanied minor makes an application for international protection'. According to Article 25(1), an application would be considered to have been made as soon as a person expresses a wish to receive international protection from a Member State.[63] However, the Committee on Civil Liberties, Justice and Home Affairs (LIBE) of the European Parliament has suggested nominating the child's guardian at 'the moment when an unaccompanied minor arrives in a Member State'.[64]

In any case, the role of the legal representative must be separated from the right to legal assistance and representation, as provided for in the articles

---

58 EU Agency for Fundamental Rights (FRA), Council of Europe, and European Court of Human Rights (ECtHR), *Handbook on European law relating to asylum, borders and immigration* (Publications Office 2014, reprinted 2016) 218.

59 European Commission, Proposal for a Regulation of the European Parliament and of the Council establishing the criteria and mechanisms for determining the Member State responsible for examining an application for international protection lodged in one of the Member States by a third-country national or a stateless person (recast), COM(2016) 270 final (2016).

60 European Commission, Proposal for a Regulation of the European Parliament and of the Council establishing a common procedure for international protection in the Union and repealing Directive 2013/32/EU, COM(2016) 467 final (2016).

61 European Commission, Proposal for a Regulation of the European Parliament and of the Council on standards for the qualification of third-country nationals or stateless persons as beneficiaries of international protection, for a uniform status for refugees or for persons eligible for subsidiary protection and for the content of the protection granted and amending Council Directive 2003/109/EC of 25 November 2003 concerning the status of third-country nationals who are long-term residents, COM(2016) 466 final (2016).

62 European Commission, Proposal for a Directive of the European Parliament and of the Council laying down standards for the reception of applicants for international protection (recast), COM(2016) 465 final (2016).

63 From the moment this wish is registered, the applicant shall lodge the application within ten working days (Art. 28 proposed Reception Conditions Directive). In the case of unaccompanied children, however, this period would start to run from the moment a guardian is appointed and they have met (Art. 32).

64 European Parliament, Committee on Civil Liberties, Justice and Home Affairs (LIBE), Report A8-0186/2017 on the proposal for a directive of the European Parliament and of the Council laying down standards for the reception of applicants for international protection (recast) (10 May 2017), Amendment 125.

from 20 to 23 of the Asylum Procedures Directive. Applicants can thus consult legal advisors at all stages of the asylum procedure, at their own cost, while they are granted free legal assistance and representation in appeals procedure against decisions taken on their application or international protection status, subject to certain conditions. Such provisions apply to child applicants, as well. Under some circumstances, mostly income requirements, they are entitled to free legal aid in all the Member States.[65]

The provision of a guardian or a legal representative should not lead to ignoring the right of children to express their views and to participate in the decision affecting their lives. The decisions by the representative or the guardian should therefore not substitute the due consideration for the child's views.

4. THE RIGHT TO BE HEARD OF CHILDREN IN ASYLUM PROCEDURES

4.1. PRIMARY EU LAW PROVISIONS

The Charter of Fundamental Rights lists among the rights of the child (Art. 24) the possibility to express their views freely. Such views shall be taken into consideration on matters concerning the child, according to their age and maturity. This formulation clearly recalls the wording of Article 12(1) of the UNCRC,[66] although the latter goes on to specify that the child shall be heard in any judicial and administrative procedure affecting them 'either directly, or through a representative or an appropriate body'. As stated above, the right to express one's views is considered by the UN Committee on the Rights of the Child as one of the four basic principles of the whole Convention. It is true that a right to freedom of expression is already acknowledged 'for everyone' in Article 11 of the Charter. Article 24, however, requires in the case of children to take these views into consideration 'on matters which concern them in accordance with their age and maturity' and has thereby an added value.[67]

The right to be heard is listed also under Article 41 of the Charter. This provision concerns the right to good administration, defined as 'the right to have his or her affairs handled impartially, fairly and within a reasonable

65 EU Agency for Fundamental Rights (FRA), 'Mapping minimum age requirements: Children's rights and justice', page 'Free legal aid for asylum seekers' (2017) <https://fra.europa.eu/en/publication/2018/minimum-age-childrens-rights-justice/legal-aid-asylum>.

66 Cf Explanations relating to the Charter of Fundamental Rights, OJ C 303/02 [2007], Explanation on Article 24.

67 Cf Simone van der Hof, 'I Agree, or Do I' (n. 1 above).

time by the institutions, bodies, offices and agencies of the Union'. Such a right includes the possibility to be heard, before any individual measure liable to adversely affect one's interests is taken, as provided for by the second paragraph and endorsed by constant jurisprudence of the CJEU.[68] Beyond the strict wording of the provision, it is discussed if this article may also bind Member States when they act within the scope of Union law.[69]

Regarding the right to be heard in judicial proceedings, it similarly may be understood as a crucial element of the principle of fair trial enshrined in Article 47 of the Charter. Indeed, children's right to be heard has found vast implementation concerning their participation in criminal proceedings;[70] both the Directive on procedural safeguards for children who are suspects,[71] as well as the Victims' Rights Directive[72] elaborate on it. In this framework, the right of a child to be heard is generally not linked to age thresholds.[73]

---

68 Amongst others: Case C-560/14 *M v. Minister for Justice and Equality Ireland and the Attorney General* [2017] ECLI:EU:C:2017:101, paras. 25 and 31; Case C-348/16 *Moussa Sacko v. Commissione Territoriale per il riconoscimento della protezione internazionale di Milano* [2017] ECLI:EU:C:2017:591, para. 34; Case C-249/13 *Boudjlida v. Préfet des Pyrénées-Atlantiques* [2014] ECLI:EU:C:2014:2431, paras. 34 and 36; Case C-166/13 *Sophie Mukarubega v. Préfet de police and Préfet de la Seine-Saint-Denis* [2014] ECLI:EU:C:2014:2336, para. 46.

69 A positive answer is provided by Paul Craig, 'Article 41' in Steve Peers/Tamara Hervey/Jeff Kenner/Angela Ward (eds.), *The EU Charter of Fundamental Rights* (Hart 2014) 1070 ff, with reference to Case C-277/11 *M.M. v. Minister for Justice, Equality and Law Reform, Ireland, Attorney General* [2012] ECLI:EU:C:2012:744, para. 83 ff. *Contra* Case C-482/10 *Teresa Cicala v. Regione siciliana* [2011] ECLI:EU:C:2011:868, para. 28.

70 Children's involvement in judicial proceedings has given rise to a considerable volume of publications, both by scholars, institutions and policy actors; amongst others, cf Helen Stalford, Kathryn Hollingsworth, Stephen Gilmore (eds.), *Rewriting Children's Rights Judgments: From Academic Vision to New Practice* (Hart 2017); Barry Goldson (ed.), *Juvenile Justice in Europe. Past, Present and Future* (Routledge 2018); EU Agency for Fundamental Rights, *Child-friendly justice – Perspectives and experiences of children involved in judicial proceedings as victims, witnesses or parties in nine EU Member States* (Publications Office 2017), and related publications; Council of Europe, *Guidelines of the Committee of Ministers of the Council of Europe on child-friendly justice* (2011).

71 Directive (EU) 2016/800 on procedural safeguards for children who are suspects or accused persons in criminal proceedings [2016] OJ L 132/1, Art. 16.

72 Directive 2012/29/EU establishing minimum standards on the rights, support and protection of victims of crime [2012] OJ L 315/57, Art. 10.

73 The Victims' Rights Directive clearly states that the right to effectively participate in their trials and express their views 'should not be precluded solely on the basis that the victim is a child or on the basis of that victim's age' (Recital 42). However, adequate safeguards need to be in place to ensure that a child-sensitive approach is applied, as required by Art. 1(2). Examples of such safeguards are the provision of suitable information, and the involvement of trained professionals. Cf EU Agency for Fundamental Rights, *Child-friendly justice – Perspectives and experiences of children and professionals* (Publications Office 2017), and related publications; Aoife Daly and Stephanie Rap, 'Children's Participation in the Justice System' in Ursula Kilkelly and Ton Liefaard (eds.), *International Human Rights of Children* (Springer 2019) 299.

4.2. SECONDARY EU LAW PROVISIONS

The whole EU *acquis* on asylum recognises, to some extent, the importance of collecting the child's views. To this end, legislative acts often resort to the wording of Article 24 of the Charter. The Dublin Regulation provides for it in Recital 13 and Article 6(3)(d), recalling the UNCRC and the need for Member States to consider the views of the minor in assessing their best interests, 'in accordance with his or her age and maturity, including his or her background'. The Qualification Directive uses a similar formulation, albeit not referring to the children's 'background'. Its Recital 18 refers to the UNCRC and the best interests, while Article 31(3) – providing for the placement of unaccompanied children – obliges Member States to take the views of the child into account in accordance with the age and degree of maturity. Also Article 23(2) of the Reception Conditions Directive resorts to the wording of the Charter, stating that the assessment of the child's best interests needs to take their views into account. Finally, the Asylum Procedures Directive entails only a general provision, not expressly referring to children. According to this, Member States shall allow any applicant to present their views, conducting a personal interview on the admissibility of the application. Remarkably, Recital 33 – concerning the best interests of the child and recalling the Charter and the UNCRC – does not entail any reference to the child's views. In assessing their best interest (singular), Member States should therefore 'take due account of the minor's well-being and social development, including his or her background'. In contrast to Recital 13 of the Dublin Regulation, the reader will not find any reference to '[safety and security considerations and] the views of the minor in accordance with his or her age and maturity' among the elements to consider in the assessment of the best interests in the Directive. Both acts of legislation were done on the same day, 26 June 2013.

Three crucial dimensions may be identified as regards the right to be heard in asylum procedures.

The first dimension concerns the right to information. All applicants have to be previously informed 'in a language they understand or are reasonably supposed to understand' (Art. 12 Asylum Procedures Directive). This applies to child applicants, too. The Dublin Regulation (Art. 4) lists several pieces of information on which competent authorities have to inform the applicant. The Reception Conditions Directive (Art. 5) elaborates on some specific aspects of such a right. Finally, regarding the beneficiaries of international protection, Article 22 of the Qualification Directive briefly refers to the need to provide them with access to information on their rights and obligations. A recurrent emphasis is put on the provision of information in a language they may understand or are supposed to understand. To this end, Article 6(3) of the proposal for a new Dublin Regulation requires the European Commission to draw up a common leaflet, as well as a specific leaflet for unaccompanied minors, containing the most important information to be conveyed to the applicant.

Secondly, the European *acquis* on asylum endows children with a right to directly present their views to the administrative authorities concerned with their application for international protection. The Asylum Procedures Directive specifies the requirements for the personal interview assessing the application. Indeed, Member States shall give applicants, such as unaccompanied children, 'the opportunity of a personal interview' (Art. 14). However, in the case of *accompanied* minors, national legislators have to determine whether or not to give them such an opportunity (Art. 14). However, under Article 21 of the proposed Asylum Procedures Regulation, the opportunity of a personal interview should be given also to children whose application has been made on their behalf, unless this is manifestly not in their best interests. In some cases, the personal interview may be omitted; consequently, its absence will not prevent the authorities from taking a decision on the application.[74]

In order to allow applicants to present their grounds 'in a comprehensive manner', the states have to ensure that interviews with minors are conducted in a 'child-appropriate' manner (Art. 15(3)(e) of the Directive). As is generally provided for by the Directive for the whole procedure examining the applications, according to Article 10(3)(d) the personnel have the possibility to seek advice from experts on child-related issues. In the case of unaccompanied minors, Article 25(3) specifies that if a personal interview takes place, a person having the necessary knowledge of the special needs of the child has to conduct it. Moreover, also the official preparing the decision is required to possess such knowledge.

Thirdly, against a decision rejecting their application as unfounded or inadmissible, applicants have the right to an effective remedy before a court or tribunal (Art. 46 Asylum Procedures Directive). Such a remedy provides for 'a full and *ex nunc* examination of both facts and points of law', according to Article 46(3). Although these provisions do not expressly mention the right of the applicant to have the own views represented before the court, such a right can be derived from the general principles of fair trial (see Art. 47(2) Charter).

5. CASE ONE: MEDICAL TESTS FOR AGE ASSESSMENT

5.1. THE PROBLEM

Age assessment in the context of international protection is the process through which authorities seek to estimate the age (or age range) of a person in order to

74 Cf Jens Vedsted-Hansen, 'Art. 14 of the Asylum Procedures Directive' in Kay Hailbronner and Daniel Thym (eds.), *EU Immigration and Asylum Law* (Beck/Hart/Nomos 2016) 1318.

establish if an individual is a child or an adult.[75] The determination if a certain applicant for international protection is below or over 18 years crucially affects the treatment they receive in a number of fields (for instance, the appointment of a guardian, special accommodation provisions, etc.). The determination of a person's age is particularly relevant for unaccompanied children, since children who have entered the European Union with their parents or relatives will be maintained with their families (principle of family unity).[76]

There are different methods to seek to determine a person's age. Those concretely used vary widely among Member States.[77] Common practice in the Member States is to allow medical tests to be carried out for this purpose. Out of the 28 States, only two do not use them.[78] Medical methods may or may not involve the use of radiations (x-ray). Among those which do not use X-rays, the most common are dental observation, magnetic resonance imaging, ultrasound, and the assessment of physical development.[79] Methods involving the use of radiations may analyse the hand or wrist (carpal X-ray), the collar bone and the teeth.[80] Generally, the assessment of the child's age is one of the most controversial issues as regards asylum law. The procedures used may involve serious risks for the person's dignity and private life. Invasive methods are sometimes used in EU Member States,[81] such as the investigation of genitalia to assess sexual maturity. In this regard, the answer to the question which countries perform sexual maturity observations differs depending on the source.[82]

---

75 European Asylum Support Office (EASO), *EASO Practical Guide on age assessment* (2nd ed., Publications Office 2018) 15 and 17.

76 Directive 2011/95/EU of the European Parliament and of the Council of 13 December 2011 on standards for the qualification of third-country nationals or stateless persons as beneficiaries of international protection, for a uniform status for refugees or for persons eligible for subsidiary protection, and for the content of the protection granted (Qualification Directive) [2011] OJ L 337/9, Art. 23.

77 European Commission, *Communication 'The protection of children in migration'*, COM(2017) 211 final (2017) 10.

78 Namely the United Kingdom and Ireland: EU Agency for Fundamental Rights (FRA), 'Mapping minimum age requirements concerning the rights of the child in the EU', page 'Consent to medical tests for age assessment' (2017) <http://fra.europa.eu/en/publication/2017/mapping-minimum-age-requirements/consent-age-assessment>. According to EASO, also Slovenia does not practically perform medical examinations either: European Asylum Support Office (EASO), *EASO Practical Guide on age assessment* (n. 75 above) 106. According to the information upon which FRA bases its study, however, paediatricians may perform a medical examination of the child.

79 European Asylum Support Office (EASO), *EASO Practical Guide on age assessment* (n. 75 above) 52 ff.

80 Ibid., 56 ff.

81 European Commission, *Communication 'The protection of children in migration'*, COM(2017) 211 final (2017) 10.

82 Denmark, Hungary, Italy, and Luxembourg, according to Council of Europe (report prepared by Daja Wenke), *Age assessment: Council of Europe's member states' policies, procedures and practices respectful of children's rights in the context of migration* (2017) 23, 28. This report

The particular protection provisions provided for unaccompanied children may be the reason for some child asylum seekers to avoid a precise determination of their age. Willing to reach relatives or acquaintances in a different Member State, children could declare themselves to be above the age of majority to prevent being subjected to those measures which may interfere with their plans. The same could happen following instructions by people-smugglers seeking to engage the child in prostitution or other criminal activities.[83] From Union law and international obligations to protect childhood therefore derives an obligation for Member States to assess the child's age and situation carefully. At the same time, asylum seekers may falsely claim to be children in order to take advantage of special protection arrangements and avoid return to their countries.

5.2. LEGAL FRAMEWORK AND ITS IMPLEMENTATION BY MEMBER STATES

Article 4 of the Qualification Directive regulates the assessment of an application for international protection, allowing Member States to consider it the duty of the applicant to submit the elements substantiating it in a timely manner.[84] Among the elements to be taken into account in assessing an application, Article 4(3) lists the 'individual position and personal circumstances of the applicant, including factors such as [...] age'.

The determination of the age of an unaccompanied child is regulated in Article 25(5) of the Asylum Procedures Directive. Member States may therefore use medical examinations 'where [...] [they] have doubts concerning the applicant's age'.[85] Although this provision does not specify that such doubts have to refer to the applicant's *minor* age, the following sentence may justify

takes into account 37 states of the Council of Europe, among them all the EU Member States but for Austria, Germany, Portugal, Romania and the United Kingdom. According to EASO, Austria, Croatia, Estonia, Germany, Hungary, Italy and Romania perform sexual maturity observations: European Asylum Support Office (EASO), *EASO Practical Guide on age assessment* (n. 75 above) 106.

83 International Organization for Migration (IOM), *Human trafficking through the central Mediterranean route: Data, stories and information collected by the International Organisation for Migration* (2017) 19; EU Agency for Fundamental Rights (FRA), *Age assessment and fingerprinting of children in asylum procedures – Minimum age requirements concerning children's rights in the EU* (n. 53 above) 10.

84 Art. 4(5) introduces an exception from the need to provide supportive documents when some conditions are met: the applicants have made a genuine effort to substantiate their application, the documents at their disposal have been submitted and a satisfactory explanation has been given as regards the missing ones, their statements are coherent, they have submitted their application as soon as possible, and their general credibility has been established.

85 Medical examination may be also used to determine if there are signs on the applicant's body that might indicate past persecution or serious harm: Art. 18 Asylum Procedures Directive.

a restrictive teleological interpretation of it. According to it, if Member States 'are still in doubt concerning the applicant's age, they shall assume that the applicant is a minor'. In this regard, the Proposal for an Asylum Procedure Regulation,[86] currently under scrutiny, lays down in Article 24(1) that medical examinations may be used to determine the age of unaccompanied minors if 'there are doubts as to whether or not the applicant is under the age of 18'.

Article 25(5) of the Asylum Procedures Directive specifies further some elements of the medical examination procedure. It shall respect the child's dignity, be the least invasive and be carried out by qualified medical professionals. Unaccompanied children have to be informed beforehand – in a language they can understand or are reasonably supposed to understand – about the methods used, the results' possible outcomes as well as about the consequences of a refusal to undergo the examination. Such a refusal, however, cannot be the only ground substantiating a rejection of the child's application.

According to Article 25(5)(b), unaccompanied children 'and/or' their representatives have to consent in order for the examination to be carried out. Despite the fact that Article 25 of the Asylum Procedures Directive only concerns unaccompanied minors, regarding this matter it has been considered providing principles of general application.[87]

In the Commission's proposal for a regulation repealing the current Asylum Procedures Directive, the medical examination shall require the child's consent 'or' the consent of their guardian: Article 24(2). Since the conjunction 'and' has been abolished, there will be no possibility to ask for the consent of both persons under the new regulation. However, the Committee on Civil Liberties, Justice and Home Affairs (LIBE) of the European Parliament has suggested amending this paragraph, substituting 'or' with 'and'.[88] As a consequence, both the consent of the child and of the guardian should be collected. Additionally, the Committee would further restrict the possibility to use medical examinations to assess the child's age and describes them as 'a measure of last resort'.[89]

The current legal provisions leave a remarkable room of manoeuvre to the Member States on the question whose consent has to be collected and at which age the child has to agree. A study recently published by the Agency of the

---

86 European Commission, Proposal for a Regulation of the European Parliament and of the Council establishing a common procedure for international protection in the Union and repealing Directive 2013/32/EU, COM(2016) 467 final (2016).

87 EU Agency for Fundamental Rights (FRA), *Age assessment and fingerprinting of children in asylum procedures – Minimum age requirements concerning children's rights in the EU* (n. 53 above) 10.

88 European Parliament, Committee on Civil Liberties, Justice and Home Affairs (LIBE), Report A8-0171/2018 on the proposal for a regulation of the European Parliament and of the Council establishing a common procedure for international protection in the Union and repealing Directive 2013/32/EU (22 May 2018), Amendment 164.

89 Ibid., Amendment 161 ff.

European Union for Fundamental Rights has provided unique insights on the concrete imposition of similar age thresholds in the national legal systems.[90] The overall project focused on how the 28 Member States resort to minimum age requirements in the most diverse fields of life.[91] The reference period of the research was until April 2016, although legislative developments since then have been included whenever relevant and known.[92]

The study provides valuable data on how Member States have implemented the obligation to request the consent of the unaccompanied child 'and/or' of their representative in order to perform a medical examination in the framework of age assessment.[93] It follows that five countries – namely Austria, Bulgaria, Latvia, Portugal and Slovakia – only require the consent of the legal representative to perform medical tests for assessing the applicant's age. Eight other Member States are satisfied with the consent of either the child or of their representative; the countries being indifferent whether they collect the one or the other. This is the case for Belgium, Cyprus, the Czech Republic, Greece, Luxembourg, Malta, Poland and Slovenia. As a consequence, in thirteen Member States a medical test to assess the child's age may be carried out without collecting the child's consent.

Conversely, eight states request the child to assent, their consent not being substitutable by the representative's. This applies in Denmark, Estonia, France, Hungary, Italy, Lithuania, the Netherlands and Spain. Five Member

---

90 The author of this chapter contributed to the development of the research project during 2017 and 2018. However, the analysis enshrined and the views expressed in this chapter are his personal opinions and cannot be referred to the EU Fundamental Rights Agency.

91 Marriage and sexual consent, citizenship, political participation, religion, health, the digital world social rights, employment and finance, education, alternative care, LGBTI rights, mobility, migration, and access to justice. Two web-publications can be accessed online, one especially concerned with children and justice, and a general one. Two reports have been published as well, providing opinions to the EU institutions and the Member States. They particularly elaborate on children's access to justice, and on age assessment in asylum procedures and children's fingerprinting. Cf EU Agency for Fundamental Rights (FRA), 'Mapping minimum age requirements: Children's rights and justice' (2017) <http://fra.europa.eu/en/publication/2018/minimum-age-childrens-rights-justice>; and 'Mapping minimum age requirements concerning the rights of the child in the EU' (2017) <http://fra.europa.eu/en/publication/2017/mapping-minimum-age-requirements-concerning-rights-child-eu>. For the reports, cf EU Agency for Fundamental Rights (FRA), *Children's rights and justice – Minimum age requirements in the EU* (Publications Office 2018); and *Age assessment and fingerprinting of children in asylum procedures – Minimum age requirements concerning children's rights in the EU* (n. 53 above).

92 The data has been collected by FRANET, the interdisciplinary research network of the Agency, composed of expert contractors in each EU Member State. Cf the general description <http://fra.europa.eu/en/publication/2017/mapping-minimum-age-requirements-concerning-rights-child-eu>.

93 EU Agency for Fundamental Rights (FRA), 'Mapping minimum age requirements concerning the rights of the child in the EU', page 'Consent to medical tests for age assessment' (2017) <http://fra.europa.eu/en/publication/2017/mapping-minimum-age-requirements/consent-age-assessment>.

States – Croatia, Finland, Germany, Romania and Sweden – oblige authorities to collect the consent of both subjects, the legal representative's and the child's.

Finally, two countries do not currently perform medical examinations and determine the child's age by other methods (the United Kingdom[94] and Ireland[95]). In this regard, it must be noted that according to the European Asylum Support Office (EASO), Slovenia, in practice, does not perform medical examinations either.[96]

6. CASE TWO: ASYLUM APPLICATIONS IN THEIR OWN RIGHT

6.1. THE PROBLEM

Applications for international protection of dependent children are usually lodged by their parents, according to the principle of family unity.[97] In the case of unaccompanied children, the question arises who should present the request for asylum. The child could lack, according to the respective Member State's laws, legal capacity, and might thus not be allowed to lodge the application. Furthermore, a child might not be able to properly assess the situation, present all the relevant documents and evidence to support the claim on time and efficiently follow the procedure.

As seen, unaccompanied children are provided with a legal representative 'as soon as possible', although European legislation does not specify a precise moment. The rules that are concretely applied by Member States differ widely. Research shows that guardians are frequently nominated quite late, with

94 More precisely, in the United Kingdom there is no direct legislation prescribing how the age assessment is to be carried out: European Asylum Support Office (EASO), *EASO Practical Guide on age assessment* (n. 75 above) 97. The Home Office policy currently does not commission paediatrician reports, dental assessments or x-rays: Home Office, *Assessing age. Version 2.0* (2011, updated October 2018) 37 ff. Physical appearance can be assessed, taking into account heights, build, facial features and voice: ibid., p. 12.

95 According to the International Protection Act 2015, Art. 24(2), the examination may be of a medical nature. Any age assessment examination requires the consent of the applicant or an adult responsible or a person appointed by the Child and Family Agency. According to EASO, medical examinations are currently not performed: European Asylum Support Office (EASO), *EASO Practical Guide on age assessment* (n. 75 above) 106.

96 European Asylum Support Office (EASO), *EASO Practical Guide on age assessment* (n. 75 above) 106. According to the information upon which FRA bases its study, however, paediatricians may perform a medical examination of the child.

97 However, there are some Member States which do allow accompanied children, from a certain age, to lodge an application on the own behalf. Cf EU Agency for Fundamental Rights (FRA), 'Mapping minimum age requirements concerning the rights of the child in the EU', page 'Asylum applications for accompanied children' (2017) <http://fra.europa.eu/en/publication/2017/mapping-minimum-age-requirements/asylum-accompanied>.

the consequence that applications are submitted late or authorities start the procedures in their absence.[98] However, important deadlines are linked to the date on which the application is lodged. By way of example, Article 14 of the Reception Conditions Directive allows Member States to postpone access to the education system for up to three months from the date on which the application for international protection was lodged. This possibility is kept in Article 14(2) of the proposal for a new Reception Conditions Directive. However, the Parliament's Committee on Civil Liberties, Justice and Home Affairs (LIBE) has suggested to limit it to one month from the moment when the application 'was made'.[99] Similarly, the right to family reunification for children having been granted asylum is linked to the application date, too.

6.2. LEGAL FRAMEWORK AND ITS IMPLEMENTATION BY MEMBER STATES

Article 7(3) of the Asylum Procedures Directive obliges Member States to allow minors to lodge an application for international protection. This may take place either on their own behalf, if they have legal capacity in the respective country to do so ('if he or she has the legal capacity to act in procedures according to the law of the Member State concerned'), or through their parents, relatives, an adult responsible by law or practice of the country, or a representative. Article 7(5) lays down further modalities as regards the submission of applications by children. National legislation may therefore determine if and when the application can be presented by the minors themselves or has to be lodged by the child's representative.

Comparative research by the EU Agency for Fundamental Rights[100] has shown that in half (14) of the Member States unaccompanied children cannot lodge an application for international protection in their own right. They therefore need a legal representative to present it. This is the case for Austria, Cyprus, Czech Republic, Estonia, France, Germany, Ireland, Lithuania, Malta, Poland, Slovakia, Slovenia, Spain and Sweden.

---

98 EU Agency for Fundamental Rights (FRA), *Key migration issues: one year on from initial reporting* (October 2016) 2.

99 As seen, under the proposed new legal framework an application is considered to have been made as soon as a person expresses a wish to receive international protection from a Member State. Cf European Parliament, Committee on Civil Liberties, Justice and Home Affairs (LIBE), Report A8-0186/2017 on the proposal for a directive of the European Parliament and of the Council laying down standards for the reception of applicants for international protection (recast) (10 May 2017), Amendment 72.

100 EU Agency for Fundamental Rights (FRA), 'Mapping minimum age requirements concerning the rights of the child in the EU', page 'Asylum applications for unaccompanied children' (2017) <http://fra.europa.eu/en/publication/2017/mapping-minimum-age-requirements/asylum-unaccompanied>. Cf also the previous section.

Conversely, in ten Member States national legislation on international protection does not set any age threshold for unaccompanied children. This is the case in Belgium, Bulgaria, Croatia, Denmark, Finland, Italy, Latvia, Luxembourg, Portugal and the United Kingdom. They can therefore apply for asylum, even if a legal representative has been appointed. National regulations on legal capacity to act in procedures, however, must be applied. Consequently, children may concretely need a legal representative to perform particular acts or engage in certain undertakings within the procedure.

Some countries do specify a minimum age for lodging an application for international protection. The Netherlands allows children aged 12 or more to lodge an application, while the age threshold is set at 14 years in Hungary and Romania and at 15 years in Greece. Below this age, children will need the application to be lodged by a person responsible for them.

The Commission's proposal for a Regulation repealing the current Asylum Procedures Directive substantially repeats in Article 31(6), with some formal amendments, the content of the current Article 7(3). However, in the proposal the clear-cut criterion is the ownership by children of legal capacity in the relevant Member State. If they have it, the request for asylum will have to be lodged by them. Where the child does not have legal capacity, the request will be lodged by an adult responsible for them, namely the guardian.

In any case, under the proposed legal framework the guardian 'shall assist and properly inform the unaccompanied minor of how and where an application is to be lodged'.[101] This duty of the guardian is listed in Article 32(1) straight after the regulation of whom is competent to lodge the application; it does not expressly refer either to the case where the child is competent to lodge the application, or the guardian. It is therefore reasonable to assume that it always applies, irrespective of who presents the application.

7. CONCLUSIONS: A LOOK AHEAD TO THE REFORM OF THE COMMON EUROPEAN ASYLUM SYSTEM (CEAS)

No matter how big the consensus may be on the principle of children as rights holders, its practical implementation in the field of asylum and migration

---

101 The Report of the Committee on Civil Liberties, Justice and Home Affairs suggests adding, before this sentence, that it shall be '[w]ithout prejudice to unaccompanied minors' right to legal assistance and representation in accordance with Articles 14 and 15'. European Parliament, Committee on Civil Liberties, Justice and Home Affairs (LIBE), Report A8-0171/2018 on the proposal for a regulation of the European Parliament and of the Council establishing a common procedure for international protection in the Union and repealing Directive 2013/32/EU (22 May 2018), Amendment 208.

is proving to be particularly challenging. While EU primary law principally recognises the autonomy of the child, secondary law on migration leaves an important margin of appreciation to the Member States as to how to concretely define it. However, national legislators have not always followed a child-rights approach. A study by the EU Fundamental Rights Agency on minimum ages in the Member States has identified important trends in this regard. Children's right to be heard is frequently not appropriately considered, while the legal representative is often expected to substitute the children's consent.

Particularly striking is the case of medical examinations for determining the age of an unaccompanied child. Five countries do not require the consent of the child at all as they consider the legal representative's sufficient. Eight Member States are satisfied with either the consent of the child or of the representative. Thus, in 13 countries a medical age assessment may be carried out without the consent of the child. Less than half the Member States always require it, alone or together with that of the representative.

In the case of asylum applications for unaccompanied children, 14 states do not allow children to lodge an application in their own right. At the same time, legal representatives are often not appointed in a timely manner. However, important deadlines are linked to the moment of the lodging of the application for international protection. As a result, the child's access to crucial services such as the education system is gravely postponed, while the delay may also thwart certain rights, such as the right to family reunification.

The ongoing reform of the Common European Asylum System is the chance for the European Union to ensure for Member States to comply with their obligations under EU law and the international human rights obligations they are bound to, both directly and as general principles of Union law.

The principle of dignity, as well as the right of the child to express their views and have these considered according to their age and maturity, are core principles in this regard. Both require the child as a rights holder to be appropriately informed, and their views and consent more widely collected. Decisions on potentially invasive tests such as those carried out for the age assessment, or on the child's life and future, cannot be taken without seriously involving the child. This does not exclude the need for the representative's assent. Especially in the case of cardinal decisions, or situations which may seriously affect the child's dignity and private sphere, the support provided by a person of trust is decisive. The involvement of a guardian should thus ensure the best interests of the child are implemented in the actual decision. Ideally, authorities should seek for the consent of both the child and the guardian.[102]

---

[102] EU Agency for Fundamental Rights (FRA), *Age assessment and fingerprinting of children in asylum procedures – Minimum age requirements concerning children's rights in the EU* (n. 53 above) 7.

Unfortunately, the Commission's proposal for an Asylum Procedures Regulation fails to provide a fully satisfying solution in this regard. In the case of asylum applications, the duties of the guardian to inform and assist the child have been positively enhanced. The identification of the subject competent to lodge the application will be found on the ownership of legal capacity by the child. While the latter criterion restricts Member States' margin of appreciation, it still allows for important decisions to be taken without properly involving the child.

The Commission's proposal is even more problematic as regards medical tests for age assessment. Requesting the child's consent 'or' the guardian's allows Member States to keep ignoring the child's opinion. An amendment suggested by the Parliament's Committee on Civil Liberties, Justice and Home Affairs (LIBE) would introduce the need to collect the consent of both subjects. Such an amendment is a step in the right direction.

Indeed, requesting the consent of the child for certain acts shall not be a way to further postpone the appointment of a representative. Member States could allow certain procedures to start only upon consent of the child, in order not to require the guardian's involvement. Already now, guardians are frequently nominated quite late, while authorities start the procedures in their absence. Speeding up the procedure is in the own interest of the applicants, in order to clarify their situation and plan their life with a far-reaching perspective. However, procedural speediness and children's rights should not be considered as intrinsically excluding each other.

The timely appointment of a legal representative is a cornerstone in this regard. A representative – better: a 'guardian' – should be promptly designated to represent and assist the unaccompanied child. A positive proposal in this regard has been made by the LIBE Committee, which requests such a guardian to be nominated from the moment when an unaccompanied minor arrives in a Member State. The guardian should make sure the child is provided with appropriate care and assistance by the competent services, and monitor how procedural safeguards – such as the provision of child-friendly information – are implemented. The representative's decisions should generally build on a shared consensus, so that the child is informed about the different possibilities at stake and involved in their assessment.

In conclusion, the ongoing reform of the European *acquis* on migration does generally provide a better recognition of the child's autonomy. However, important amendments need to be made, in order to ensure that the Union and the Member States fully implement the principle of children being rights holders, as requested by EU primary law and the international obligations they are bound to.

THE RIGHTS OF MINOR SIBLINGS IN MIGRATION

Why Migration Policies should Stop Systematically Separating Siblings

Marit BUDDENBAUM* and Julia SLOTH-NIELSEN**

1. INTRODUCTION

While the peak in the number of asylum seekers was reached in 2015, recent years have continued to present high numbers of asylum requests. In 2016, UNICEF estimated that one in every 200 children in the world today is a refugee.[1] In 2017, over 31,000 unaccompanied minors registered in the EU.[2] The number of child refugees and beneficiaries of subsidiary protection is large, but an anticipated threat to states is that these numbers are bound to increase when children apply for family reunification. In order to ensure states are able to

* Doctoral candidate at the Department of Private Law at VU Amsterdam, the Netherlands.
** Professor of law at the Faculty of Law, University of the Western Cape, South Africa, and the Department of Child Law, Leiden Law School, Leiden University, the Netherlands.

1 UNICEF, 'Uprooted: The growing crisis for refugee and migrant children' (UNICEF 2016) 6.

2 European Commission, 'Over 31,000 unaccompanied minors among asylum seekers registered in the EU in 2017' (EUROSTAT 2018).

care for the children in their territory, they call for strict migration policies that ensure that no one is able to groundlessly reunify with third-country nationals (TCNs) seeking protection in the EU. By law, EU Member States are granted a wide margin of discretion to identify who falls within or outside the scope of family reunification of TCNs.

The Council of Europe Commissioner for Human Rights wrote in 2017 that

> '[i]n most states, the right to family reunification of unaccompanied minor refugees *only extends to their parents*. Where it does not extend to other family members, this often leads to great hardship and family separation, as parents must choose to leave behind other children if they wish to avail themselves of the right to reunification with an unaccompanied minor'.[3]

While the Commissioner endorses the tough position that parents of multiple children are in, the fact that the bond between siblings is permanently disrupted as a result of migration policies, as described above, seems neglected or at the least overlooked. Currently, it is up to the discretion of states whether non-parental family relationships of the unaccompanied minor will be eligible for reunification in the host state. Also, it will be up to the discretion of states whether they will strive to keep siblings together and reunite siblings in cases of their separation as a result of migration.

In contrast to strict family reunification policies on a national or regional level, international children's rights law puts its focus on the best interests of children. This general principle is put forth in Article 3 of the UN Convention on the Rights of the Child (UNCRC) and states that in all actions concerning a child, the best interests of the child (BIC) should be a primary consideration.[4] Full application of the BIC in state decisions requires a rights-based approach and a holistic BIC assessment which secures, among other dimensions, the psychological well-being of the child.[5] Policies and state decisions that exclude siblings from family reunification or that overlook the sibling tie might not take the BIC as a primary consideration. This chapter questions whether sibling-separating migration policies could amount to a violation of international children's rights law. Furthermore, this chapter will address whether the strategy of minimising reunions between non-parental family members in a territory bears negative consequences for states in the long term, when it comes to minors' integration, mental health and economic burden/contribution.

3 Council of Europe Commissioner for Human Rights, 'Realising the Rights to Family Reunification of Refugees in Europe' (Council of Europe 2017) 36, *emphasis added.*

4 The United Nations Convention on the Rights of the Child (adopted 20 November 1989, entered into force 2 September 1990) UNTS 1577 (UNCRC) Art. 3(1).

5 UN Committee on the Rights of the Child, 'General Comment No. 14 (2013) on the right of the child to have his or her best interests taken as a primary consideration (art. 3, para. 1)' (2013) CRC/C/GC/14 [5].

This chapter aims to promote an evaluation of current family reunification policies related to TCNs in Europe by defining the rights of siblings under international and European law and reviewing the relevance of intact sibling relationships from a psycho-social perspective. The latter aims to provide states with an incentive to invest in the protection of sibling ties, as this might not only be in children's interest, but also in that of states.

2. THE LEGAL DEFINITION OF SIBLING

The various different types of sibling relationships that can be identified (varying from full biological siblings to half-sisters, adopted brothers and so on) possibly pose a challenge to legally defining 'sibling', which is a prerequisite for recognising rights for siblings in migration law. The Oxford English Dictionary elegantly defines sibling as '[e]ach of two or more children or offspring having one or both parents in common; a brother or sister'.[6] Taking into account that siblings can both be children and adults and that they can share one or both parents, this definition already illustrates the heterogeneity of the group. Age is generally an issue in family reunification cases, even if it is not a sibling but a parent who applies – 'family reunification of adult children is not permitted, unless there is some particular need'.[7] Article 4 paragraph 2(b) of the Family Reunification Directive of the European Union (FRD) refers to authorising entry and residence of 'adult unmarried children of the sponsor or his or her spouse, where they are objectively unable to provide for their own needs on account of their state of health'.[8] It is questionable whether children who would like to apply for family reunification with their adult siblings will be able to procure proof of their sibling's needs – if they would be allowed at all to extend the right to family reunification to their siblings.

Also, in today's world with so-called modern family formations and artificial reproductive technology (ART) it is possible that two children are not biologically related, but grew up together as siblings nonetheless. Even though the FRD includes adopted children in the scope of parent-child family reunification, concerns are voiced that some states require formal proof of the adoption that may be difficult to procure for TCNs who fled their countries.[9] It is safe to say that having to provide proof of the adoption of their brother or sister would be

---

6 *Sibling* <https://en.oxforddictionaries.com/definition/sibling>.

7 Commissioner for Human Rights, 'Realising the Rights to Family Reunification of Refugees in Europe' (n. 3 above) 38.

8 Council Directive (EC) 86/2003 on the right to family reunification [2003] OJ L251/12, Art. 4(2)(b).

9 Commissioner for Human Rights, 'Realising the Rights to Family Reunification of Refugees in Europe' (n. 3 above) 38.

especially difficult for siblings to procure. Another question that relates to this issue, is the possibility that children who fled from Islamic countries are part of a *kafalah* arrangement – which is an Islamic alternative care arrangement similar to adoption, but without the child being entitled to the family name or an automatic right of inheritance from the family.[10] On top of their possible inability to present a legal contract explaining their ties, there is the question of whether the children would be considered siblings at all? Even though they have a shared history similar to that of siblings, cultural differences in looking at a relationship might exclude children who are neither biological siblings nor legal siblings, in spite of their close bond. All of these questions indicate the need for a sound definition of the term 'sibling', as well as a difficulty in finding one that fits all possible (and sometimes very vague) sibling relationships. In order for states to deal with this heterogenous family relationship in a non-discriminatory manner, it seems necessary to determine the importance of the sibling bond on an individual basis, along the lines of a flexible definition in which the core component of sharing or – in the case of deceased parents having shared – at least one parent is a minimal requirement:

> A sibling shares or has shared at least one parent and:
>
> a) is biologically related (or shares genetic information), and/or;
> b) has another relationship that can be proven to be of significant importance to the individual child.

3. THE RIGHTS OF SIBLINGS UNDER INTERNATIONAL CHILDREN'S RIGHTS LAW

3.1. THE UNCRC

The extensive ratification of the UNCRC by all but one Member State since 2015[11] signifies an international consensus on states' obligations to protect children, provide certain safeguards for children and give children the opportunity to participate in decisions that directly or indirectly concern them. At the same time, states have been given autonomy to shape and realise their shared commitment in practice at the national and/or regional level. In light of the great numbers of people migrating to Member States in the EU, the biggest

---

10 U.M. Assim and J. Sloth-Nielsen, 'Islamic kafalah as an alternative care option for children deprived of a family environment' (2014) 14(2) African Human Rights Law Journal 329.

11 OHCHR, 'UN Committee hails Somalia's ratification of Convention on the Rights of the Child' (2015) OHCHR <https://www.ohchr.org/EN/NewsEvents/Pages/DisplayNews.aspx?NewsID=16556&LangID=E>.

concern in the balancing of states' and individual families' interests, is the possible losing sight of the child's best interests along the way.

The UNCRC defines explicitly the roles, rights and responsibilities of three actors: parents and/or caregivers, the state and the child. In cases where the interests of these actors conflict, it is the best interests of the *child* that is stipulated to be the primary consideration. In providing for this, the UNCRC focuses on individual children and does not mention the roles and rights of siblings, nor is any legal position for siblings identified within the UNCRC. This causes potential issues in cases that involve nuclear families with multiple children, be it two or even six siblings (see Figure 1).

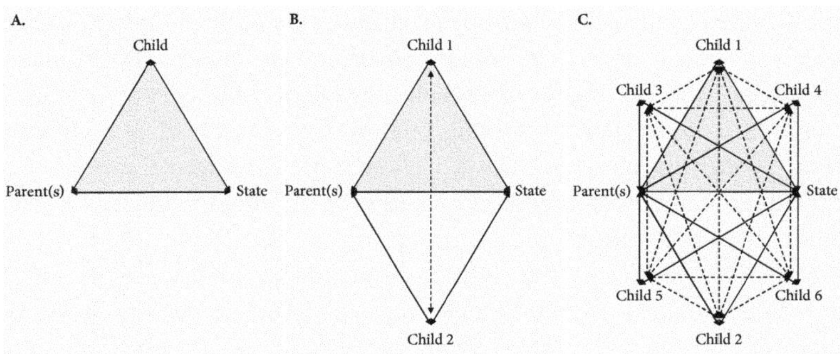

Figure 1. Adding sibling ties to the child-parent(s)-state triangle

A. displays the classic child-parent(s)-state triangle, which is more commonly embraced under US law.[12]
B. displays the triangle when a case concerns two children, such as two siblings. They both have their individual rights within the UNCRC, and parents and states each have obligations towards these individual children. But, added to this is also their relationship (the dashed line).
C. displays that the more children there are, the more complicated any balancing act would become.

It should be noted that from mid-childhood onwards, children spend, on average, more time with their siblings than with their parents, making it odd

---

12 'Family Law in the U.S. has long embraced the image of a triangle to describe the allocation of legal authority over child-rearing. Parents, children and the State stand at the three points of the triangle' (L.A. Rosenbury, 'Between Home and School' (2007) 155(4) University of Pennsylvania Law Review 1). Rosenbury highlights also other American authors who use the same triangle to visualise the triangular relationship between children, parents and the state. In the UNCRC, the triangle is also sometimes referred to, even though during the drafting process of the treaty, Finland noted that this relationship between the three is bound to change (OHCHR, Legislative History of the Convention on the Rights of the Child Vol. 2 (United Nations 2007) 869 [211]).

to neglect this family relationship in the law.[13] Even though the term 'sibling' is not explicitly mentioned in the Convention, the relationship between siblings impacts individual children's well-being and sense of identity to the extent that the separation of siblings can negatively affect their rights under Articles 3, 8 and 16 UNCRC.

Article 8 UNCRC addresses the child's right to identity. Following the findings of Branje et al. and Herrick & Piccus, siblings shape each other's (sense of) identity.[14] Depending on the type of sibling, the sibling is a part of the children's biological identity and/or of the child's family identity.[15] One's (sense of) identity, Page explains, is both fixed and dynamic, meaning that certain aspects are continuous, and others can fluctuate over time.[16] It is clear that biological siblings will always be part of each other's fixed biological identity, but children who become step-siblings later in life, could for instance start identifying as a step-sibling, making their new relationship part of their identity. As such, failing to protect the sibling relationship could lead to a violation of the right to identity under Article 8 UNCRC, meaning that the protection of or information about sibling relationships is indirectly safeguarded in the child's right to the preservation of identity.[17]

The UNCRC addresses the right to privacy and family under Article 16, which is similar to Article 8 on the right to private and family life of the European Convention on Human Rights (ECHR).[18] The body of case law regarding Article 8 of the ECHR provides an in-depth and well-established definition of family life. For Article 16 UNCRC, however, this is not yet the case. In point of fact, the UNCRC specifically mandates non-separation from a child with his or her parents under Article 9(1) and this right to non-separation is not directed at any other members of the family, such as siblings. Even though the emphasis on the parent-child relationship could be interpreted as finding this relationship more important than other family relationships, the UNCRC implemented Article 16 on the child's right to privacy and family to include 'the child's wider family, such as siblings or grandparents, *who may be as important to the child*'.[19] As such, the definition of the right to family under the UNCRC stresses that siblings are an important part of the family environment, which is also recognised under

13 D. Wolke and others, 'Bullying in the family: siblings bullying' (2015) 2(10) Lancet Psychiatry 917.

14 See section 4 of this chapter.

15 C. Page 'Artificial Womb Technology and the Safeguarding of Children's Rights Through an Analysis of the Right to Identity' (LL.M. thesis, Leiden University 2017) 7.

16 Ibid.

17 UNCRC (n. 4 above) Art. 8(1).

18 Convention for the Protection of Human Rights and Fundamental Freedoms (European Convention on Human Rights, as amended) (ECHR) Art. 8.

19 R. Hodgkin and P. Newell, 'Implementation Handbook for the Convention on the Rights of the Child' (UNICEF 2007) 210 [emphasis added].

the right to family life of the ECHR. Also, Article 5 UNCRC implies that the guidance of and responsibility for individual children extends to parents *and other family members*, which in the context of child-headed households, foster children and siblings in migration, could very well be the sibling.

3.2. GENERAL COMMENTS AND BIC ASSESSMENTS

Even though the UNCRC does not mention siblings in the Convention itself, through the adoption of General Comments, the United Nations Committee on the Rights of the Child (hereinafter CRC Committee), the monitoring body of the UNCRC, can extend the *corpus juris* of international children's rights for purposes of interpretation of the UNCRC.[20] These General Comments are not legally binding, but provide authoritative guidance to states parties on the implementation of the UNCRC. Eight General Comments (GCs) mention siblings explicitly (namely GCs 3,[21] 6,[22] 7,[23] 14,[24] 16,[25] 17,[26] 21[27] and 23[28]) in the contexts of children's family environment. One paragraph in the latest General Comment, No. 23, does not only mention siblings, but also provides explicit guidance to states on the interpretation of siblings as a part of the family, when it writes that:

> 'in compliance with international legal obligations in terms of maintaining family unity, which includes siblings, States should prevent separation in accordance with the Guidelines on Alternative Care of Children.'[29]

---

20 OHCHR, 'Committee on the Rights of the Child' (1996–2019) OHCHR <https://www.ohchr.org/EN/HRBodies/CRC/Pages/CRCIntro.aspx>.

21 UN Committee on the Rights of the Child, 'General Comment No. 3 (2003) on HIV/AIDS and the rights of the child' (2003) CRC/C/GC/3 [34], [36].

22 UN Committee on the Rights of the Child, 'General Comment No. 6 (2005) on the treatment of unaccompanied and separated children outside their country of origin' (2005) CRC/C/GC/6 [31ii], [40].

23 UN Committee on the Rights of the Child, 'General Comment No. 7 (2005) on implementing child rights in early childhood' (2005) CRC/C/GC/7 [19], [20c], [36e].

24 GC 14 (n. 5 above) [65].

25 UN Committee on the Rights of the Child, 'General Comment No. 16 (2013) on State obligations regarding the impact of the business sector on children's rights' (2013) CRC/C/GC/16 [19].

26 UN Committee on the Rights of the Child, 'General Comment No. 17 (2013) on the right of the child to rest, leisure, play, recreational activities, cultural life and the arts (art. 31)' (2013) CRC/C/GC/17 [48].

27 UN Committee on the Rights of the Child, 'General Comment No. 21 (2017) on children in street situations' (2017) CRC/C/GC/21 [4].

28 UN Committee on the Rights of the Child and Committee on the Protection of the Rights of All Migrant Workers and Members of their Families, 'Joint General Comment No. 4 (2017) of the Committee on the Protection of the Rights of All Migrant Workers and Members of their Families and No. 23 (2017) of the Committee on the Rights of the Child on the human rights of children in the context of international migration in countries of origin, transit, destination and return' (2017) CMW/C/GC/4-CRC/C/GC/23 [27], [32], [37–38].

29 Ibid., [27].

It should be understood that this particular phrase was written in the specific context of migration. Furthermore, this GC was jointly written together with the Committee on the Protection of the Rights of All Migrant Workers and Members of their Families, and it is to be questioned whether that committee's definition of 'family' happens to include siblings, or whether the CRC Committee actively chose to include siblings in this context too. Still, the CRC Committee agreed on the wording of this paragraph, otherwise it would have been rewritten. Therefore, this is an extremely important finding for the way sibling relationships need to be viewed in international children's rights law: as part of the family environment. Taking all the Comments together, the Committee clearly ascribes to the sibling relationship a pivotal role in a child's development. Still, there is room for an additional and specific General Comment on inter-child relationships or even one specific to siblings in order to ensure authoritative guidance to states on how to treat siblings and incorporate the rights of siblings into their national jurisdictions. General Comments Nos. 6 and 23 explain the rights of children in the context of migration and were published in 2005 and 2017 respectively. Several paragraphs dealt with siblings and give an important insight into how the Committee would like them to be treated in the context of migration.

In GC 6, the Committee established that, first, siblings are part of the (definition of) family.[30] Second, registration of children in migration by a receiving state, including bio-data assessment, includes identifying (if there are) siblings.[31] Third, in accordance with the principle of family unity, siblings should be kept together.[32] These three points were repeated in GC 23. This GC addressed cases in which the child's relations with parents and siblings are interrupted by migration. Two important remarks regarding the sibling tie under such conditions were, first, that preservation of the family unit (which includes siblings) should be part of a BIC assessment in decisions on family reunification.[33] Secondly, the GC encourages states to provide adequate financial support for sibling reunification.[34]

Not only in General Comments, but also by monitoring the implementation of the UNCRC at the national level through periodic state reports, the Committee presents its view on the importance of protecting the sibling relationship from arbitrary and systematic separation clearly. In previous reports, the Committee expressed concern to multiple Muslim countries who 'award custody of young

---

30 GC 6 (n. 22 above) [40] and GC 23 (n. 28 above) [27].

31 GC 6 (n. 22 above) [31ii].

32 Ibid., [40].

33 GC 23 (n. 28 above) [32].

34 Ibid., [37].

children to mothers and older children to fathers'.[35] In its response to the state report of Pakistan, the CRC Committee expressed concern

> 'that the State Party's legislation uses age limits, instead of the best interests of the child, as criteria in determining custody in cases of divorce. Such permission, in addition to *implying that siblings can be separated*, discriminates between the sexes and fails to acknowledge the child's right to express her/his views and have them taken into account'.[36]

By literally expressing its concern for systematic sibling separation, the CRC Committee shows that sibling separation for other reasons than it being in the BIC of the children concerned, should be discouraged. Similar expressions can be found directly on the topic of siblings in migration in the CRC Committee's Concluding Observations to Denmark of October 2017:

> '41. The Committee notes with concern that:
>
> (a) Unaccompanied children may, under certain circumstances, be placed in detention when awaiting deportation and, as of age 17, they are not placed in the specialized children's asylum centres but in centres for adults. *Unaccompanied siblings are accommodated according to their age and may thus be separated*.'[37]

The lack of legal recognition of siblings explains why many states have failed to put this important family tie in the balance when cases concern siblings directly[38] and indirectly.[39] Given the importance of sibling relationships,[40] there is a need for legal practitioners to include siblings as an important factor in the BIC – even if the sibling relationship concerned occurs in a non-classical family form, such as half-siblings and adopted siblings.

A very important way to find out whether the sibling relationship is important for the children at hand, is by asking the individual children. A BIC assessment normally requires children's participation and, especially for young and disabled children who cannot (yet) participate, a child-centered approach. The United Nations High Commissioner for Refugees (UNHCR) includes siblings in their definition of family and encourages a best-interests-of-the-child assessment in

---

35 UNICEF (n. 19 above) 128.

36 Ibid., [emphasis added].

37 UN Committee on the Rights of the Child, 'Concluding Observations on the fifth periodic report of Denmark' (2017) CRC/C/DNK/CO/5 [41a].

38 Cf Extending the right to family reunification for unaccompanied minors only to their parents and making siblings unable to reunify.

39 Cf family reunification cases which do not apply to (all) the siblings.

40 See section 4 of this chapter.

all proceedings affecting a child. However, also the UNHCR focused its BIC assessment tool on individual children and their parents and failed to include siblings explicitly.[41] This shows that the focus on the parent-child relationship in legal documents and guidelines can result in overlooking or neglecting one of the most important relationships for children, their brothers and sisters, in the law. Therefore, adding an explicit enquiry about the sibling relationship as a factor in a BIC assessment could be a necessary step to ensure that siblings are recognised in the balancing of interests in migration cases. By anchoring siblings in individual children's BIC assessments, Article 3 UNCRC could offer a direct legal protection for sibling's rights to family reunification. That is, if states agree that preservation of the family unit (including siblings) should be part of a BIC assessment in decisions on family reunification, as General Comment No. 23 recommends. It should be stressed, too, that BIC assessments are in most legal systems an obstacle in migration cases, due to the great amount of asylum and family reunification applications and states' lack of resources to assess them thoroughly.

3.3. RECOGNITION OF SIBLINGS THROUGH BIC ASSESSMENTS

Still, the importance of a BIC assessment is recognised by regional courts and international legal bodies as became visible in a recent case ruling by the Inter-American Court of Human Rights (IACtHR). In this case, also the legal acknowledgement of siblings is visible. Without there being a direct legal text that mentions siblings, the IACtHR ruled on behalf of the family life of two half-brothers in *Ramirez v. Guatemala (2018)*.[42] 18 years ago, two half-brothers (age 7 and 2) were removed from their home and placed in an institution due to suspicion of neglect by their parents. While the parents attempted to regain the custody over their boys, the children were separated from each other in the institution. After the parents (and other family members) failed to regain custody, the decision was made to place the boys for international adoption into separate families. Fifteen years later, the oldest brother was able to trace his biological family and decided to file a case against Guatemala. He felt the separation from his family, especially from his younger brother was an unjustified interference with his right to family life and identity. The IACtHR ruled that Guatemala was indeed in violation of his rights to equal protection of the family, name and identity and even of humane treatment. The Court expressly stated that Guatemala should have done a BIC assessment in every decision regarding the

41 UNHCR, UNHCR Guidelines on Determining the Best Interests of the Child (UNHCR 2008).

42 IACtHR, *Caso Ramírez Escobar y Otros v. Guatemala* (2018).

boys, which would have either justified the decisions to separate the brothers or would have hampered their separation.

Similarly, a BIC assessment was missing in the determination of a family reunification case in Belgium.[43] In 2006, an Iraqi family of two parents, a daughter of 17 and a son of 11 fled their war-torn country. At the end of 2007, the mother of the family was granted subsidiary protection in Belgium. The father and both children, who had fled to Syria by that time, applied for family reunification with the mother in Belgium. In the meantime, the daughter had turned 18 and reached the age of majority. Because the mother was unable to prove sufficient financial means to support her daughter, only the father and the son were granted a visa and arrived in Belgium in 2009. The daughter was still (financially) dependent and her file demonstrated that her personal circumstances were similar to those of her brother. Even though in this case the sibling separation occurred indirectly, the strict migration policies aimed at keeping the influx of migrants at a minimum overlooked the permanent disruption of a family relationship between a brother and sister, on the basis of the sister having reached the age of majority before she could apply for family reunification with her mother. This case highlights that family reunification policies primarily focus on the age of children, financial means of the parents and the type of family tie (parental and spousal). It is debatable whether a BIC assessment of the brother in this case would have prevented a negative reunification decision for the daughter and sister of the family, but the fact that such an assessment has not been made highlights the potential danger that decisions will be taken that counter children's best interests and jeopardise their rights.

Even though the FRD has been in place since 2003 and specifies in Article 4 that adult children could be allowed entry and residence based on their dependence and needs, the case above is a perfect example of the danger that lies in not ensuring BIC assessments and not recognising the importance of the sibling tie through law: it can result in failing to protect vulnerable families and violate the rights of children. Since 2011, Article 31(4) of the Qualification Directive of the European Union has established important progress in recognising sibling bonds through law and reinforced the need for a BIC assessment for unaccompanied minors: 'As far as possible, *siblings shall be kept together, taking into account the best interests of the minor concerned* and, in particular, his or her age and degree of maturity. Changes of residence of unaccompanied minors shall be limited to a minimum.' In 2017, recommendations by the Council of Europe Commissioner on Human Rights included to 'strengthen the position

43 A. Bathily and A.F. Atger, 'Disrupted Flight: The Realities of Separated Refugee Families in the EU' (Red Cross EU Office and European Council on Refugees and Exiles 2014) 12.

of children in the family reunification process', and specifically numbers 5 and 6 recommend for states to:

5. Ensure that the best interests of the child is a primary consideration in all family reunification decisions and that refugee children's requests for family reunification are dealt with in a positive, humane and expeditious manner.
6. Avoid family separation and allow both parents and siblings to reunite when an unaccompanied minor is the sponsor, that is, the first family member arriving in a host state.[44]

It is questionable whether these laws and recommendations are always in mind in migration cases and decisions, and whether the importance of the sibling relationship is recognised by authorities and decision-makers. In the next section, therefore, the importance of the sibling tie will be presented.

4. THE RELEVANCE OF INTACT SIBLING RELATIONSHIPS FROM A SOCIO-PSYCHOLOGICAL PERSPECTIVE

The presence of a legal basis for sibling rights under international children's rights law was described above. It is from the socio-psychological perspective, however, that the importance of a sibling bond becomes clear. The sibling relationship is a unique and a potentially life-long family relationship that has been a subject of interest for decades in the field of (Developmental) Psychology. The importance of the sibling bond for healthy or unhealthy development is well established for various types of siblings, including full biological siblings, but also half-siblings, step-siblings, foster siblings and adopted siblings. Sibling relationships are important because the interaction between siblings influences the social and emotional context in which the children grow up.[45] The number, age and common history of siblings varies between different sibling relationships, making every sibling group unique.[46] Despite these differences, a positive sibling relationship is associated with a reduced risk of poor peer relationships and other adverse life events.[47] Siblings can contribute

---

44 Commissioner for Human Rights, 'Realising the Rights to Family Reunification of Refugees in Europe' (n. 3 above) 7.

45 G.H. Brody, 'Sibling Relationship Quality: Its Causes and Consequences' (1998) 49(1–24) Annual Review of Psychology 19.

46 R. Scelles, 'Accueil des fratries: analyse de l'expérience de professionnels travaillant dans le cadre de l'association SOS Villages d'Enfants' in H. Kutin (ed.), 'Because we are sisters and brothers: siblings in alternative care' (SOS Children's Villages International 2012) 9.

47 Wolke, 'Bullying in the family' (n. 13 above) 917.

to the development of each other's cognitive and language skills.[48] Intact sibling relationships allow children to fulfil an important role in each other's lives, as teachers and caregivers, but also as companions.[49] Growing up with a sibling helps the development of psychological skills (e.g. effective coping strategies or empathy) in a child.[50] Although sibling relationships can be negative or even harmful as a result of other problems in the familial sphere, the positive influence of a positive sibling relationship on the development of the child is widely acknowledged in academic literature. The development and protection of sibling relationships in childhood should be perceived as investments for the future of the child.[51] This is illustrated by many elderly people, who report feeling closer to their siblings than to any other member of the family, except for maybe their own children.[52]

When their family environment becomes unstable, children value their sibling relationships even more highly. US attorney and *guardian ad litem*[53] Jenny R. Stevens describes the increasing significance of the sibling relationship in a stressful divorce scenario: 'many time siblings become each other's best, and maybe only, friends'.[54] When other family relationships are crumbling the sibling relationship becomes especially important, because it provides 'solace, nurturing, care-taking and secure emotional attachments'.[55] In alternative care settings, sibling relationships are often 'the only constants' and therefore become extra valuable to the child.[56] Siblings growing closer together when their relationship with one or both parents is threatened is not a surprising phenomenon, because siblings naturally seek each other's help 'in the process of gaining autonomy and defining their identity'.[57] Minors in migration face an extreme form of unstable family environment while potentially dealing with trauma and uncertainty. Looking at the examples of alternative care and parental divorce, it is inevitable that in the context of migration the importance and value of intact sibling bonds will be increased significantly. Therefore, especially in

48 M. Azmitia and J. Hesser, 'Why siblings are important agents of cognitive development: A comparison of siblings and peers' (1993) 64(2) Child Development 442.

49 J. Dunn and S. McGuire, 'Sibling and peer relationships in childhood' (1992) 33(1) Journal of Child Psychology and Psychiatry 71.

50 Brody, 'Sibling Relationship Quality' (n. 45 above) 19.

51 M. Kosonen, 'Sibling relationships for children in the care system' (1994) 18(3) Adoption and Fostering 23.

52 J.E. Hasday, 'Family Law Reimagined' (Harvard University Press 2014).

53 A '*guardian ad litem*' is appointed by a court to investigate which solutions would be in the BIC.

54 J.R. Stevens, 'The Importance of Sibling Relationships for Children of Divorce' (The Stevens Firm, PA Family Law Center, 18 February 2014) <https://www.scfamilylaw.com/importance-sibling-relationships-children-of-divorce>.

55 Hasday, 'Family Law Reimagined' (n. 52 above) 166.

56 Kutin, 'Because we are sisters and brothers' (n. 46 above) 32.

57 S.J.T. Branje and others, 'Perceived support in sibling relationships and adolescent adjustment' (2008) 45(8) Journal of Child Psychology and Psychiatry 1395.

migration cases when the state performs a BIC assessment, no sibling ties should be overlooked.

Separating siblings would put an end to the positive influence they had on each other, but it is not only the potential benefits of the relationship that are lost. Unjustified sibling separation itself is described as negatively impacting children in multiple ways. Despite acknowledgement of the importance of sibling relationships for children's short-term and long-term welfare, a large proportion of children in alternative care live separated from one or more siblings.[58]

> 'Because of the significant relationships that children may have with their parents and siblings before being removed from their home, children who enter the child welfare system may [feel unwanted or unloved and] experience anxiety, trauma, grief, guilt and loss of identity.'[59]

Herrick and Piccus explored that maintaining sibling relationships through placement together – as long as the safety of all siblings allows for placement together – can have 'ameliorating effects' on the negative impact that placement in alternative care can have on a child.[60] In alternative care settings, siblings take on the role of 'mutual supporters' to compensate to some extent their loss of parents.[61] Also, they can provide each other with stability, love and permanence.[62] When siblings live apart from each other, they cannot positively influence each other's development, in the ways that were described above. In other words, the potential of the sibling relationship is (partly) wasted in such a situation. In addition to this loss of potential, involuntary separation of siblings results in loneliness negatively affecting the child.[63] Separating children from their sibling(s) (on top of separating them from their parents) whilst they wish to remain together intensifies children's weakened psychological well-being upon entering the welfare system.

These negative effects are very relevant in the context of migration. Child and adolescent migrants express the importance of their sibling relationships in conversations with mental health workers of the National Health Services in the United Kingdom.[64] Some express their fear that something bad will

58 Kosonen, 'Sibling relationships for children in the care system' (n. 51 above) 845.

59 M.A. Herrick and W. Piccus, 'Sibling connections: The importance of nurturing sibling bonds in the foster care system' (2005) 27(7) Children and Youth Services Review 84.

60 Ibid., 858.

61 Kutin, 'Because we are sisters and brothers' (n. 46 above) 32.

62 Herrick and Piccus, 'Sibling connections' (n. 59 above) 858.

63 Ibid., 849.

64 During the 'Lost in Migration II: from European priorities to local realities' conference on 12 April 2018 in Brussels, Belgium, Dr. Ana Draper provided all participants of her workshop

happen to their siblings if they have to go through the same, horrible, journey the child concerned went through before arrival. Uncertainty and worry over the life, survival and health of their sibling(s) forms a recurring cause for anxiety disorders, sleep deprivation and anger issues among unaccompanied and separated minors. In Luxembourg, the children's ombudsman recognised this phenomenon and recently witnessed a case where an Afghan boy could not wait to be reunited with his (minor) siblings.[65] The boy feared for his vulnerable siblings more than he did for any other relative. These examples illustrate that in addition to losing the developmental benefits of an intact sibling relationship, involuntary separation has additional detrimental effects. This phenomenon seems EU-wide to say the least and suggests that legal recognition of the sibling bond might improve children's development and mental health. Since poor mental health is a major obstacle for integration in the host country, improving mental health of children in migration by protecting their sibling relationship might be an attractive and even cost-effective approach for host states. Obviously for large extended families with many siblings, the cost-effectiveness for host states is questionable, but if the legal framework cannot justify keeping the siblings separated, and their separation would amount to children's rights violation for the child within a state's jurisdiction, abiding by law would still be the way to go.

Given the described significance of the sibling relationships – that only increase when they are in an unstable family environment – adults (parents as well as states authorities) should not think lightly about these ties. As such, sibling separation as a result of social workers' intent to save children from unstable family environments (cf through their separate placement, like in the case of the Ramírez Brothers (n. 42 above)) could be harmful and their relationship and the impact of separation should therefore be assessed prior to the decision that leads to sibling separation. There is a justified need to protect the sibling relationship as one crucial to children's well-being, identity and psychological health. This is because brothers and sisters can shape each other's identity, be beneficial for the (social) development and well-being of the child, and are in general considered an important member of the child's family environment. All types of sibling relationships require protection if this is found to be in the individual children's best interest, as much as their separation would be justified if *that* is in their best interest.

---

with some of her daily encounters as a child psychiatrist for unaccompanied and separated children.

65 During the 'Safeguarding Children's Rights in Migration' conference on 22 November 2018 at Leiden Law School, the Netherlands, the Children's Ombudsman of Luxembourg mentioned this in a conversation with the authors after the presentation.

5. CONCLUSION

As rights holders, children in migration situations have the right to reunify with family and integrate into society as soon as they receive a permit to stay. Family reunification laws intend to enable children to build a life outside the country of origin without any permanent separation from family left behind or lost during their migratory journey. However, today states are presented with extremely high numbers of child and adolescent refugees and try to minimise the influx of third-country nationals through strict reunification policies. Most states extend the right to family reunification for unaccompanied minors only to their parents, and thereby *de facto* disrupt opportunities to reunite siblings.

Especially since siblings in migration are in need of protection independently from their parents, but with a focus on the parent-child relationship, laws and policies on a national and regional level lack sufficient regard for sibling ties. This chapter explored to what extent, internationally, UNCRC Member States should protect ties between siblings in the context of migration and strive to reunite siblings who have been separated as a result of migration. Strictly construed, also the UN Convention on the Rights of the Child focuses primarily on the rights of individual children and their parent(s) or legal caregiver(s), and not on siblings or other inter-child relationships. But, even though siblings are not explicitly mentioned in the UNCRC, the CRC Committee established that siblings are part of the family environment, also in the context of migration, and that sibling separation is cause for concern when it occurs outside the scope of the children's best interests or because of a difference in age. Also, from an analysis of cases and jurisdictions concerning brothers and sisters, it is submitted that the rights to identity, to private and family life as well as the general principle to have one's best interests taken as a primary consideration, are at risk of being violated if siblings are separated because of restrictive policies. As such, the relationship between siblings impacts individual children's sense of identity and well-being to the extent that the separation of siblings can negatively affect their rights under Articles 3, 8 and 16 of the UNCRC.

This chapter has indicated that the sibling relationship is important in the lives of children. The multiplicity of different types of sibling bonds with half-siblings and adopted siblings potentially poses difficulties for legally defining siblings, because family relationships are sometimes not legally established nor biologically identifiable. This chapter recommends using a broad definition for sibling ties, excluding solely looking at full biological ties, with the burden of proving siblinghood not resting on the siblings, but embedded in the states' mandatory assessment of the best interests of the child. Including siblings explicitly in BIC assessments can ensure that this important family tie is not overlooked in migration decisions, but it should be stressed that this inclusion would only help if BIC assessments are carried out thoroughly for every child at stake, which, unfortunately, is mostly not the case due to states' constraints in resources and time.

Studies in the field of developmental psychology revealed that protecting the sibling bond is of urgent importance in the context of stressful family circumstances, making it particularly important to protect siblings in migration. Where siblings are part of children's identity and have a positive potential on each other's development, mental health and social skills (such as sharing, empathy and understanding, coping and negotiating), separating siblings in times of stressful circumstances intensifies their weakened psychological well-being, and forms an obstacle to the integration of children and adolescents in host states.

In contrast to strict migration policies, there is a justified need to protect the sibling relationship as one crucial to children's well-being, identity and psychological health. States have the responsibility to protect siblings under international (children's rights) law. Acting on this responsibility might benefit the host society in economic and other ways. Due regard for the importance of sibling relationships is essential for effectively safeguarding children's rights in migration. As a solution, the sibling relationship should be included in BIC assessments for all children in the context of migration, in order to ensure a fair balancing of the interests of children involved, without sibling separation being a matter of collateral damage, because the sibling bond was not factored into any migration or family reunification policy. As such, this chapter submits that children should not be (kept) separated from their siblings unless the state can justify that such separation will be in the child's best interests.

THE (LIMITED) ROLE OF CHILDREN'S RIGHTS IN EU FAMILY REUNIFICATION LAW FOR BENEFICIARIES OF INTERNATIONAL PROTECTION

Mark KLAASSEN* and Gerrie LODDER**

1. INTRODUCTION

The 1951 Convention on the Status of Refugees does not contain a state obligation to allow for family reunification of refugees. In the Final Act of the Conference of Plenipotentiaries states are recommended to take the necessary measures to protect the family life of refugees.[1] The right to family reunification has been discussed a lot ever since, but this has never resulted in a binding legal obligation to allow for family reunification in international law. The Human

* Assistant professor of immigration law at the Institute of Immigration Law, Leiden University, the Netherlands.

** Researcher and lecturer at the Institute of Immigration Law, Leiden University, the Netherlands.

1 United Nations, *Final Act of the United Nations Conference of Plenipotentiaries on the Status of Refugees and Stateless Persons*, 25 July 1951, United Nations, Treaty Series, vol. 189, p. 137, https://www.refworld.org/docid/3e2becbb4.html, Recommendation B.

Rights Committee has held based on the International Covenant on Civil and Political Rights (ICCPR) that states should take the appropriate measures 'to ensure the unity or reunification of families, particularly when their members are separated for political, economic or similar reasons'.[2] The Convention of the Rights of the Child (UNCRC) does contain an explicit reference to the importance of family reunification. In Article 10(1) it is stated that states shall deal with applications for family reunification by a child or his or her parents in a positive, humane and expeditious manner. In European human rights law, Article 8 European Convention on Human Rights (ECHR) protects the right to respect for private and family life. Even though no right to family reunification is provided for in the ECHR, the European Court of Human Rights (ECtHR) has laid down specific safeguards for the exercise of the right to family reunification in the context of Article 8.[3]

In European Union (EU) law, a substantive right to family reunification is laid down in the EU Family Reunification Directive (FRD).[4] The Directive was adopted in 2003 and entered into force in 2005. It harmonises the right to family reunification in the EU and is applicable in all EU Member States, except Denmark, Ireland and the United Kingdom.[5] It lays down that third-country national family members of third-country national sponsors residing lawfully on the territory of the Member States shall be granted family reunification if they comply with the substantive requirements that the Member States are allowed to impose in accordance with the Directive. The FRD includes a separate regime for persons who have been recognised as a refugee in the Member State concerned. The FRD is the only instrument in supranational law which grants a substantive right to family reunification to refugees.[6] The FRD prescribes that when examining an application for family reunification, the Member States shall have due regard to the best interests of minor children.[7]

The focus of this chapter is on the right to family reunification for beneficiaries of international protection in the EU. The central question that is

---

2 UNHRC, *CCPR General Comment No. 19: Article 23 (The Family) Protection of the Family, the Right to Marriage and Equality of the Spouses*, 27 July 1990, available at: http://www.refworld.org/docid/45139bd74.html, para. 5.

3 See e.g. Ciara Smyth, 'The Best Interests of the Child in the Expulsion and First-Entry Jurisprudence of the European Court of Human Rights: How Principled Is the Court's Use of the Principle?' (2015) 17 European Journal of Migration and Law 70.

4 Council Directive 2003/86/EC of 22 September 2003 on the right to family reunification (Family Reunification Directive).

5 These Member States have opted out of the Directive.

6 Mark Klaassen, *The Right to Family Unification: Between Migration Control and Human Rights* (Meijers Instituut 2015), https://openaccess.leidenuniv.nl/handle/1887/36049.

7 Art. 5(5) FRD. See for an analysis of the use of the best interests concept in EU family reunification law, Mark Klaassen and Peter Rodrigues, 'The Best Interests of the Child in EU Family Reunification Law: A Plea for More Guidance on the Role of Article 24(2) Charter' (2017) 19 European Journal of Migration and Law 191.

addressed in the chapter is what the role of the best interests of the child in the different aspects of the right to family reunification for sponsors with some form of international protection is. This chapter is – after the introduction – divided into two parts. The first part gives a general overview of the most relevant international and regional legal rules for family reunification with an international protected sponsor in the EU. Firstly, section 2.1 analyses the implications of the right to respect for family life under Article 8 ECHR and Article 7 Charter and the best interests of the child as laid down in Article 3(1) UNCRC and Article 24(2) Charter for family reunification of refugees in EU law. After that, section 2.2 discusses the family reunification of refugees and beneficiaries of subsidiary forms of protection under the FRD. The second part of the chapter discusses in more detail three problematic aspects of the right to family reunification for beneficiaries of international protection in the EU. Firstly, the lawfulness of the distinction that is made in EU family reunification law between refugees and subsidiary forms of protection is assessed in section 3.1 The next issue is child marriage in relation to the right to family reunification. The FRD does provide for the family reunification of the spouse of a refugee, but the Directive allows Member States to exclude spouses below the age of 21. Several Member States make use of this option to exclude child spouses from the scope of family reunification. The compatibility of excluding child spouses from the scope of the Directive with the current legal framework is discussed in section 3.2. The last specific issue addressed, in section 3.3, is the right to family reunification of unaccompanied minors. Unaccompanied minors who obtain refugee status are eligible to be reunited with their parents.

2. THE INTERNATIONAL AND REGIONAL RULES FOR FAMILY REUNIFICATION IN THE EU

This section gives a general overview of the legal rules in international and regional law which regulate the right to reunification with a sponsor who is a beneficiary of international protection in the EU.

2.1. THE RIGHT TO RESPECT FOR FAMILY LIFE AND THE BEST INTERESTS OF THE CHILD

Before discussing the particular legal norms prescribed by the FRD, first the implications of the right to respect for family life under Article 8 ECHR and Article 7 EU Charter of Fundamental Rights (Charter) and the best interests of the child under Article 3(1) UNCRC and Article 24(2) Charter for family reunification are analysed.

The right to respect for family life under Article 8 ECHR does not include a right to family reunification as such. The ECtHR reiterates in each and every immigration case that immigration control is a state prerogative.[8] The ECtHR takes a different approach in various types of immigration cases. Generally, the ECtHR holds that only in exceptional circumstances the state is under a positive obligation under Article 8 to allow for family reunification.[9] An important element in the considerations of the ECtHR is whether family life is possible in the country of origin of the applicant.[10] In the context of family reunification to sponsors who are beneficiaries of international protection, it can generally not be held that family life in the country of origin is possible, as it can be assumed that there are insurmountable obstacles to exercise family life in the country of origin as the sponsor was provided with international protection in the host state.[11]

In determining whether a refusal of family reunification to a sponsor who is a beneficiary of international protection is justified, the ECtHR attaches significant weight to the circumstances under which the sponsor has left behind family members in the country of origin and the efforts that were made to reunite with the family members swiftly after arrival in the host state. In this context, the ECtHR takes into account whether family members were left behind by the sponsor of his or her own free will.[12] The ECtHR further takes into account whether the application for family reunification was lodged promptly after arrival or after status recognition. In a case in which the family separation continued for a number of years without clear efforts of the sponsor to reunite with her children, the ECtHR held that the refusal of family reunification did not amount to a violation of Article 8.[13] However, the ECtHR has also held that family life remains intact in cases in which family members are separated for a long period.[14]

In the specific context of the right to respect for family life of refugee sponsors, the ECtHR had held that the right to respect for family unity is an essential right of refugees of which the right to family reunification is an essential element.

---

8 The origin of this formulation can be traced back to the seminal *Abdulaziz* ruling. See *Abdulaziz, Cabales and Balkandali v. United Kingdom* (1985) 7 EHRR 471.

9 Mark Klaassen, 'Between Facts and Norms: Testing Compliance with Article 8 ECHR in Immigration Cases' (2019) 37(2) Netherlands Quarterly of Human Rights 165.

10 Marie-Bénédicte Dembour, *When Humans Become Migrants : Study of the European Court of Human Rights with an Inter-American Counterpoint* (1st ed., OUP 2015).

11 See e.g. *Gül v. Switzerland* (1996) 22 EHRR 93, para. 38; *Tuquabo-Tekle v. Netherlands* (2010) EHRR 1454, para. 42. In *Jeunesse v. Netherlands* (2014) ECHR 1309, the Court adopted a different approach, noting that there were no insurmountable obstacles to exercising family life in the country of origin, but that the minor children of the applicant would experience a certain degree of hardship were they to relocate.

12 *Tuquabo-Tekle* (n. 11 above) para. 42.

13 *IAA v. United Kingdom* (2016) 6 EHRR SE19.

14 *Saleck Bardi v. Spain* App no 66167/09 (ECHR 24 May 2011).

The Court notes that there is an international consensus on the need for a more favourable treatment of family reunification to refugee sponsors. Considering the vulnerability of refugees and their family members, applications for family reunifications must be ruled on promptly without excessive delays.[15]

As laid down in Article 3(1) UNCRC, the best interests of the child must be a primary consideration in all decisions affecting children. This is codified in EU law in Article 24(2) Charter. There is no provision in the ECHR on the best interests of the child. However, the principle is frequently invoked by the ECtHR in the interpretation of Article 8 ECHR in immigration cases. The ECtHR has emphasised that the best interests of the child in the context of the right to family reunification requires the consideration of the age of the children, their situation in the country of origin and the extent to which they are dependent on their parents.[16] The best interests of the child must be placed at the heart of the considerations. However, the best interests of the child cannot be regarded as a 'trump card' requiring the admission of all children which would be better off in the host state.[17] The Committee on the Rights of the Child (CRC Committee) has emphasised the need for expeditious and humane family reunifications repeatedly, especially for unaccompanied minors.[18] Furthermore, the CRC Committee has held that the Contracting Parties are under the obligation to use an inclusive definition of the family in domestic family reunification laws.[19]

The human right to respect for family life and the best interests of the child are minimum safeguards that must be respected in the context of domestic laws and practices on family reunification. The FRD acknowledges in the Preamble the importance of the right to family life in general and Article 8 ECHR in particular.[20] The Charter is applicable to the EU Member States when implementing and applying EU law.[21] That means that in the implementation of the FRD the Member States are bound to respect the safeguards from the Charter. It is laid down in the Charter that the Charter provisions that are comparable

15 *Mugenzi v. France* App no 52701/09 (ECHR 10 October 2014); *Tanda-Muzinga v. France* App no 2260/10 (ECHR 10 October 2015).

16 *El Ghatet v. Switzerland* (2016) ECHR 963.

17 *IAA* (n. 13 above) para. 46.

18 UN Committee on the Rights of the Child (UNCRC), General Comment No. 6 (2005): Treatment of Unaccompanied and Separated Children Outside their Country of Origin, 1 September 2005, CRC/GC/2005/6.

19 *Y.B. and N.S.* [2018] CRC/C/79/D/12/2017 (Committee on the Rights of the Child). The Committee did not go as far as ruling that Belgium is under an obligation to allow for Kafalah adoptions in domestic family reunification policy based on Art. 10 UNCRC. See for further discussion: G. Erdem Türkelli and W. Vandenhole, Communication 12/2017: Y.B. and N.S. v Belgium, Leiden Children's Rights Observatory, Case Note 2018/3, Leiden Law School, 10 December 2018.

20 Recital 2 FRD.

21 Art. 51 Charter.

to provisions from the ECHR – such as the provision on the right to respect for family life in Article 8 ECHR and Article 7 Charter – must be interpreted in the same manner as the ECHR provision is interpreted. However, the role of the Charter vis-à-vis the ECHR is different. Especially in the context of the right to family reunification, the FRD provides for a subjective right to family reunification where Article 8 ECHR merely provides a minimum standard based on the more general right to respect for family life. Article 5(5) FRD) states that the Member States shall have due regard to the best interests of the child, mirroring Article 24(2) Charter.

2.2. HARMONISING REFUGEE FAMILY REUNIFICATION IN THE FAMILY REUNIFICATION DIRECTIVE

In the Preamble of the Directive, it is stated that

> 'special attention should be paid to the situation of refugees on account of the reasons which forced them to flee their country and prevent them from leading a normal family life there. More favourable conditions should therefore be laid down for the exercise of their right to family reunification.'[22]

Eligibility for family reunification depends on the status of the sponsor and of the migrating family members. The FRD obliges the Member States to allow for family reunification to family members of sponsors who are eligible under the Directive when the requirements which the Member States may impose based on Article 7 are complied with.[23] With regard to the substantive requirements, the Court of Justice of the EU (CJEU) has consistently held that any limitations placed on the right to family reunification must be interpreted strictly as family reunification is considered to be the general rule.[24] The CJEU emphasises that the competence of the Member States to impose such requirements may not be applied in a manner which would undermine the effectiveness of the legal protection provided for by the Directive.[25] Asylum seekers, temporary protection holders and beneficiaries of a subsidiary form of protection are explicitly excluded from the scope of the Directive.[26] The eligible family members under the Directive are divided in two categories. The Member States shall authorise

22 Recital 8 FRD.

23 Art. 7(1) FRD gives the Member States state competence to require sponsors to meet income, accommodation and health care insurance requirements. Additionally, Art. 7(2) FRD allows Member States to impose integration measures.

24 Case C-578/08 *Chakroun* [2010] ECR I-1839, para. 47; Joined Cases C-356/11 and C-357/11 *O. and S. & L.* [2012].

25 Ibid.

26 Art. 3(2) FRD See section 4 of this chapter for further analysis on the exclusion of beneficiaries of subsidiary protection from the right to family reunification.

family reunification to the sponsor's spouse and minor children of the sponsor and the spouse.[27] The Member States may allow for the family reunification of first-degree dependent relatives in the direct ascending line and adult unmarried children, but are not under an obligation to do so.[28]

The safeguards for the family reunification of sponsors who are recognised by the host state as refugees are laid down in Chapter V of the Directive. The Member States may limit the application of the more liberal regime for refugees to family relationships that predate the refugee's entry into the Member States.[29] Under the Directive, the Member States are authorised to allow for family reunification of dependent family members which are not included in the definition of the family.[30] However, the Member States are under no obligation to do so. Unaccompanied minors which have been granted refugee status are entitled to family reunification of their first-degree relatives in the direct ascending line (their parents).[31] In case the unaccompanied minor has no parents or the parents cannot be traced, the Member States may allow for the family reunification of legal guardians or other family members.[32] Siblings of the unaccompanied minor are not stated in the Directive as eligible to be reunited. The Directive prescribes that in case a refugee cannot provide documentary evidence of the family relationship, the Member States shall take into account other evidence, to be assessed in accordance with national law.[33] Refugee sponsors are exempted from the substantive requirements for family reunification.[34] The Member States may require refugee sponsors to apply for family reunification within a period of three months after the granting of refugee status for the exemption from the substantive requirements to apply.[35]

An important element of the family reunification procedure is the administrative delay in the processing of applications. The Directive prescribes that the Member States shall provide the applicant for family reunification with a written notification of the decision within nine months from the date on which the application for family reunification was lodged.[36] The Directive allows for the extension of this period in exceptional circumstances linked to the complexity of the examination of the application. For the realisation of the right to family reunification of refugees this is not the only administrative delay as the sponsor must be recognised as a refugee before the application for family

27 See Art. 4(1) for an exact definition of the children that included in the definition of the family.
28 Art. 4(2) FRD.
29 Art. 9(2) FRD.
30 Art. 10(2) FRD.
31 Art. 10(3)(a) FRD.
32 Art. 10(3)(b) FRD.
33 Art. 11(1) FRD.
34 Art. 12(1) FRD.
35 Art. 12(1) last para. FRD.
36 Art. 5(3) FRD.

reunification may be lodged. The asylum procedure may take up to 15 months.[37] This means that in case the maximum administrative periods are complied with, it may take up to two years before an asylum seeker who is recognised as a refugee is issued a decision on the application for family reunification. This creates a significant waiting period in which the refugee sponsor is separated from his family members who remained in the country of origin. Especially considering the fact that the sponsor is recognised as a refugee, this waiting period is problematic. In the first place because of the inhuman and possible life-threatening situation for family members of a refugee and secondly, because living together with your family members is an essential precondition for the refugees' integration in host state society.[38]

3. ISSUES IN FAMILY REUNIFICATION LAW

In this section three different legal issues in respect of the right to family reunification of beneficiaries of international protection are discussed, namely the differentiation between refugees and beneficiaries of subsidiary protection.

3.1. DIFFERENTIATING BETWEEN REFUGEES AND BENEFICIARIES OF SUBSIDIARY PROTECTION

The FRD explicitly excludes beneficiaries of subsidiary forms of protection as sponsors.[39] During the negotiation of the Directive, the EC sought to include beneficiaries of subsidiary protection as sponsors, but this was removed because subsidiary protection status was insufficiently harmonised at that time.[40] In its Guidelines for application of the FRD, the EC expressed that it

> 'considers that the humanitarian protection needs of persons benefiting from subsidiary protection do not differ from those of refugees, and encourages [Member States] to adopt rules that grant similar rights to refugees and beneficiaries of temporary or subsidiary protection.'[41]

---

37 Art. 31(3) Directive 2013/32/EU of the European Parliament and of the Council of 26 June 2013 on common procedures for granting and withdrawing international protection (Asylum Procedures Directive).

38 Commissioner for Human Rights, Time for Europe to get Migrant Integration Right, Issue paper by the Commissioner for Human Rights of the Council of Europe, 2016.

39 Art. 3(2)(c) FRD.

40 EC, Amended proposal for a Council Directive on the right to family reunification, COM(2000) 624 final, pp. 2–3; UNHCR (n. 42 below) 28.

41 EC, Communication from the Commission to the European Parliament and the Council on Guidance for application for Directive 2003/86/EC on the right to family reunification, COM(2014) 210 final, pp. 24–25.

Despite this guideline from the European Commission 15 States in the EU+ region make a distinction between refugees and beneficiaries of subsidiary forms of protection in their national family reunification laws.[42] Some Member States have excluded beneficiaries of subsidiary forms of protection from the preferential treatment for refugees at the moment of implementation of the FRD in their national law,[43] other states introduced limitations on the right to family unification of subsidiary protected persons, after the increase of asylum application in the period 2015–2017. There are different manners in which the (Member) States make this differentiation. Some (Member) States have introduced mandatory waiting periods before a beneficiary of subsidiary protection can lodge an application for family reunification.[44] Other (Member) States have temporarily suspended the right to family reunification.[45] Two (Member) States have excluded beneficiaries of subsidiary protection from family reunification altogether, while two other (Member) States exclude beneficiaries of subsidiary protection from more favourable provisions applicable to refugees.[46]

The differentiation between refugees and beneficiaries of subsidiary forms of protection creates either a significant waiting period on top of administrative delays or excludes beneficiaries of subsidiary protection from family reunification altogether. This is problematic from both the perspective of the prohibition of discrimination enshrined in Article 14 ECHR as from the perspective of the best interests of the child.

Article 14 ECHR prohibits discrimination on various grounds in the enjoyment of the Convention rights. This prohibition of discrimination can only be invoked in combination with another substantive provision. In the context of the distinction between refugees and beneficiaries of subsidiary protection, the ECtHR has held that the refusal of family reunification yields an arguable claim under Article 8 ECHR.[47] The distinction based on international protection status qualifies under the discrimination ground 'other status'.[48] The differential

42 UNHCR, 'Families Together: Family Reunification in Europe for Refugees' (2018) 28, https://www.unhcrorg/nl/wp-content/uploads/Familiestogether_20181203-FINAL.pdf. The EU+ Region (as defined by the UNHCR in this report) contains apart from the 28 EU countries: Iceland, Liechtenstein, Norway and Switzerland, p. 6.

43 Kees Groendendijk and others, *The Family Reunification Directive in EU Member States; the First Year of Implementation* (Centre for Migration Law, 2007) pp. 41–42: one year after the implementation period passed, eight Member States had no special regime for subsidiary protected persons and one Member State only for a limited group.

44 UNHCR 2018 (n. 42 above) p. 28. These Member States are Austria, Denmark, Latvia, Liechtenstein and Switzerland.

45 Ibid. These Member States are Germany and Sweden.

46 Ibid., p. 30. These Member States are Cyprus, Greece and Malta.

47 See e.g. *Mugenzi v. France* (n. 15 above).

48 *Hode and Abdi v. United Kingdom* (2013) 56 EHRR 27; *Bah v. United Kingdom* (2012) 54 EHRR 21.

treatment may be justified if it pursues a legitimate aim and the treatment is proportionate to this aim.[49]

Generally, three possible justifications for differentiating between refugees and beneficiaries of subsidiary forms of protection can be brought forward. Firstly, the argument could be made that the distinction is allowed for under the FRD. A similar argument was brought forward regarding the differential treatment based on other status in spousal family reunification where the spousal relationship predated and post-dated arrival in the host state.[50] Regarding this differential treatment, the respondent state argued that it sought to honour its international obligations without providing any further incentives for asylum seekers to choose the respondent state over other possible countries of refuge. This race-to-the-bottom argument was explicitly rejected by the ECtHR, which ruled that the fact that the respondent state honoured its international obligations was no justification for differential treatment.[51] Secondly, the argument can be made that refugees and beneficiaries of subsidiary forms of protection have different protection needs – subsidiary protection being of a more temporary nature than refugee protection – and that therefore beneficiaries of subsidiary forms of protection are less in need of family reunification. This argument does not hold. Both refugee protection and subsidiary forms of protection share the core principle of the prohibition of refoulement. Equally, essentially both statuses are temporary, as the need for international protection depends on the situation in the country of origin.[52] From the perspective of the right to family reunification – the context in which the distinction is made – refugees and beneficiaries of subsidiary forms of protection are in a similar situation regarding possible family members that remained in the country of origin. A third argument that could be made for justifying the difference in treatment is that the sudden increase of applications for international protection made it necessary to limit the scope of the right to family reunification in order to manage the reception of all beneficiaries of international protection. There is some merit in this argument, especially considering the relatively unequal distribution of asylum applicants in the EU Member States. The right to respect for family life is

49 The ground of discrimination in order to fall within the ambit of 'other status' is the particular status of international protection that is afforded to the applicant by the host state. This is not a 'suspect ground' in the sense that it is based on an innate and immutable characteristic of the applicant. See Janneke Gerards, 'The Discrimination Grounds of Article 14 of the European Convention on Human Rights' (2013) 13 Human Rights Law Review 99, 116. This, however, does not alleviate the need for the host state to justify the differential treatment.

50 *Hode and Abdi* (n. 48 above).

51 Ibid., para. 55.

52 Art. 1C(5) Refugee Convention states that a refugee ceases to be a refugee in case the circumstances in connection with which he has been recognised as a refugee have ceased to exist.

not absolute and the state has the prerogative to control immigration. A sudden increase in the number of applications for international protection puts the national asylum system under pressure. In limiting family reunification rights of beneficiaries of subsidiary protection, Member States should, however, make an individual examination of the circumstances of each case, taking the best interests of the child into account in this assessment. A blanket refusal of the right to family reunification for the sole reason that the applicant is a beneficiary of subsidiary protection amounts to an arbitrary interference with the right to respect for family life and is in breach of the principle of the best interests of the child. An increased number of asylum applicants may not serve as a justification to arbitrarily interfere with the right to respect for family life and children's rights in a discriminatory manner.

3.2. CHILD MARRIAGES

The issue of child marriage became more urgent in Europe due to the rise in applications for asylum and family reunification which involved – mostly Syrian – child brides as a result of the Syrian civil war. Several European countries such as Denmark,[53] Germany,[54] the Netherlands[55] and Sweden[56] adopted laws which not only put a ban to the conduct of a marriage in which one, or both of the partners is under the age of 18, but which also do not recognise child marriages concluded abroad, even if a marriage has been concluded in accordance with the relevant national law. The non-recognition of a child marriage has several consequences. A couple can be separated, and the minor marital partner can be placed in custody. Although the measure is meant to protect the minor it can also lead to harassment of the girl by her environment.[57]

---

53 See: https://www.independent.co.uk/news/world/europe/denmarkban-under-18-marriage-under-18-asylum-seeking-teens-arrive-spouses-minors-a7537441.html.

54 Fassung des Gesetzes zur Bekämpfung von Kinderehen vom 17. Juli 2017 (BGBl. I S. 2429). See also Sabine Witting, '"Girls belong in school, and not in front of the altar": Is the German Bill on child marriages violating international law?', Verfassungsblog, 19 April 2017, and Christian Rath, 'Underage, Married, Separated. A German law abolished child marriage in general – not always in the interests of those affected', Max-Planck-Gesellschaft, 19 March 2019.

55 Wet Tegengaan Huwelijksdwang (adopted 6 October 2015, entered into force 5 December 2015) *Staatsblad* (2015) 354. See also Anne Wijffelman, 'Child marriage and family reunification: an analysis under the European Convention on Human Rights of the Dutch Forced Marriage Prevention Act' (2017) 35(2) Netherlands Quarterly of Human Rights 104–121.

56 Förbud mot erkännande av utländska barnäktenskap, Civilutskottets betänkande 2018/19:CU4. See also Socialstyrelsen, About child marriage laws and rules in Sweden, https://www.socialstyrelsen.se/globalassets/sharepoint-dokument/artikelkatalog/vagledning/2019-2-3-about-child-marriage.pdf/.

57 Rath, 'Underage, married, separated' (n. 54 above).

Child marriage is defined as a marriage where at least one of the partners is under the age of 18.[58] Most child marriages concern girls and child marriage is still a high frequency phenomenon.[59] At the same time, the United Nations has made the abolition of all child marriage by 2030 one of the sustainable policy goals.[60] So far, there is no univocal prohibition of child marriages in the international legal framework.[61] The Convention on the Elimination of All Forms of Discrimination against Woman (CEDAW) explicitly addresses this issue. According to Article 16 CEDAW, the marriage or betrothal of a child should have no legal effect and the convention urges states parties to specify a minimum age for marriage. The African Charter on the Rights and Welfare of the Child contains a prohibition of child marriages.[62] From other legal instruments, a prohibition of child marriage can be construed. The UNCRC does not contain a specific provision on child marriages, but several other rights are at stake in case of a child marriage, such as the right to education and the right to health.[63] In a Joint General Comment the UN Committees of the CEDAW and the UNCRC, consider child marriages in principle to be forced marriages.[64] In the Supplementary Slavery Convention of 1956, forced marriages are listed as a practice compared to slavery.[65] The special rapporteur of the United Nations Commission on Human Rights in 2007 stated that child marriage is by definition a forced marriage because children are incapable of refusal or consent. As such, a child marriage violates fundamental human rights and should therefore be prohibited.[66] In Europe, the Parliamentary Assembly of

---

58 UN Committee on the Elimination of Discrimination against Women/Committee on the Rights of the Child Joint General Comment No. 31 of the CEDAW/No 18 of the UNCRC on harmful practices (2014) UN Doc CEDAW/C/GC/31-CRC/C/GC/18, 7.

59 According to the United Nations Population Fund (UNPF) worldwide one out of five girls is married at an age under 18. See: https://www.unfpa.org/child-marriage-frequently-asked-questions#why%20does%20child%20marriage%20happen.

60 The elimination of all child, early and forced marriages by 2030 is listed under the sustainable development goals of the United Nation: United Nations, Transforming our world: the 2030 agenda for sustainable development, A/RES/70/1, UN 2015.

61 See for an overview of international and regional legal instruments which directly or indirectly address the issue of child marriage: Girls not Brides, 'Provisions of International and Regional Instruments Relevant to Protection from Child Marriage', 2013, https://www.girlsnotbrides.org/wp-content/uploads/2013/06/International-and-Regional-Standards-for-Protection-from-Child-Marriage-June-2013.pdf.

62 See Art. 21(2) ACRWC 1990. See also the Protocol to the African Charter on Human and Peoples' Rights on the Rights of Women in Africa 2003, Art. 6(b).

63 See also the Joint General Comment No. 31 of the CEDAW/No. 18 of the UNCRC on harmful practices, (2014) UN Doc CEDAW/C/GC/31-CRC/C/GC/18, 7.

64 UN Doc CEDAW/C/GC/31-CRC/C/GC/18, p. 7.

65 Art. 1(c) Supplementary Convention on the Abolition of Slavery, the Slave Trade, and Institutions and Practices Similar to Slavery.

66 Sigma Huda, Report of the Special Rapporteur on the human rights aspects of the victims of trafficking in persons, especially women and children, A/HRC/4/23, pp. 9, 21.

the Council of Europe passed a resolution against forced marriages and child marriages. In this resolution child marriages are denounced in strong wordings:

> 'It is outraged by the fact that, under the cloak of respect for the culture and traditions of migrant communities, there are authorities which tolerate forced marriages and child marriages although they violate the fundamental rights of each and every victim.'[67]

However, this section is not concerned with child marriage as such but with child marriage from the perspective of the right to family reunification. As discussed in section 2.2, the FRD gives third-country nationals a right to family reunification if the substantive criteria are fulfilled. The FRD offers Member States the possibility to refuse applications of child marital partners with the optional clause to set a minimum age for a spouse. The minimum age may not be set above 21 years.[68] A second option Member States can use to refuse applications for family reunification of minor marital partners, is the annulment of child marriages or the denial of the existence of a family relationship, when one of the partners is a minor. This section offers an evaluation of whether these two options to refuse family reunification applications of marital partners on the sole ground that at least one of the marital partners is a minor, are allowed under EU law and is in accordance with the ECHR.

The first issue is the 21-year condition of the FRD. Member States are allowed to refuse applications for family reunification if one of the spouses is under the age of 21.[69] According to the wording of this provision, the purpose of this optional condition is to better the integration and prevent forced marriages. The minimum age requirement may also be applied to the spouse of a refugee sponsor. Although Chapter V of the FRD provides for the more favourable treatment of family reunification applications of sponsors who are a refugee, this more favourable regime does not include a derogation of the 21-year rule. The European Commission (EC) stated in the guidance for application of the FRD that in applying the age limit, a refusal of an application should always be based on an individual assessment of the case. The EC based this interpretation of Article 4(5) on the ruling of the CJEU in *Chakroun*.[70] In this case, the Court ruled that Article 17 FRD requires various individual circumstances to be taken into account when a decision is taken.[71] This precludes a blanket application of any abstract threshold without regard to the circumstances of the case, according to the Court. Article 17 FRD states that in every decision the nature and solidity

67 Parliamentary Assembly Council of Europe Resolution 1468 (2005) 3.
68 Art. 4 (5) FRD.
69 Art. 4(5) FRD.
70 See ECJ 3 March 2010, C-578/08 (*Chakroun*).
71 Ibid., para. 49.

of the family relationship should be taken into account. This provision is inspired by Article 8 ECHR and should be interpreted in accordance with the interpretation of the ECtHR. According to the EC it follows from *Chakroun* that if the circumstances of the case show that the justification of Article 4(5) FRD, i.e. ensuring better integration and preventing forced marriages, is not applicable, Member States should consider making an exception to the application of the minimum age requirement.[72]

So far, the CJEU has ruled in just one case about the age limit and did not confirm this interpretation of Article 4(5) FRD of the EC.[73] The issue in this case was whether the minimum age requirement had to be considered by reference to the date when the application seeking family reunification was lodged, or the date when the application is ruled upon. In *Noorzia*, the CJEU acknowledged that a national rule that provides that spouses must be 21 years old on the moment of *lodging* the application for family reunification is in accordance with Article 4(5) FRD.[74] The CJEU did not question the legality of the requirement itself, but did recognise the general purpose of the age requirement. Although in general the Court stresses the importance of Article 17 FRD,[75] in *Noorzia* the CJEU did not make any reference to this provision. A possible reason for this could be that in this case the application of the age requirement itself was not put into question, but only the date by which this requirement had to be fulfilled. At the other hand, the Court explicitly acknowledged the general purpose of the age requirement of bettering the integration and preventing forced marriages. In combination with the views of the HRC[76] and the Joint General Comment of the committees of the CEDAW and UNCRC[77] that child marriages are in principal forced marriages, this provides for a strong argument to apply the age requirement to refuse family reunification applications of a minor marital spouse.

The second issue to discuss is whether the annulment of a marriage in which at least one of the spouses is a minor, constitutes a valid reason to refuse a family reunification application under EU law. The FRD gives criteria for which family members are eligible for family reunification. If a child marriage is not recognised as a valid marriage, the spouses can be excluded from the scope

---

72 Communication from the Commission to the European Parliament and the Council on guidance for application of Directive 2003/86/EC on the right to family reunification, COM(2014) 210 FINAL, pp. 7–8.

73 ECJ 17 July 2014, Case C-338/13 (*Noorzia*).

74 ECJ 17 July 2014, Case C-338/13 (*Noorzia*) para. 19.

75 See ECJ 3 March 2010, C-578/08 (*Chakroun*).

76 Sigma Huda, Report of the Special Rapporteur on the human rights aspects of the victims of trafficking in persons, especially women and children, A/HRC/4/23, pp. 9, 21.

77 UN Committee on the Elimination of Discrimination against Women/Committee on the Rights of the Child Joint General Comment No. 31 of the CEDAW/No. 18 of the UNCRC on harmful practices (2014) UN Doc CEDAW/C/GC/31-CRC/C/GC/18, 7.

of eligible family members and an application for family reunification can be denied. However, according to the Preamble, the FRD is an instrument to protect family life.[78] In applying the Directive, Member States should respect Article 8 ECHR. Furthermore, Article 17 prescribes that in any decision family ties are taken into account. The FRD does not define the concept of 'family life'. For the notion of what constitutes family life, the case law of the ECtHR is instructive. In *Al-Nashif*, the ECtHR summarised its previous case law regarding the meaning of the concept of family life.[79] In principle, the relationship between spouses in a marriage is always considered to constitute family life. The ECtHR has not yet explicitly ruled on whether a marriage in which one of the spouses is a minor, constitutes family life. In a case concerning a 14-year-old girl who was married to her 18-year-old cousin, the ECtHR stated that:

> 'Article 8 of the Convention cannot be interpreted as imposing on any State party to the Convention an obligation to recognise a marriage, religious or otherwise, contracted by a 14 year old child.'[80]

However, the Court is silent about the question whether this particular marriage constituted family life in the sense of Article 8 ECHR. This is why Judge Nicolaou is critical about the ruling of the Court. In a concurring opinion, he argued that the Court should look at the facts of the case in order to determine whether there is family life: 'What is important here is that the non-recognition of the purported marriage could not exhaust the question of whether the applicants did or did not have a family life together.'[81]

Based on the concurring opinion of Judge Nicolaou it can be argued that the conclusion that a child marriage does not constitute family life, deserves a better motivation. This argument keeps the option open that in certain circumstances a child marriage might constitute family life. From this argument it follows that a refusal of a family reunification needs an individual assessment.

This leads us to the last issue: in an application of family reunification of a child marital spouse, Member States should have due regard to the best interests of children. The best interests of the child principle is also laid down in the FRD.[82] It can be argued that leaving a minor spouse behind in a country of origin by the refusal to be reunited with the refugee sponsor in the host Member State in an unsafe situation could be in violation of the best interests of the child

---

78 See Preamble FRD no. 6.

79 ECtHR 20 Juni 2002, *Al-Nashif*, no. 50963/99, para. 112. The ECtHR stated that 'In so far as relations in a couple are concerned, "family life", encompasses both families based on marriages and also de facto relationships. When deciding whether a relationship can be said to amount to "family life", a number of factors may be relevant (...)'.

80 ECtHR 8 December 2015, *Z.H.* en *R.H. v. Switzerland*, para. 44.

81 Ibid., concurring opinion of Judge Nicolaou.

82 Art. 5(5) FRD.

principle. At the other hand, also the decision to allow for family reunification can put the child in a dangerous and abusive situation. This requires an individual assessment of all relevant factors.

If no automatic denial of a family reunification application of a child marital spouse is allowed under EU law, which factors should be taken into account to decide on such an application? First, the age of the minor and the age difference between the spouses can be taken into account. This is also listed as a possible exception to declaring a child marriage of 16- or 17-year-old- children a forced marriage, according to the CEDAW/UNCRC Joint General Comment. Secondly, the presence of children born out of the relationship should be take into account. This follows from the EC guidelines and is also recognised by the ECtHR in *Al Nashif* as a factor of importance in deciding if a non-marital relationship can be classified as family life. Even if no family life exists between the child partner and the sponsor, there will, in principle, be family life between both of the parents and the children. The best interests of these children should also be taken into consideration. Finally, other family and social bonds of the child partner in the country of origin or residence and the country of destination are important considerations. This follows from both Article 8 ECHR and Article 17 FRD.

In conclusion, the automatic refusal of a family reunification application of a child marital spouse – either by applying the minimum age requirement or by the non-recognition of the child marriage – is not in accordance with EU law. This application needs an individual assessment.

3.3. UNACCOMPANIED MINORS AND FAMILY REUNIFICATION

For unaccompanied minors that have been granted international protection in a host state, the right to family reunification is often the only manner in which family life with parents can be effectively exercised. After the granting of international protection to an unaccompanied minor, action must be taken promptly for protection and continuation of the full development of the child.[83] The state hosting the unaccompanied minor is therefore under the obligation to end the separation between the unaccompanied child and his or her parents through authorising and facilitating family reunification.[84]

The FRD prescribes that the Member States shall authorise the family reunification of the first-degree relatives in the direct ascending line (the parents) of unaccompanied minor refugees.[85] The negotiation history of the Directive

[83] Guy S. Goodwin-Gill, 'Unaccompanied Refugee Minors: The Role and Place of International Law in the Pursuit of Durable Solutions' [1995] International Journal of Children's Rights 407.

[84] Art. 10(3)(a) FRD.

[85] Art. 10(3)(a) FRD.

shows that the right to family reunification to the parents of unaccompanied minors is based on Article 22 UNCRC.[86] At the time of the adoption of the Directive, most Member States did not allow for the family reunification of the parents of unaccompanied minors.[87] The United Kingdom, which is not bound by the Directive, does not grant the right to family reunification to the parents of unaccompanied minor sponsors.[88]

The CJEU has ruled that the date on which the application for asylum was lodged should be used to determine whether the applicant qualifies as an unaccompanied minor for the family reunification of family members in the ascending line.[89] In the ruling, the Court emphasises that the Member States have no margin of discretion to determine on which date the applicant should be a minor to establish eligibility for family reunification as the relevant provision of the Directive does not refer to the national law of the Member States in this regard and that therefore there is a need for the uniform interpretation of EU law.[90] The Court rejects the arguments for establishing that the date on which the application for family reunification is lodged is decisive for eligibility for the family reunification of parents, as this would make eligibility directly dependent on the duration of the asylum procedure – considering that an application for family reunification can only be lodged after the positive decision on the asylum claim. Any other reading could frustrate the objective of the Directive of ensuring that the best interests of the child is in practice a primary consideration.[91]

The Directive does not provide for the family reunification of the siblings of unaccompanied minors. This means that the Member States are not obliged under the Directive to allow for the family reunification of siblings. This omission in the Directive is problematic. Not extending the right to family reunification to the siblings of unaccompanied minors where the parents are allowed to reunite in the host state can create the separation of the parents and the children that were left behind in the country of origin. This would lead to a situation that is not in accordance with the right to respect for family life under Article 8 ECHR and would violate the prohibition under Article 9 UNCRC to

86 European Commission, Proposal for a Council Directive on the right to family reunification, COM(1999) 638 final, p. 16. Art. 22 UNCRC obliges the contracting parties to provide children seeking refugee status with appropriate protection and humanitarian assistance in the enjoyment of applicable rights set forth in the UNCRC and other human rights treaties.

87 Groenendijk and others, *The Family Reunification Directive in EU Member States: The First Year of Implementation* (n. 43 above).

88 Gina Clayton, *Textbook on Immigration and Asylum Law*, (6th ed., OUP 2014) 301.

89 Case C-550/16 *A. and S.* [2018].

90 Ibid., para, 41. The CJEU refers in this regard to Case C-22516 *Ouhrami* [2017], in which it held that in a situation where secondary legislation does not make an express reference to the national law of the Member States, there must normally be an autonomous and uniform interpretation throughout the EU. See para. 38.

91 Case C-550/16 *A. and S.* [2018] para. 58.

prevent the separation of parents and children except in (a) situation(s) when this is in the best interests of the child.

4. CONCLUSION

Although there is no general right to family reunification in international law, beneficiaries of international protection are entitled to a more favourable treatment in international law and can in certain situations derive a right to family reunification. However, the right to family reunification is under pressure in the EU. The FRD offers those who fulfil the conditions a right to family reunification, but contains some omissions and leaves some room for restrictive policies for Member States. After the increased number of applicants for asylum between 2015 and 2017, some Member States have introduced new restrictive family reunification policies. These policies apply a general approach to a certain group. The different examples discussed in this chapter have highlighted that the best interests of the child – which should be a primary consideration – hardly played any role in this development. This is problematic. Sponsors who have been granted international protection are separated from their family members who were left behind in the country of origin or in a transit country. Firstly, the family members remain in an unsafe place. Secondly, this is detrimental for the integration of the sponsor in the host state. Whereas in family reunification applications without an international protection component, there are often no insurmountable obstacles to exercising the right to respect for family life in the country of origin of the family members, beneficiaries of international protection who are separated from their family members have no other possibility to end the separation of the family than family reunification in the host Member State. Each application for family reunification should be considered individually on its merits and in this assessment the best interests of the child must be a primary consideration. Furthermore, due to the specific position that sponsors who have been granted international protection find themselves in, applications should be considered promptly without undue delays. An application for family reunification may not be rejected without an individual examination of the circumstances involved in the case.[92] In this personal assessment of the circumstances involved, the Directive itself explicitly prescribes that the Member States shall have due regard for the best interests of the child. Both at the level of individual cases as well as in the sphere of the development of family reunification policies in the EU, it seems that the best interests of the child is often not a primary consideration.

92 Art. 17 FRD.

COMBATTING CHILD SMUGGLING AND TRAFFICKING

A Comparative Study of the Situation in Nine European States

Dagmara RAJSKA*

1. INTRODUCTION

Child smuggling and trafficking had hardly been discussed before and during the 1990s, despite it having always existed. The fact that, in the last few years, the issue of child smuggling and trafficking has been brought into the public arena of national and international bodies is a significant accomplishment.

* Postdoctoral researcher at the UCERF, Molengraaff Institute for Private Law, Utrecht University, the Netherlands (2018–2019).

It can also be considered that there has been some progress towards the elimination of criminal activities related to child smuggling and trafficking. At the same time, academics consider that these achievements are far from satisfactory.[1]

There is a correlation between the phenomenon of migration and child trafficking. Children who are recruited and transported for the purpose of exploitation are considered as trafficked[2] no matter whether or not they consented to the move.[3] The reason for this is that the questions about choice, consent and agency are irrelevant when children are concerned.[4] The correlation between child migration and child trafficking has been noticed by the Special Rapporteur on the sale and sexual exploitation of children and the Special Rapporteur on trafficking in persons, especially women and children, and they have published a joint study on this subject. More particularly, they have found that:

> 'As one of the main destinations for children on the move who are fleeing violence, conflict and humanitarian crisis, Europe is at the heart of the sale of, trafficking in and other forms of exploitation of children. In Europe, child trafficking has increased sharply owing to the migration crisis.'[5]

This chapter aims to determine how the existing international legal framework, in particular the Council of Europe Convention on Action against Trafficking in Human Beings, protects migrants – often unaccompanied children – against

---

1 Morawska E., 'Trafficking into and from Eastern Europe' in Lee M. (ed.), *Human Trafficking*, Willan Publishing 2007, pp. 92–116.

2 Some academics do not agree with this principle, stating the thesis that an illegal migrant child, leaving his/her country because of the dream of a foreign land, paying a smuggler for a boat-trip, voluntarily working in one of the only sectors accessible to them and giving part of their income to a third person, is not a victim of trafficking: Oude Breuil B., 'Bienvenue chez les grands! Border-Crossing of Young Migrant Cigarette Vendors in Marseille' in Craig G., *Child slavery now. A contemporary reader*, The Policy Press 2010, pp. 189–203.

3 Art. 3 Protocol to Prevent, Suppress and Punish Trafficking in Persons, Especially Women and Children, supplementing the United Nations Convention against Transnational Organized Crime available at: https://www.ohchr.org/EN/ProfessionalInterest/Pages/ProtocolTrafficking InPersons.aspx. UNODC, The role of consent in the trafficking in persons protocol, Vienna 2014, p. 7: 'Consent, in the case of adults, is always irrelevant to determining whether the crime of human trafficking has occurred, whether means such as force or abduction are used, or whether more subtle means such as "abuse of a position of vulnerability" are used. In the case of children, consent is irrelevant regardless of whether any means were used or not.' Available at: https://www.unodc.org/documents/human-trafficking/2014/UNODC_2014_ Issue_Paper_Consent.pdf.

4 O'Connell Davidson J., 'Telling Tales: Child Migration and Child Trafficking. Stories of Trafficking Obscure the Realities for Migrant Children. Child Abuse and Neglect' The International Journal, 37 (2013), pp. 1069–1079, for this reference p. 1071.

5 'Sale and sexual exploitation of children, including child prostitution, child pornography and other child sexual abuse material; and trafficking in persons, especially women and children', 18 July 2017, available at: https://reliefweb.int/sites/reliefweb.int/files/resources/N1721883.pdf.

child smuggling and trafficking.[6] In accordance with the UN Convention against Transnational Organized Crime Trafficking Protocol to Prevent, Suppress and Punish Trafficking in Persons, especially Women and Children, the key elements of human trafficking are: recruitment and facilitated movement of a person within or across national frontiers by means of coercion, threats or deception for the purpose of exploitation. Human smuggling, under the UN Convention against Transnational Organized Crime, Protocol against the Smuggling of Migrants by Land, Sea and Air, is the illegal movement of persons across international borders in order to obtain a financial benefit. Smuggling finishes when the person arrives at a destination while trafficking results in exploitation. Finally, trafficking is a crime against a victim whose rights were violated, and smuggling is a crime against the political interest of the state.

The chapter takes a new approach, because it reinterprets the understanding of national mechanisms established to combat child smuggling and trafficking on basis of the outcome of comparative analysis of nine Group of Experts on Action against Trafficking in Human Beings (GRETA) country reports and their interpretation in the light of above-mentioned international legal instruments.

It investigates and identifies what the existing challenges and obstacles are for the implementation of the legal framework by raising awareness, training professionals, working with childhood education, and by providing appropriate accommodation for children, adequate border measures, effective identification of child trafficking victims, legal guardianship, age assessment procedures and the criminalisation of child trafficking.

Based on existing empirical research, the author compares the situation in countries with the highest rate of child trafficking (the UK, Romania, Bulgaria), as well as in the most affected destinations (Sweden, Germany) and the most frequently used transit countries (Serbia, Italy). The Netherlands and France were also included in the comparative study due to their high rate of human trafficking.[7]

The Council of Europe Convention on Action against Trafficking in Human Beings provides that each state party to the Convention shall take specific measures to reduce children's vulnerability to trafficking and re-trafficking, in particular by creating a protective environment for them.[8]

---

6 See more: 'Introduction: Understanding human trafficking', Lee M., in Lee, *Human trafficking* (n. 1 above) pp. 1–26.

7 Research has been conducted on the basis of country reports provided by experts of the Council of Europe Group of Experts on Action against Trafficking in Human Beings (GRETA), available at: https://www.coe.int/en/web/anti-human-trafficking/home. To conduct this research, the author refers mainly to one source of information, the GRETA reports, which impose limits on this research.

8 There are, in particular, numerous general and specific international instruments protecting and combatting child smuggling and trafficking, which apply to the states that signed and ratified them: European Convention on Human Rights (Art. 4); Council of Europe Convention on

2. AWARENESS RAISING ON CHILD TRAFFICKING

National authorities in Europe have made available many mechanisms and tools in order to raise awareness that will contribute to the prevention and combatting of child smuggling and trafficking.

The role to be played by the state (national authorities), NGOs and other organisations should be clarified in the context of child trafficking. It is often the NGOs that act on the ground and that is good, in the sense that they probably have the right skills and know the terrain, but the prevention of trafficking still comes first and foremost from the obligations of the states. However, the NGOs must be supported, financially for example, by the state. Otherwise the state implicitly defers its responsibilities to other actors, private in particular, and completely discharges its obligations.

Three mechanisms will be analysed below: information campaigns, education and schooling and the training of legal professionals. As stated before, the information on the varying countries comes from the empirical research reports drafted by (GRETA).

2.1. INFORMATION CAMPAIGNS

According to GRETA information campaigns aimed at the competent institutions, relevant professionals, children – in particular those exposed to the risk of human trafficking – and their parents play an important role in the context of the prevention of and combatting child trafficking and smuggling.[9] It has been suggested in the literature that effective intervention requires a multidisciplinary approach that brings different societal groups together – for example, social workers, doctors and lawyers – to facilitate the exchange of information about their experience with child victims of trafficking.[10] However, the rest of society has to be informed in more general terms about the risks of child trafficking.

Action against Trafficking in Human Beings, Convention on the Rights of the Child (Art. 32); Protocol to Prevent, Suppress and Punish Trafficking in Persons Especially Women and Children, supplementing the United Nations Convention against Transnational Organized Crime (Palermo Protocol); Optional Protocol to the Convention on the Rights of the Child on the sale of children, child prostitution and child pornography; EU Charter of Fundamental Rights (Art. 5); and Directive 2011/36/EU of the European Parliament and of the Council of 5 April 2011 on preventing and combatting trafficking in human beings and protecting its victims. The author examined these instruments and chose to refer to the provisions of the Council of Europe Convention on Action against Trafficking in Human Beings.

9 Arts. 5 and 6, The Council of Europe Convention on Action against Trafficking in Human Beings, 2005, https://rm.coe.int/168008371d.

10 West A., Loeffler Diane N., 'Understanding Victim Resistance: An explanatory Study of the Experiences of Service Providers Working with Victims of Child Trafficking' 6(1) Journal of Applied Research on Children: Informing Policy for Children at Risk, TMC Library, 2015, p. 1.

On the one hand, these information campaigns develop the skills of each adult, so that they can better react when faced with child trafficking and identify a child victim of trafficking. On the other hand, a child who is aware can also defend him or herself when he or she is approached by a trafficker.[11]

The term 'child trafficking' covers a wide range of child labour migration issues.[12] However, the perception of child trafficking in society is often very narrow and restricted to sex trafficking,[13] in particular involving girls.[14] This perception of child trafficking restricted to the sex trade is indirectly reinforced if the existing information campaigns focus only on child sexual exploitation and do not refer to other sectors of child exploitation.

Among bad practices, in Sweden, for example, there has been a lack of information campaigns on child trafficking for exploitation purposes other than sexual exploitation.[15] However, making more information available to Swedish citizens, such as explaining that those who sexually exploit children abroad can be prosecuted in Sweden, has made Swedish society more aware and, at some point, has probably reduced future demand. In this country, there is also a lack of awareness on trafficking for the purpose of sexual exploitation of men and boys, particularly unaccompanied and separated migrants and asylum-seeking boys. There are other countries in which information campaigns do not exist at all. The last information campaign in Italy[16] was organised in 2008. In France, despite a national plan of action against trafficking human beings, no national information campaigns have been organised. Some local initiatives have succeeded in publishing books, brochures and press articles[17] on the prevention of trafficking of human beings.[18]

---

11 Jovanovic J., *Challenges to Preliminary Identification of Romani 'Victims of Trafficking': The Serbian Case*, CEU Center for Policy Studies 2015, p. 24.

12 Whitehead, A. and Hashim I., 'Children and Migration Background paper for DfID migration team', Critical Social Policy 2005, pp. 454–477.

13 Hynes P., 'No Magic Bullets: Children, Young People, Trafficking and Child Protection in the UK', International Migration, John Wiley and Sons Ltd. 2015; Van Reisen M., Stefanovic A., *Lost Kids, Lost Futures, The European Union's Response to Child Trafficking*, International Federation Terre des Hommes 2004, p. 28.

14 Huijsmans R. and Baker S., 'Child Trafficking: Worst Form of Child Labour or Worst Approach to Young Migrants?' Development and Change, 43(4) (2012), p. 921.

15 Report concerning the implementation of the Council of Europe Convention on Action against Trafficking in Human Beings by Sweden, GRETA, March 2018, p. 16, available at: https://rm.coe.int/greta-2018-8-fgr-swe-en/16808b1cd7.

16 Report concerning the implementation of the Council of Europe Convention on Action against Trafficking in Human Beings by Italy, GRETA, July 2014, p. 29, available at: https://rm.coe.int/CoERMPublicCommonSearchServices/DisplayDCTMContent?documentId=0900001680631cc1.

17 E.g. Gallini P., 'Entre 100 et 200 esclaves enchainées dans la ville ?' La Provence, Marseille, 7 May 2007.

18 Report concerning the implementation of the Council of Europe Convention on Action against Trafficking in Human Beings by France, GRETA, March 2017, p. 20, available at: https://rm.coe.int/greta-2017-17-fgr-fra-en/16807454bf.

There may be good practices established in countries where information campaigns are organised. Nationwide campaigns on child trafficking presumably change societal perception. In the Netherlands, a campaign about victims of human trafficking, called '*Schijn Bedriegt*' ('Appearances deceive'), aimed to raise awareness among the general public and more specifically among clients of prostitutes.[19] In Serbia,[20] information is delivered by representatives of public institutions, trade unions, employers' associations and civil society for labour inspectors and representatives of institutions involved in the detection and prevention of child labour.[21] In Bulgaria,[22] a number of national and local commissions were organised to inform the general public and target groups about the risks of human trafficking, recruitment methods used by traffickers, ways for prevention and the criminalisation of the use of services of victims of trafficking. NGOs organised preventive activities for students and young people.[23] In Romania,[24] the National Agency Against Trafficking in Persons (ANITP)[25] and civil society are actively engaged in organising information campaigns.[26]

Among other interesting awareness-raising initiatives, German facilitators have been appointed in counselling centres for immigrants to raise awareness and focus on the manifestations of human trafficking and victim support

---

19 Report concerning the implementation of the Council of Europe Convention on Action against Trafficking in Human Beings by the Netherlands, March 2014, GRETA, p. 32, available at: https://rm.coe.int/CoERMPublicCommonSearchServices/DisplayDCTMContent?documentId=0900001680632199.

20 Report concerning the implementation of the Council of Europe Convention on Action against Trafficking in Human Beings by Serbia, November 2017, GRETA, p. 17, available at: https://rm.coe.int/greta-2017-37-frg-srb-en/16807809fd.

21 See also Awareness and the issue of trafficking in people and measures to be taken, in Trafficking in people in Serbia, OSCE 2004, pp. 208–235.

22 Report concerning the implementation of the Council of Europe Convention on Action against Trafficking in Human Beings by Bulgaria, GRETA, November 2015, p. 17, available at: https://rm.coe.int/CoERMPublicCommonSearchServices/DisplayDCTMContent?documentId=0900001680630d6c.

23 The awareness-raising activities of the NGOs are most often based on funding by donors. Therefore, it happens that donors demand the creation of anti-trafficking projects based on their conceptualisation of human trafficking (Huijsmans R. and Baker S., 'Child Trafficking: Worst Form of Child Labour or Worst Approach to Young Migrants?', Development and Change43(4) (2012), pp. 924–925).

24 Report concerning the implementation of the Council of Europe Convention on Action against Trafficking in Human Beings by Romania, GRETA, p. 13, July 2016, available at: https://rm.coe.int/CoERMPublicCommonSearchServices/DisplayDCTMContent?documentId=09000016806a99b1.

25 GRETA, Serbia (n. 20 above), 91 campaigns organised in 2012–13. The implementation of campaigns in Romania is classical (meetings, posters, flyers, audio-video spots, distribution of materials with anti-trafficking messages and information) and internet-based as using Facebook and online platforms.

26 GRETA, Serbia (n. 20 above). The projects specifically target youth awareness of human trafficking through music, art, dance, film, animation, sport, creative and social media.

strategies.[27] In the UK, in partnership with the Border Force's Safeguarding and Trafficking Team, NGOs organised a day of activity at Heathrow Airport to raise awareness about child trafficking among support airport staff and passengers in order to detect and protect vulnerable children.[28]

In conclusion, the existence of nationwide information campaigns on child smuggling and trafficking, such as those organised in the Netherlands, Serbia, Bulgaria, the UK, Germany and Romania is an appropriate measure in the quest to make society aware of the importance of the problem and to have a good perception of the character and scale of the phenomenon. This measure should be seen as good practice and implemented in other countries such as France, Sweden and Italy.

2.2. EDUCATION ON CHILD TRAFFICKING

Migrant children exposed to trafficking have often fled from war or from the poor and disadvantaged communities[29] in which they had been born. In this second case, most of them had no access to education or dropped out of school shortly before being trafficked.[30]

The UN Convention on the Rights of the Child (UNCRC) establishes a right to education for each child.[31] The European Court of Human Rights (ECtHR) has also highlighted the importance of education for children with an irregular status and the need to scrutinise strictly any restrictions on this right.[32] Education as well as educational information campaigns to raise awareness of children and their close environment are strong preventive measures for vulnerable migrant children who are exposed to a risk of becoming child trafficking victims, are forced into criminality or are being radicalised.[33] The general education system

---

27 Report submitted by the German authorities on measures taken to comply with the Committee of the Parties Recommendation CP(2015)2 on the implementation of the Council of Europe Convention on Action against Trafficking in Human Beings, GRETA, June 2017, p. 6, available at: https://rm.coe.int/cp-2017-21-rr-deu-en-pdf/168073fdf2.

28 Report concerning the implementation of the Council of Europe Convention on Action against Trafficking in Human Beings by the United Kingdom, GRETA, July 2016, p. 30, available at: https://rm.coe.int/CoERMPublicCommonSearchServices/DisplayDCTMContent?documentId=09000016806abcdc.

29 Rafferty Y., 'Child Trafficking and Commercial Sexual Exploitation: A Review of Promising Prevention Policies and Programs' American Journal of Orthopsychiatry, 83(4) (2013), pp. 559–575.

30 Dottridge M., *Action to prevent child trafficking in South Eastern Europe. A preliminary assessment*, UNICEF & Terre des Hommes, Geneva, 2006.

31 Arts. 20 and 22 UN Convention on the Rights of the Child (UNCRC), 20 November 1989, https://www.ohchr.org/en/professionalinterest/pages/crc.aspx.

32 *Ponomaryovi v. Bulgaria* App no. 5335/05, para. 57 (ECtHR, 21 June 2011).

33 Communication from the Commission to the European Parliament and the Council. The protection of children in migration, 12 April 2017, https://ec.europa.eu/home-affairs/

plays an important role in raising awareness about human trafficking and discouraging future demand.[34] Most often, the information on human/child trafficking is included in primary and secondary school curricula, as a part of civic education, human rights, philosophy or history lessons.[35] Particular attention should be given to girls' participation in education and schooling, which is a protective factor for girls against gender-based violence and child trafficking.[36]

Firstly, education should be provided in the countries of origin of the migrant children, because only peace and development are a solid foundation for a stable society and the rule of law.[37] Secondly, education should be provided in the country of arrival of minor migrants.

Across Europe, the provision of such education varies. Bulgaria,[38] Serbia[39] and Romania[40] provide positive examples of countries where educational programmes are implemented at schools. These programmes cover the topic of human trafficking. In France,[41] the UK[42] and Serbia[43] educational programmes are implemented by the NGOs. In the Netherlands[44] and in Germany,[45] similar education for children is provided in the shelters for child trafficking victims.

In contrast, Italy[46] and Sweden[47] have no materials for schoolteachers on the subject of human trafficking and it is not part of the national educational curricula.

Consequently, Italy and Sweden should establish educational programmes for children, including activities with a focus on child trafficking, taking examples of good practice where it exists in France, Romania, Bulgaria, Serbia, the Netherlands, the UK and Germany.

---

sites/homeaffairs/files/what-we-do/policies/european-agenda-migration/20170412_communication_on_the_protection_of_children_in_migration_en.pdf.

34 Arts. 12 and 16 The Council of Europe Convention on Action against Trafficking in Human Beings, 2005, https://rm.coe.int/168008371d.

35 Arts. 5 and 6 The Council of Europe Convention on Action against Trafficking in Human Beings, 2005, https://rm.coe.int/168008371d.

36 United Nations Development Fund for Women (UNIFEM), 'Investing in gender equality: Ending violence against women and girls', 2011, available at: https://eur-lex.europa.eu/legal-content/en/ALL/?uri=CELEX%3A52017DC0211.

37 UN Security Council 8111th Meeting, Security Council Open Debate on Maintenance of international peace and security, Trafficking in persons in conflict situations, 21 November 2017.

38 GRETA, Bulgaria (n. 22 above) p. 20.

39 GRETA, Serbia (n. 20 above) pp. 16–17.

40 GRETA, Romania (n. 24 above) p. 44.

41 GRETA, France (n. 18 above) p. 23.

42 GRETA, the UK (n. 28 above), p. 30.

43 GRETA, Serbia (n. 20 above) pp. 16–17.

44 GRETA, the Netherlands (n. 19 above), p. 5.

45 GRETA, Germany (n. 27 above) p. 11.

46 GRETA, Italy (n. 16 above) p. 29.

47 GRETA, Sweden (n. 15 above) p. 19.

2.3. TRAINING OF PROFESSIONALS ON CHILD TRAFFICKING

The frontline practitioners working with child victims of trafficking, such as police officers and social workers, often lack awareness of the phenomenon of child trafficking. They might theoretically know the procedure, but they regularly have difficulty applying it in practice and identifying which indicators they should be looking for.[48]

This lack of knowledge and practical skills of frontline practitioners could lead to wrong conclusions. For example, some cases of child victims of trafficking were hidden. By hidden cases, it should be understood that the officers working on the child trafficking cases, deliberately dissimulated them, because they did not give faith to the existence of child trafficking or because they did not wish to deal with the burden and difficulty of work in situations of occurrence of child trafficking. In the case of a 15-year-old child brought into a country to work in domestic servitude, the officers reported that the child is intelligent, manipulates the system and cannot be considered as a child victim of trafficking. In another case, a different professional reported that a young girl made pregnant by traffickers, became pregnant to extract money from those traffickers.[49] Some other practitioners treat cases of child victims of trafficking as hot-potato cases and pass them on to other agencies rather than identifying the child victims of trafficking.[50]

The lack of coordination and cooperation at the national and international level among government officials, law enforcement officers, social workers and other practitioners, arising from lack of clear boundaries specifically in terms of roles and responsibilities is also an important obstacle to the smooth functioning of the system of child protection against child smuggling and trafficking.[51]

Taking all of the above into account, the persons concerned should be trained and guided to develop necessary knowledge and practical skills. Professionals working in government and nongovernment institutions and organisations do not know that they treat cases involving human trafficking because they do not have adequate information on the issues involved.[52] Consequently, government officials are uninformed regarding the causes and consequences of trafficking,

---

48 Warria A., Nel H., Triegaardt J., 'Challenges in Identification of Child Victims of Transnational Trafficking Practice', Practice, British Association of Social Workers, Taylor and Francis, Routledge, 2015, 27(5), p. 323.

49 Pearce Jenny J., *Working with Trafficked Children and Young People: Complexities in Practice*, Oxford University Press 2011, p. 8.

50 Ayeer P. and Preston-Shoot M. (eds.), *Children's Services at the Crossroads*, Russell House Publishing 2010.

51 Harvey J.H., Hornsby R.A., and Sattar Z., *Disjointed service: An English case study of multiagency provision in tackling child trafficking*, Oxford University Press 2015, p. 500.

52 Rafferty, 'Child Trafficking and Commercial Sexual Exploitation' (n. 29 above).

and thus the appropriate rights-based legal responses and the necessary actions and interventions are overlooked.[53] The training provided to a variety of professionals makes them recognise the signs of trafficking and enables them to detect children who are at risk of falling victim or are already in the process of being trafficked.[54]

The training, apart from the relevant content, has to fulfil two conditions: choose the adequate methodology and involve persons really concerned. There are different good practices existing in all countries. In some of them, such as the Netherlands,[55] Italy,[56] Germany[57] and the UK,[58] law enforcement officers are trained on how to identify child victims of trafficking. In other countries, such as France,[59] Bulgaria[60] and Serbia,[61] educational staff, teachers, school nurses and doctors become trainees on the development of skills that are necessary in order to identify children at risk. In Sweden, the National Board of Health and Welfare has developed well-based training and brochures on the risks of sexual exploitation, one of which focuses on children. The County Administrative Board of Stockholm (CABS) has cooperated with hotels and taxi companies to raise awareness among their staff on human trafficking.[62]

In France, the Netherlands, Serbia, Italy, Germany, Romania, the UK, Sweden and Bulgaria, training on the identification of child victims of trafficking is provided to practitioners. The training should probably involve broader groups and involve, for example, law enforcement agents in France, Bulgaria and Serbia, where the priority is given to educational staff and teachers. It should stay regular to be effective instead of being a singular ad hoc activity.

3. PROCEDURES RELATED TO CHILD TRAFFICKING

The right to access the territory is not protected as such by international legal instruments. On the one hand, preventing access to territory, including via land

---

53 Jordan A., 'Human rights or wrongs? The struggle for a rights-based response to trafficking in human beings' (2002) Gender and Development, 10, pp. 28–37.

54 Arts. 5 and 29 The Council of Europe Convention on Action against Trafficking in Human Beings, 2005, https://rm.coe.int/168008371d; Security Council Resolution 2331(2016) on trafficking in persons in armed conflicts, available at: https://www.refworld.org/docid/587f71514.html; see also Global Report on Trafficking in Persons, Policy implications, UNODC, 2018, pp. 13–14, available at: http://www.unodc.org/documents/data-and-analysis/glotip/2018/GLOTiP_2018_BOOK_web_small.pdf.

55 GRETA, the Netherlands (n. 19 above) pp. 26–28, 33.

56 GRETA, Italy (n. 16 above) pp. 13–16.

57 GRETA, Germany (n. 27 above) pp. 5, 8, 12.

58 GRETA, the UK (n. 28 above) p. 16.

59 GRETA, France (n. 18 above) p. 23.

60 GRETA, Bulgaria (n. 22 above) p. 20.

61 GRETA, Serbia (n. 20 above) p. 18.

62 GRETA, Sweden (n. 15 above) p. 19.

borders, may engage state responsibility.[63] On the other hand, the state has to establish and implement immigration policies in order to protect safety and security.

Unaccompanied children, in particular child victims of smuggling and trafficking, should be promptly identified,[64] in order to have their rights effectively applied. Identification needs to take place as soon as an individual comes into contact with a state's authorities.

To accomplish the 'right of the child to preserve his or her identity',[65] it is necessary to identify first whether the person is a child or not. Ordinarily, the age assessment procedures consist of an interview with a child to estimate his/her psychological maturity and the examination of his/her physical appearance. There is no determinative examination for age currently available and there is no common agreement as to how to assess a person's age.[66]

Child smuggling and trafficking is punishable under criminal law in the majority of European countries.

3.1. BORDER MEASURES TO PREVENT CHILD TRAFFICKING

There is no doubt that child trafficking is a human rights violation through exploitation, and child smuggling is a crime against the state.[67] The role of border guards and police officers as frontline practitioners to be in contact with migrant children is very important. Law enforcement officers, in particular border guards, perform border controls, implementing a state's immigration policies in order to protect safety and security.[68] In recent years, immigration policies have become more restrictive and the introduction of tighter border controls has led to the growth in the illegal market of clandestine migration services. The cruel reality of this situation is that an important number of refugee children are found dead, drowned, frozen to death in refrigerated lorries, suffocated in cargo containers or shot by police, because of border militarisation, asylum laws or deportations.[69] Other migrating children are at risk of rape or fall victim to

63 *Hirsi Jamaa and others v. Italy* App no. 27765/09 (ECtHR, 23 February 2012).

64 *Abdullahi Elmi and Aweys Abubakar v. Malta* App nos. 25794/13 and others (ECtHR, 22 November 2016).

65 Art. 8 UNCRC.

66 Refugee and migrant children, HELP online course, Council of Europe, available at: http://help.elearning.ext.coe.int/course/index.php?categoryid=356&browse=courses&perpage=20&page=1.

67 Pearce, *Working with Trafficked Children and Young People* (n. 49 above) p. 10.

68 Piotrowicz R., 'Irregular migration networks: The challenge posed by people traffickers to states and human rights' in *Irregular migration and human rights: Theoretical, European and International Perspectives*, Martinus Nijhoff Publishers 2004, pp. 137–159.

69 O'Connell Davidson J., 'Telling Tales: Child Migration and Child Trafficking', Child Abuse & Neglect 37(13) pp. 1074–1075.

demands for sex from criminals or government officials in exchange for onward passage.[70] Finally, border guards do not always believe the stories told to them by migrating children: 'The way the screening unit [...] interviews children means that they do not always disclose the information that professionals need in order to identify a child as trafficked.'[71] Furthermore, they say: 'We often hear the same story again and again and it is only if something is different about the case that trafficking is suspected.'[72] The border measures are important, firstly, for safety and security, and, secondly, for the identification of child victims of trafficking.[73] The prevention of transnational trafficking through measures to detect possible victims at the border should also be applied without prejudice to international commitments in relation to freedom of movement.[74]

In most of the countries, police or border guards are assigned to border controls. They are responsible for informing the competent immigration service if, at the border checkpoint, there is a suspicion that a child is a victim of trafficking. As an example of good practice, this system functions in France,[75] the Netherlands,[76] Serbia,[77] Sweden,[78] and the UK.[79] Sometimes, good initiatives are not effective. In Romania, a child travelling abroad without both parents must have a notarial certificate confirming consent for his/her travel given by the child's parent remaining in Romania. However, the system does not efficiently prevent child trafficking, because it does not contain the expected date of return of the child, the child's photograph and information in languages other than Romanian.[80]

The GRETA report does not provide information on border measures on the prevention of human trafficking in Germany.[81] In Italy,[82] there are still failures in the mechanism of detecting and preventing human – and in particular child – trafficking through border control measures, which need to be improved.

70 Ibid.
71 Hynes 'No Magic Bullets' (n. 13 above) p. 66.
72 Ibid., p. 66.
73 *Antislavery, Trafficking for Forced Criminal Activities and Begging in Europe, Explanatory Study and Good Practice Examples*, September 2014, p. 94, available at: http://www.antislavery.org/wp-content/uploads/2017/01/trafficking_for_forced_criminal_activities_and_begging_in_europe.pdf; circumstances that point to trafficking crime potentially being committed: a person appears to be in control of another; using false identities and documents; a person is in possession of someone else's identity documents; children travelling with adults who speak a different language or who are not their legal guardians.
74 Art. 7 The Council of Europe Convention on Action against Trafficking in Human Beings, 2005, https://rm.coe.int/168008371d.
75 GRETA, France (n. 18 above) p. 31.
76 GRETA, the Netherlands (n. 19 above) pp. 35–36.
77 GRETA, Serbia (n. 20 above) pp. 22–23.
78 GRETA, Sweden (n. 15 above) p. 23.
79 GRETA, the UK (n. 28 above) p. 35.
80 GRETA, Romania (n. 24 above) p. 16.
81 GRETA, Germany (n. 27 above) p. 11.
82 GRETA, Italy (n. 16 above) p. 31.

In particular, they need to introduce a checklist,[83] which helps to identify child victims of smuggling and trafficking, for example by: conducting screenings of potential trafficking victims among those incarcerated and in immigration detention centres, as victims are sometimes incarcerated for crimes committed as a result of their trafficking; adopting programmes to screen vulnerable immigrant populations, including asylum seekers and unaccompanied children at borders, for indicators of human trafficking. Indicators such as these do exist, for example, in *Sweden*, during the visa application system. Here, training is being provided to relevant staff to help them detect possible human trafficking victims.

In conclusion, France, the Netherlands, Serbia, Romania, the UK, Sweden and Bulgaria have established border procedures in order to identify potential trafficking victims, including child trafficking victims. There is no information provided on specific border procedures against human trafficking in Germany. In Italy, the procedures are not effective and need to be reviewed in order to establish the indicators and checklists that will help to identify child trafficking victims at the Italian borders.

3.2. IDENTIFICATION OF CHILD VICTIMS OF TRAFFICKING

It is essential to identify child victims in order to combat child trafficking and prevent re-trafficking. However, the identification of child victims of internal and international trafficking is a very difficult task, and many victims are never identified.[84] This can be illustrated by the fact that even the victims themselves do not always understand that they are victims of trafficking. For this, they would need to know what is wrong and what is right, and have an understanding of life without abuse. In most of the cases, the children lack the emotional maturity to process the nature of the abuse which they are experiencing.[85] It happens also that the children are attached to traffickers and have formed a positive relationship with them.[86]

The identification is most often made by law enforcement officers, in particular border and police officers, social workers and health professionals.

---

83 See the example of 'Human Trafficking Protection Checklist established by the US', available at: https://2009-2017.state.gov/documents/organization/259307.pdf.

84 Okech D., Morreau W., Benson K., 'Human trafficking: Improving victim identification and service provision', (2011) International Social Work, 55, pp. 488–503.

85 West A., Loeffler Diane N., 'Understanding Victim Resistance: An explanatory Study of the Experiences of Service Providers Working with Victims of Child Trafficking' Journal of Applied Research on Children: Informing Policy for Children at Risk, 6(1) (TMC Library, 2015) p. 10.

86 Cohen J., Mannarino A., Deblinger E., *Treating trauma and traumatic Grief in Children and Adolescents*, Guilford Press 2006.

It is a crucial step in helping trafficking victims to escape from the traffickers and restore their lives.

There are certain indicators that can serve to identify a child victim of trafficking. Firstly, situational indicators are contextual markers for human trafficking victims:[87] absence of documentation, the constant presence of another individual, signs of physical abuse, a lot of people living together or frequent changes of address. Secondly, story indicators may suggest the existence of trafficking.[88] Thirdly, emotional demeanour, including signs of fear or depression or a tendency to answer questions evasively, are all indicators of trafficking.[89] There is also little empirical understanding of how these indicators should be incorporated into the identification and the assessment process.[90]

The additional difficulty in the formal identification of child trafficking is a hidden character of the crime.[91] There are many stories in which the trafficking of a child does not come up in formal registers. For example, the employees of shelters for children understand well the issue of forced marriage or trafficking for marriage. However, the practice is that the girl is 'kept in a shelter for two months, until she has reached the age [for legal marriage]. She does not want to go back to her mom's; there she has to dumpster dive and here she cooks'.[92]

In accordance with Article 10 of the Council of Europe Convention on Action against Trafficking in Human Beings,[93] the states should provide training and ensure that the relevant stakeholders, such as government officials, law enforcement officers and prosecutors, child specialists and child protection services take into account the special circumstances and needs of child victims of trafficking, and collaborate to identify these children. On the one hand, the identification of the victims of trafficking requires specialised training to ensure that, where a child is unable to explicitly articulate a concrete fear of trafficking, such risks are recognised, and protection provided without delay. On the other hand, the legislator should establish clear procedures to be followed

87 Alvarez M.B., Alessi E.J., *Human trafficking is more than sex trafficking and prostitution: Implications for social work*, (2012) Affilia 27, pp. 142–152.

88 Macy R.J., Graham L.M., 'Identifying domestic and international sex-trafficked victims during human service provision' (2012) Trauma, Violence and Abuse 13(2), pp. 59–76.

89 Logan T.K., Walker R., Hunt G., 'Understanding human trafficking in the United States,' (2009) Trauma, Violence and Abuse 10(1), pp. 3–30; Hodge D.R., 'Assisting Victims of Human Trafficking: Strategies to Facilitate Identification, Exit from Trafficking and the Restoration of Wellness' Social Work, 4 April 2014, pp. 3–4.

90 Rigby P., 'Separated and Trafficked Children: The challenges for Child Protection Professionals,' Child Abuse Review, 20 (2011) pp. 332–334.

91 Ibid., pp. 332–334.

92 Jovanovic J., *Challenges to Preliminary Identification of Romani 'Victims of Trafficking': The Serbian Case,* CEU Center for Policy Studies; 2015, pp. 18–19.

93 Also Art. 19 para. 2 UNCRC.

in cases in which suspected victims of child trafficking have been identified – the so-called National Referral Mechanism (NRM).[94]

The NRM makes the identification more effective because the reporting procedure on the potential child victims of trafficking is clearer and faster. In a case in which the identification system is complex and bureaucratic, it 'defeats the goal of finding and serving trafficked children, and the more pieces to a system, the more possible cracks for children to fall through'.[95] Sometimes, it happens that there are parallel systems of protection and identification making the whole process even less clear.[96] The lack of clear definitions in national legislations and large discretionary powers when identifying victims affects under-identification.[97]

Examples of good practices are Sweden,[98] Romania,[99] Bulgaria,[100] the UK[101] and the Netherlands.[102] They have all established their own NRM. The main burden of identification of child victims of trafficking rests with law enforcement agencies in France,[103] the Netherlands,[104] Sweden,[105] Romania,[106] the UK,[107] Germany[108] and Bulgaria.[109] However, these countries could also improve and strengthen their compliance with international obligations in the prevention of child trafficking. For example, the UK should allow its medical staff to report directly any identified human trafficking victims.

---

94 National Referral Mechanism (NRM) is a framework for identifying and referring potential victims of modern slavery and ensuring they receive the appropriate support, see the example of NRM established for the UK, available at: https://www.gov.uk/government/publications/human-trafficking-victims-referral-and-assessment-forms/guidance-on-the-national-referral-mechanism-for-potential-adult-victims-of-modern-slavery-england-and-wales.

95 Goździak E.M., 'Identifying child victims of trafficking. Towards solutions and resolutions' Criminology & public policy, 9(2) (2010), pp. 245–255, for this reference p. 251.

96 Nanou K., 'Protecting children in migration in Europe, Alternatives to institutional care and detention' Public Policy Exchange, 24 October 2018. To learn more about Eurochild, see: https://www.eurochild.org.

97 Warria, Nel, Triegaardt, 'Challenges in Identification of Child Victims of Transnational Trafficking Practice' (n. 48 above) pp. 315–333.

98 GRETA, Sweden (n. 15 above) p. 24.

99 GRETA, Romania (n. 24 above) p. 21.

100 GRETA, Bulgaria (n. 22 above) p. 29.

101 GRETA, the UK (n. 28 above) p. 41, See also Hynes, 'No Magic Bullets' (n. 13 above) p. 65.

102 GRETA, the Netherlands (n. 19 above) p. 57. See more for the National Referral Mechanism in the Netherlands, Implementation of anti-trafficking policy in the Netherlands, European Commission, available at: https://ec.europa.eu/anti-trafficking/member-states/netherlands-3-implementation-anti-trafficking-policy_en. Consequently, the author considers that the NRM has already been established in the Netherlands.

103 GRETA, France (n. 18 above) p. 32.

104 GRETA, the Netherlands (n. 19 above) p. 57.

105 GRETA, Sweden (n. 15 above) p. 24.

106 GRETA, Romania (n. 24 above) p. 21.

107 GRETA, the UK (n. 28 above) p. 24.

108 GRETA, Germany (n. 27 above) p. 12.

109 GRETA, Bulgaria (n. 22 above) p. 29.

In Italy, the NRM is being established.[110] The Italian authorities still need to introduce a clear NRM to provide frontline staff with operational indicators and training and to strengthen multi-agency involvement in victim identification, in order to ensure that they adopt a proactive and harmonised approach towards detecting and identifying victims of trafficking. Increased attention should be paid to detecting victims of trafficking among unaccompanied minors, irregular migrants and asylum seekers. The NRM does not exist in France,[111] Serbia[112] or Germany.[113]

In conclusion, the NRM has been established to identify the victims of human trafficking in Sweden, Romania, Bulgaria, the UK and the Netherlands. In Italy, the NRM is being established. Finally, this mechanism does not exist – and should be established – in three countries, more particularly France, Serbia and Germany.

3.3. AGE ASSESSMENT

In accordance with Article 8 of the UNCRC,[114] states are obligated to respect a child's identity, and this can involve an age assessment based on the physical appearance of the child and his or her psychological maturity.[115] According to the CRC Committee, this assessment should be conducted 'in a scientific, safe, child- and gender-sensitive and fair manner, avoiding any risk of a violation of the physical integrity of the child, and giving due respect to human dignity'.[116] Under the European Convention on Human Rights (ECHR), the authorities should restrain from and prevent third persons from committing acts resulting in torture or inhuman or degrading treatment of children during age assessment procedures (Art. 3 ECHR). In parallel, the authorities can

110 GRETA, Italy (n. 16 above) p. 7; *Mutatis mutandis:* Report concerning the implementation of the Council of Europe Convention on Action against Trafficking in Human Beings by Italy, GRETA, January 2017, p. 6, https://rm.coe.int/16806edf35. See for more concerning the plan to establish the National Referral mechanism in Italy: https://ec.europa.eu/anti-trafficking/member-states/italy-3-implementation-anti-trafficking-policy_en.

111 GRETA, France (n. 18 above) p. 32.

112 GRETA, Serbia (n. 20 above) pp. 33–34.

113 GRETA, Germany (n. 27 above) p. 12.

114 Art. 8 UNCRC.

115 UNHCR Guidelines on Policies and Procedures in Dealing with Unaccompanied Children Seeking Asylum, February 1997, para. 5.11.; General Comment No. 6 (2005), Treatment of unaccompanied and separated children outside their country of origin, Committee on the Rights of the Child, Thirty-ninth session, 17 May–3 June 2005, p. 10, available at: https://www2.ohchr.org/english/bodies/crc/docs/GC6.pdf.

116 UN Convention on the Rights of the Child, General Comment No. 6 (2005): Treatment of unaccompanied and separated children outside their country of origin, UN Doc. CC/GC/2005/6, 1 September 2005, (V)(a)(31)(A).

legitimately interfere with a child's right to privacy and conduct age assessments if, in accordance with the law, it is necessary to protect one of the legitimate aims stated in Article 8 paragraph 2 of the ECHR.[117] A child should be informed that an age assessment will be carried out in a language that he or she understands. Furthermore, his or her consent should be obtained before any examination is done.[118]

In accordance with Article 10 paragraph 3 of the Council of Europe Convention on Action against Trafficking in Human Beings, the states should establish special protection measures pending verification of the victim's age when the age of the victim is uncertain. Furthermore, he or she shall be presumed to be a child until his or her age has been assessed. Benefit of the doubt should be applied in such a manner that, in a case of uncertainty, the individual will be considered to be a child. Given that the consequences of an erroneous assessment may lead to children being placed in accommodation with adults with potentially heightened risks of trafficking or re-trafficking, an age assessment is critical to effective protection.

According to GRETA reports, there is significant variation in the nature and scope of age assessment procedures in European countries.

Firstly, among good practices, there are countries such as France,[119] the Netherlands,[120] Bulgaria,[121] Italy,[122] Sweden[123] and the UK,[124] which have established age assessment procedures. An interview aims to assess the physical appearance and the maturity of a child. If the age cannot be confirmed in this way, a medical test is done through an age assessment method based on the making and appraisal of one X-ray of the left hand and wrist and three X-rays of the medial clavicular epiphyses, which is an end of the long bone that serves as a strut between the shoulder blade and the breastbone. The extent to which the epiphyses in these bones have disappeared determines the skeletal age of the young person in question. For example, in the Netherlands, the closure of the

---

117 'Migration and asylum' in *Handbook on European law relating to the rights of the child, migration and asylum*, FRA, ECtHR, Council of Europe, 2014, pp. 167–169.

118 As required in accordance with Art. 25(5) Directive 2013/32/EU of the European Parliament and of the Council of 26 June 2013 on common procedures for granting and withdrawing international protection (recast), OJ 2013 L180/60, Art. 25(5), available at: https://eur-lex.europa.eu/legal-content/EN/ALL/?uri=CELEX:32013L0032.

119 GRETA, France (n. 18 above) p. 43.

120 Keunen A.M., Roscam Abbing H.D.C., Schumacher J.H., 'Age assessment of unaccompanied minor asylum seekers in the Netherlands, Radiological examination of the medial clavicular epiphysis' Dutch Association of Age Assessment Researchers, p. 10, available at: http://scep.sitespirit.nl/images/21/266.pdf.

121 GRETA, Bulgaria (n. 22 above) p. 33.

122 GRETA, Italy (n. 16 above) p. 35.

123 GRETA, Sweden (n. 15 above) p. 31.

124 GRETA, the UK (n. 28 above) p. 54.

radius of the left hand had previously been assumed to correspond to a minimum age of 15 in girls and of 16 in boys; these lower limits have now been reduced to 12.9 years in girls and 14.5 years in boys.[125] There are still challenges with age assessment even in these countries. In Bulgaria, age assessment procedures exist in practice, but should now be established in legislation. In France, a number of NGOs have emphasised that a worrying number of Nigerian girls were victims of sexual exploitation without having been identified as such by the police on the ground, partly because they claimed to be adults. In accordance with French law, if these girls claim to be adults, the authorities cannot further verify the age of these girls and protect them against exploitation by traffickers. The societal reality of these adolescents is very difficult in the context of age assessment and its consequences; it is well illustrated by Oude Breuil:

> '[...] in Marseille these "border controls" are exercised directly on young migrants' bodies. Their bodies are used in legal procedures as medical sites from which to gather evidence against their own claims to their identity. Skeletal tests inscribe the selective truth of French or Marseille politics in young migrants' bodies and point out on which side of the border they belong: "child" or "adult", "deserving" or "underserving", "in need of protection" or "to be protected against." By using medical knowledge, the low position in the societal hierarchy of young migrant cigarette vendors is exposed and they are appointed their "proper" place in the societal universe: the general message is, "go back home, we do not want you here."'[126]

In the UK,[127] whenever there are reasonable grounds to believe that the person has not reached 18 years of age, until an age assessment has been carried out, there is a presumption that a possible victim is under 18 years of age. If it comes to an age assessment medical examination, dental and bone age testing is carried out by a small number of physicians and dentists who are contracted and paid by the government. In the UK, there were several cases in which Vietnamese nationals were held at an immigration centre on the basis of having allegedly received incorrect age assessments and despite having shown clear signs of having been trafficked.[128]

Secondly, bad practices in Germany, Serbia and Romania are among those pointed out in GRETA reports. In Germany,[129] though they might have

125 See more for medical explanation of this change: Keunen, Roscam Abbing, Schumacher, 'Age assessment of unaccompanied minor asylum seekers in the Netherlands' (n. 120 above).

126 Oude Breuil B., 'Bienvenue chez les grands! Border-Crossing of Young Migrant Cigarette Vendors in Marseille' in Craig G., *Child slavery now. A contemporary reader*, The Policy Press 2010, pp. 189–203.

127 GRETA, the UK (n. 28 above) p. 54.

128 Age assessment practices: a literature review & annotated bibliography, Smith T., Brownlees L., UNICEF, 2011, p. 27, available at: https://www.unicef.org/protection/Age_Assessment_Practices_2010.pdf.

129 GRETA, Germany (n. 27 above) p. 14.

considerable importance, the 'age assessments' are often based on quick visual appraisals during the interview process for asylum-seeking children.[130]

In Serbia,[131] there is no formalised age assessment procedure. If the age of a person is not known, but there are reasons to believe that he or she has not reached 18, there is a presumption that the person is a child. In Romania,[132] if the age of the victim is not known and when there are reasons to suspect that the victim is a child, the Romanian authorities have indicated that it will be assumed that the person is a child and he or she shall be granted specific protection measures. The Romanian authorities have explained that, because of the very low number of identified foreign victims of human trafficking in Romania, there has never been a situation of doubt as regards a trafficking victim's age. The fact that the age determination process leaves room for informal assessment based on physical appearance, performed by untrained administrative or social staff out of their sphere of competence, is a reason why the age assessment procedures should be formalised in these countries. In the frame of asylum procedure, this age assessment acts against a child, who is beneficiary of presumption of minority. In the context of trafficking, the age assessment procedure is supposed to prove that the person is a minor and to guarantee a stronger protection by the state.[133]

France, the Netherlands, the UK, Bulgaria, Sweden, and Italy have established a medical examination based on dental and bone testing for the age assessment of unaccompanied presumed minors. In Germany, clear guidelines are necessary for age assessment procedures. In Serbia and Romania there are no established age assessment procedures and it would be good for them to be implemented.

3.4. CRIMINALISATION OF CHILD TRAFFICKING AND RELATED OFFENCES

As 'certainty of punishment is more important than its severity [...]'[134] prosecuting presumed traffickers and those who exploit children is a strong preventive measure against child trafficking.[135]

---

130 Feltz V., Age assessment for unaccompanied minors, Doctors of the World, 2015, p. 8, available at: https://mdmeuroblog.files.wordpress.com/2014/01/age-determination-def.pdf.

131 GRETA, Serbia (n. 20 above) p. 30.

132 GRETA, Romania (n. 24 above) p. 27.

133 There are recent trends towards rejecting medical age assessment procedures conducted by X-ray of the wrist as not sufficiently precise, see Observatoire romain du droit d'asile et des étrangers, 'Réfugiés mineurs traités comme des adultes : la Société suisse de pédiatrie dénonce les examens médicaux de détermination de l'âge', 2 June 2017, available at: https://odae-romand.ch/breve/refugies-mineurs-traites-comme-des-adultes-la-societe-suisse-de-pediatrie-denonce-les-examens-medicaux-de-determination-de-lage/.

134 Beccaria, (1963) in Meehl P., *Selected Philosophical and Methodological Papers*, University of Minnesota Press 1991.

135 Hughes D.M., *Best practices to address the demand side of sex trafficking*, 2004, available at: http://citeseerx.ist.psu.edu/viewdoc/download?doi=10.1.1.523.2857&rep=rep1&type=pdf;

In *accordance* with Article 18 of the Council of Europe Convention on Action against Trafficking in Human Beings, each state party shall adopt such legislative and other measures as may be necessary to establish human trafficking as a criminal offence.[136] The states should also expand criminal sanctions on persons and businesses commercialising trans-border child sexual services[137] or for other forms of trans-border child exploitation, for example, forced labour.[138]

The states which are covered by the comparative study: France,[139] Germany,[140] Bulgaria,[141] Romania,[142] the UK,[143] the Netherlands,[144] Sweden,[145] Serbia[146] and Italy[147] have criminalised human trafficking and related offences. In all of these countries, there is a mechanism established to allow the trafficking victim to claim compensation. In some countries, such as Bulgaria,[148] it is already a criminal offence to use the services of trafficking victims if it is known that the person is a trafficking victim,[149] while other countries have changed their legislation in order to criminalise such acts. This is the case for Italy[150] and the Netherlands.[151]

However, firstly, the collection of data[152] and bringing to justice of criminals is very difficult and the rate of prosecutions stays globally very low.[153]

---

a contrario the prosecution of child victims of trafficking is a completely different subject; concerning minors exploited for forced criminality, see e.g. Rapport Uitbuiting van minderjarigen in de criminaliteit in Nederland, onderzoek naar de signalering van kinderhandel, de aanpak en de samenwerking door professionals, Faculty of Law, Economics and Governance, Utrecht University, available at: https://www.rijksoverheid.nl/documenten/rapporten/2016/12/14/tk-bijlage-definitieve-rapportage-uitbuiting-van-minderjarigen-in-de-criminaliteit-in-nl, pp. 132–133.

136 See also Arts. 18, 19 and 20 of the Council of Europe Convention on Action against Trafficking in Human Beings; Arts. 1, 3 and 4 Optional Protocol to the Convention on the Rights of the Child on the sale of children, child prostitution and child pornography; Art. 5 EU Charter of Fundamental Rights; Art. 4 European Convention on Human Rights.

137 Rafferty, 'Child Trafficking and Commercial Sexual Exploitation' (n. 29 above).

138 Zerfata E., 'Human trafficking in Malta' Agenzija Appogg, FSWS, Presentation at Public Policy Exchange, Brussels, 24 October 2018.

139 GRETA, France (n. 18 above) p. 58.

140 GRETA, Germany (n. 27 above) p. 2.

141 GRETA, Bulgaria (n. 22 above) pp. 38–39.

142 GRETA, Bulgaria (n. 22 above) pp. 34–36.

143 GRETA, the UK (n. 28 above) pp. 65–71.

144 GRETA, the Netherlands (n. 19 above) p. 25.

145 GRETA, Sweden (n. 15 above) pp. 39–40.

146 GRETA, Serbia (n. 20 above) pp. 35–38.

147 Report concerning the implementation of the Council of Europe Convention on Action against Trafficking in Human Beings by Italy, GRETA, January 2017, p. 6, https://rm.coe.int/16806edf35.

148 GRETA, Bulgaria (n. 22 above) p. 9.

149 Art. 19 The Council of Europe Convention on Action against Trafficking in Human Beings.

150 GRETA, Italy (n. 16 above) p. 30.

151 GRETA, the Netherlands (n. 19 above) p. 51.

152 *Child trafficking in Europe: The State of Play, Lost kids, lost futures, The European Union's Response to Child Trafficking*, 'International Federation Terre des Hommes' pp. 11–15;

Consequently, involvement in child trafficking criminal groups is not very risky, and even when there has been an investigation, more often than not, the outcome is negative, leading to the traffickers being acquitted. Even if traffickers are sentenced, the prison sentences are short and the imposed fines are low.[154]

Secondly, public perception of child trafficking and exploitation plays an important role. Sex tourists are rarely prosecuted in their own countries and they feel unpunishable if their country of origin does not criminalise the use of child sexual services made abroad.[155] Sweden is an example of a country which has criminalised the use of child sexual services by its own citizens in other countries.[156]

Thirdly, practitioners, including law enforcement officers, facing the problem of child trafficking, sometimes think that victims willingly participate in this activity and no crime has been committed.[157] As mentioned in section 2.3, this lacuna can be aligned or eliminated if relevant training is provided to concerned practitioners.

Finally, massive corruption undermines the capacity of the legal system, because police, border officers and customs officials might have been bought by smugglers and traffickers.

In conclusion, child trafficking is a criminal offence and punishable with a criminal sanction in all nine examined countries. However, taking account of the transnational character of child trafficking, low detectability of this crime, high level of corruption and its wrong perception in society, the law enforcement policies should be reinforced by, for example, establishing more effective and detailed databases, and increasing the number of border and police officers allocated to pursue trafficking crimes.

4. ASSISTANCE TO CHILD VICTIMS OF TRAFFICKING

An adequate standard of living means that, at a minimum, every child should have access to some basic means of subsistence including water, food and shelter

Piotrowicz R., 'Trafficking of human beings and their human rights in the migration context' in *International migration law. Developing paradigms and key challenges*, Cholewinski R., Perruchaud, MacDonald E. (eds.), IOM 2007, pp. 275–291.

153 Hill A., Carey R., 'The trade in human lives' (2010) Americas Quarterly, 4(2), pp. 84–89.

154 Shelley L., 'Human trafficking as a form of transnational crime' in Lee, *Human trafficking* (n. 1 above) pp. 116–137.

155 Andrews S., 'United States domestic prosecution of the American international sex tourist: Efforts to protect children from sexual exploitation' The Journal of Criminal Law and Criminology, 94 (2004) pp. 415–454.

156 GRETA, Sweden (n. 15 above) p. 16.

157 Shelley, 'Human trafficking as a form of transnational crime' (n. 154 above) 137.

under conditions of dignity. In all cases, housing in temporary shelters is a sustainable solution only if a child is to be relocated in a reasonable time.[158] Each child should be housed with its family unless it is against the child's best interest[159] or foster care if a child has no own family. In the context of migration, it is particularly important that, in the light of the right to liberty[160] read together with the principle of the best interests of the child[161] and the right to development[162] children should never be detained. The detention of a child is not prohibited under human rights law if substantial and procedural safeguards are met. There is, however, broad international consensus that the detention should not be applied to refugee and migrant children, in particular victims of child smuggling and trafficking. Unfortunately, there are still situations in which migrant children are detained.[163]

The states have a responsibility to look after the unaccompanied children and appoint, without undue delay, a legal guardian to represent the child in all necessary procedures and life situations. Lack of compliance with this human right standards can result e.g. in violation of provisions of the ECHR.[164]

4.1. ACCOMMODATION OF CHILD VICTIMS OF TRAFFICKING

The right to an adequate standard of living is a fundamental right of all children. The states have an obligation to take adequate measures to assist child trafficking victims. In particular, the states need to develop necessary legislation, adopt administrative measures and establish judicial mechanisms, in order to place child trafficking victims in appropriate and secure accommodation.[165]

According to the UN Human Rights Office of the High Commissioner (OHCHR), housing assistance, food stamps and other support programmes are either not available or are limited, temporary or dependent on a child's migration status.[166]

---

158 *DCI v. the Netherlands* App no. 47/2008 (ECSR, 20 October 2009).

159 *Tarakhel v. Switzerland* App no. 29217/12 (ECtHR, 4 November 2014); *DCI v. Belgium* App no. 69/2011 (ECSR, 23 October 2012).

160 Art. 37 UNCRC.

161 Art. 3 UNCRC.

162 Art. 6 UNCRC.

163 *Mohamad v. Greece* App no. 70586/11 (ECtHR, 11 December 2014).

164 *Rahimi v. Greece* App no. 8687/08 (ECtHR, 5 April 2011).

165 Art. 12 of the Council of Europe Convention on Action against Trafficking in Human Beings, 2005, https://rm.coe.int/168008371d.

166 'The right to an adequate standard of living, including housing, water and sanitation, and food' in *The economic, social and cultural rights of migrants in an irregular situation*, OHCHR, p. 60–80, available at: https://www.ohchr.org/Documents/Publications/HR-PUB-14-1_en.pdf; see also Kulu-Glasgow I., Noyon S.M., Smit M., Unaccompanied minor

Separated accommodation should be established for vulnerable migrant children, because it protects them from abuse, smuggling and trafficking by foreign adults if these children are placed in common shelters with them. Such separated accommodation is available for children in France,[167] Sweden,[168] the UK,[169] the Netherlands[170] and Italy.[171]

In the UK, unaccompanied minors are placed in a different kind of accommodation, in particular residential care homes, shared flats and houses, bedsits, bed and breakfast emergency housing and foster care. Children over 16 are placed in semi-independent accommodation. There is a lack of special accommodation for child victims of trafficking. Undocumented, unaccompanied minors are not registered, and that is why 60% of children go missing, among them children going missing in one part of the UK and exploited in another part of the UK.[172]

In the Netherlands,[173] after an interview with the police, the Nidos Foundation provides guardianship for unaccompanied minors. These minors are placed in protected shelters, where they receive special guidance and support, and are informed of the risks linked to trafficking. The children stay under supervision in the shelter, but they can leave shelters with a supervisor, and outside programmes are organised for them. The minors received in the shelter fill in special forms with detailed personal information in case the minor goes missing.[174]

There is a lack of places for children in the shelters in France and in Italy. They stay outside at night or they are even detained,[175] such as happens in Romania[176] and Bulgaria.[177] In certain exceptional cases, under Rule 39,[178] the ECtHR has ordered interim measures in order to ensure that asylum-seeking families are provided with shelter while their claims before the ECtHR are pending.[179]

---

asylum seekers in the Netherlands: choice or chance?, Wettenschappelijk Onderzoek-en Documentatiecentrum Ministrie van Justitie en Veiligheid, Cahier 2018–18, p. 21.

167 GRETA, France (n. 18 above) p. 25.

168 GRETA, Sweden (n. 15 above) p. 18.

169 GRETA, the UK (n. 28 above) p. 51.

170 GRETA, the Netherlands (n. 19 above) p. 17.

171 GRETA, Italy (n. 16 above) pp. 31–32.

172 GRETA, the UK (n. 28 above) p. 51.

173 GRETA, the Netherlands (n. 19 above) p. 17.

174 Verstegen T., 'Towards a European Guardianship Network' Public Policy Exchange, 24 October 2018. To learn more about the Nidos Foundation, see: https://www.nidos.nl.

175 *Migration and International Human Rights Law*, Practitioners Guide No. 6, International Commission of Jurists, Geneva, 2011.

176 GRETA, Romania (n. 24 above) p. 25.

177 GRETA, Bulgaria (n. 22 above) p. 28.

178 Rules of the Court, 1 August 2018, https://www.echr.coe.int/Documents/Rules_Court_ENG.pdf.

179 'Housing,' *Handbook on European law relating to asylum, borders and immigration*, FRA, ECtHR, Council of Europe, 2014, pp. 198–203.

The European Committee of Social Rights (ECSR) has stated that, if the enforcement of a right is particularly complex or expensive, steps must be taken in order for states to realise the right within a reasonable time, with measurable progress, whilst prioritising the needs of the most vulnerable.[180]

Once placed in residential or closed-type institutions, migrant minors, in particular unaccompanied minors[181] such as orphans, neglected or abused children and children in conflict with the law, still represent a group which is particularly vulnerable to human trafficking during and after their placement in competent institutions.[182] Among bad practices, one is the placement of children in common accommodation with adults, exposing them to a higher risk of becoming a victim of trafficking. This is the situation in Serbia,[183] Bulgaria,[184] Romania[185] and Germany.[186]

Eurochild,[187] which is an NGO of organisations and individuals working in and across Europe to promote the rights and well-being of children and young people, considers that alternative measures to detention for migrant children and deinstitutionalisation can improve the situation. They understand it as the transformation of national structures for the protection of children, in order to create necessary and suitable alternative care solutions for children unable to stay with their biological families. This vulnerability also persists when young people leave such institutions after their coming of age.

In conclusion, Serbian, Bulgarian, Romanian and German authorities place minors in the same accommodation as adults. Consequently, they should take measures to improve the situation and adapt the accommodation. In France, Sweden, the UK, the Netherlands and Italy, there is separated accommodation for children. However, there is a lack of places for children in the shelters in France and Italy, and it is crucial that places are urgently created for children who risk spending the night outside or under detention.

---

180 *Defence for Children International (DCI) v. Belgium*, no. 69/2011, ECSR, paras. 70–73.

181 See also Thematic Report on migrant and refugee children prepared by the Special Representative of the Secretary General on migration and refugees, SG/Inf(2017)13, 10 March 2017, available at: https://search.coe.int/cm/Pages/result_details.aspx?ObjectId=09000016806fdd08; Recommendation 1985 (2011), 'Undocumented migrant children in an irregular situation: a real cause for concern', 7 October 2011, available at: http://www.assembly.coe.int/nw/xml/XRef/Xref-XML2HTML-en.asp?fileid=18041&lang=en.

182 In a situation of migrant children, these rights are also recognised in Art. 20 UNCRC.

183 GRETA, Serbia (n. 20 above) p. 18.

184 GRETA, Bulgaria (n. 22 above) p. 28.

185 GRETA, Romania (n. 24 above) p. 25.

186 GRETA, Germany (n. 27 above) p. 25.

187 Nanou K., 'Protecting children in migration in Europe' (n. 96 above). To learn more about Eurochild, see https://www.eurochild.org.

4.2. LEGAL GUARDIANSHIP FOR UNACCOMPANIED CHILDREN

Unaccompanied children arriving in Europe are deprived of their family environment and they have limited legal capacity. They do not have parents or they are separated from their parents, so their interests are not defended by them. That is why their rights should be defended by an independent person[188] who can safeguard the child's best interests and his or her general well-being.

If neither parent nor other family members can be found, the child should be accorded the same protection as any other child permanently or temporarily deprived of his or her family environment for any reason. The CRC Committee has explained that this means that states are required to create the underlying legal framework in order to take necessary measures to secure proper representation of an unaccompanied or separated child's best interests, in particular in asylum proceedings. This means appointing a legal guardian who should be consulted and informed regarding all actions taken in relation to the child.[189] The guardian protects the child's best interests in different areas covered by the ECHR. For example, child protection against inhuman or degrading treatment (Article 3), appealing a detention order against a child (Article 5 paragraph 4), or tracing a child's family in order to facilitate family reunification (Article 8).[190] Unaccompanied children's rights are also protected by the Asylum Procedures Directive, which implements a child's right to asylum and protects his or her best interests.[191]

In the context of child victims of trafficking, Article 10 paragraph 4a of the Council of Europe Convention on Action against Trafficking in Human Beings obligates national authorities to provide a child victim of trafficking with a legal guardian, an organisation or an authority which shall act in the best interests of the child.[192] The timely appointment of a legal guardian who can act independently with authority and uphold the child's best interests is

---

188 On regular and independent check-ups of the legal guardians, see e,g, Resolution 1810 (2011), Unaccompanied children in Europe: issues of arrival, stay and return, Parliamentary Assembly 15 April 2011, available at: http://assembly.coe.int/nw/xml/XRef/Xref-XML2HTML-en.asp?fileid=17991&lang=en.

189 UN Convention on the Rights of the Child, General Comment No. 6 (2005) para. 33.

190 The *per se* non-appointment of the guardian was sanctioned by the ECtHR in *Rahimi v. Greece*, 5 April 2011, no. 8687/08 (Art. 3 and 5 ECHR); and the ECSR, *European Committee for Home-Based Priority Action for the Child and the Family (EUROCEF) v. France*, 24 January 2018, no. 114/2015 (Art. 17(1) ESC).

191 As required in accordance with Art. 25 Directive 2013/32/EU of the European Parliament and of the Council of 26 June 2013 on common procedures for granting and withdrawing international protection (recast), OJ 2013 L180/60, available at: https://eur-lex.europa.eu/legal-content/EN/TXT/HTML/?uri=CELEX:32013L0032&from=EN.

192 In a situation of migrant children, these rights are also recognised in Art. 20 and 22 UNCRC.

essential for ensuring the protection and rehabilitation of unaccompanied children who are identified as victims of trafficking, breaking the links with traffickers and minimising the risk of children going missing. In countries of origin, the appointment of legal guardians to child victims of trafficking who cannot be returned to their families because the families were involved in the trafficking is an important factor for minimising the risk of re-trafficking and supporting the child's integration.[193] Most countries' legislation provides for the appointment of legal guardians to child victims of trafficking, but the procedure is cumbersome, there are delays in the guardians' appointment and the guardians often cannot be seen as being independent and acting in the best interests of the child. They cannot provide legal advice and protect the rights of such children because of the nature of their responsibilities and/or due to the fact that they do not have legal training.

Good practices exist in many countries in Europe. France, Germany,[194] the Netherlands, Serbia, Italy and Sweden have established systems of legal guardianship for unaccompanied minors. These systems are, however, very diverse and it is worth looking more closely at some of them. In France,[195] the cases of unaccompanied minors are notified by police to the public prosecutor, who takes the decision on appropriate protection measures. Child trafficking victims are placed under the general child protection framework of the departmental councils and child welfare services. If there is no person with parental authority, an ad hoc administrator is appointed without delay to protect the best interests of the child. In the Netherlands,[196] unaccompanied minors must be under guardianship. The minors who apply for asylum without a parent in the Netherlands are placed under temporary guardianship of the Nidos Foundation. In Serbia,[197] guardians for unaccompanied minors are assigned from among staff of the competent centres for social work. However, the centres are understaffed and lack human resources. That is why it can happen that 50 children are under the legal guardianship of one person. In Sweden,[198] unaccompanied children, without a residence permit, are provided with a *guardian ad litem* ('god man'). If a child is granted asylum in Sweden, a specially appointed custodian will normally be appointed instead of the *guardian ad litem*. Some *guardians ad litem* are responsible for too many children, others are appointed with considerable delays, limiting their capacity to safeguard the best interests of the child. Communication between guardians and migrant children is sometimes limited because of the low quality of interpretation in Sweden. In Italy,[199] the mayor in

193 Rap S., Buddenbaum M., *Lost in migration*, Missing Children Europe 2018, pp. 31–34.
194 GRETA, Germany (n. 27 above) p. 14.
195 GRETA, France (n. 18 above) p. 42.
196 GRETA, the Netherlands (n. 19 above) pp. 40, 43, 48.
197 GRETA, Serbia (n. 20 above) p. 18.
198 GRETA, Sweden (n. 15 above) p. 29.
199 GRETA, Italy (n. 16 above) p. 38.

the place of arrival of unaccompanied minors must appoint a temporary legal guardian before the child is transferred to the relevant accommodation centre.

In Romania, Bulgaria, and the UK there is no legal guardianship system for unaccompanied minors. There are some other forms of legal representatives for children. In Bulgaria,[200] the Law on Asylum and Refugees provides that if the child does not have an appointed guardian, it shall be represented by the Agency for Social Assistance. The director of the local Social Assistance Directorate appoints a social worker who is personally responsible for the child and acts as his or her legal representative in administrative proceedings. The social worker's legal representation is limited to the application for international protection and does not guarantee that unaccompanied minors exercise their rights to education or health care. In the UK,[201] there is no system of legal guardianship applying across the UK. In England and Wales, to represent and support children who are possible victims of human trafficking, there are independent child trafficking advocates. In Romania,[202] the General Directorate for Social Assistance and Child Protection (GDSACP) designates an educated and qualified person with legal or social assistance experience for the entire duration of the refugee status application process. A private body authorised to support children's rights may also be assigned.[203]

In conclusion, in France, Germany, the Netherlands, Serbia, Italy and Sweden, there is an established system of legal guardianship for unaccompanied minors. However, the number of legal guardians is often very limited, such as in Serbia. Among the obstacles to the effective functioning of legal guardianship, is the long time it can take to appoint a legal guardian, and the low quality of the translation provided for communication between a child and the guardian. This is the case in Sweden. In Romania and Bulgaria, there is no legal guardianship system for unaccompanied minors. There are some other forms of legal representation for children. These legal representatives have limited power and cannot always act in the best interests of the child. All delays in appointment, and the lack of a guardian for a child, make the child more vulnerable to becoming a victim of trafficking.

5. CONCLUSION

As a result of the refugee crisis of the past years, there are a considerable number of migrant children, and they often travel unaccompanied or become separated

200 GRETA, Bulgaria (n. 22 above) p. 32.
201 GRETA, the UK (n. 28 above), p. 53.
202 GRETA, Romania (n. 24 above) p. 27.
203 Synthesis Report, Overview of guardianship systems for unaccompanied minor asylum-seekers in Central Europe', IOM, 2012, available at: https://kidsempowerment.org/overview-of-guardianship-systems-for-unaccompanied-minor-asylum-seekers-in-central-europe.

during their journey. This means that they become exposed to the risk of being exploited by smugglers and traffickers through forced criminality, street begging or forced labour – mainly in the sex industry – and can become victims of forced marriages or organ transplants.

The research study was based on existing research reports for France, Germany, the Netherlands, the UK, Bulgaria, Romania, Sweden, Serbia and Italy. It revealed that child smuggling and trafficking often happen because the mechanisms established in international treaties to protect children do not protect children's rights effectively, or in some rare cases, they even do not exist at the national level.

Firstly, measures need to be taken even before child trafficking has occurred. Improving awareness of the risks of child trafficking among the victims or potential victims and their relatives, among the practitioners working with child victims of trafficking and society is a strong preventive measure. Awareness can be raised particularly by a couple of mechanisms. Nationwide information campaigns presumably have a preventive impact on the society and they have been already organised in the Netherlands, Serbia, Bulgaria, the UK, Germany and Romania. Education and schooling can enhance knowledge of potential child smuggling and trafficking. The specific educational programs have been already implemented in all countries covered by this research. Relevant training of professionals working on child trafficking, as has been organised in France, the Netherlands, Serbia, Italy, Germany, Romania, the UK, Sweden and Bulgaria, should be regular and involve a broad group of professionals.

Secondly, the procedures related to child trafficking cover a wide range of border measures. The identification of children, age assessment and the criminalisation of child trafficking should always be implemented with the highest respect for the human rights of vulnerable groups of migrant – often unaccompanied – children.

Border measures are established by the states to prevent and detect child and human trafficking. The specific procedures to follow if there is a suspicion of child trafficking have been established in France, Serbia, Romania, the Netherlands, the UK, Sweden and Bulgaria. However, the fact that these procedures have been established in these countries, does not mean that they always function efficiently (Romania, Italy).

The identification of victims requires the existence of rules on how to proceed in order to inform the competent authorities about a potential child trafficking victim, the so-called National Referral Mechanism (NRM). The NRM, however, does not exist in all countries (France, Serbia and Germany).

The next step is to determine whether a trafficking victim is a minor. The presumed minors who do not have any identification documents and raise a doubt concerning their age should be submitted, upon their agreement, to an age assessment procedure, necessary for the minors to have their rights respected.

There are two countries, Romania and Serbia, which do not have any established age assessment procedures.

Child trafficking and related offences are criminalised in all countries covered by this research. On the one hand, the criminalisation is essential for individual prevention. It means that the potential offender is made aware of and discouraged from getting criminally involved in child trafficking and in getting involved in child trafficking again after being sentenced. On the other hand, the criminalisation of these acts also serves a broader general prevention measure among third parties in society.

Thirdly, the next step towards the elimination of child smuggling and trafficking is taking adequate measures to place the child in appropriate and secure accommodation. The children should not be placed in the same accommodation as adults, because it has been considered as a factor that increases the risk of a child becoming a victim of trafficking (Serbia, Bulgaria, Romania and Germany). A problem of lack of places in shelters for children, like in France and Italy, should be solved by finding alternative accommodation for the children concerned, such as, for example, in foster families, which would also enhance the integration of children into society.

As minors do not have legal capacity, legal guardians should be appointed without undue delay. Each guardian should be appointed to represent and protect the rights of a reasonable number of children, to represent them and to protect their rights. In Romania, Bulgaria and the UK, legal guardians are not appointed. In the UK, children do have legal representatives, but they have limited power and they cannot always act in the best interests of the child.

The above-mentioned measures are milestones in the eradication of child smuggling and trafficking. It has been scientifically proven that the implementation of these measures can improve the situation of vulnerable – often unaccompanied or separated – children.

IS IMMIGRATION DETENTION OUT OF THE QUESTION?

A Child-Based Approach to Immigration Detention and Family Unity

Charis Pasiourtidou*

* Lawyer at the Research and Documentation Directorate, Court of Justice of the European Union, Luxembourg. This chapter constitutes part of the thesis submitted in partial fulfilment of the requirements for the degree of Advanced LL.M in European and International Human Rights Law, Leiden University, under the supervision of Professor Dr. Ton Liefaard, Vice-Dean for Education and UNICEF Chair in Children's Rights at Leiden Law School. The opinions expressed in this chapter are those of the author and do not purport to reflect the opinions or views of the Court of Justice of the European Union or its members.

1. INTRODUCTION

Child immigration detention remains a disconcerting reality of our times. This chapter focuses on the detention of asylum-seeking children accompanied by their family, in light of their right to liberty, family unity and the best interests of the child (BIC). It considers the extent to which these three rights support the extension of non-custodial alternatives not only to children, but to their entire family.

The right to liberty is safeguarded by all international and regional human rights instruments[1] and also by child-specific norms, most notably, the United Nations Convention on the Rights of the Child (UNCRC).[2] When people are arbitrarily deprived of their liberty, they can also be deprived of other rights, depending on the conditions of detention.[3] Moreover, the negative effects of detention are solidly recognised,[4] with the effects exacerbated when children are involved. Tens of thousands of asylum-seeking children worldwide are 'captive' in different forms of detention, with or without their families, and are effectively stripped of their childhood.[5]

---

1 See e.g. Arts. 3 and 9 Universal Declaration of Human Rights (UDHR), 10 December 1948, 217A (III); Art. 9 ICCPR, 16 December 1966, UN, Treaty Series, vol. 999, 171; Art. 14 Convention on the Rights of Persons with Disabilities (CRPD): *resolution/adopted by the General Assembly*, 24 January 2007, A/RES/61/106; Art. 31 Refugee Convention, 28 July 1951, United Nations, Treaty Series, vol. 189, 137; Art. 5 ECHR, 4 November 1950, ETS 5; Art. 7 American Convention on Human Rights (ACHR), *'Pact of San Jose', Costa Rica*, 22 November 1969; Art. 6 Banjul Charter, 27 June 1981, CAB/LEG/67/3 rev. 5, 21 I.L.M. 58 (1982); Art. 6 Charter of Fundamental Rights of the European Union (OJ C 326, pp. 391–407) (Charter).

2 Art. 37(b), UN General Assembly, *Convention on the Rights of the Child*, 20 November 1989, United Nations, Treaty Series, vol. 1577, p. 3.

3 E.g. the right to a prompt trial before a competent and impartial tribunal or the right to freedom from torture and inhuman or degrading treatment or punishment. See, inter alia, Alfred de Zayas, 'Human rights and indefinite detention' (2005) 85(857) International Review of the Red Cross 19, who goes as far as to argue that indefinite detention involves, with little doubt, inhuman treatment and even a form of torture *per se*.

4 UNHCR 'Guidelines on the Applicable criteria and standards relating to the detention of asylum-seekers and Alternatives to Detention' (2012) ('Detention Guidelines').

5 Exact statistics are hard to obtain due to the fluctuating nature of migration. Human Rights Watch, 'Children Behind Bars: The Global Overuse of Detention' (March 2016);

Against this backdrop, it becomes imperative that the contours of the obligations of states vis-à-vis asylum-seeking children are elucidated. The focus of this chapter is specifically on accompanied asylum-seeking children, although the analysis pertaining to the right to liberty is equally relevant for unaccompanied minors. However, in contrast with unaccompanied children,[6] human rights law has not yet definitively rejected the use of detention for accompanied children. It is still widely used, often in the pretext of maintaining family unity, with the legal status of the child often being subsumed into their parents' migratory status.[7]

This chapter evaluates the increased significance that the BIC has come to acquire in the international and European arenas, and how this has contributed to a shift in approach regarding child immigration detention. The main proposition of this chapter is that immigration detention can no longer be an option for children, and that, because all children's rights are inextricably linked, including the rights to liberty and family unity, non-custodial alternatives should be extended to the children's entire family.

2. THE BEST INTERESTS OF THE CHILD: FROM 'PRIMARY' TO 'PARAMOUNT' CONSIDERATION

The significance of the following analysis lies in the fact that the BIC is closely connected with all other children's rights and always remains a relevant consideration that can inform immigration decision-making. The added value of the BIC-dimension in the context of immigration detention is appreciated if set against the heightened importance that the principle has come to acquire in the international and European contexts.

Firstly, Article 3 UNCRC makes the BIC a 'primary consideration' in every decision and action that concerns children by any private, judicial, legislative or administrative body.[8] Applying the guidance offered by the CRC Committee

---

CoE Commissioner for Human Rights, 'Human Rights Comment by Thomas Hammarberg, Migrant Children should not be detained' (Strasbourg, 8 February 2011).

6 The CRC Committee dedicates a whole General Comment to unaccompanied and separated children stating therein that unaccompanied children 'should not, as a rule, be detained'. UNCRC Committee, General Comment No. 6 (2005): Treatment of Unaccompanied and Separated Children Outside their Country of Origin, 1 September 2005, CRC/GC/2005/6, para. 61.

7 UNCRC Committee, 'Report of the 2012 Day of General Discussion: The Rights of All Children in the Context of International Migration' (November 2012), para. 32; Angenietha E. Zijlstra, 'In the best interest of the child: A study into a decision-support tool validating asylum-seeking children's right from a behavioural scientific perspective' (University of Groningen, 2012).

8 The principle also features in several other UNCRC provisions: Art. 9 UNCRC clarifies that the non-separation of children from his/her parents and the preservation of family relations

in its General Comment No. 14[9] to the immigration context, the BIC should guide decisions and policies that might impact the individual asylum-seeking child or children as a group, even if the decision does not specifically target them.[10] In individual cases, the Committee has non-exhaustively identified the child's views; identity; maintenance of family relations and environment; the child's care, safety, protection, and situation of vulnerability; and his/her health and education as factors to be taken into account.[11] Moreover, the UNHCR's Executive Committee has provided guidelines to determine the BIC whenever children 'at risk' are involved,[12] which arguably covers accompanied asylum-seeking children.[13]

The CRC Committee has also clarified that even though the BIC is not the decisive factor in each and every case, it should nonetheless be given priority and 'larger weight' vis-à-vis other considerations.[14] At the same time, it has been urging states to give the BIC paramountcy in national laws and policies.[15] The high degree of priority that should be attached to the BIC is also demonstrated by the Committee's proposition that the BIC can only be superseded by equally

---

and direct regular contact of the child with both parents should be the default position, except if the BIC command otherwise; Art. 18(1) UNCRC postulates that the BIC is the 'basic concern' of the parents; Art. 21 makes the BIC a 'paramount consideration' in the adoption context; Arts. 37 and 40 UNCRC call for the separation of children and adults in detention and for the presence of parents in criminal proceedings involving children in conflict with the law, respectively, unless it is against their best interests.

9 UNCRC Committee, General Comment No. 14 (2013) on the right of the child to have his or her best interests taken as a primary consideration (Art. 3, para. 1), 29 May 2013, CRC/C/GC/14, para. 48; UNCRC Committee, General Comment No. 11, 'Indigenous children and their rights under the Convention', UN Doc. CRC/C/GC/11 (2009), para. 30; UNCRC Committee, General Comment No. 7, 'Implementing child rights in early childhood', UN Doc. CRC/C/GC/7/Rev. 1 (2005), para. 13.

10 UNCRC Committee, General Comment No. 14, ibid., para. 6; *Rahimi v. Greece*, no. 8687/08, ECHR 2011. In the case, even though the provision on detention was not specifically directed at children but at all illegal immigrants in general, it had nonetheless implications for the unaccompanied minor at issue and thus his best interests had to be primarily considered, taking into account his dual vulnerability as a 'child' and as an 'unaccompanied minor', para. 108.

11 UNCRC Committee, General Comment No. 14 (n. 9 above), paras. 52–79.

12 UNHCR Executive Committee of the High Commissioner's Programme, Conclusion on children at risk, No. 107 (LVIII) – (2007) (c) (ii).

13 Ciara M. Smyth, *The Common European Asylum System and the Rights of the Child: An Exploration of Meaning and Compliance* (doctoral thesis, University of Leiden, 's-Hertogenbosch: Uitgeverij Boxpress, 2013) 5, 48.

14 UNCRC Committee, General Comment No. 14 (n. 9 above) paras. 37, 39.

15 E.g. in its Concluding Observations to Romania in 2003, the CRC Committee criticised Romania for its failure to make the BIC a 'paramount consideration in all legislation and policies affecting children'. UNCRC Committee, Concluding Observations to Romania in 2003, UN Doc. CRC/C/15/Add.199, para. 29. On the same footing, the Committee urged the UK to recognise the BIC as a 'paramount consideration' in all its laws and policies, and specifically within the immigration action frames. UNCRC Committee, Concluding Observations to the United Kingdom of Great Britain and Northern Ireland in 2002, UN Doc. CRC/C/15/Add. 188, paras. 25–26.

rights-based considerations,[16] as upheld by the UNHCR.[17] The Committee has unequivocally opined that general immigration imperatives do not constitute rights-based considerations and cannot thus take precedence over the BIC when detention is envisaged.[18] Such an approach does not completely negate states' margin of appreciation, and leaves some room for preponderant countervailing interests, albeit exceptional.[19] However, a principled approach to the BIC means that it is expected that the BIC will consistently take precedence over general immigration control interests,[20] which may in turn increase the chances of decisions consistent with the BIC.[21]

2.1. BIC IN THE EUROPEAN CONTEXT

The BIC is gaining significance at the European level, too. Article 24 of the Charter explicitly protects the BIC as one of the rights of the child that should be given 'primary consideration'.[22] The BIC is also made a 'primary consideration' in the implementation of EU asylum Directives,[23] such as the Reception Conditions Directive,[24] the Dublin Regulation,[25] the Asylum Procedures Directive,[26] the

---

16 UNCRC Committee, General Comment No. 6 (n. 6 above), para. 86, in the context of the expulsion of unaccompanied and separated children.

17 UNHCR 'Guidelines on Determining the Best Interests of the Child' (May 2008) 76.

18 UNCRC Committee, General Comment No. 6 (n. 6 above), para. 86. This has been reiterated in the more recent Joint General Comment No. 3 (2017) of the Committee on the Protection of the Rights of All Migrant Workers and Members of Their Families and No. 22 (2017) of the Committee on the Rights of the Child on the general principles regarding the human rights of children in the context of international migration, UN Doc. CMW/C/GC/3-CRC/C/GC/22 (2017), para. 33.

19 UNCRC Committee, General Comment No. 6 (n. 6 above), para. 86.

20 Such a principled approach was developed in Ciara M. Smyth, 'The Best Interests of the Child in the Expulsion and First-entry Jurisprudence of the European Court of Human Rights: How Principled is the Court's Use of the Principle?' (2015) 17 *European Journal of Migration and Law* 102.

21 Ibid., 103.

22 However, it should be noted that the CJEU had already identified the BIC as a general principle of EU law, even before the entry into force of the Charter in 2009. See Case C-540/03 *European Parliament v. Council* [2006] ECR I-5769.

23 These asylum directives cumulatively form the so-called Common European Asylum System (CEAS).

24 Art. 23 Directive 2013/33/EU of the European Parliament and of the Council of 26 June 2013 laying down standards for the reception of applicants for international protection (OJ L 180, pp. 96–116) (Reception Conditions Directive).

25 Art. 6, Regulation (EU) No. 604/2013 of the European Parliament and of the Council of 26 June 2013 establishing the criteria and mechanisms for determining the Member State responsible for examining an application for international protection lodged in one of the Member States by a third-country national or a stateless person (recast) (OJ L. 180/31-180/59) (Dublin III).

26 Recital 33 Directive 2013/32/EU of the European Parliament and of the Council of 26 June 2013 on common procedures for granting and withdrawing international protection (OJ L 180, pp. 60–95) (Asylum Procedures Directive).

Qualification Directive,[27] as well as the Return Directive.[28] A number of factors for BIC determination are also identified therein,[29] although the weight to be attributed to the BIC is somewhat undermined due to normative restrictions.[30]

The BIC concept is gaining ground in CJEU jurisprudence, albeit not specifically in the context of immigration detention. Nevertheless, it signals how the principle is to be applied in future relevant jurisprudence. For instance, in both *Zambrano*[31] and *Chavez-Vilchez*, the CJEU attributed decisive weight to the child's interests over state considerations, taken in conjunction with the child's right to family, age, physical and emotional development, and his/her ties with both parents.[32]

For its part, the ECtHR already appears to have transcended the narrow scope of the CEAS instruments by affirming that Article 23(1) of the Reception Conditions Directive is equalised to Article 3 UNCRC in the context of child immigration detention despite the fact that the Directive provision pertaining to detention is normatively age-neutral.[33] Notwithstanding the absence of the BIC in the text of the ECHR, the ECtHR often refers to the BIC when interpreting substantive provisions in cases involving children,[34] such as Articles 5[35] and 8. In immigration cases, the ECtHR is seen downgrading the state interests, such

---

27 Art. 20(5) and Recital 18 Directive 2011/95/EU of the European Parliament and of the Council of 13 December 2011 on standards for the qualification of third-country nationals or stateless persons as beneficiaries of international protection, for a uniform status for refugees or for persons eligible for subsidiary protection, and for the content of the protection granted (OJ L 337, pp. 9–26) (Qualification Directive).

28 Recital 22, Arts. 5(a) and Art. 17(5) Directive 2008/115/EC of the European Parliament and of the Council of 16 December 2008 on common standards and procedures in Member States for returning illegally staying third-country nationals (OJ L 348, pp. 98–107) (Return Directive).

29 With the exception of the Asylum Procedures Directive, other CEAS instruments include factors such as family reunification possibilities; the well-being and social development of children given their backgrounds; safety and security matters and the child's views given his/her age and level of maturity. See Art. 23(2) Reception Conditions Directive; Art. 6(3) Dublin III; Recital 33 Asylum Procedures Directive; Recital 18 Qualification Directive (incl. 'family unity').

30 E.g. the Asylum Procedures Directive only provides for BIC primacy in a Recital (33) but not a substantive provision, with the exception of Art. 25(6), which specifically concerns unaccompanied children. No reference to the BIC whatsoever exists in its child-specific provisions either. See Art. 7(a) and 14(1); Art. 20(5) Chapter VII of the Qualification Directive.

31 Case C-34/09 *Zambrano v. ONem (Belgium)* [2011] ECR I-1177.

32 Case C-133/15 *Chavez-Vilchez and Others* [2017] ECR I, para. 40. Case C-82/16 *K.A and Others v. Belgium* [2018] ECR I represents an important development since the same assessment factors as *Chavez* were held applicable, including the BIC assessment, even in the lack of the exercise of an EU freedom and even though national security was at the other end of the balancing scale. For previous case law on how the BIC principle was used in the CJEU jurisprudence, see Case C-356/11 *O, S and L* (2012) ECR I and Case C-165/14 *Alfredo Rendon Marin and C.S* (2016) ECR I.

33 *Popov v. France*, nos. 39472/07 and 39474/07, ECHR 2012, para. 141.

34 See *Demir and Baykara v. Turkey*, no. 34503/97, ECHR 2008, paras. 98–105 and 147–150; George Letsas, 'Strasbourg's Interpretive Ethic: Lessons for the International Lawyer' (2010) 21 European Journal of International Law 509–541.

35 *Rahimi v. Greece* (n. 10 above).

as the economic well-being of the country, to a secondary consideration when judged against the BIC.[36] This may lead one to conclude that the ECtHR has elevated the importance attached to the BIC in the immigration context, making it, *prima facie*, a consideration that takes precedence over other state interests.[37] In an even bolder statement, the ECtHR invoked an existing '*broad consensus – including in international law*' that the BIC must be a 'paramount' consideration in all decisions concerning children.[38]

2.2. BIC AND THE RIGHTS OF THE CHILD: LINKING THE PIECES

The multiple references to the BIC both in the UNCRC text, as well as its use as an interpretive principle, leave no doubt that there is a close nexus between the BIC and other children's rights. Indeed, the rights enshrined in the UNCRC can arguably be viewed as a consensus of the international community as to what the BIC are.[39] The CRC Committee clearly emphasised this connection by stressing the universality, interdependence and interrelatedness of all rights enshrined in the UNCRC[40] and specifically highlighted that the BIC always remains a relevant consideration when implementing UNCRC rights.[41] Building on this interrelationship, it has been clearly stated that an action cannot be said to be in the BIC if that contradicts any of the rights of the child; that would be, *ipso facto*, against the BIC.[42] Thus, compliance with the BIC means compliance with all rights enshrined in the UNCRC.[43] Accordingly, in the immigration context,

36 *Rodrigues Da Silva and Hoogkamer v. the Netherlands*, App No. 50435/99, ECHR 2006, para. 44.

37 To appreciate the magnitude of the ECtHR's leap in this regard, it is worth tracing the Court's initial stance according to which, when both family life and immigration are at stake, border control remains a state's sovereign right, as a matter of 'well established international law and subject to its treaty obligations', *Abdulaziz et al*, nos 9214/80, 9473/81, 9474/81 (1985) Series A no. 74.

38 *Neulinger and Shuruk v. Switzerland*, no. 41615/07, ECHR 2010, para. 135, although the case concerned parental abduction. In 2014, the ECtHR reiterated the preeminence of the BIC principle in the expulsion case of *Jeunesse v. The Netherlands*, no. 12738/10, ECHR 2014, paras. 109, 120. The importance of this development is more succinctly understood if contrasted again with previous jurisprudence, whereby the significance attached to the BIC was dependent upon the other factors surrounding the case, see also *Josef v. Belgium*, no. 70055/10, ECHR 2014, para. 142.

39 John Eekelaar, 'The Importance of Thinking That Children Have Rights' (1992) 6 International Journal of Law and the Family 57.

40 UNCRC Committee, General Comment No. 14 (n. 9 above) para. 6.

41 Concluding Observations to, inter alia, Jordan in 2006, UN Doc. CRC/C/JOR/CO/3, para 37.

42 UNCRC Committee, General Comment No. 14 (n. 9 above) para. 4; furthermore, the Committee emphasised that the BIC 'must be consistent with the whole Convention' and the concept 'cannot be used to justify practices … which conflict with the child's human dignity and right to physical integrity'. UNCRC Committee, General Comment No. 8 (2006) The Right of the Child to Protection from Corporal Punishment and Other Cruel or Degrading Forms of Punishment (Arts. 19, 28, para 2, and 37, inter alia), 2 March 2007, CRC/C/GC/8, para 26.

43 Smyth, *The Common European Asylum System and the Rights of the Child* (n. 13 above) 31.

whether the national authorities have undertaken an action, such as detention, having the BIC as a primary consideration will be assessed against the degree to which the child's rights overall have been respected.

As per the above analysis, a shift can be observed in the international and regional approaches to BIC. Through evolutive interpretations, the concept has come to acquire an increased significance to the point of arguably transcending treaty boundaries and incrementally growing into a general principle of international law.[44] Indeed, a comprehensive assessment of the BIC while considering the interrelationship of the concept with other core children's rights can inform national decision-making when it comes to immigration detention. In this context, the specific relationship between the BIC and the right to liberty and family unity, respectively, are explored below.

3. IMMIGRATION DETENTION AND THE RIGHT TO LIBERTY

The rights that are implicated in any given context serve as useful indicators for what the BIC are in that specific context.[45] Accordingly, in order to determine the BIC in the immigration context and, more specifically, whether detention can ever be in the BIC, one must examine the rights that are at stake in the said context, starting with the right to liberty.

3.1. INDIVIDUALS DEPRIVED OF LIBERTY

The right to liberty constitutes one of the fundamental rights of human beings and as such, it has a prominent position in international and regional human rights frameworks.

3.1.1. International Standards

Article 31 of the Refugee Convention begins with the presumption against the imposition of punitive measures to asylum seekers who make an unauthorised entry into another country when their life and freedom are at risk,[46] due to

---

44 For an extensive analysis on the evidence pointing to the conclusion that the BIC principle has acquired customary status, see Dina Imam Supaat, 'The Principle of the Best Interests of the Child as the Basis of State Obligation to Protect Refugee Children in Malaysia' (2012) SEAJCBEL, Vol. 1, ISSN 2289-1560.

45 Smyth, *The Common European Asylum System and the Rights of the Child* (n. 13 above) 86.

46 UNHCR Excom. Conclusion No. 44 (XXXVII), Detention of Refugees and Asylum-Seekers, 13 October 1986, in which it is mentioned that detention should be avoided due to the hardship involved and sets out grounds and conditions of detention, should it be applied.

their vulnerable position and their often traumatic background, which inhibits their ability to conform to legal entry formalities.[47] This also finds support in Article 8(1) of the Reception Conditions Directive according to which no one shall be detained for the sole reason of being an asylum seeker. Similarly, it has been held that criminalising the illegal entry of asylum seekers, inter alia, 'exceeds the legitimate interest of States to control and regulate illegal immigration and leads to unnecessary detention'.[48]

For its part, the UNHCR has identified a number of legitimate justifications for detention.[49] However, the blanket use of detention on the basis of these justifications, without an individualised assessment that also takes into account the particular situation and needs of certain categories of asylum seekers, including children,[50] can potentially infringe the principles of necessity and proportionality and thus be arbitrary.

Human rights treaties do leave room for depriving asylum seekers of their liberty, but in only limited circumstances and only if such deprivation is accompanied by clearly defined justifications and safeguards.[51] For instance, Articles 9 and 10 ICCPR only allow deprivation of liberty if the grounds thereof are prescribed by law, a determination that involves an assessment of reasonableness and predictability,[52] while providing a series of procedural safeguards and detention conditions to which detained persons are entitled. In this regard, 'inappropriateness, injustice, lack of predictability and due process of law',[53] as well as necessity and proportionality, are elements to be assessed

---

47 UNHCR 'Revised Guidelines on Applicable Standards and Criteria relating to the Detention of Asylum-Seekers' (February 1999), Guidelines 2 and 3.

48 Working Group on Arbitrary Detention, Report on the Promotion and Protection of all Human Rights, Civil, Political, Economic, Social, and Cultural Rights, Including the Right to Development to the 7th Session of the HRC, A/HRC/7/4, 10 January 2008, para. 53. This was most recently echoed in Joint General Comment No. 4 (2017) of the Committee on the Protection of the Rights of All Migrant Workers and Members of their Families and No. 23 (2017) of the CRC Committee on State obligations regarding the human rights of children in the context of international migration in countries of origin, transit, destination and return, UN Doc. CMW/C/GC/4-CRC/C/GC/23, para. 7.

49 UNHCR Detention Guidelines (n. 4 above), Guidelines 4.1 and 4.1.3; HRC, *A v. Australia*, Communication No. 560/1993, UN Doc. CCPR/C/59/D/560/1993, Views adopted on 3 April 1997, para. 9.4; *A and Others v. UK*, no. 3455/05, ECHR 2009, para. 185. For the meaning of national security, see UN Commission on Human Rights, The Siracusa Principles on the Limitation and Derogation Provisions in the International Covenant on Civil and Political Rights, 28 September 1984, E/CN.4/1985/4, paras. 29–32; *Geleri v. Romania*, no. 33118/05, ECHR 2011, paras. 35–36.

50 UNHCR Detention Guidelines (n. 4 above), Guidelines 4 and 9.2.

51 See e.g. Arts. 3 and 9 UDHR; Art. 9 ICCPR; Art. 14 CRPD; Art. 31 Refugee Convention; Art. 5 ECHR; Art. 7 ACHR; Art. 6 African Charter of Human and People's Rights; Art. 6 Charter.

52 HRC, *Hugo van Alphen v. The Netherlands*, Communication No. 305/1988, UN Doc. CCPR/C/39/D/305/1988, Views adopted on 23 July 1990, para. 5.8.

53 HRC, *F.K.A.G. v. Australia*, Communication No. 2094/2011, UN Doc. CCPR/C/108/D/2094/2011, Views adopted on 20 August 2013, para. 9.3.

when determining whether such deprivation is 'prescribed by law' or is otherwise arbitrary.[54] This inevitably implies that an evaluation of individual circumstances is required when authorities purport to apply or prolong detention. Moreover, failure to apply less intrusive measures to reach the same objectives, when available, reaches the arbitrariness threshold.[55] Beyond a justified initial period of detention for the purposes of registration and identity checks, any further detention of asylum seekers must be based on individual-specific risks of absconding, of committing crimes against others or acts against national security.[56] Thus, the above-described standards can be said to rule out mandatory or indefinite immigration detention since it inevitably lacks an individualised case-by-case assessment approach, while detention as an option is confined to very narrowly-defined parameters.[57]

3.1.2. European Standards

Article 5 ECHR, which secures the right to liberty, does not include an arbitrariness clause as such, but rather includes an exhaustive list of grounds that can justify deprivation thereof. Most pertinently, Article 5(1)(f) allows administrative detention of people who seek to make an unauthorised entry into another country or who are subject to deportation proceedings, provided that it is prescribed by law and thus has a foreseeable and 'sufficiently accessible and precise' legal basis[58] and is accompanied by procedural safeguards.[59] However, in contrast with the Human Rights Committee's (HRC) approach, the ECtHR has not yet consistently established an individual assessment requirement as part of its necessity or proportionality tests under Article 5(1)(f) ECHR,[60] as long as 'due diligence' is observed in deportation proceedings[61] or as long a detention

54 HRC, *A v. Australia* (n. 49 above) para. 9.2.

55 HRC, *C. v. Australia*, Communication No. 900/1999, UN Doc. CCPR/C/76/D/900/1999, Views adopted on 28 October 2002, para. 8.2; HRC, *Saed Shams and Others v. Australia*, Communications Nos. CCPR/C/90/D/1255, 1256, 1259, 1260, 1266, 1268, 1270 & 1288/2004, Views adopted on 11 September 2007, para. 7.2.

56 HRC, *F.K.A.G. v. Australia* (n. 53 above), para. 9.3.

57 Ibid., para. 9.3; Smyth, *The Common European Asylum System and the Rights of the Child* (n. 13 above) 274.

58 *Amuur v. France*, no. 19776/92 ECHR 1996-II, para. 50; *Del Rio Prada v. Spain*, no. 42750/09, ECHR 2013, para. 125.

59 Art. 5(2)–(5) ECHR. Additional requirements such as the court setting time limits to detention and providing detainees with legal, humanitarian or social assistance have also been established jurisprudentially, see *Amuur v. France*, ibid., para. 53.

60 Whilst the ECtHR has been seen requiring such an individualised assessment as part of the application of Art.5(1)(f) ECHR, this approach has not always found support in subsequent jurisprudence, *Popov v. France* (n. 33 above), para. 120. See also *Jusic v. Switzerland*, no. 4691/06, ECHR 2010, paras. 71–73; *Raza v. Bulgaria*, no. 31465/08 (2010), para. 74.

61 *Chahal v. The United Kingdom*, no. 22414/93, ECHR 1996-V, paras. 112–113.

is closely linked to the objective of averting unauthorised entry in a country.[62] There is therefore room for the ECtHR to take a more assertive stance, making individualised assessment an outright requirement, in line with the HRC and CRC Committee's approaches, discussed below.

The right to liberty and security is also guaranteed in Article 6 of the Charter, although no further reference is made to additional safeguards. In the EU asylum context, detention may be implicated during the process of the asylum procedure, for which the Reception Conditions and the Asylum Procedures Directives are relevant as well as pending transfer under Dublin III or return pursuant to a rejection of the asylum application. In the case of transfers, Article 28 of Dublin III makes clear that asylum seekers cannot be detained merely on the basis that they are subject to the Regulation, except if there is a 'significant risk of absconding', established on the basis of objective criteria defined by law (Art. 2(n)), individual circumstances and proportionality assessment as warranted by Article 52(1) of the Charter, as well as consideration of less coercive measures.[63]

In *Al Chodor*,[64] the CJEU aligns its interpretation on the arbitrariness element with that of the ECtHR and HRC in that detention on the basis of a domestic legal provision does not automatically make the detention lawful[65] unless it is sufficiently accessible, precise and foreseeable.[66] On this basis and in accordance with Article 25 of the Charter, which proclaims that no restrictions should be applied that would hinder the essence of the right, it follows that the prerequisites of lawfulness and non-arbitrariness in situations of immigration detention can in no circumstances be overlooked.[67]

3.2. CHILDREN DEPRIVED OF THEIR LIBERTY

Although the above-mentioned standards are age-neutral and apply equally to children and adults, further international and regional standards specifically focus on the implications of detention on children's rights.

---

62 *Saadi v. UK* [GC], no. 13229/03, ECHR 2008, para. 74.

63 Similar provisions are found in Art. 15 and Recital 26 Return Directive under which detention is only justified if a person's conduct will likely jeopardise the enforcement of a deportation order or there are fears of absconding. In any case, detention should be used only if 'strictly relevant', for the shortest possible time and with due diligence. Case C-61/11 PPU, *Hassen El Dridi*, Judgment of 28 April 2011, para. 39; Case C-534/11 *Arslan v. Policie ČR* [2013] ECR I, paras. 62–63; Case C-18/16 *K. v. Staatssecretaris van Veiligheid en Justitie* [2017] ECR I, Opinion of AG Sharpston, para. 73.

64 Case C-528/15 *Al Chodor* [2017] ECR I, para. 40.

65 *Mooren v. Germany*, no. 11364/03, ECHR 2009, paras. 76–77; HRC, *Hugo van Alphen v. The Netherlands* (n. 52 above), para. 5.8.

66 *Del Rio Prada v. Spain* (n. 58 above), para. 125; *Al Chodor* (n. 64 above), para. 40.

67 Case C-18/16, Opinion of AG Sharpston (n. 63 above), para. 73.

3.2.1. *International Standards*

While admitting that Article 24 ICCPR does not preclude the detention of minors *per se*,[68] the HRC has underlined that whenever children are involved, the requisite individualised assessment should be guided by the best interests and needs of children[69] and their mental health state,[70] or else there could be a violation of Articles 9 and 24 ICCPR.[71] The special position of children in general is also recognised by Article 10(3) ICESCR, which calls for 'special measures of protection and assistance' for children.

Most notably, the UNCRC establishes strict standards both to protect children from detention in the first place but also *in detention*. Thus, Article 37(b) UNCRC states that children shall not be deprived of their liberty unlawfully or arbitrarily whilst, in the cases where detention is deployed, it should only be used as a measure of last resort and only for the shortest possible time. This phraseology implies a requirement for individualised assessment to determine the lawfulness or arbitrariness of child detention, since the 'last resort and shortest possible time' requirement cannot be satisfied without examining the particular situation of the child concerned. This inference is also supported by the statement in Article 37(c) that the needs of children should be taken into account as per their age.[72] At a minimum, the above standards impliedly prohibit mandatory child immigration detention.

3.2.2. *European Standards*

ECtHR jurisprudence appears to be taking steps towards a more child-based approach to immigration detention, influenced by the UNCRC. In the absence of a general individual assessment requirement, it could follow that no BIC assessment is required to determine the lawfulness of detention under Article 5(1)(f) either.[73] Nevertheless, the ECtHR had already recognised in previous Article 8 case law that the BIC should be a primary consideration whenever a decision concerns children,[74] in light of the international consensus in this regard. However, the effect of Article 37(b) UNCRC in conjunction with

---

68 HRC, *Jollah v. The Netherlands*, Communication No. 794/1998, UN Doc. CCPR/C/74/D/794/1998, Views adopted on 15 April 2002, para. 8.3.

69 Ibid.; HRC, *Bakhtiyari v. Australia*, Communication No. 1069/2002, UN Doc. CCPR/C/79/D/1069/2002, Views adopted on 29 October 2003, para. 9.5.

70 HRC, *F.K.A.G. v. Australia* (n. 53 above), para. 9.3.

71 HRC, *Bakhtiyari v. Australia* (n. 69 above), para. 9.7.

72 William Schabas and Helmut Sax, 'A commentary on the United Nations Convention on the Rights of the Child, Article 37, Prohibition of Torture, Death Penalty, Life Imprisonment and Deprivation of Liberty' (Martinus Nijhoff Publishers 2006) 89.

73 Ibid.

74 *Neulinger and Shuruk v. Switzerland* (n. 38 above) para. 135.

the BIC principle is more notable in recent Article 5 ECHR jurisprudence. Firstly, in *Rahimi v. Greece*, the ECtHR, despite its traditional stance of not looking into the reasonableness, necessity and proportionality of detention within the scope of Article 5(1)(f), creates an exception for unaccompanied children, noting that the unaccompanied minor applicant's particular situation must have been taken into account by the administrative authorities combined with an assessment of his best interests as a matter of primacy.[75] The ECtHR recognised that accompanied minors are equally subject to individual assessment that should also encompass a BIC evaluation, notwithstanding the fact that they are with their parents or even accommodated in special 'family' wings.[76] The need for individual assessment is also alluded to in the Reception Conditions Directive. Although the provision on detention therein is age-neutral,[77] the special reception needs of vulnerable persons such as minors should be taken into account, including their (mental) health and best interests.[78]

What can be deduced at this point is that both international and European standards do allow a leeway for immigration detention of both children and adults, although within strictly defined parameters. As for asylum-seeking children, the standards are even more rigorous, with detention constituting an exceptional recourse.

3.3. CONDITIONS IN DETENTION

It should also be noted that a series of other children's rights might be breached when in detention, depending on the conditions.[79] Even when in detention, children enjoy the totality of their rights under the UNCRC.[80] In order for children to be treated 'with humanity and respect for the inherent dignity of the human person' when in detention,[81] their age-specific needs must be considered.[82] One potential interpretation of this statement is that 'needs' equates

75 *Rahimi v. Greece* (n. 10 above) para. 109.

76 *Popov v. France* (n. 33 above) paras. 119, 140.

77 Art. 8 Reception Conditions Directive.

78 Art. 11 Reception Conditions Directive.

79 Illustratively, the International Detention Coalition (IDC) highlights that poor health care and sanitation while in detention can impair the physical development of children whilst lack of education and recreational activities, combined with the disruption of family, can inhibit their cognitive, psychological and skills development, IDC, 'Captured Childhood' (2012) 51.

80 Most pertinently, detained children enjoy at all times the rights enshrined in Arts. 6, 11(2), 22, 19, 24, 27, 29, 31 and 34. See also Art. 17(3) Return Directive; UNHCR Detention Guidelines (n. 4 above), Guideline 9.2, para. 56. There is also a specific obligation enshrined in Art. 39 UNCRC according to which states must place children who have been victims of abuse or inhuman and degrading treatment of any kind in an environment that is conducive to their 'health, self-respect and dignity'.

81 As proclaimed by Art. 10 ICCPR and Art. 37(c) UNCRC.

82 Art. 37(c) UNCRC.

to 'rights', since all the rights enshrined in the UNCRC provide an unfaltering hint of what children's needs are.[83] It follows that if any right is violated, this may signal that the treatment received by the child amounts to inhuman and degrading treatment.[84]

As per the ECtHR, whether or not the requisite degree of severity to constitute inhuman or degrading treatment is reached will be judged according to all the circumstances of the case, including the duration and mental and physical effects of such treatment as well as the 'sex, age and state of health of the victim',[85] implying that the ill-treatment threshold for children asylum seekers could be lower. In the case of *Mayeka Mitunga*, the ECtHR found that placement in closed detention facilities that were not designed for children and did not take into account their extreme vulnerability breaches Article 3 ECHR.[86] The Court made clear that states bear a positive obligation under Article 3 ECHR to provide care and protection to vulnerable people, including children, which will always take precedence over their (illegal) migratory status,[87] with no relevance being attached to whether children are accompanied or unaccompanied.[88] Rather, the focal point is their extreme vulnerability as children, especially asylum-seeking children, reinforced by the need to give their best interests primary consideration.[89] The ECtHR in *Popov* recognised that this reasoning is in line with the Reception Conditions Directive, which does not distinguish between unaccompanied or accompanied children in terms of their degree of vulnerability,[90] as well as with Article 22 UNCRC, which assigns the responsibility to states to protect and provide humanitarian assistance to asylum-seeking children in general, notwithstanding them being with or without their parents.[91] Moreover, in *Zherdev*, the ECtHR found that keeping children with adults in detention can amount to ill-treatment given that it can cause detained children 'feelings of fear, anguish, helplessness and inferiority [and diminishment of] dignity'.[92]

83 Smyth, *The Common European Asylum System and the Rights of the Child* (n. 13 above) 280.

84 Art. 37(1) UNCRC; Art. 3 ECHR; Art. 7 ICCPR; Art. 4 Charter.

85 *Raninen v. Finland*, no. 20972/92 ECHR 1997-VIII, para. 55.

86 *Mubilanzila Mayeka and Kaniki Mitunga v. Belgium*, no. 13178/03, ECHR 2006, paras. 55, 59.

87 Ibid., para. 55; *Rahimi v. Greece* (n. 10 above), para. 87.

88 *Muskhadzhiyeva v. Belgium*, no. 41442/07, ECHR 2010, paras. 57–58.

89 *Kanagaratnam and Others v. Belgium*, no. 15297/09, ECHR 2011.

90 Art. 21 Reception Conditions Directive.

91 *Popov v. France* (n. 33 above), para. 91.

92 *Zherdev v. Ukraine*, no. 34015/07, ECHR 2017, paras. 92–93. In the same vein, Art. 10(2)(b) ICCPR as well as other international and European instruments specifically argue for separation of accused juveniles from adults in detention, from which it could also be argued that the separation principle applies in immigration detention involving children, as well. See, inter alia, Beijing Rules, r. 13.4; CoE Recommendations on European Rules for Juvenile Offenders Subject to Sanctions or Measures, CM/Rec (2008)/11, 5 November 2008, para. 59(1); CPT Standards, CPT/Inf/E (2002) 1, Rev. 2011, para. 100.

3.4. BEYOND 'LAST RESORT' AND TOWARDS ABOLITION?

As per the above, the UNCRC does allow room for child detention: it is permissible as a measure of last resort. However, an international consensus among human rights experts and organisations is starting to build up towards complete abolition of detention for migrant children.[93]

Already in 1997, the UNHCR advocated that asylum-seeking children should not be detained.[94] The UNHCR reiterated this position in 1999, which it justifies with reference to Articles 2, 3, 9, 22 and 37 UNCRC.[95] The UNHCR's strong commitment against child detention was echoed again in its 2012 Detention Guidelines,[96] as well as in its statement amid concerns over Hungary's amended laws in favour of mandatory detention. It highlighted that children should not be detained under any migration-related circumstances because detention can never be considered to be in the BIC[97] and cannot be justified on the basis that it is a measure of 'last resort', since Article 37(b) UNCRC does not apply to the immigration context.[98]

Both the CRC Committee and the Committee on the Protection of the Rights of All Migrant Workers and Members of their Families (CMW Committee) repeatedly stood against child detention on the basis of the child's or the parent(s)'s migratory status.[99] They recently established, for the first time, resonating with the UNHCR's position, that detention of children for immigration-related purposes is not permissible, not even 'as a measure of last resort' since Article 37(b) does not envisage situations that do not involve the commission of a crime, clarifying that irregular entry or stay do not constitute a crime.[100] The imposition of detention in such circumstances would

---

93 Marta Maurás Pérez, Vice-Chairperson of the CRC Committee in UNCRC Committee, Report of the 2012 Day of General Discussion (n. 7 above) para. 10.

94 UNHCR 'Guidelines on Policies and Procedures in Dealing with Unaccompanied Children Seeking Asylum' (February 1997) paras. 7.6 and 7.7.

95 UNHCR Revised Guidelines (n. 47 above) Guideline 6.

96 Ibid., Guideline 9.2, para. 51.

97 UNHCR deeply concerned by Hungary plans to detain all asylum seekers, Summary of UNHCR spokesperson Cécile Pouilly (press briefing at the Palais des Nations, Geneva, 7 March 2017) <http://www.unhcr.org/news/briefing/2017/3/58be80454/unhcr-deeply-concerned-hungary-plans-detain-asylum-seekers.html>.

98 UNHCR's position regarding the detention of refugee and migrant children in the migration context, Division of International Protection (January 2017) fn 11.

99 Joint General Comment No. 4 (2017) and No. 23 (2017) (n. 48 above), para. 5; UNCRC Committee, General Comment No. 6 (n. 6 above) paras. 40, 61. For a critical overview of the rather ambiguous stance of the CRC Committee on immigration detention, see Ciara M. Smyth, 'Towards a Complete Prohibition on the Immigration Detention of Children' (2019) 19 Human Rights Law Review 4–9.

100 Joint General Comment, ibid., para. 10. The UNHCR had already reached this conclusion earlier, UNHCR (n. 98 above) 2. On this basis, the CRC Committee recently called upon the EU and its Member States to establish an EU-wide ban on child immigration detention

contravene the BIC and the child's right to development.[101] A similar view was taken during the Committee's 2012 General Day of Discussion; participants clearly recognised that the lack of an absolute prohibition of child immigration detention constituted a 'significant protection gap'[102] and culminated in the CRC Committee itself urging states to 'expeditiously and completely' stop detaining children based on their or their parents' immigration status, since detention, *ipso facto*, goes against their rights and best interests, and thus cannot be justifiable.[103]

Finally, the CRC Committee takes a clear and unequivocal stance against child immigration detention. Although its recommendations remain non-binding, it now clearly urges its immediate prohibition, in law and in practice, even when children are accompanied.[104]

4. IMMIGRATION DETENTION AND FAMILY UNITY

Since this contribution is concerned with asylum-seeking children accompanied by their families, the implications that detention measures have on the family life and unity of those involved merits exploration.[105] The following analysis examines and questions the extent to which the preservation of family unity can be used to justify detention of the whole family, or whether family unity can, alternatively, support diversion of families away from detention.

---

that should clearly be reflected in EU law and notably in a revised version of the CEAS. See OHCHR, 'UN Child Rights Experts call for EU-wide ban on child immigration detention' (Geneva/Brussels, 21 February 2018) <https://www.ohchr.org/EN/NewsEvents/Pages/DisplayNews.aspx?LangID=E&NewsID=22681>.

101 Joint General Comment No. 4 (2017) and No. 23 (2017) (n. 48 above).

102 CRC Committee, Report of the 2012 Day of General Discussion (n. 7 above) para. 37.

103 Ibid., paras. 32, 78. This was more authoritatively repeated in the Joint General Comment No. 4 (2017) and No. 23 (2017) (n. 48 above), para. 5. This position was also upheld by the General Rapporteur for the CoE Parliamentary Campaign to End immigration detention of Children, Doris Fiala, calling child immigration detention 'a serious violation of children rights'. Inaugural Speech of Doris Fiala at the Launch of the Parliamentary Campaign to End immigration detention of Children (20 April 2015). Similarly, the UN Special Rapporteur on Torture strongly added that child immigration detention 'exceeds the requirement of necessity, becomes grossly disproportionate and may constitute cruel, inhuman or degrading treatment of migrant children', UN Human Rights Council, Report of the Special Rapporteur on torture and other cruel, inhuman or degrading treatment or punishment, 5 March 2015, A/HRC/28/68, para. 80.

104 Joint General Comment No. 4 (2017) and No. 23 (2017) (n. 48 above), paras. 5, 12.

105 There are different scenarios that are unfolding when accompanied asylum-seeking children are being processed by immigration authorities. For a comprehensive analysis, see Sarah Campbell, Antigoni Boulougari and Youngeun Koo, 'Fractured childhoods: the separation of families by immigration detention' (Bail for Immigration Detainees 2013).

4.1. THE RIGHT TO FAMILY UNITY

It should be noted from the outset that there is no universal definition of 'family'. The term has a broad meaning;[106] 'family' can be established taking into account the close ties[107] or dependency relationships shared between people,[108] and can encompass *de jure* or *de facto* carers of the child,[109] having regard to the BIC.[110] The following analysis sheds light on the central position of family life and unity at the international and European levels.

4.1.1. Family Unity: International Standards

The fundamental position of the family unit in society is entrenched in Article 23 ICCPR and Article 10(1) ICESCR.[111] Article 17 ICCPR further establishes the general right to privacy and family, while Article 24 ICCPR assigns the responsibility to the family, as well as the state and society in general, to protect children. The vital role of family in the asylum context is also recognised by

---

106 E.g. the UNCRC text alternates between different terms to describe family relations, such as 'parents', 'or other members of the family', 'members of the extended family or community as provided by local custom', 'legal guardians', 'other individuals [or] persons legally responsible for the child', 'others having financial responsibility for the child', 'persons having responsibility for the maintenance of the child', 'others responsible for the child' and 'any other person who has the care of the child'.

107 *K. and T. v. Finland [GC]*, no. 25702/94, ECHR 2001-VII, para. 150. Thus, 'family' has been held to encompass husband, wife and dependent children, with no distinction made for illegitimate children (see *Marckx v. Belgium*, no. 6833/74 (1979) Series A no. 31, para. 31), or adopted children (see *X v. Belgium and Netherlands* no. 6482/74, Decision of 10 July 1975; *Pini and Others v. Romania*, App nos. 78028/01 and 78030/01, ECHR 2004-V, para. 140), siblings (*Moustaquim v. Belgium*, no. 12313/86 (1991) Series A no. 193, para. 36), grandparents (see *Marckx v. Belgium*, para. 45) and even 'young adults [with] their parents and other close family members' (*Osman v. Denmark*, no. 38058/09, ECHR 2011, para. 55).

108 Art. 2(c) Reception Conditions Directive; Art. 2(j) Qualification Directive; Art. 2(g) Dublin III.

109 Art. 2(c) Reception Conditions Directive; Art. 2(j) Qualification Directive; Art. 2(g) Dublin III. It should be noted that, in the context of the CEAS, family relations must have existed in the country of origin. However, see the proposal of the European Commission, 'Proposal for a Regulation on the European Parliament and of the Council on standards for the qualification of third-country nationals or stateless persons as beneficiaries of international protection, for a uniform status for refugees or for persons eligible for subsidiary protection and for the content of the protection granted and amending Council Directive 2003/109/EC of 25 November 2003 concerning the status of third-country nationals who are long-term residents', COM(2016) 466 final, 2016/0223 (COD) Brussels, 13.7.2016, 16.

110 Recital 19 Qualification Directive: 'It is necessary to broaden the notion of family members, taking into account […] the special attention to be paid to the BIC.'

111 Similar articulations feature in other regional human rights instruments as well. See Art. 17(1) ACHR, Art. 16 European Social Charter, Art. 18(1) ACHPR.

the Refugee Convention, which recognises family unity as a fundamental right of refugees that should be protected by States[112] as a 'minimum basic human standard'.[113]

From a children's rights perspective, the right to family unity can be seen as a fulcrum of other children's rights. It holds a dominant position in the UNCRC text, which has earned it the description of a 'meta-norm'.[114] Article 16 UNCRC contains the general child's right to privacy, family and home, which states must protect from arbitrary or unlawful interference. Article 7(1) establishes children's right to know and be cared for by their parents, with Article 18(1) clarifying that it is (both) parents, or legal guardians where applicable, who have the primary and common responsibility 'for the upbringing and development' of their child(ren), with the BIC as their guiding and basic concern. Article 18(2) also attributes to the state a supporting role in childrearing, through the provision of all necessary assistance to parents. Article 8 provides for the preservation of the child's identity, which includes the maintenance of family relations and requires states to offer all appropriate assistance and protection against unlawful deprivation of such identity or elements thereof.

Article 9 UNCRC is the epitome of family unity: it contains a prohibition of separation of children from their parents against their will, unless such separation is in their best interests. The provision mentions two instances in which separation would serve the BIC, related to abuse/negligence factors and residence arrangements in case of parental separation. The wording of this provision implies that family unity is what the BIC requires, with the only impediment to family unity being the BIC *per se*, essentially turning the principle into a paramount consideration in this regard.[115] It can further be deduced from these examples that separation can only be justified on the basis of the BIC, if it is related to family relations and circumstances, ostensibly to the exclusion of any unrelated state-based considerations.[116]

4.1.2. Family Unity: European Standards

4.1.2.1. Council of Europe and Family Unity

Article 8 ECHR protects the right to private and family life, which encompasses a positive obligation to ensure that family life is effectively respected.[117] Several

---

112 Refugee Convention 1951, Recommendation B.

113 Excom Conclusion No. 22 ((XXXII), Protection of Asylum-Seekers in Situations of Large-Scale Influx (1981), para. II.B.2.(h)).

114 Smyth, *The Common European Asylum System and the Rights of the Child* (n. 13 above) 87.

115 Ibid., 176.

116 Ibid., 177.

117 *Maire v. Portugal*, no. 48206/99, ECHR 2003, para. 159.

principles have been identified in ECtHR jurisprudence that remain informative when assessing the importance attached to family life and unity at the Council of Europe (CoE) level, although they do not specifically pertain to the context of immigration detention.

The ECtHR reiterates that parents and children should be able to mutually enjoy each other's company, which constitutes a fundamental element of an effective family life.[118] In *Neulinger*, the ECtHR seems to confirm that the severance of family ties is a matter of exceptionality, confined to situations 'where the family has proved particularly unfit', and that all efforts must be undertaken to maintain family relations.[119] The growing tendency of the ECtHR to attach great weight to family unity, considering it a determinant factor of the BIC, can also be observed in the deportation case of *Nunez*, where the need to keep the children close to their mother took precedence over her deportation for immigration offences.[120] Thus, it appears that the ECtHR recognises family unity as a well-entrenched right that can trump immigration imperatives,[121] potentially even detention.

4.1.2.2. EU and Family Unity

The emphasis on the protection of family life and unity is also evident in the EU asylum context. Beyond the right to family life enshrined in Article 7 of the Charter in conjunction with Articles 33(1) and 24(3) thereof, the Reception Conditions, the Return and Qualification Directives all provide that family unity should be maintained in their respective areas.[122] While not excluding the detention of families, the Reception Conditions Directive places emphasis on the detention in 'separate accommodation, guaranteeing adequate privacy'[123] and family life is to be taken into account 'as far as possible' in the provision of housing.[124] The recitals to both the Return Directive and Dublin III make family life a 'primary consideration' in accordance with the Charter and ECHR, when considering return or transfer proceedings, respectively.[125] As regards minors, the Qualification Directive cites family unity as one of the factors to be taken

118 *Olsson v. Sweden (no. 1)*, no. 10465/83 (1988) Series A no. 130, para. 59; *Johansen v. Norway*, no. 17383/90 ECHR 1996-III, para. 52.

119 *Neulinger and Shuruk v. Switzerland* (n. 38 above) para. 136.

120 *Nunez v. Norway*, no. 55597/09, ECHR 2011, para. 84.

121 Although the Court tried to confine this finding to the 'concrete and exceptional circumstances of the case'. Ibid.

122 Art. 12 Reception Conditions Directive; Art. 23 Qualification Directive, pending determination of the status of asylum-seekers; Art. 14(a) Return Directive, pending return of asylum-seekers.

123 Art. 11(4) Reception Conditions Directive.

124 Art. 18(2)(a) Reception Conditions Directive.

125 Recital 22 Return Directive; Recital 14 Dublin III.

into account when determining the BIC.[126] This is in line with the presumption of the UNCRC, discussed above, that family unity is, *ipso facto*, in the BIC.[127]

4.2. FAMILY UNITY AND BIC DIMENSION

It should be recalled that all the rights enshrined in the UNCRC are considered to be in the BIC.[128] In other words, the extent to which states protect children's rights in the immigration context act as signposts of the extent to which immigration-related decisions are, in fact, in the BIC. Accordingly, an exploration of the relationship between family unity and the BIC may set states on the right track on what they are expected to do in this regard.

Articles 5 and 18 UNCRC recognise the responsibility of the parents or other guardians, broadly understood, to direct and guide children in the realisation of their rights enshrined therein as well as vest them with the primary responsibility of raising and assisting the development of their children, in line with their best interests. Thus, the right to family unity is not only a stand-alone obligation, but is also closely connected with the child's right to development.[129]

According to the BIC-model developed by Kalverboer and Zijlstra, in order to realise the child's right to development, bonds of attachment need to be established between parents or caregivers and the child, which is only possible if the former are actually available for the child.[130] Thus, the establishment of such bonds is a prerequisite for his/her best interests.[131] Moreover, the opportunity to have parents or guardians serve as examples of behaviour, values and cultural norms is also a precondition for compliance with the right to development,[132] which is also in line with Article 9 UNCRC, which stipulates the maintenance of regular and direct contact between parents and children.

At this point, it should be emphasised that the need to focus on what would be in the BIC does not automatically mean that no regard should be given to the situation of the children's parents when detained. This analysis is particularly relevant for the scenario whereby asylum-seeking parents or caregivers are kept in detention and how this has implications for the children and their rights, even if not themselves detained.[133]

---

126 Recital 18 Qualification Directive.

127 Smyth, *The Common European Asylum System and the Rights of the Child* (n. 13 above) 176.

128 UNCRC Committee, General Comment No. 14 (n. 9 above) para. 4.

129 François Crépeau, Preface to IOM, Children on the Move (2013) 3.

130 Kalverb Kalverboer and Zijlstra, 'Best Interest of the Child – model (BIC-Model)' (2006), no. 7.

131 Ibid., no. 3.

132 Ibid., no. 5.

133 It is worth taking note as well as interpretative inspiration from the African Committee of Experts on the Rights and Welfare of the Child (ACERWC) and its General Comment No. 1 focusing on the incarceration of parents and/or caregivers, whereby it clarifies that the BIC

In fact, any attempt to disassociate the needs of parents from their children's or to completely exclude the parents' situation from the BIC determination has been characteristed as a 'fallacy'.[134] This characterisation is based on the premise that the well-being of caregivers influences heavily the well-being of children.[135] The CRC Committee itself has recognised this interdependency.[136] In order for children to be provided with a family environment conducive to their development, appropriate care and protection should be afforded to their primary caregivers,[137] as recognised in Article 18(2) UNCRC. A potential consequence of separation or 'handicapped' parenting is that it makes children more vulnerable to the types of abuse and exploitation[138] against which states are obligated to protect them.[139]

In relation to families in detention, the child's right to an adequate standard of living 'appropriate for the child's physical, mental, spiritual, moral and social development',[140] can be interpreted to extend to his/her caregivers, since they need to be in a position to provide such conditions to their children. The placement in detention, in often deplorable conditions, essentially curtails the ability of parents to parent in a way that would be adequate to their child's development, either due to being separated altogether or due to the mental and psychological effects associated with detention.[141] Another argument that can be raised is that by keeping parents or caregivers in detention, even if the children are not detained themselves, the disruption of family unity that ensues serves as punishment of both the 'illegally migrating' parents and the children.[142] This arguably goes against not only the right to family unity, but also the non-discrimination clause.[143]

---

do not automatically exclude the possibility of parent detention but rather, what the BIC require are adequately trained judicial officers who are in a position to appropriately balance the BIC against the gravity of the offence that is on the other end of the scale and public security. See ACERWC, General Comment No. 1 (Article 30 of the African Charter on the Rights and Welfare of the Child) on Children of incarcerated and imprisoned parents and primary caregivers (2013), ACERWC/GC/01, para. 39.

134 Barbara Bennett Woodhouse, 'Hatching The Egg: A Child-Centered Perspective on Parents' Rights' (1993) 14 Cardozo Law Review 1747–1864, at 1825.

135 Zijlstra, 'In the best interest of the child' (n. 7 above) 30.

136 UNCRC, General Comment No. 7 (n. 9 above) para. 20.

137 Michael Freeman, 'Why It Remains Important to Take Children's Rights Seriously' (2007) 15 International Journal of Children's Rights 16.

138 Ibid.

139 Art. 19 UNCRC.

140 Art. 27(1) UNCRC. This provision also provides that the state must furnish caregivers with material support and assistance via, inter alia, the provision of housing.

141 IDC, 'Captured Childhood' (n. 79 above) 48.

142 Smyth, *The Common European Asylum System and the Rights of the Child* (n. 13 above) 90.

143 Art. 2(2) UNCRC protects children against discrimination and punishment on the basis of, inter alia, their parents, legal guardians, or family members' activities; UNCRC Committee, General guidelines regarding the form and content of initial reports to be submitted by

Ultimately, maintaining family unity is, in fact, essential for the protection and realisation of a series of other rights.[144]

4.3. FAMILIES IN IMMIGRATION DETENTION

In recognition of the reality that children are detained daily despite the documented legal and psychological implications involved, standards have been developed at both the international and European levels calling for the preservation of family unity while in detention. The ECtHR has recognised that irrespective of whether children are accompanied by their families, they should still be treated as children first, over and above their (illegal) migratory status.[145] To this effect, international and European standards urge the placement of families together in separate,[146]open facilities conducive to the meaningful enjoyment of their family life.[147] However, certain restrictions are permissible in the EU context, whereby states are to observe family unity only 'as far as possible'[148] and not necessarily when families are detained in border or transit zones.[149] Family unity is thus contingent upon what is 'possible', rather than on what the BIC require, which would be the only justification for separation under the UNCRC.[150] In the absence of CJEU case law, to affirm the primacy of family unity and the BIC in the implementation of Directives, it is suggested that it should take an assertive stance on the question, at the first opportunity, and that any future recast of the CEAS instruments restrict justifications for interference with family unity to circumstances consistent with the UNCRC's child-based approach.

At this time, the focus appears to be on assessing the suitability of detention facilities and conditions rather than on the unsuitability of detention as a measure to protect family unity *per se*. This is illustrated in the case of *Popov*, where the ECtHR did not consider the length of detention of accompanied children as excessive on its own; the finding of excessiveness was rather due to the inappropriateness of the detention facilities for children of that age.[151] Both the Luxembourg and Strasbourg courts have yet to clarify whether detention

States Parties under Article 44, paragraph 1(a) of the Convention, UN Doc. CRC/C/5 (1991), para. 13.

144 Smyth, *The Common European Asylum System and the Rights of the Child* (n. 13 above) 87.

145 *Mayeka and Mitunga v. Belgium* (n. 86 above) para. 55; *Muskhadzhiyeva v. Belgium* (n. 88 above) para. 62.

146 Art.23(5) Reception Conditions Directive.

147 UNCRC Committee, Report of the 2012 Day of General Discussion (n. 7 above) para. 39.

148 Art. 12 Reception Conditions Directive.

149 Art. 11(6) Reception Conditions Directive.

150 Smyth, *The Common European Asylum System and the Rights of the Child* (n. 13 above) 187.

151 *Popov v. France* (n. 33 above) para. 100.

of families with children in closed facilities constitutes *per se* a violation of the ECHR and Charter, respectively, regardless of the specific conditions encountered therein.[152] In this regard, it is suggested that both courts should, at the earliest opportunity, focus their reasoning on the outright prohibition of detention as a suitable option for children; this prohibition, in conjunction with the children's need to stay united with their family for the effective enjoyment of the totality of their rights, should lead to the diversion of the entire family away from detention as the only possible solution that is consistent with the BIC.

4.4. RIGHT TO FAMILY UNITY AND RIGHT TO LIBERTY: CONFLICTING OR CONCURRING RIGHTS?

The final point that merits consideration is whether the right to family life can justify the deployment of immigration detention. Such an approach appears to coincide with the UNHCR's initial stance according to which detention should not be applied for accompanied asylum-seeking children 'unless this is the only means of maintaining family unity'.[153] However, this should in no way imply that children should be detained for the purposes of family unity without having regard to the requirements of Article 37(b) UNCRC, which always requires an individualised assessment. In fact, there appears to be a suggestion, on the part of the CRC Committee, that if detaining children will not comply with the Article 37(b) requirements, then Article 9(1) should be used to justify the diversion of the whole family away from detention.[154]

This position is the starting point for a shift that can be observed in recent international and regional standards. This shift rests on the assumption that there is no hierarchy between UNCRC rights, and that a decision or practice cannot be interpreted to be in the BIC if it violates other children's rights.[155] A variation in approach can be observed in the more recent UNHCR guidelines pertaining to the detention of asylum seekers, which does not mention the maintenance of family unity as a viable justification for child detention.[156] Instead, the UNHCR takes a stronger stance in favour of taking into account the whole family's

152 Stijn Smet, 'ECtHR v Belgium on detention of children: part II' (Strasbourg Observer Blog, 13 April 2010) <https://strasbourgobservers.com/2010/04/13/ecthr-v-belgium-on-detention-of-children-part-ii/>.

153 UNHCR Revised Guidelines (n. 47 above) Guideline 6.

154 UNCRC Committee, Concluding Observations to Belgium in 2010, UN Doc. CRC/C/BEL/CO/3-4, para. 77, whereby the Committee urges Belgium to stop detention in closed centres and introduce alternatives to detention for asylum-seeking families.

155 UNCRC Committee, General Comment No. 14 (n. 9 above) para. 4.

156 UNHCR Detention Guidelines (n. 4 above).

right to private and family life, in conjunction with the BIC and the extent that detention facilities are suitable for children.[157] The CRC Committee's 2012 General Day of Discussion also revealed a consensus against the use of detention measures in the pretext of maintaining family unity and a preference for diversion of the entire family from detention.[158]

The ECtHR has embraced the same approach in its *Popov* judgment, emphasising that maintaining family unity does not necessarily mean respecting family life.[159] It made clear that the BIC called not only for the maintenance of family unity but also for the diversion from custody, 'as far as possible', of families with children. It signalled that, in the absence of risks of absconding, detention of families would be disproportionate and a violation of Article 8 ECHR.[160] The shift in approach can more clearly be understood if seen against the earlier judgment of *Muskhadzhiyeva*. Given that in that case the ECtHR found a violation of Articles 3 and 5(1)(f) ECHR due to the conditions endured in detention,[161] states may be required to not detain children with their families, but rather take steps to release them altogether as the only way to comply with Articles 8, 3 and 5(1)(f) ECHR.

The above analysis culminates in the conclusion that the right to family unity should no longer be used to justify the deployment of detention of the whole family. Instead, a child-based approach to family unity supports the diversion of the whole family away from detention.

5. CONCLUSION

This chapter presents a child-based approach to immigration detention, taking accompanied asylum-seeking children as the point of reference in an attempt to clarify the legal obligations of state immigration authorities. In light of the ever-persisting use of detention measures as a deterrent to migration flows,[162] it becomes imperative not to lose sight of the fact that asylum-seeking children

157 Ibid., Guideline 9.2, para. 53.

158 UNCRC Committee, Report of the 2012 Day of General Discussion (n. 7 above) para. 39; Joint General Comment No. 4 (2017) and No. 23 (2017) (n. 48 above) provides clear authoritative guidance to this effect, para. 11.

159 *Popov v. France* (n. 33 above) para. 134.

160 Ibid., paras. 147–148.

161 *Muskhadzhiyeva v. Belgium* (n. 88 above), para. 98. Note that in the case, the ECtHR did not find a violation of Art. 8 ECHR, given that the children were detained along with their mother.

162 See, inter alia, Thomas Gammeltoft-Hansen and Nikolas F. Tan, 'The End of the Deterrence Paradigm? Future Directions for Global Refugee Policy' (2017) 5 Journal on Migration and Human Security 28; Alice Edwards, 'Detention under scrutiny in Forced Migration Review: Detention, alternatives to detention, and deportation', Refugee Status Centre, Issue 44, September 2013, 4.

are children first and foremost, and are thus entitled, at all times, to the totality of their rights stemming from human rights law as well as the UNCRC, including their rights to liberty and family unity.

Deprivation of liberty is already confined to narrowly-defined circumstances and is subject to individual assessment, which rules out the mandatory and/or indefinite detention of migrant children as, *ipso facto*, arbitrary. Although the ECtHR is lagging in making individualised assessment a prerequisite for detention under Article 5(1)(f), such assessment seems essential when children are involved, in light of the BIC. The added value of the BIC principle in the context of child immigration detention is better grasped if seen against the heightened importance that the concept has come to acquire in the international and European contexts, which incrementally seem to embrace the paramountcy of the BIC vis-à-vis non-human-rights-based considerations,[163] including immigration control imperatives.[164]

On their face, international and European norms still leave room for child detention as a measure of last resort. However, there appears to be a growing international consensus that complete abolition of child immigration detention is required. Detention *per se*, as well as the conditions endured therein, may contravene other children's rights, such as the right to be free from inhuman and degrading treatment and their right to development and, as such, can never be considered in the BIC, not even as a last resort.[165] Thus, in light of this shift in approach at both the international and European levels, it can be concluded that child immigration detention *should* be out of the question.

The chapter also shed light on the centrality of family unity as a fundamental prerequisite for the realisation of children's rights, and, by extension, as part and parcel of the BIC. In light of the disruptive effects of detention on family unity, it can be concluded that immigration detention contravenes not only the principle of family unity *per se*, in case of separation, but also leads to violations of other children's rights. Most notably, the subversion of family relations that ensues breaches their right to development, inextricable as it is, with all the UNCRC rights.[166] Accordingly, states should no longer justify the deployment of detention policies on the basis of maintaining family unity. Family unity cannot and should not trump children's right to liberty. Both rights must be respected and realised concurrently.

In light of the growing international consensus against detention of children for immigration purposes, the centrality of family unity, and the increasing

163 *Neulinger and Shuruk v. Switzerland* (n. 38 above) para. 135.

164 UNCRC Committee, General Comment No. 6 (n. 6 above), para. 86; UNHCR, Guidelines on Determining the Best Interests of the Child (n. 17 above).

165 UN Human Rights Council, *Report of the Special Rapporteur* (n. 103 above); UNHCR's position (n. 98 above); Joint General Comment No. 4 (2017) and No. 23 (2017) (n 48 above).

166 See the discussion in section 4.2.

weight attributed to the BIC, non-detention and resort to alternative non-custodial measures should be the default position for both children and their families. A number of such alternatives have been introduced thus far.[167] Their implementation, if carried out properly, with due regard to procedural guarantees, cannot only contribute to a more humane asylum process that is more respectful of children's rights, but may also satisfy immigration control imperatives, proving that the two are not mutually exclusive objectives.

[167] See e.g. Joint General Comment No. 3 (2017) and No. 22 (2017) (n. 18 above); Joint General Comment No. 4 (2017) and No. 23 (2017) (n. 48 above), para. 12, both suggesting community-based care solutions; UNHCR Detention Guidelines (n. 4 above); UNHCR and OHCHR, Global Roundtable on Alternatives to Detention of Asylum-Seekers, Refugees and Migrants and Stateless Persons: Summary Conclusions, May 2011; Geert Verbauwhede, 'Alternatives to Detention for Families with Minor Children – The Belgian Approach', a discussion paper for EU Asylum Conference 13–14 September 2010.

THE DETENTION OF UNACCOMPANIED MINORS IN EU ASYLUM LAW

What is Left of Children's Rights?

Audrey PLAN*

1. INTRODUCTION

Child migrants are not a phenomenon specific to the EU, nor is detention the only issue that unaccompanied children face. But in 2017, minors still accounted

* Doctoral candidate and research assistant at the Department of Political Science, Trinity College Dublin, Ireland. I would like to thank the organising committee of the conference, as well as the editors and reviewers for their advice and feedback in the preparation of this chapter.

for a third of all asylum seekers in the EU; among them, almost 15 per cent were unaccompanied, for a total of more than 30,000 asylum applications from unaccompanied minors in the EU.[1] This number has only just started to decrease, following the general trend of first-time asylum applications in the EU, but had been rising constantly ever since the 1990s.[2] Unaccompanied children are becoming a population which therefore must be factored into the EU asylum system, and their vulnerability must be considered. Moreover, asylum laws and policies can no longer be considered purely from a national, domestic perspective, as these competences have started to be transferred by Member States to the EU ever since the Amsterdam Treaty and the communautarisation of the 1985 Schengen Agreements and their 1990 Implementing Convention. Regarding the focus on detention of this chapter, it appears to be one of the most pressing issues for unaccompanied minors seeking asylum: detention is a total deprivation of liberty, here inflicted on one of the most vulnerable parts of the population. It seems to have been normalised in the context of immigration laws and policies in the EU since the 1990s,[3] but any authority which wishes to use this mechanism outside of a punitive context needs to tread very carefully, or risk violating the fundamental rights of a very vulnerable population.[4]

In this chapter, it will be examined whether or not the EU does tread carefully when it comes to allowing or demanding the placement of unaccompanied minors in detention by national authorities. Does the Common European Asylum System (CEAS) properly uphold international human rights and children's rights standards in its detention system for unaccompanied minors?

To begin with, the CEAS is made up of multiple instruments, and most of them were recast in 2013. However, concerning detention, the only ones relevant and which will be studied here are the Reception Conditions Directive (for asylum applicants whose claim is being processed (RCD)),[5] the Dublin

---

1 Eurostat, 'Over 31 000 Unaccompanied Minors among Asylum Seekers Registered in the EU in 2017' (16 May 2018) Press Release 84/2018.

2 European Commission, 'Background Paper for the 10th European Forum on the Rights of the Child: The Protection of Children in Migration' (5 February 2018); Jyothi Kanics and Daniel Senovilla Hernandez, 'Protected or Merely Tolerated? Models of Reception and Regularization of Unaccompanied and Separated Children in Europe' in Jyothi Kanics and others (eds.), *Migrating Alone: Unaccompanied and Separated Children's Migration to Europe* (UNESCO 2010).

3 Mary Bosworth and Sarah Turnbull, 'Immigration Detention, Punishment, and the Criminalization of Migration' in Sharon Pickering and Julie Ham (eds.), *The Routledge Handbook on Crime and International Migration* (Routledge 2014).

4 UN Committee on the Rights of the Child, 'General Comment No. 6 on the Treatment of unaccompanied and separated children outside their country of origin' (2005) in 'Note by the Secretariat, Compilation of General Comments and General Recommendations Adopted by Human Rights Treaty Bodies' (8 May 2006) UN Document HRI/GEN/1/Rev.8.

5 European Parliament and Council Directive 2013/33/EU laying down standards for the reception of applicants for international protection [2013] OJ L180/96.

Regulation (which indicates which country is responsible for processing the claim, and allows for the transfer of an asylum seeker from one Member State to another)[6] and the Return Directive (for those whose asylum claim has been denied and will be returned to their country of origin, or a 'safe country').[7] These instruments are all, however, undergoing a reform, for which negotiations are still ongoing within the EU.[8] As a result, throughout this study and for each instrument, reference will be made to the recast proposal of the Commission.

Some precision must then be given regarding the specific vocabulary which will be used throughout this study. To begin with, the EU provides a definition of 'unaccompanied minor' as

> 'a minor who arrives on the territory of the Member States unaccompanied by an adult responsible for him or her whether by law or by the practice of the Member State concerned, and for as long as he or she is not effectively taken into the care of such a person; it includes a minor who is left unaccompanied after he or she has entered the territory of the Member States.'[9]

This definition is in line with the UN Guidelines on unaccompanied minors.[10] The concept of 'detention' under EU law is also defined within the CEAS as 'confinement of an applicant by a Member State within a particular place, where the applicant is deprived of his or her freedom of movement',[11] meaning that any place where an asylum seeker is not allowed to leave is synonymous with a detention facility, even without having this specific name (e.g. a 'reception centre').

It must also be specified that a few elements are not discussed in this chapter. First of all, as unaccompanied minors not seeking asylum are not included in the EU framework, their situation will not be studied here. EU competences

---

6 European Parliament and Council Regulation 604/2013 establishing the criteria and mechanisms for determining the Member State responsible for examining an application for international protection lodged in one of the Member States by a third-country national or a stateless person [2013] OJ L180/31.

7 There are other texts from various European institutions on the topic of child migrants, unaccompanied migrants, migration detention, such as the EU Plan of Action for unaccompanied minors, or the Agenda for the Rights of the Child; however, they are interpretative and indicative rather than normative.

8 Council of the European Union, 'Reform of the Common European Asylum System and Resettlement – Progress report 6600/19' (26 February 2019): no definite agreement has been reached for the recast any of the instruments so far.

9 European Parliament and of the Council Directive 2013/33/EU laying down standards for the reception of applicants for international protection [2013] OJ L180/96; the exact same definition is used in ever EU instruments in the CEAS.

10 UNHCR 'Guidelines on Policies and Procedures in dealing with Unaccompanied Children Seeking Asylum' (1997).

11 Ibid.

are currently limited to asylum seekers, and immigration policies and norms, although at least partly integrated in the EU, are still mainly the competence of Member States.[12] Secondly, the issue of detention is linked with many other fundamental rights, especially for children, such as the rights to education, to family unity or to have legal representation. Lastly, the focus of the chapter will be the CEAS itself, and not the issues related to its implementation by Member States or the oversight of the implementation by the Commission.

As a result, the goal of this chapter will first be to clarify the framework of detention of unaccompanied minors in the CEAS, and research whether this status is in line with international standards; if not, what the reasons of the shortcomings are, and how those issues can be solved, what are the changes that must be implemented. This will allow us to cast a critical eye over the elements of reform currently made public by EU institutions, examining them from the perspective of children's rights, and try to extrapolate what can be expected from the EU on the detention of unaccompanied minors who will seek asylum in an EU Member State in the future.

The legal framework laid down by the CEAS regarding the detention of unaccompanied minors will be confronted with international norms on human and children's rights, to assess and identify the possible shortcomings of the CEAS. The study will break down the unaccompanied minors detention framework into three categories, after first identifying what are the norms of international law which will be used as reference (section 2): the possible motives allowing for detention; (section 3); the duration of the detention (section 4), and the conditions and facilities of the detention (section 5). We will conclude by trying to classify the various shortcomings in specific categories and propose possible solutions to the shortcomings identified.

2. INTERNATIONAL STANDARDS ON THE DETENTION OF UNACCOMPANIED MINORS SEEKING ASYLUM

The first reference will be the UN Convention on the Rights of the Child (UNCRC), as it is the most relevant regarding children's rights.[13] The EU is not party to this Convention; however, all the Member States are, and Article 3 of the Treaty on European Union mentions that the EU shall 'contribute to the

---

12 This is an odd repartition of competences which has been criticised (see Raphaëlle Faure, Mikaela Gavas and Anna Knoll, *Challenges to a Comprehensive EU Migration and Asylum Policy* (Overseas Development Institute 2015)) but the EU still has to find a solution to this issue.

13 Guy S. Goodwin-Gill, 'Unaccompanied Refugee Minors: The Role and Place of International Law in the Pursuit of Durable Solutions' (1995) 3 Int'l J Child Rts 405.

protection of human rights, in particular the rights of the child' in its external actions. Other documents published by the Commission indicate that, while not strictly legally bound by the UNCRC, the EU's normative action is 'is firmly associated with the CRC'.[14] Article 37 of the UNCRC is relevant regarding detention, dealing with the right to protection against torture and deprivation of liberty of children. Moreover, General Comment No. 6 on the treatment of unaccompanied and separated children outside their country of origin[15] will also be taken into account.

The European Convention on Human Rights (ECHR) and the jurisprudence of the European Court on Human Rights (ECtHR) will be the second reference, given the Treaty on the European Union states plainly that 'Fundamental rights, as guaranteed by the European Convention for the Protection of Human Rights and Fundamental Freedoms (…) shall constitute general principles of the Union's law'.[16] The main point of reference here will be Article 5 on the right to protection against deprivation of liberty, but also Article 3 on the right to protection against torture, and inhuman or degrading treatment or punishment. Concerning Article 5, reference will be made to all possible five grounds given for detention, and not only the ground specific to minors (Art. 5(f)).[17]

As for the EU Charter, its Article 24 on the rights of the child could be used as another standard to measure the quality of the CEAS regarding detention (especially paragraph 2 on the best interest of the child and paragraph 1 on the rights to protection and care), given that both EU institutions and national authorities implementing EU law must comply with it.[18] However, given the lack of jurisprudence expanding on the notion of 'best interest of the child' and 'right to protection and care' under EU law,[19] the use of the charter will be

14 EU Agency for Fundamental Rights and Council of Europe, *Handbook on European Law Relating to the Rights of the Child* (Publications Office of the European Union 2015).

15 UNCRC, General Comment No. 6 (n. 4 above).

16 The interactions between the ECtHR and the European Union are unfortunately more complex than this chapter allows for; for a more detailed analysis, see Turkuler Isiksel, 'European Exceptionalism and the EU's Accession to the ECHR' (2016) 27 Eur. J. Int. Law 565.

17 *Mubilanzila Mayeka and Kaniki Mitunga v. Belgium* ECHR 2006-XI 267: 'The Court does not agree with the second applicant's submission that paragraph (d) of Article 5 §1 of the Convention is the only provision which permits the detention of a minor. It in fact contains a specific, but not exhaustive, example of circumstances in which minors might be detained, namely for the purpose of their educational supervision or for the purpose of bringing them before the competent legal authority to decide.'

18 Art. 51, Charter of Fundamental Rights of the European Union (2000) OJ C326/39.

19 Mark Klaassen and Peter Rodrigues, 'The Best Interests of the Child in EU Family Reunification Law: A Plea for More Guidance on the Role of Article 24(2) Charter' (2017) 19 European Journal of Migration and Law 191.

scarce here, and the ECHR and UNCRC provisions will be the most relevant for this study.

The 1997 UNHCR Guidelines on Policies and Procedures in dealing with Unaccompanied Children Seeking Asylum will also be used, as despite being 20 years old and being only interpretative, they continue to be one of the most specific documents provided by the UN.

3. THE MOTIVES FOR DETENTION: FROM UNSOUND VAGUENESS TO PROFOUND VIOLATIONS

Table 1. Overview of the ground for the detention of unaccompanied minors in the ECAS

Norm	General Detention Regime	Supplementary conditions for unaccompanied minors
RCD	✓ Individual assessment ✓ No other less coercive measure possible ✓ One of the 6 following situation:[20] ◦ ID Verification ◦ Verification of elements required to assess the asylum claim ◦ At the border, to assess the right to enter the territory ◦ Possibly abusive asylum claim for someone already detained under the Return Directive ◦ Threat to national security/public safety ◦ Detention under the Dublin Regulation	✓ Last resort ✓ Exceptional circumstances
Dublin Regulation	✓ Non negligible risk of absconding ✓ Individual assessment ✓ Proportionality of the placement in detention ✓ No other less coercive effective measure	*None*
Return Directive	✓ No other less coercive effective measure ✓ To prepare the return/removal process	✓ Last resort

Regarding the possible grounds for detention, the comparison of EU law with international standard is paradoxical. Indeed, the Directives' and Regulation's wording make them mostly in line with most international texts, but this wording allows for little to no actual safeguard for the rights of the unaccompanied

20 Another ground for detention has been added to the Recast RCD, in case of violation of the assignation to residence: Commission, 'Proposal for a Directive of the European Parliament and of the Council laying down standards for the reception of applicants for international protection (recast)' COM(2016) 465 final, Art. 8.3(c).

minors (section 2.1). However, when faced with the standards set specifically by the ECtHR, it appears that the detention framework set by EU law is sometimes in clear violation of human rights (section 2.2).

3.1. A SOLELY FORMAL COMPLIANCE OF THE CEAS WITH INTERNATIONAL NORMS

Regarding the possible grounds for the detention of unaccompanied minors, the one common idea found in international texts is 'last resort'. The UNCRC only mentions that detention 'shall be used only as a measure of last resort'. General Comment No. 6 does not give much more precision concerning the possible motives for detention, stating that it can be 'exceptionally justified for other reasons', and be in accordance with the previously mentioned provision of the UNCRC.[21] In the same line, the 1997 UNHCR Guidelines takes a slightly different approach, giving the clear recommendation that unaccompanied minors should not be kept in detention; it does not give specific grounds allowing detention, only acknowledging that some states do not follow the recommendation, and that for these states, the detention of unaccompanied minors should be used 'only as a measure of last resort'.[22]

Going back to the CEAS, the concept of 'last resort' for the detention of unaccompanied minors is explicitly mentioned in both the RCD and the Return Directive. In the Dublin Regulation, where there is no specific disposition for the detention of unaccompanied minors, the general framework applicable to them conditions the detention to the fact that 'other less coercive alternative measures cannot be applied effectively'.[23] The first problem which appears here is the lack of a proper definition given to these two terms under EU law; it can only be assumed that they do not have the same meaning, since in the RCD, the condition to place an adult in detention is lack of 'less coercive alternative measures', and for unaccompanied minors, 'last resort'. As a result, it seems that for the Dublin Regulation, the child-specific concept of 'last resort' is missing, preventing proper protection against the detention of unaccompanied minors, and cannot simply be replaced by the requirement for a lack of less coercive measure, which appears to be the 'adult' standard.

Moreover, the lack of definition of 'last resort' under EU law, the lack of criteria or guidelines to help authorities evaluate what is considered 'last resort', especially compared to the usual regime applicable to adults, makes it difficult

21 UNCRC, General Comment No. 6 (n. 4 above) para. 61.

22 UNHCR, Guidelines on Policies and Procedures in dealing with Unaccompanied Children Seeking Asylum (n. 10 above) para. 7.7.

23 European Parliament and Council Directive 2013/33/EU laying down standards for the reception of applicants for international protection [2013] OJ L180/96, Art. 28.2.

to ensure that the specific vulnerability of children will be taken into account. In other words, by using the very expression 'last resort', the RCD and the Return Directive are, on a textual basis, in line with the international norms. However, contrary to international conventions, the CEAS set up an actual detention regime, and should be expected to provide better safeguards, beyond respecting purely formal the letter of the conventions. As it is, there is no certainty as to the legal meaning of 'last resort', meaning no certainty that there is a real child-specific regime.

This issue of formal respect of international standards and yet lack of substantial safeguards in the actual detention regime is due to the inherent vagueness of international standards. As a result, it is essential to refer to the more comprehensive and elaborate ECHR and the jurisprudence of its Court.

3.2. SPECIFIC VIOLATIONS OF THE EUROPEAN CONVENTION ON HUMAN RIGHTS

In the last years, the ECtHR has developed quite a comprehensive jurisprudence on migration detention, even if there has been only a limited amount of cases involving unaccompanied minors so far. Two will here be used to examine the compatibility of EU law with the ECHR: the *Mubilanzila* ruling (2006)[24] and the *Rahimi* ruling (2011).[25] In the latter especially, the Court lays down the conditions for possible detention under Article 5: the ground for detention must be among one of the five motives listed by Article 5 of the ECHR, and detention must lawful and not be arbitrary. Moreover, the *Mubilanzila* case, though older, gives more specific guidelines on the detention regime of unaccompanied minors specifically.

3.2.1. The Textual Violation of Article 5 of by the CEAS

Article 5 of the ECHR provides five possible ground for detention, and two are relevant to the current study:

> 'b. the lawful arrest or detention of a person for non-compliance with the lawful order of a court or in order to secure the fulfilment of any obligation prescribed by law'

---

24 *Mubilanzila Mayeka and Kaniki Mitunga v. Belgium* (n. 17 above).

25 *Rahimi v. Greece* App no. 8687/08 (ECtHR, 5 April 2011). As there is no official English translation of this ruling, we will refer to the press release of the ECHR on this case (Registrar of the ECtHR, 'Press Release N°297: Inadequate Care and Unlawful Detention of an Unaccompanied Minor Seeking Asylum') and the Note on unaccompanied minors under the ECHR (ECtHR Press Unit, 'Factsheet – Unaccompanied Migrant Minors in Detention' 2018).

and

> 'f. the lawful arrest or detention of a person to prevent his effecting an unauthorized entry into the country or of a person against whom action is being taken with a view to deportation or extradition.'

As a result, what must be assessed is whether each ground for detention in the different instruments of the CAES is in line with one of these two provisions, as the list the article provides is exhaustive.[26]

Detention under the Dublin Regulation[27] and the Return Directive[28] fits with Article 5(f), as the goal of the detention is to ensure the removal from the national soil or the transfer to another state. As for the RCD, each of the five motives must be analysed individually, minus the one which is simply a reference to the Dublin Regulation.[29] First of all, detention for the sake of verifying the identity or any other documentation required to assess the asylum claim seems to fit within the boundaries of Article 5(b) (ensuring fulfilment of a legal obligation),[30] even if the vagueness of it has been criticised.[31] Detention at the border before entering the territory fits within Article 5(f). The two remaining provisions prove to be more questionable.

Allowing for an asylum seeker already detained under the Return Directive to remain in detention under the RCD for the reason that the asylum claim might be simply a means to delay the return means that the person is placed in detention on the ground of his/her asylum claim, and no longer for the sake of removal.[32] However, detention on the ground of an asylum claim is not only in violation of the ECHR (as this is not one of the possible grounds for detention according to Article 5), the General Comment no. 6[33] but also of Article 8(1) of

---

26 *Saadi v. UK* ECHR 2008-I 31, para. 43.

27 European Parliament and Council Regulation 604/2013 establishing the criteria and mechanisms for determining the Member State responsible for examining an application for international protection lodged in one of the Member States by a third-country national or a stateless person [2013] OJ L180/31, Art. 28.

28 European Parliament and Council Directive 2008/115/EC of 16 December 2008 on common standards and procedures in Member States for returning illegally staying third-country nationals [2013] OJ L 348/98, Art. 15.

29 European Parliament and Council Directive 2013/33/EU laying down standards for the reception of applicants for international protection [2013] OJ L180/96, Art. 8.3(f).

30 Phillippe de Bruycker and others, 'Alternatives to Detention in the EU – Time for Implementation' (Odysseus Network 2015) 50–51.

31 Ibid.

32 Contrary to the interpretation of the EU Fundamental Rights Agency, which considered this disposition to fall under Art. 5.f on removal of the territory (see EU Agency for Fundamental Rights, *Handbook on European Law Relating to the Rights of the Child* (n. 14 above) 44.

33 UNCRC, General Comment No. 6 (n. 4 above) para. 61.

the RCD itself, which prevents placing someone in detention simply because of their status as an asylum seeker.[34]

The other questionable disposition is the possibility to detain someone to protect national security or public safety, which currently exists under the RCD, and has been added to the Recast Return Directive still being negotiated.[35] There is no such ground under the ECHR, a problem which has already been raised both by scholars[36] and within the EU itself.[37] It could be argued that this disposition falls Article 5(c) of the ECHR, which allows for:

> 'the lawful arrest or detention of a person effected for the purpose of bringing him before the competent legal authority (...) when it is reasonably considered necessary to prevent his committing an offence (...).'

However, the Court specified that this preventive detention is a ground for detention to prevent someone from committing a specific offence, for pre-trial detention. In the words of the Court:

> 'Article 5 §1 (c) does not, thereby, permit a policy of general prevention directed against an individual or a category of individuals who are perceived by the authorities, rightly or wrongly, as being dangerous or having propensity to unlawful acts. That ground of detention does no more than afford the Contracting States a means of preventing a concrete and specific offence [...]. Under the Court's well-established case-law, detention to prevent a person from committing an offence must, in addition, be "effected for the purpose of bringing him before the competent legal authority", a requirement which qualifies every category of detention referred to in Article 5 §1 (c).'[38]

As a result, detention for a possibly abusive asylum claim is questionable, and detention to protect national security or public safety as organised by the CAES is in plain violation of the ECHR. But the other conditions set by the ECtHR to ensure proper respect of the right to liberty must now be analysed.

---

34 A way to use this article in a way which respects fundamental rights would be to raise it jointly with the dispositions on detention to prevent absconding, or to ensure identity or an element necessary to process the asylum claim (De Bruycker and others, 'Alternatives to Detention in the EU' (n. 30 above)). However, there is currently no obligation for Member States to do so, which therefore constitutes a threat to unaccompanied minors' rights.

35 European Commission, Proposal COM(2018) 634 final for a Directive of the European Parliament and of the Council on common standards and procedures in Member States for returning illegally staying third-country nationals (recast) [2018], Art. 18(c).

36 Ibid.

37 EU Agency for Fundamental Rights and Council of Europe, *Handbook on European Law Relating to the Rights of the Child* (n. 12 above).

38 *Ostendorf v. Germany* App no. 15598/08 (ECtHR 7 March 2013) paras. 66–67.

3.2.2. Lawfulness and Protection against Arbitrariness

First, the *Rahimi* case simply uses the conditions already laid out in the *Saadi* case to define what would characterise the arbitrariness of the detention. The Court states that detention must be 'carried out in good faith', 'closely connected to the purpose of preventing unauthorized entry of the person to the country', in 'the place and conditions of detention had to be appropriate', and 'the length of the detention should not exceed that reasonably required for the purpose pursued'.[39,40] It must be noted that in case of Article 5(b), there is also a requirement for necessity of the detention[41] (as opposed to Article 5(f) for which there is no such requirement).

Good faith can only be examined *in concreto*, as it relies on the course of action decided on by the authorities enforcing the norms; as for the second condition, it is Article 5(f) of the ECHR which was relevant in both the *Saadi* and the *Rahimi* cases, which means that this condition of an existing link between the goal of the detention and the actual detention holds whether the goal is to prevent entry or to ensure removal from the territory. One can wonder if the same test can be used when detention is on the ground of Article 5(b), as shown previously for some provisions of EU law. The rationale of the *James, Wells and Lee v. UK* case seems to indicate that it is the case: the point is that detention must be connected with its goal, this goal varying according to which ground for detention has been used.[42] As a result, whatever is the motive invoked under EU law, there must be a link between this motive and the detention itself. However, once again these elements are also appreciated *in concreto*; as a result, to properly assess whether children's rights are respected here, analysing the enforcement of EU law by national authorities would be necessary.

It is therefore more relevant to focus on the 'lawfulness' of the detention, meaning that the detention must be done under a specific provision, and that this legal provision must have a certain legal certainty. The first criterion is met, as there are specific provisions allowing for detention in the CEAS, but it is possible to question the 'quality of the law', which should allow for 'legal certainty', meaning 'a national law authorizing deprivation of liberty must be sufficiently accessible and precise, in order to avoid all risk of arbitrariness'.[43] However, one can question whether the CEAS checks this criterion, given the vagueness of many provisions, as seen previously, concerning the grounds for

39 *Rahimi v. Greece* (n. 25 above) para. 106.

40 For the provisions regarding the conditions and duration of the detention, see sections 3 and 4 of this chapter.

41 *Chahal v. The United Kingdom* ECHR 1996-V para. 112.

42 *James, Wells and Lee v. The United Kingdom* App no. 25119/09, 57715/09 and 57877/09 (ECHR 18 September 2012) para. 191.

43 *Mubilanzila Mayeka and Kaniki Mitunga v. Belgium* (n. 17 above) para. 97.

detention: the lack of definition of many expressions, and the differences in their meaning, such as 'last resort', 'no other less coercive means' and 'exceptional circumstances'.[44] It is reasonable to question whether an unaccompanied minor could be able to know exactly what he or she can expect concerning the possible ground for detaining him/her.

3.2.3. *Protection Afforded Specifically to Unaccompanied Minors*

The ECtHR does not set a different standard specifically for (unaccompanied) minors, but its jurisprudence requires taking into account the vulnerability of unaccompanied minors. In the *Rahimi* case, it was held that Greece violated Article 5 of the ECHR because the authorities had automatically enforced the national law allowing for the unaccompanied minor to be placed in detention. The Court considered that the obligation of good faith, to ascertain the arbitrariness of the detention, included the obligation to take into account the specific situation of these minors, their best interests, and the obligation to conduct an individual assessment of their needs.[45] Comparatively, EU law always requires taking into account the best interests of children, and always requires an individual assessment, whether the person placed in detention is an adult or a minor,[46] except in the Return Directive, where no such obligation of individual assessment exists, but the best interests of the child is still a 'primary consideration'.[47] As a result, any violation of this specific disposition comes not from the EU framework, but from either national law or the enforcement by national authorities.

The second relevant disposition can be found is the *Mubilanzila* ruling: in this case, Belgium found itself in violation of Article 5, as 'the Belgian legal system at the time and as it functioned in this instance did not sufficiently protect the second applicant's right to liberty', especially given that '[at that time, the [Belgian detention regime] did not contain any provisions specific to minors'.[48]

---

44 The limits of analysing EU law through the filter of the ECHR reaches, however, its limits here. Indeed, this analysis requires the assimilation of EU law to traditional national law. If this assimilation is possible for Regulations, which are enforced *as is* by Member States, this may not be the case for Directives, which, by their essence, are not specific and always give a certain leeway to Member States.

45 *Rahimi v. Greece* (n. 25 above), para. 108.

46 European Parliament and Council Directive 2013/33/EU laying down standards for the reception of applicants for international protection [2013] OJ L180/96, Art. 8.2; European Parliament and Council Regulation 604/2013 establishing the criteria and mechanisms for determining the Member State responsible for examining an application for international protection lodged in one of the Member States by a third-country national or a stateless person [2013] OJ L180/31, Art. 28.2.

47 European Parliament and Council Directive 2008/115/EC of 16 December 2008 on common standards and procedures in Member States for returning illegally staying third-country nationals [2013] OJ L 348/98, Art. 17.5.

48 *Mubilanzila Mayeka and Kaniki Mitunga v. Belgium* (n. 17 above), para. 99 and para. 104.

This is very relevant, concerning EU law, for the Dublin Regulation, which does not contain any specific provision for unaccompanied children regarding the grounds for detention. This appears to be in clear violation of the standards set by the ECHR.

The grounds for detention within the EU, despite their appearance of compliance with most international standards, prove to provide to insufficient safeguards and guarantees regarding the detention of unaccompanied minors, and are even in violation of the ECHR and its related jurisprudence. With these shortcomings having been identified, the same course of study can be followed for the framework on the duration of detention in the CEAS.

4. THE DURATION OF DETENTION: THE NECESSITY OF AN *IN CONCRETO* APPROACH

Table 2. Overview of the duration of the detention of unaccompanied minors in the CEAS

Norm	General Detention Regime	Supplementary conditions for unaccompanied minors
RCD	✓ Detention as short as possible ✓ As long as the motives for detention still stand	✓ Release as soon as possible
Dublin Regulation	✓ Detention as short as possible ✓ No detention beyond what is required to proceed with the administrative formalities ✓ 53 days maximum, broken down in shorter deadlines	✓ None
Return Directive	✓ Reasonable prospect of removal ✓ Original grounds for detention still stand ✓ As long as necessary to organise the return/ removal ✓ 6 months maximum, up to 18 months if: - Lack of cooperation by the person - Lack of cooperation by the state of return	✓ Shortest period of time possible

When looking at the norms regulating the duration of migration detention for unaccompanied minors, the EU framework raises immediately the two following questions:

- Is there a requirement for the norm organising detention to set a maximum duration of detention? (section 3.1).
- Is there a maximum duration of immigration detention set in international law, and if not, what are the criteria to qualify an excessive duration, including for unaccompanied minor? (section 3.2).

It must be highlighted that the UNCRC, the General Comment No. 6 and the UN guidelines all only indicate that the detention must be for 'the shortest time possible', and once again, EU law uses the exact same expression. As a result, no real legal comparison can be made using these norms, and it is mainly the ECtHR jurisprudence which will be taken as a reference in this part.

4.1. THE LACK OF MAXIMUM DURATION SET IN THE NORM

It is possible to wonder if the obligation of 'legal certainty' set by the ECtHR requires the norm to indicate the maximum duration of detention, since the goal is for the law to be predictable. However, the jurisprudence of the ECtHR is very clear on the point: there is no requirement to set a maximum duration of detention in the law under Article 5(f) of the ECHR; the existence of such duration is only an indication among others to ascertain the arbitrariness of the detention for detentions on the Article 5(f) ground;[49] there is no case specifying a time limit for detention on the ground of Article 5(b) of the ECHR, but it can be inferred that the approach would be the same, with an individualised approach to examining the possibility of excessive duration. In doing so, the Court, following the approach of the Council of Europe, does not require a specific time limit.[50] It is noteworthy, however, that the UNHCR has a different approach and requires strict legal time limits to be set in for detention.[51] As a result, the lack of time limit for the detention under the Reception Condition Directive does not disregard human rights by ECHR standards, which the EU is bound by,[52] but it is questionable regarding UN standards.

4.2. THE ONLY TEST FOR EXCESSIVE DURATION: THE DUE DILIGENCE OF AUTHORITIES

The *role* of the assessment of the excessive duration in the examination of the arbitrariness of the detention by the Court is difficult to determine with certainty.

---

49 *JN v. UK* App no. 37289/12 (ECHR 19 May 2016) para. 90.

50 See Council of Europe, Committee of Ministers, 'Twenty Guidelines on Forced Returns' (4 May 2005) and Council of Europe, PACE Resolution 1707 (2010) on the retention of asylum seekers (28 January 2010).

51 UNHCR, 'Detention Guidelines – Guidelines on the Applicable Criteria and Standards Relating to the Detention of Asylum-Seekers and Alternatives to Detention' (2012) guideline 6. The UNHCR refers in this document to 'national law' only, but it can be inferred that any safeguards necessary for a detention regime organised at national level will also be applicable for a detention regime set up at a supranational, namely European, level.

52 Consolidated Version of the Treaty on European Union [2008] OJ C115/13, Art. 6.

In the *Rahimi* case, following the rules laid out in *Saadi*, the duration of the detention is one of the criteria of the arbitrariness test, alongside the good faith of the authorities.[53] In the *Abdullahi* case, however, the duration of the detention is part of the assessment of the good faith.[54] However, in the end, the *approach* of the Court to determine the excessiveness of the detention itself is always the same.

To begin with, it must be highlighted that the ECtHR never found one specific duration of immigration detention as being always excessive.[55] In assessing whether the duration of detention is excessive, the Court relies on the behaviour of the authorities during the detention. They have obligation make the detention as short as possible, and as a result, must undertake due diligence regarding the proceedings they are supposed to conduct.[56] As a result, even a very short duration can prove to be excessive if the authorities did not show such due diligence.[57] Concerning the requirement for a detention duration specific to children, it can be highlighted that following the *Mubilanzila* ruling, there is a requirement for a detention regime specific to (unaccompanied) children;[58] this is an issue for the Dublin Regulation, which does not contain any disposition regulating the detention duration differently for adults and for unaccompanied minors.

However, beyond this element of a mandatory, child-specific regime, there is no set standard concerning the length of the detention for unaccompanied minors under ECtHR jurisprudence. This can make it difficult to assess the quality of EU law, since the only appreciation possible is *in concreto*. The maximum time limits of 53 days in the Dublin Regulation and of 18 months in the Return Directive are not, in themselves, compliant or not with international norms; the issue of excessive duration of detention is purely a case-by-case evaluation.

---

53 *Rahimi v. Greece* (n. 25 above) para. 106.

54 Ibid., para. 146: 'even accepting that the detention was closely connected to the ground of detention relied on, namely to prevent an unauthorized entry, and in practice to allow for the applicants' asylum claim to be processed with the required prior age assessment, the delays in the present case, particularly those subsequent to the determination of the applicants' age, raise serious doubts as to the authorities' good faith'.

55 It must be noted, however, that this possible lack of absolute time limit, with a purely *in concreto* approach, does not make consensus within the Court, as proved by a concurring opinion in the *Abdullahi* case (*Abdullahi Elmi and Aweys Abubakar v. Malta* App no. 25794/13 and 28151/13 (ECHR, 22 Nov 2016)), Judge Pinto de Albuquerque: 'A period of 18 months is per se contrary to the exceptional character of detention under Article 5 §1 (f), as no deportation procedure lasting that long can be said to have been undertaken with due diligence' 31; this makes for a particular interesting statement, as the maximum duration of detention under the Return Directive is 18 months.

56 *Chahal v. The United Kingdom* (n 41) para. 113; *Amie and others v. Bulgaria* App no. 58149/08 (ECHR 12 February 2013) para. 78.

57 See e.g. the *Rahimi* case, where Greece was deemed in violation of Art. 5 for a detention lasting two days.

58 *Mubilanzila Mayeka and Kaniki Mitunga v. Belgium* (n. 17 above), para. 56 and para. 82.

As a result, the CEAS seems to have the necessary safeguards to be in line with international standards concerning the duration of the detention. The only elements left to confront concerning international standards are the detention conditions.

5. THE INADEQUACIES OF THE CEAS REGARDING THE DETENTION CONDITIONS OF UNACCOMPANIED MINORS

Table 3. Overview of the detention conditions of unaccompanied minors in the CEAS

Norm	General Detention Regime	Supplementary conditions for unaccompanied minors
RCD and Dublin Regulation	✓ Specialised detention centre, or if not possible, prison facility with separation from the other detainees.	✓ No detention in prison facility ✓ Separation from adults (except if over 16 and in the best interests of the child) ✓ 'As far as possible': with facilities and personnel which take into account their specific needs
Return Directive	✓ Specialised detention centre, or if not possible, prison facility with separation from the other detainees.	✓ 'As far as possible': with facilities and personnel which take into account their specific needs

The examination of the provisions regarding the detention conditions of unaccompanied minors in the CAES, in light of international standards, sheds lights on clear shortcomings from a normative standpoint.

Indeed, Article 37(c) of the UNCRC requires that children must be detained 'in a manner which takes into account the needs of persons of his or her age. In particular every child deprived of liberty shall be separated from adults unless it is in their best interest not to do so [...]'. General Comment No. 6 is more specific, stating that states must ensure that children must be placed in 'living quarters that are suitable for children and that separate them from adults, unless it is considered in the child's best interests not to do so'.[59] In addition, the ECtHR has highlighted the importance of keeping unaccompanied minors separate from adults, at the risk of violating not Article 5 but Article 3 on the prohibition of torture or inhuman or degrading treatment or punishment.[60]

59 UNCRC, General Comment No. 6 (n. 4 above) para. 63.

60 *Mubilanzila Mayeka and Kaniki Mitunga v. Belgium* (n. 17 above) para. 103.

As a result, two elements appear to be imperative concerning the facilities, the conditions, in which unaccompanied minors are detained: separation from adults, except if it is in their best interests, and quarters specifically adapted to the needs of children.

Two main shortcomings of EU law can be identified here: the first one is the lack of obligation, under the Return Directive, to keep unaccompanied minors separated from adults. This separation from adults is mandatory[61] in the RCD and the Dublin Regulation; it was mandatory in the initial proposition of the Commission for the Return Directive as well,[62] but in the final version of the Directive, as agreed on by the Parliament and the Council, this disposition was removed, and the preparatory documents do not give any justification for this modification.

The second shortcoming consists in the wording of EU law concerning the type of facilities required. Under the RCD, which also regulates detention under the Dublin Regulation, 'all efforts shall be made to release the detained minors and place them in accommodation suitable for minors' (Art. 11(2)); the Return Directive requires that '[u]naccompanied minors shall as far as possible be provided with accommodation in institutions provided with personnel and facilities which take into account the needs of persons of their age'.[63] Both these forms of wording indicate not the obligation for the state to actually provide minors with adequate facilities, but to *try* to provide those facilities. In other words, Member States will not be in violation of the CEAS if they prove that they tried to provide proper accommodation but were not able to. The issue here lies in the fact that under international law, as seen previously, providing minors with facilities specifically taking into account their needs is not optional. As a result, while Member States will be bound by international treaties in their implementation of EU law, the standard set by EU law itself is significantly lower than the one set by international human rights law.

The last element which should be noted concerns the reform of the CEAS: the word 'facilities [taking their need into account]' has been removed in the new RCD proposal[64] (but not in the Return Directive Recast proposal), keeping only 'personal [taking their need into account]'. This modification is questionable

61 Except when a lack of separation is in the best interests of the child.

62 Commission, 'Proposal for a Directive of the European Parliament and of the Council on common standards and procedures in Member States for returning illegally staying third-country nationals' COM/2005/0391 final, Art. 15.3.

63 European Parliament and Council Directive 2013/33/EU laying down standards for the reception of applicants for international protection [2013] OJ L180/96, Art. 17.4.

64 European Commission, 'Proposal for a Directive of the European Parliament and of the Council on common standards and procedures in Member States for returning illegally staying third-country nationals' (n. 62 above).

regarding children's rights, as it opens the door to the detention of children in adult facilities under the new RCD, in violation of the UNCRC and the General Comment No. 6.

Having said this, some elements of the CEAS do comply with international law, such as the obligation, under the RCD and the Dublin Regulation, to keep unaccompanied minors and adults separated in general.

6. CONCLUSION

While it clearly takes into account many international standards and treaties related to human rights and children's rights, the CEAS does have clear normative shortcomings when it comes to fully upholding them in the area of immigration law, especially, regarding the detention of unaccompanied minors seeking asylum. By breaking down the detention regime of unaccompanied minors under EU law into three components (ground, duration, conditions), many shortcomings can be identified. In the end, however, they can be classified in three categories, all calling for a different approach to better safeguarding children's rights in the CEAS.

First, there are isolated but very clear and dire violations of international standards, such as the lack of separation from adults under the Return Directive, detention on the ground of threat to public order and detention for presumed abusive asylum claim. These dispositions place the EU in direct violations of international standards it is meant to uphold, and as a result, call for clear modifications in the upcoming reform.

Then, some provisions, or lack thereof, do not fully take into account the necessity to include child-specific norms. If these provisions are not violations of human or children's rights by themselves, they are very likely to lead to violations when implemented by Member States: for example, the non-binding obligation to provide for facilities adapted to children, or the lack of a child-specific regime under the Dublin Regulation. It could be argued that the proper execution of EU laws and policies goes to Member States, which are all bound by the various international treaties used as a reference in this chapter, and that as a result, national authorities will have to comply with them when they decide on the detention of an unaccompanied minor seeking asylum, no matter what the content of EU law is. However, EU law presents the advantage of having its own implementation sanction mechanism,[65] which cannot always be said of international law, especially for countries of dualist tradition, where the fact

65 Consolidated version of the Treaty on the Functioning of the European Union [2007] OJ C 115/47, Art. 258–260.

that a state is party to an international convention does not always guarantee the proper implementation of this treaty.[66,67] As a result, EU law and the CEAS should be the level at which all safeguards are present.

The last normative issue is the use of vague concepts, poorly ensuring a real protection and specific treatment of unaccompanied minors beyond the letter of the law, which makes them at risk of being treated as adults, or being treated differently depending on the Member State where they are; the issues are mainly here the lack of definition or proper difference between 'last resort', 'no other less coercive measure' and 'exceptional circumstances', and of any indication as to what the 'shortest amount of time' is. These issues do not necessarily require the modification of the Directives and Regulations making up the CEAS, as they are not rights violations *per se*, but could benefit from clarifications from the EU institutions, to ensure the coherence of the CEAS and an implementation by Member States in line with children's rights.

66 Pieter van Dujk, 'Comments on the implementation of international human rights treaties in domestic law and the role of Courts', CDL(2014)050* (European Commission for Democracy through law 2014).

67 This is not to say that implementation of the CEAS by Member States is exemplary; however, the challenges in the implementation of EU law, especially regarding the CEAS, would require more thorough research of its own.

HOW *PROTECTIVE* IS CUSTODY FOR UNACCOMPANIED MINORS IN GREECE?

Protecting Children's Rights within Detention

Ioannis PAPADOPOULOS*

1. INTRODUCTION

Protecting the human rights of children under the scope of the UN Convention on the Rights of the Child (UNCRC) and embodying them in the domestic policy of the ratifying Member States, has always been a goal to be achieved. In the meantime, due to the massive migration flows arriving in the area of the Mediterranean, literature and research have excessively focused upon Greece for being a stepping-stone to safety for the majority of those in quest of refuge in Europe. Among those asylum-seeking individuals arriving in Greece, unaccompanied minors (UAM) are particularly in need of certain UNCRC rights to be granted to them at arrival, given their youth and their unique socio-legal status. Currently, the situation UAM experience in Greece is particularly complex, as all migrant minors, regardless of whether or not they apply for international protection, are, by law, to be immediately apprehended for entering the country in an irregular manner and consequently to be placed under what is known as *protective custody*, in specially designed short-term hosting facilities

* Doctoral candidate at the Institute of Criminal Justice Studies, University of Portsmouth, United Kingdom.

provided by the state, where they are also to be provided with sufficient care and assistance until referred to appropriate hosting units.

However, due to the state's inability to adequately and promptly cover the accommodation needs of all UAM arriving in the country, this procedure is often replaced by *administrative detention*, until these minors are further referred to suitable long-term accommodation structures. Hence, in the meantime, UAM are most commonly placed in detention facilities, usually under police administration, where they are often subjected to highly inappropriate and clearly problematic conditions, thus raising crucial questions in the area of protecting children's rights under the scope of the UNCRC provisions. In addition to the above, this form of detention often exacerbates existing medical, psychological and social needs arising from being an asylum seeker in the first place, eventually corroborating the country's failure to provide ample and suitable refuge to UAM at arrival, leading to a custody regime euphemistically considered to be *protective*, while in reality UAM are simply placed under procedures of detention. The question therefore still lies on whether or not *protective custody* for UAM successfully manages to protect children's rights as enshrined in the UNCRC.

Attempting to address and respond to these issues, this chapter will define the terms 'unaccompanied minor' and 'separated child', as well as add special focus on the basic characteristics and unique status of UAM in the Greek legal context, based on provisions of both international and domestic legislation, coupled with bibliographical sources and statistical data. Starting from the moment of irregular entry in the country, it will focus on UAM detention as a form of protective custody, under the scope of the UNCRC and its implementation in the Greek legal context. To this end, it will elaborate on the differentiation between the terms 'administrative detention' and 'protective custody', followed by an analysis of the current state of affairs in Greece, with regard to UAM, based both on reviews of the literature as well as references to the applicable law. Moreover, it will add further emphasis to the issue of effectively applying the UNCRC provisions in the case of detained UAM and focus on protecting children's rights in detention, with the main aim being, firstly, to analyse the UNCRC implementation within the Greek legal context and, subsequently, to examine humanitarian and migration policing issues that arise regarding UAM detention.

2. DEFINING A MINOR AS 'UNACCOMPANIED'

The term 'unaccompanied minor' has been thoroughly remarked upon in the literature, especially in the most recent past, as issues in the area of human rights and migration policing appear more often both in theory and research, mainly due to the fact that the number of asylum-seeking individuals, including UAM, is increasing significantly throughout Europe (UNHCR;[1] National Centre of Social Solidarity – EKKA[2]). More specifically, the literature has shown that minors and adolescents below the age of 18 represent almost half of the worldwide refugee population[3] and based on information provided by the UNHCR, the majority of them are *unaccompanied*.[4] Therefore, following the definition provided by the UNHCR, 'unaccompanied minors' are 'children below the age of eighteen who have been separated from both parents and are not being cared for by an adult, including a distant relative, who, by law of custom, is responsible to do so'.[5] However, the term 'unaccompanied' should not be considered as defining only children who are separated from their parents or guardians.[6] Hence, the term 'unaccompanied' should never be confused with the term 'separated', which refers to children under the age of 18 who are indeed separated from their parents or from their previous legal or customary primary caregiver, albeit accompanied by a temporary caretaker, or most commonly, a distant relative.[7] Based on the above, in order to differentiate accurately between the terms 'unaccompanied minor' and 'separated child', one must focus on the status of these children at the moment they cross the national borders of the host country, in which case, 'separated' are those minors usually accompanied by a guardian, whereas, according to the definition provided by the European Council, which was subsequently embodied in the Greek legal framework, 'unaccompanied' is

> 'a minor who arrives in the territory of a Member State unaccompanied by an adult responsible for him or her whether by law or by the practice of the Member State

---

1 UNHCR, *Displacement, The New 21st Century Challenge UNHCR Global Trends 2012* (The UN Refugee Agency 2013) 6, available at: https://www.unhcr.org/statistics/country/51bacb0f9/unhcr-global-trends-2012.html.

2 EKKA National Centre for Social Solidarity, *Situation Update: Unaccompanied Children (UAC) in Greece* (Reliefweb, 15 November 2018), available at: https://reliefweb.int/sites/reliefweb.int/files/resources/EKKA%20Dashboard%2015-11-2018.pdf.

3 Marianne Vervliet, Cecile Rousseau, Eric Broekaert and Ilse Derluyn, *Multilayered Ethics in Research Involving Unaccompanied Refugee Minors* (28(4) Journal of Refugee Studies 2015) 468–485.

4 UNHCR, *Displacement* (n. 1 above) 28.

5 UNHCR, *Refugee Children: Guidelines on Protection and Care UNHCR Geneva 1994* (The UN Refugee Agency 1994) 52, available at: https://www.unhcr.org/protection/children/3b84c6c67/refugee-children-guidelines-protection-care.html?query=Refugee%20Children:%20Guidelines%20on%20Protection%20and%20Care; UNHCR, *Trends in Unaccompanied and Separated Children Seeking Asylum in Industrialized Countries 2001–2003 United Nations High Commissioner for Refugees Geneva* (The UN Refugee Agency 2004) 2, available at: https://www.unhcr.org/40f646444.pdf.

6 UNHCR, *War's Human Cost, UNHCR Global Trends 2013* (The UN Refugee Agency 2014) 29, available at: https://www.unhcr.org/statistics/country/5399a14f9/unhcr-global-trends-2013.html.

7 UNGA, *Report of the Secretary General on Protection and assistance to unaccompanied and separated refugee children* UN GAOR 56th Session Item 126 of the provisional agenda UN Doc. A/56/333 (2001) 3, available at: http://www.refworld.org/pdfid/3d58c6147.pdf.

> concerned, and for as long as he or she is not effectively taken into the care of such person; it includes a minor who is left unaccompanied after he or she has entered the territory of the Member States'.[8]

In the case of UAM, research has shown that in most cases they originate from areas affected by armed conflicts and warfare activities, commonly paired with an unstable socio-political regime, for which reason they often become targets of multiple human rights abuses, including gender-based violence and sexual or labour exploitation.[9] Therefore, their main purpose in fleeing their country of origin is, most commonly, to seek refuge away from conflicts and to avoid persecution, for which reason they aim primarily at applying for international protection in the host country and to eventually be granted the status of the refugee, as stipulated in the Geneva Convention, relating to the status of refugees 1951 (Refugee Convention) and implemented accordingly in the Greek legal context, according to which, a 'refugee' is

> 'a third country national who, owing to a well-founded fear of being persecuted for reasons of race, religion, nationality, political opinion or membership of a particular social group, is outside the country of nationality and is unable or, owing to such fear, is unwilling to avail himself or herself of the protection of that country, or a stateless person, who, being outside of the country of former habitual residence for the same reasons as mentioned above, is unable or, owing to such fear, unwilling to return to it'.[10]

---

8 Regulation (EU) No. 604/2013 of the European Parliament and of the Council of 26 June 2013 establishing the criteria and mechanisms for determining the Member State responsible for examining an application for international protection lodged in one of the Member States by a third-country national or a stateless person (recast) [2013] OJ 2 180/31 Art. 2(j) 38, available at: http://www.refworld.org/docid/51d298f04.html; Codification of Legislation (GR) No. 3386/2005 Entry Residence and Social Integration of Third Country Nationals on Greek Territory [Greece] GG A 212 Art. 1(h) 1, available at: http://www.refworld.org/docid/4c5270962.html.

9 UNGA, *Note by the Secretary General on Promotion and Protection of the Rights of Children Impact of armed conflict on children* UN GAOR 51th Session Item 108 of the provisional agenda UN Doc. A/51/306 (1996) 29–33, available at: http://www.refworld.org/docid/3b00f2d30.html.

10 National Legislative Bodies/National Authorities (GR) Presidential Decree No. 141/2013 Transposition into the Greek legislation of Directive 2011/95/EU of the European Parliament and of the Council of 13 December 2011 (L 337) on minimum standards for the qualification of third-country nationals or stateless persons as beneficiaries of international protection, for a uniform status for refugees or for persons eligible for subsidiary protection and for the content of the protection granted (recast) [Greece], GG A 226 Art. 2(e) 2, available at: http://www.refworld.org/docid/54eb4e774.html; National Legislative Bodies/National Authorities (GR) Presidential Decree No. 113/2013 Establishment of a single procedure for granting the status of refugee or of subsidiary protection beneficiary to aliens or to stateless individuals in conformity with Council Directive 2005/85/EC 'on minimum standards on procedures

To this end, due to the unique status of UAM, combined with the obvious lack of care and support both in their country of origin as well as throughout their journey, scholars have excessively focused on the vulnerability of UAM, especially when compared to other groups of asylum-seeking individuals, including separated children.[11] Additionally, the Greek law also considers UAM to be particularly vulnerable, placing them along with

> 'the disabled; elderly; pregnant women; women in a post-natal situation; single parent families with minors; victims of torture, rape or other serious psychological, physical or sexual violence or exploitation and victims of trafficking'.[12]

Furthermore, according to the relevant provisions of EU law, as embodied in the Greek legal context, Member States shall 'take measures to ensure that a representative assists the unaccompanied minor to enable him or her to benefit from the rights and comply with the obligations provided for in this Directive'.[13] As a result, according to the law, UAM are to be provided with effective reception procedures at arrival, including suitable and appropriate accommodation, coupled with effectual legal aid, especially when it comes to applying for international protection upon the host country's competent authorities.

---

in Member States for granting and withdrawing refugee status (L 326/13.12.2005)' and other provisions [Greece] GG A 146 Art. 2(f) 3, available at: http://www.refworld.org/docid/525e84ae4.html.

11 Janice H. Goodman, *Coping with trauma and hardship among unaccompanied refugee youth from Sudan* (14(9) Qualitative Health Research 2004) 1117–1196, available at: https://doi.org/10.1177/1049732304265923; Sara Thommessen, Fiorenzo Laghi, Claudia Cerrone, Roberto Baiocco and Brenda K. Todd, *Internalizing and externalizing symptoms among unaccompanied refugee and Italian adolescents* (35(1) Children and Youth Services Review 2013) 7–10, available at: https://doi.org/10.1016/j.childyouth.2012.10.007; Sara Thommessen, Paula Corcoran and Brenda K. Todd, *Experiences of arriving to Sweden as an unaccompanied asylum-seeking minor from Afghanistan: An interpretative phenomenological analysis* (5(4) Psychology of Violence 2015) 374–383, available at: http://dx.doi.org/10.1037/a0038842; Ioannis Papadopoulos and Aaron Pycroft, *Detention as protective custody for Unaccompanied Migrant Minors: A social and legal policy overview of the Greek framework on conditions of detention, under the scope of the UNCRC* in E.M. Guzik-Makaruk and E.W. Pływaczewski (eds.), *Current Problems of the Penal Law and Criminology*, C. H. Beck, Warsaw 2019 (in press).

12 National Legislative Bodies/National Authorities (GR) Presidential Decree No. 141/2013 (n. 10 above) Art. 20(3) 7.

13 Directive (EU) No. 2013/33/EU of the European Parliament and of the Council of 26 June 2013 laying down standards for the reception of applicants for international protection (recast) [2013] OJ L 180/96 Art 24(1) 12, available at: https://eur-lex.europa.eu/legal-content/EN/TXT/?uri=celex%3A32013L0033; Codification of Legislation (GR) No. 4540/2018 on the Transposition of the Greek legislation to the provisions of Directive 2013/33/EU of the European Parliament and of the Council of 26 June 2013 on the requirements for the reception of applicants for international protection (recast) and other provisions [Greece] GG 91 Art. 22(5) 8, available at: http://asylo.gov.gr/wp-content/uploads/2018/05/ΝΟΜΟΣ-4540-22.05.2018.pdf.

3. APPLYING THE UNCRC TO UAM IN DETENTION

The issue of drafting an internationally binding document focusing on protecting human rights, started with the establishment of the United Nations and the adoption of the Universal Declaration of Human Rights (1948). Up until 1984, the UN General Assembly adopted several human rights treaties of crucial importance,[14] leading to 1989 when the UNCRC was adopted in resolution 44/25[15] and subsequently came into force on 2 September 1990, as stated by the UN Committee on the Rights of the Child (CRC Committee),[16] creating a landmark in a century-long struggle for social reform.[17] Until this day, the UNCRC is considered to be the longest UN human rights treaty in force, as well as the most ratified international convention in history,[18] focusing both on asserting the value of children as legal persons,[19] as well as on promoting their legal interests and human rights.[20] As a result, it has become the most complete legal instrument in the field of securing children's rights, having successfully incorporated previous declarations and international regulations,[21] while making its provisions more effective[22] towards protecting children's rights on an international level. However, with regard to protecting the interests and aims of UAM, it has been discussed in the literature[23] that international jurisprudence

---

14 Barry Goldson and John Muncie, *Towards a global 'child friendly' juvenile justice?* (40(1) International Journal of Law Crime and Justice 2012) 40–64, available at: https://doi.org/10.1016/j.ijlcj.2011.09.004.

15 Sharon Detrick, *A commentary on the UNCRC* (Martinus Nijhoff Publishers 1999) 619–712.

16 UNGA *Report of the Committee on the Rights of the Child* UN GAOR 55th Session Supplement No. 41 UN Doc. A/55/41 (2000) available at: https://undocs.org/A/55/41(SUPP).

17 Michael Jupp, *The UN Convention on the Rights of the Child: An Opportunity for Advocates* (12(1) Human Rights Quarterly 1990) 130–136, available at: https://www.jstor.org/stable/762171.

18 John Muncie, *The 'Punitive Turn' in Juvenile Justice: Cultures of Control and Rights Compliance in Western Europe and the USA* (8(2) The National Association for Youth Justice 2008) 107–121, available at: https://doi.org/10.1177/1473225408091372.

19 Thomas Hammarberg, *The UN Convention on the Rights of the Child – And how to make it work* (12(1) Human Rights Quarterly 1990) 97–105, available at: https://www.jstor.org/stable/762167.

20 Goldson and Muncie, *Towards a global 'child friendly' juvenile justice?* (n. 14 above).

21 Hammarberg, *The UN Convention on the Rights of the Child* (n. 19 above); Jonathan Todres, *Emerging Limitations on the Rights of the Child: The UN Convention on the Rights of the Child and its early case law* (30(1) Columbia Human Rights Law Review 1990) 159–200; Paroula Naskou-Perraki, *The Implementation of the UN Convention on the Rights of the Child in Greece* (11(2) Revista de Asistenta Sociala 2012) 39–50, available at: https://www.academia.edu/10249373/The_implementation_of_the_UN_Convention_on_the_Rights_of_the_Child_in_Greece_2012.

22 Stan Meuwese, Mirjam Blaak and Majorie Kaandorp, *Handboek Internationaal Jeugdrecht* (1st ed., Ars Aequi Libri 2005) 543.

23 Jacqueline Bhabha and Wendy Young, *Not Adults in Miniature: Unaccompanied Child Asylum Seekers and the New US Guidelines* (11(1) International Journal of Refugee Law 1999) 84–125, available at: https://doi.org/10.1093/ijrl/11.1.84.

has considerably neglected these matters, proving that the UNCRC is also the most violated UN human rights treaty in force, as in most cases it has not been fully or correctly incorporated into the domestic policy of the ratifying Member States.[24] In the case of Greece, the UNCRC was signed in 1990 and ratified by law in 1992,[25] taking precedence over any conflicting and pre-existing domestic legislation, without however making any reservations with regard to its content, nevertheless binding the Greek state to take all necessary measures for the establishment and the advocacy of the rights enshrined in the UNCRC.[26]

Analogously to the issues of UNCRC applicability on the European continent, when it comes to the situation of UAM on the ground in Greece, the literature shows that Greece clearly suffers from a poorly structured legal and procedural framework, for which reason the country is often considered to be incapable of protecting the rights of UAM.[27] In consequence, Greece is considerably, to this day, failing to provide suitable care and legal assistance to asylum-seeking individuals who apply for international protection, especially when excessive detention practices, applied to UAM who are arrested for entering the country in an irregular manner, are omnipresent. With regard to the issue at hand, namely children in detention, certain UNCRC provisions apply, thus raising important questions in the area of protecting children's rights. Starting from the overarching principle concerning the welfare of the world's children, which is the *best interests of the child*, Article 3(1) UNCRC states that:

> 'In all actions concerning children, whether undertaken by public or private social welfare institutions, courts of law, administrative authorities or legislative bodies, the best interests of the child shall be a primary consideration.'[28]

In addition to Article 3, the general principles of the UNCRC include the principle of non-discrimination (under Art. 2), the right to life, survival and

---

24 Muncie, *The 'Punitive Turn' in Juvenile Justice* (n. 18 above).

25 Codification of Legislation (GR) No. 2101/1992 on the Ratification of the International Convention on the Rights of the Child [Greece] GG A 192, available at: https://www.e-nomothesia.gr/kat-anilikoi/nomos-2101-1992-phek-192-a-2-12-1992.html.

26 Paroula Naskou-Perraki, Kostas Chrysogonos and Charalambos Anthopoulos, *The UN Convention on the rights of the Child and its implementation in the national legal order Article by article interpretation* (1st ed. Ant N Sakkoulas Athens-Komotini 2002).

27 Andriani Fili and Virginia Xythali, *The Continuum of Neglect: Unaccompanied Minors in Greece* (15(2) Social Work and Society International Online Journal 2017) 1–14, available at: https://www.socwork.net/sws/index; Nikolaos Sitaropoulos and Achilles Skordas, *Why Greece is Not a Safe Host Country for Refugees* (16(1) International Journal of Refugee Law 2004) 25–52, available at: https://ssrn.com/abstract=2152866.

28 Ronald K. Bullis, *The Convention on the Rights of the Child: A Young Legal Regime for the World's Youngest Citizens* (8(3) Child and Adolescent Social Work 1991) 239–251, available at: https://doi.org/10.1007/BF00756094; Hammarberg, *The UN Convention on the Rights of the Child* (n. 19 above).

development (under Art. 6), and the right of children to participate in all matters affecting them, or, as most commonly known, the right to be heard (under Art. 12), which apply to all children. However, according to research,[29] in the case of children in conflict with the law, i.e. within detention centres, Article 37 UNCRC (containing guarantees for children deprived of their liberty) and Article 40 UNCRC (containing specific provisions concerning juvenile justice) are of particular importance, setting forth most of the substantive and procedural guarantees so that the ratifying Member States can eventually work towards developing successful and comprehensive juvenile justice procedural frameworks, which will operate within the overall goals of the UNCRC.[30] However, even though Article 37 and Article 40 UNCRC apply when it comes to children being held detained, the question still remains as to whether or not the same provisions apply when it comes to UAM being kept in detention centres, even as a form of *protective custody*. As correctly stated in research, the fact that children are held in detention is also a basis for extra efforts on the part of the state to guarantee the protection of all the rights recognised in the UNCRC.[31] As a result, there should be no doubt that all of the UNCRC provisions also apply to migrant minors, including Article 22 UNCRC, which is considered to be the first legally binding provision that acknowledges the unique needs and risks of refugee and asylum-seeking children.[32] In detail, according to Article 22(1) UNCRC,

> 'States Parties shall take appropriate measures to ensure that a child who is seeking refugee status or who is considered a refugee … receive appropriate protection and humanitarian assistance in the enjoyment of applicable rights set forth in the present Convention and in other international human rights or humanitarian instruments to which the said States are Parties',

whereas according to Article 22(2) UNCRC,

> 'States Parties shall provide … co-operation … to protect and assist such a child … in order to obtain information necessary for reunification with his or her family.

29 Defence for Children International Netherlands, *Kids Behind Bars. A study on children in conflict with the law: towards investing in prevention, stopping incarceration and meeting international standards* (International Juvenile Justice Observatory, 2004) 21–31, available at: https://defenceforchildren.org/wp-content/uploads/2010/04/Kids-Behind-Bars.pdf.

30 Wallace J. Mlyniec, *The Implications of Articles 37 and 40 of the Convention on the Rights of the Child for US Juvenile Justice and US Ratification of the Convention* (89(5) Child Welfare 2010) 103–120, available at: https://www.ncbi.nlm.nih.gov/pubmed/21361160.

31 Defence for Children International Netherlands, *Kids behind bars* (n. 29 above).

32 Christoph Bierwirth, *Protection of Refugee and Asylum-Seeking Children: The Convention on the Rights of the Child and the Work of the Committee on the Rights of the Child* (24(2) Refugee Survey Quarterly 2005) 98–124, available at: https://doi.org/10.1093/rsq/hdi029.

> In cases where no parents or other members of the family can be found, the child shall be accorded the same protection as any other child permanently or temporarily deprived of his or her family environment for any reason, as set forth in the present Convention'.

Ergo, in the case of Article 22(1) UNCRC strong emphasis is added on the principle of non-discrimination, as enshrined under Article 2 UNCRC, especially due to the fact that the issue of subjecting UAM to discriminatory and often abusive treatment in the host country is considered to be quite common, including incidents of mistreatment and abuse towards UAM, as stated by the Greek Ombudsman.[33] For this reason, Article 22(2) UNCRC adds special focus to the cooperation of the host country with the UN, as well as humanitarian organisations, in order to ensure that all UAM will be adequately assisted and supported throughout their application procedure for international protection, i.e. either aiming for family reunification processes as enshrined in the provisions of the Dublin Regulation,[34] or when applying for asylum at the host country.

4. CURRENT STATUS OF UAM IN GREECE

According to the law in Greece, anyone entering the country irregularly, i.e. without valid travel documents, is to be apprehended and legal charges are to be pressed against him or her, for violating Article 83(1) of Act 3386 of 2005, as mentioned above,[35] according to which,

> 'A third-country national who leaves or attempts to leave or enters or attempts to enter the Greek territory without legal formalities shall be punished by imprisonment of at least three months and a penalty of at least EUR 1,500'.

With regard to the followed legal process in the case of illegal entry, according to Article 76(1)(b) of Act 3386 of 2005, followed by the recently amended

33 The Greek Ombudsman Department of Children's Rights, *Parallel Report to the UN Committee on the Rights of the Child – Findings and recommendations of the Independent Authority 'the Greek Ombudsman' on the implementation of Children's Rights in Greece (July 2003 – September 2011)* (The Greek Ombudsman Children's Rights, April 2012) 6–8, 18–22, available at: https://www.synigoros.gr/?i=childrens-rights.en.recentinterventions.82331; The Greek Ombudsman Department of Children's Rights, *The Greek Ombudsman's Intervention for unaccompanied children, refugees and immigrants* (The Greek Ombudsman Children's Rights, 30 March 2016), available at: https://www.synigoros.gr/resources/dt-asynodeytoi-anilikoi-3032016.pdf.

34 Regulation (EU) No. 604/2013 (n. 8 above).

35 Codification of Legislation (GR) No. 3386/2005 (n. 7 above).

Act 4375 of 2016,[36] building on Act 4251 of 2014,[37] as well as on Act 3907 of 2011,[38] when a third-country national is arrested for entering the country in an illegal manner, a decision of *administrative detention* is issued upon them, usually followed by a decision for deportation, unless the individual follows voluntary departure procedures, as stipulated under Article 30(1) of Act 3907 of 2011, according to which, '[t]hird-country nationals are to be held detained until their deportation is completed, unless the individual follows the procedure of voluntary departure'. Interestingly enough, however, when it comes to *administrative detention*, the same procedure applies for UAM, without any differentiation made whatsoever, even though both the Convention (1951) and the Greek Ombudsman are clear on the matter, the former stating under Articles 31 and 32 that asylum seekers should never be prosecuted for illegal entry, whereas the latter has declared that '[u]naccompanied children seeking asylum should never be detained for entering the country illegally'.[39] To this end, during the time UAM are kept under *administrative detention* and in an effort to meet the child's needs and protect their best interests, the CRC Committee supports that 'any disciplinary measure must be consistent with upholding the inherent dignity of the juvenile' at every point of the justice process and furthermore, recourse to judicial proceedings and, more specifically, arrest and detention should only ever be operationalised as measures of last resort and for the shortest period of time.[40] Additionally, with regard to the deportation procedure applied on UAM, Article 25(1) of the aforementioned Act 3907 of 2011[41] is clear on the matter, stating that, '[b]efore taking a decision on the return of an unaccompanied minor and taking into account his or her best

---

36 Codification of Legislation (GR) No. 4375/2016 Codification of Legislation on the organization and operation of the asylum service, the appeals authority, the reception and identification service, the establishment of the general secretariat for reception, the transposition into Greek legislation of the provisions of Directive 2013/32/EC [Greece] GG A 51, available at: http://www.refworld.org/docid/573ad4cb4.html.

37 Codification of Legislation (GR) No. 4251/2014 Codification of Legislation on the Code for Migration and Social Integration and other provisions [Greece] GG A 80, available at: http://www.refworld.org/docid/54eb40114.html.

38 Codification of Legislation (GR) No. 3907/2011 on the Establishment of an Asylum Service and a First Reception Service, transposition into Greek legislation of Directive 2008/115/EC 'on common standards and procedures in Member States for returning illegally staying third country nationals' and other provisions [Greece] GG A 7, available at: http://www.refworld.org/docid/4da6ee7e2.html.

39 The Greek Ombudsman Department of Children's Rights, *Conclusions on the situation of unaccompanied minors in Pagani-Mitilini: report on administrative detention and removal of minors from October 2005* (The Greek Ombudsman Children's Rights, 2006), available at: https://www.synigoros.gr.

40 UNCRC, *General Comment 10 Committee on the Rights of the Child*, 44th Session UN Doc. C/GC/10 (2007) 10, 24, available at: http://www.refworld.org/docid/4670fca12.html.

41 Codification of Legislation (GR) No. 3907/2011 (n. 38 above).

interests, assistance is provided by appropriate bodies, other than the authorities responsible for the return', whereas according to Article 25(2),

> 'Before an unaccompanied minor is removed from the country, the competent authorities shall verify that he or she will be returned to a member of his / her family, to designated guardians or to appropriate reception facilities in the State of return'.

In practice, the only way to postpone deportation is if the individual decides to follow legal procedures against the deportation decision itself, as these procedures are stipulated by law, or file an application for international protection upon the competent state authorities.

In this case, however, the applicant will probably be facing an arbitrary and time-consuming detention period, until the completion of certain administrative procedures,[42] including the referral of UAM to suitable accommodation units or them being assigned to legal guardians or organisations, either governmental or non-governmental (NGOs), through official procedures followed by EKKA. More specifically, under Article 25(1) of Act 3907 of 2011, UAM in Greece are being assisted by EKKA upon arrival, the latter being based on the coordination of a social support services network, including, but not restricted to, care and support for vulnerable groups or individuals and generally populations experiencing crises or in need of emergency social aid, as stated under Article 6(2) of Act 3106 of 2003.[43] In the case of UAM specifically, EKKA, in collaboration with the Greek Ministry for Migration Policy provides child-appropriate and UAM-friendly accommodation and support services, in order to replace UAM detention as soon as possible, a procedure that starts the moment a minor is registered as *unaccompanied* in the Greek territory. Based on referrals made to EKKA by national services, as well as domestic and foreign NGOs, EKKA is able to provide its services, including providing accommodation to those in need, as well as conduct monthly statistical data analyses on socio-political matters, such as calculating the estimated number of UAM in Greece; the total number of places available in UAM shelters; as well as the numbers of UAM on the waiting list for shelter.

Thus, according to the most recent statistical information of EKKA[44] at the time this chapter was drafted, the estimated number of UAM located in Greece

---

42 Human Rights Watch, *Left to Survive Systematic Failure to Protect Unaccompanied Migrant Children in Greece* (Refworld 22 December 2008) 53–64, available at: http://www.refworld.org/docid/4950a7382.html.

43 Codification of Legislation (GR) No. 3106/2003 Codification of Legislation on the reformation of the national social care system [Greece] GG A 30, available at: https://www.e-nomothesia.gr/kat-ygeia/n-3106-2003.html.

44 EKKA National Centre for Social Solidarity (n. 2 above).

is 4,616 and the total number of places available in long-term accommodation units for UAM is only 1,196, whereas the total number of places in temporary accommodation is only 650. Hence, the total number of UAM on the waiting list for a shelter or any other appropriate accommodation scheme is 2,976 (including 291 separated children). This includes for 1,416 children located at the state borders, either in the mainland (Fylakio, Evros) or the islands (Kos, Leros, Lesvos, Samos, Chios), where the current First Reception and Identification Centres (RICs) in operation are located, and with 238 children held in protective custody, as well as detention centres. In detail, there are currently only 48 long-term UAM shelters with a total of 1,136 places and 10 short-term safe zones (i.e. designated supervised spaces within accommodation sites, providing UAM with 24/7 emergency protection and care, giving priority to UAM in detention as well as other vulnerable children, in line with their best interests and in light of the insufficient number of available shelters), with a total of 300 places. Additionally, there are currently 15 Supported Independent Living (SIL) apartments for UAM older than 16 years of age, with a total of 20 places, as well as 12 hotels (i.e. emergency accommodation spaces being used as a measure to care for UAM due to the insufficient number of available places, giving priority to UAM in RICs) with a total of 604 places. Based on the above information, we can have a clear picture of the urgent need for Greece to focus on providing UAM with appropriate accommodation, especially at arrival, in order to cover their basic needs and successfully implement the UNCRC provisions in the Greek legal context, while protecting the 'best interests of the child' principle, as depicted under Article 3(3) UNCRC.

5. PROTECTING UAM RIGHTS WITHIN DETENTION

In times when particularly high numbers of asylum-seeking individuals arrive in Greece,[45] the Greek Government introduced Act 4636 of 2019[46] on November 1st 2019. The recently introduced law was originally concerned with incorporating three EU Directives within the Greek domestic policy,

---

45 EKKA National Centre for Social Solidarity (n. 2 above).

46 Codification of Legislation (GR) No. 4636/2019 on the amendments of the Greek legislation in accordance with the provisions of Directive 2011/95/EU of the European Parliament and of the Council of Europe of December 13 2011, on 'International Protection, provisions on the qualification and the status of third country nationals or stateless persons as beneficiaries of international protection, for a single status for refugees or persons eligible for subsidiary protection and for the content of protection granted, unification of provisions for the reception of applicants for international protection, the procedure for granting and revoking of the status for international protection, restructuring of judicial protection of asylum seekers and other provisions' [Greece], available (in Greek) at: https://www.e-nomothesia.gr/kat-allodapoi/prosphuges-politiko-asulo/nomos-4636-2019-phek-169a-1-11-2019.html.

namely 2013/32/EU, 2013/33/EU and 2011/95/EU, as already discussed, and redesigning the currently defective Greek asylum system, in accordance to the requirements of the EU law, thus aiming to respect the rights of asylum seekers. However, despite the strict procedural requirements and formalities which were introduced with regard to the current operational context of Greece, the law ignored the element of vulnerability that characterises UAM. The latter was particularly evident due to the fact that the new law has made no changes whatsoever with regard to the current legal context governing UAM detention. To this end, given the fact that Act 4636 of 2019 will enter into force on January 1st 2020, the references that will be made to the applicable legal provisions in this part of the chapter, will be based on the current legal framework on UAM detention, followed by a short remark on the relevant provisions of the recently introduced legal Act on the same issue.

Based on the above, migrant minors can be placed in detention under the Greek law, either for deportation purposes, or in order to undergo screening procedures at a RIC, as set under Article 14 of Act 4375 of 2016 (as amended by Act 4540 of 2018 and Act 4636 of 2019), building on Act 3907 of 2011, which involves primarily first registration processes, coupled with identity and nationality verification and age assessment procedures for UAM. In both scenarios, UAM are to be held temporarily under what is known as *protective custody*, until they are placed in a more permanent child-appropriate accommodation scheme, specifically designed to host UAM, as suggested by EKKA. However, when UAM reach the Greek borders, a RIC can only provide a limited number of accommodation places for UAM under the *protective custody* regime, for which reason UAM are usually transferred either to shelters/safe zones, or to detention centres right after their initial registration. However, when detention procedures apply, custody ceases to maintain its protective character and UAM are in reality placed in detention facilities, pre-removal centres (originally created for adults), or police stations, experiencing circumstances that are overall inappropriate and unsuitable for minors,[47] involving incidents of oppressive behaviour towards UAM by the Greek law enforcement authorities.[48] For this reason, as addressed in the EU Action Plan on UAM,[49] the CRC Committee has concluded on the matter that 'Detention cannot be justified solely on the basis of the child being

---

47 The Greek Ombudsman Department of Children's Rights (The Greek Ombudsman Children's Rights, April 2012) (n. 32 above).

48 Victoria Galante, *Greece's Not-So-Warm Welcome to Unaccompanied Minors: Reforming EU Law to Prevent the Illegal Treatment of Migrant Children in Greece* (39(2) Brooklyn Journal of International Law 2014) 745–791, available at: https://brooklynworks.brooklaw.edu/bjil/vol39/iss2/5/.

49 European Commission COM(2010)213 final Communication from the Commission to the European Parliament and the Council Action Plan on Unaccompanied Minors (2010–2014) [2010] SEC(2010)534, available at: http://eur-lex.europa.eu/LexUriServ/LexUriServ.do?uri=COM:2010:0213:FIN:en:PDF.

unaccompanied or separated, or on their migratory or residence status, or lack thereof', and further urges Member States to 'expeditiously and completely cease the detention of children on the basis of their immigration status'.[50]

Apart from the excessive number of Acts and binding European Directives on the matter, the issue of UAM detention remains to this day a particularly complex topic in the Greek legal context, especially when it comes to applying the law in practice. More specifically, detention for UAM in Greece is allowed under certain circumstances (Articles 9 and 10 of Act 4540 of 2018, building up on Article 46(10) of Act 4375 of 2016; Article 48(2) of Act 4636 of 2019), i.e. only as a measure of last resort and only for 25 days, which can be further extended for an extra 20 days and only until an appropriate place in a shelter for minors is found. Moreover, with regard to the conditions of detention for UAM, Article 32(2) of Presidential Decree 141 of 2013 states that national authorities shall ensure that the minors' needs are adequately covered and that they shall 'regularly assess the situation of the minor', while Article 32(3) states that national authorities shall ensure the accommodation of unaccompanied minors in special centres or any other appropriate hosting facilities. Besides the issue of duration, Article 10(b) of Act 4540 of 2018 focuses on UAM rights within detention, for example keeping detained UAM separately from adults and providing minors with age-appropriate activities. Moreover, under Article 9 (e, f and g), minors are also to be provided with adequate medical care, legal aid and detailed information in a language they fully understand regarding the reasons and the duration of their detention, as well as their rights and means to challenge the administrative decision for detention. Sadly, however, reality in Greece lies far from the letter of the law. More specifically, when UAM are apprehended for illegal entry, they usually end up in detention facilities and police stations, as a first and immediate response to their arrival, often sharing the same space with adults. Moreover, the detention period for UAM is usually longer than 25 and/or 45 days, as described above, often lasting several months.[51] Hence, *administrative detention* is considered to be the new *protective custody*, for which reason the Committee of Ministers of the Council of Europe strongly invited the authorities to pursue their efforts, so that all unaccompanied minors are referred to special accommodation centres immediately upon arrival. Additionally, several reports

---

50 UNCRC, *General Comment 6 Treatment of Unaccompanied and Separated Children Outside Their Country of Origin*, 39th Session UN Doc. CRC/GC/2005/6 (2005) 61, available at: http://www.refworld.org/docid/42dd174b4.html; UNCRC *Report of the 2012 Day of General Discussion The rights of all Children in the Context of International Migration* (UNHR Office of the High Commissioner 2012) 78, available at: https://www2.ohchr.org/english/bodies/crc/docs/discussion2012/2012CRC_DGD-Childrens_Rights_InternationalMigration.pdf.

51 European Union Agency for Fundamental Rights *Separated, asylum-seeking children in European Union Member States Comparative Report* (FRA December 2010) 66–70, available at: https://fra.europa.eu/en/publication/2012/separated-asylum-seeking-children-european-union-member-states.

were made on this issues by the Greek Ombudsman calling for a complete ban on detention of minors, both unaccompanied and separated, due to the fact that such practices represent a clear violation both of the UNCRC as well as domestic law, due to the highly problematic and adverse detention conditions within police stations.[52] In detail, according to the UN Office of the High Commissioner of Human Rights:

> 'Unaccompanied children locked in police station cells 24/7 without access to the outdoors for over two weeks and was informed that some may stay for a month ... the children were manifestly traumatised and distressed by the experience, as compared to children met in open reception centres and informal camps ... As determined by the Committee on the Rights of the Child, detention can never be in the best interest of a child. Even under the guise of protective custody, it is utterly unacceptable for children to be administratively detained ....'[53]

Based on the above, it is evident that the current procedures of *administrative detention* that apply on UAM at arrival on Greek ground, come to unsuccessfully replace *protective custody* for the reasons already discussed. To this end and even though such practices have always been at the forefront of the police's choices and promoted by the competent ministry, UAM detention inevitably leads to a clear distortion and breach of children's rights, which clearly contradicts several human rights instruments and legal Acts, including the UNCRC, as well as the Greek legal framework.[54] The above are also evident in a plethora of decisions of the European Court of Human Rights, such as in *M.S.S v. Belgium and Greece*,[55] as well as in *Rahimi v. Greece*,[56] where the Court focused on the clear violations of Article 3 UNCRC because of the dreadful detention circumstances and because of the applicants' extremely vulnerable situation in each individual case, coupled with the fact that the state authorities never examined whether or not detention was in the applicants' best interests and if it was used as a measure of last resort, for which reason detention was found to be in violation both of the UNCRC and the European Convention of Human Rights.

---

52 The Greek Ombudsman Department of Children's Rights (The Greek Ombudsman Children's Rights, April 2012) (n. 33 above).

53 UNHCR *UN Special Rapporteur on the human rights of migrants concludes his follow up country visit to Greece* (United Nations Human Rights Office of the High Commissioner, 16 May 2016), available at: https://www.ohchr.org/EN/NewsEvents/Pages/DisplayNews.aspx?NewsID=19972&LangID=E.

54 The Greek Ombudsman Department of Children's Rights, *Conclusions on the situation of unaccompanied minors in Pagani-Mitilini* (n. 39 above).

55 *MSS v. Belgium and Greece* App no. 30696/09 (ECHR 21 January 2011).

56 *Rahimi v. Greece* App no. 8687/08 (ECHR 5 July 2011).

6. CONCLUSION

Accepting and hosting children among other asylum-seeking individuals in European countries under the scope of the UNCRC provisions is a difficult process as it is based mainly on legal procedures differing among Member States, depending entirely on national law and the level of UNCRC implementation within each individual country's legal context. To this end, the UNCRC is correctly considered to be a critical landmark in the process of protecting the general child welfare, as well as providing legal protection to all children, including UAM seeking refuge far from their country of origin. Unfortunately, however, the implementation of the UNCRC within the Greek legal context is often problematic, especially when it comes to the issue of UAM detention, thus leading to children being deprived of certain UNCRC rights both at arrival and during the first administrative steps in the host country. To this day Greece is characterised by a clear absence of an efficient legal and procedural framework, responsible for protecting and covering the basic needs of UAM at arrival. For this reason, *protective custody* is often replaced by *administrative detention*, leading to minors being placed in detention and treated like adults regardless of their asylum status.

Consequently, even though *detention* is considered to be the harshest method of securing an illegal alien's deportation, practice in Greece has shown that this form of *custody* still lies far from being considered as *protective* when it comes to safeguarding UAM rights, which is evident by the excessive reports and the repeated condemnations both from the ECtHR and the Greek Ombudsman, on the grounds of violation of the 'best interests of the child' principle. Hence, the humanitarian issue of keeping UAM in detention is still a matter to be solved and it is the extensive use of prolonged *detention* overthrowing *protective custody*, characterised by clearly unsuitable detention conditions for UAM, that clearly highlights the severe deficiencies in the Greek legal context, when it comes to protecting children's rights under the scope of the UNCRC. For that reason and in order to overcome the above-discussed issues, Greece must focus its attention and resources on reinventing the national legal framework, so that it reaches a higher level of applicability and effectiveness, combined with policies that support the rights of UAM at arrival, including a protective and sound referral pathway that will replace the currently applied procedures regarding UAM detention. Only then Greece will be able to take a first step towards reinstating a series of effective migration policing techniques with a view to protecting the rights of UAM, through facilitating positive adjustment and integration of the UNCRC provisions within the Greek legal context.

APPELLATE ASYLUM AND MIGRATION PROCEEDINGS IN BELGIUM

Challenges for the Best Interests of the Child Principle and Unity of Jurisprudence

Ellen DESMET*

1. INTRODUCTION

This chapter analyses two strands of case law of the Council for Alien Law Litigation (CALL or Council) in Belgium from the perspective of children's rights and the need to ensure unity of jurisprudence.[1] On the one hand, it looks into appeals against decisions of the Commissioner General for Refugees and

* Assistant professor of migration law and member of the Migration Law Research Group/Human Rights Centre/CESSMIR at Ghent University, Belgium.

1 The analysis of the asylum case law in this chapter is based on Ellen Desmet, 'Minderjarigen in de volle rechtsmachtprocedure van de Raad voor Vreemdelingenbetwistingen' [2018] Tijdschrift voor Vreemdelingenrecht 198.

Stateless Persons (CGRS) denying a minor or his/her parent(s) the refugee and/or subsidiary protection status, in which the CALL undertakes a full judicial review. On the other, it scrutinises appeals against return orders delivered by the Immigration Office in the context of the durable solution procedure to the guardian of an unaccompanied minor (UNAM), for which the CALL only has an annulment competence.

First, in a quantitative analysis, the relationship between the outcome of the case (accepting or rejecting the appeal) and the language of the proceedings (French or Dutch) is analysed. Even though the necessary caution is warranted, the findings do reveal a different approach between the French-speaking and the Dutch-speaking Chambers, especially in the asylum case law. The second part of the chapter concerns a qualitative analysis, assessing the legal weight attached to the principle of the best interests of the child in both strands of case law. It is demonstrated, among others, that the legal weight attached to the best interests principle in the asylum case law of the CALL varies on a continuum from non-applicable/non-relevant, to a procedural application and (exceptionally) a substantive application. In the annulment cases under review, there seems more coherence in how the best interests principle is interpreted, which may be related to its incorporation in the relevant national legal provisions. These quantitative and qualitative findings of divergence within the Belgian asylum and migration case law involving (unaccompanied) minors raise questions from a children's rights perspective, as well as from the perspective of legal certainty and unity of jurisprudence. This is an exploratory research, however: the research design does not allow formulation of definitive explanations of the findings. Only correlations are identified, no causal explanations are given. Where possible and relevant, hypotheses are formulated as to the interpretation of certain findings.

After a short presentation of the Council for Alien Law Litigation, the methodology adopted is discussed. Thereinafter follow the quantitative and qualitative analyses, discussing each time first the asylum case law, and then the appeals against return orders in the context of the durable solution procedure for unaccompanied minors. The chapter closes with some final reflections.

2. THE COUNCIL FOR ALIEN LAW LITIGATION

The Council for Alien Law Litigation[2] is an independent administrative court in Belgium, competent for handling appeals against individual decisions taken on the basis of the Aliens Act of 15 December 1980.[3] The CALL currently

[2] Also referred to as the Aliens Appeals Board, for instance by the European Court of Human Rights.

[3] Art. 39/1 Act of 15 December 1980 regarding the entry, residence, settlement and removal of aliens (Aliens Act).

consists of 54 judges,[4] who are divided over nine Chambers: one Chamber is presided by the First President, one by the President, three Chambers handle cases in Dutch, three Chambers deal with cases in French, and one Chamber handles bilingual cases.[5]

The case law of the Council is divided in two branches: the full judicial review appeal and the annulment appeal. The full judicial review appeal consists of appeals against decisions of the Commissioner General for Refugees and Stateless Persons regarding the granting of the refugee and/or subsidiary protection status. Here, the Council can take three types of decisions: confirm the decision of the CGRS (which in the majority of cases[6] will come down to a denial of international protection status); reform the decision (and grant refugee or subsidiary protection status);[7] or annul the decision and send it back to the CGRS.[8] A decision of the CGRS is annulled when it is vitiated by a substantial irregularity which cannot be remedied by the Council, or because essential elements are lacking to the effect that the Council cannot confirm or reform the decision without additional investigative measures.[9] Against any other decision based on the Aliens Act, only an annulment appeal can be lodged, limited to a legality control. Either the Council rejects the appeal, or it annuls the decision and sends it back to the Immigration Office, for violation of substantial or under penalty of nullity prescribed formalities, or for exceeding or disposing of power.[10]

One of the legal obligations of the Council for Alien Law Litigation is to safeguard unity of jurisprudence – which is not self-evident given the large number of judgments that the Council has already issued since the start of its activities on 1 June 2007.[11] At the level of the Council, the First President and the President are entrusted with this task, and take the necessary measures to that end.[12] Within each Chamber, its President, with the support of a coordinator, watches over the unity of jurisprudence; he or she may order that a case be dealt with by three judges instead of by one judge, when the legal difficulties or the

4 C. Bamps et al., 'Présentation du Conseil du Contentieux des Étrangers – Voorstelling van de Raad voor Vreemdelingenbetwistingen' in C. Adam et al. (eds.), *10 jaar Raad voor Vreemdelingenbetwistingen: daadwerkelijke rechtsbescherming – 10 ans du Conseil du Contentieux des Étrangers: la protection jurisdictionnelle effective* (die Keure 2017) 34.

5 Art. 39/9 §1 Aliens Act.

6 The Minister or the Immigration Office can also appeal against a decision of the CGRS granting international protection status, but this is very rare. Art. 39/56, 2nd al. Aliens Act.

7 Except in the rare cases where the appeal was introduced by the Minister or the Immigration Office, see n. 6.

8 Art. 39/2 §1 Aliens Act. See also Art. 39/76 §§1–2 Aliens Act.

9 Art. 39/2 §1, 2nd para., 2° Aliens Act. The CALL does not have investigative competence itself.

10 Art. 39/9 §2 Aliens Act.

11 In March 2019, the Council had already adopted more than 217,000 judgments, see http://www.rvv-cce.be/nl/arr.

12 Art. 39/6 §1 Aliens Act.

importance of the case so demand.[13] When the First President or the President, after having obtained the advice of the judge involved, consider it necessary for the unity of the case law or for the development of the law, that a case be heard by the United Chambers, he or she orders the referral to these Chambers.[14] The United Chambers consist of six judges of the CALL, three French-speaking and three Dutch-speaking.[15] When both parties request a referral to the United Chambers with a view to ensuring unity of jurisprudence, the First President or the President are obliged to accept this.[16] When the latter assess, however, that the importance of the case so demands, they can decide to refer the case to the General Assembly of the CALL, which is composed of all judges.[17] The General Assembly holds hearing in even numbers, with a minimum of ten judges. Like in the United Chambers, both linguistic registers are equally represented. Judgments adopted by the United Chambers and – especially – the General Assembly are considered to set out the lines for subsequent case law, and in this way guarantee unity of jurisprudence. In addition, the – also legally required[18] – publication of the judgments of the CALL potentially contributes to a greater unity of case law. This makes a more exhaustive analysis possible than of the decisions issued by the ordinary judiciary in Belgium, or of migration case law in some other countries,[19] which are not published systematically.

This chapter analyses two specific strands within the full judicial review and annulment appeals of the Council respectively, in which minors are involved. On the one hand, it looks into appeals against decisions of the CGRS denying a minor or his/her parent(s) the refugee and/or subsidiary protection status. On the other, the chapter scrutinises appeals against 'orders to be brought to the border' ('Annex 38') delivered by the Immigration Office to the guardians of unaccompanied minors. These are specific orders for minors, whereas adults who are irregularly staying in Belgium receive an 'order to leave the territory'.[20] For unaccompanied minors, Belgium has established a specific residence procedure, which aims to ensure a 'durable solution' for the minor concerned.[21] The Aliens Act identifies three possible durable solutions: (i) family

---

13 Art. 39/10 Aliens Act.

14 Art. 39/12 §1 Aliens Act.

15 Art. 39/12 §2 Aliens Act.

16 Art. 39/12 §1 Aliens Act.

17 Art. 39/11 Aliens Act.

18 Art. 39/65 Aliens Act.

19 See e.g. on asylum case law in Ireland, Samantha Arnold, 'Child refugee and subsidiary protection appeals in Ireland' (2018) 30 Child and Family Law Quarterly 35.

20 Art. 61/18 Aliens Act.

21 For more information, see Katja Fournier, 'Duurzame oplossingen voor niet-begeleide minderjarige vreemdelingen: pistes voor de toekomst' in Ellen Desmet, Jinske Verhellen and Steven Bouckaert (eds.), *Rechten van niet-begeleide minderjarige vreemdelingen in België* (die Keure, 2019); Katja Fournier, *Durable Solutions for Separated Children in Europe. National Report: Belgium* (Service Droit des Jeunes 2016); Veerle Peeters, 'Niet-begeleide

reunification, in accordance with Articles 9 and 10 of the UN Convention on the Rights of the Child (UNCRC), in the country of legal residence of the parents; (ii) return to the country of origin or the country where the unaccompanied minor has legal residence, with guarantees of adequate reception and care according to his age and degree of maturity, either by his parents or other adults who will take care of him, or by public authorities or non-governmental bodies; (iii) or legal residence in Belgium.[22] If the Immigration Office decides that family reunification or return is the durable solution, it issues an order to be brought to the border to the guardian of the unaccompanied minor, requiring him to do so within 30 days. This order is not forcibly executed, however, as long as the person is a minor, but he or she does not have a legal stay in Belgium anymore. When turning 18, these young people can receive an order to leave the territory, and be forcibly removed.[23] The judgments under scrutiny here are the appeals against these orders to be brought to the border.

3. METHODOLOGY

A two-step methodology was adopted to analyse both strands of case law. A first selection was made on the basis of relevant keywords[24] entered in the case law database of the CALL,[25] within a specific time frame.[26] This yielded 536 judgments within the full judicial review appeal, and 179 judgments within the annulment appeal (even though a larger time span was taken).[27] In a second step, this sample was reduced to 'relevant' judgments. For the full judicial review appeal, the 'relevance' criterion was defined as 'involvement of a minor as an applicant or child of the applicant'. This can be as an unaccompanied minor,

---

minderjarige vreemdelingen in de praktijk van de Dienst Vreemdelingenzaken: de bijzondere verblijfsprocedure' in Desmet, Verhellen and Bouckaert (eds.), *Rechten van niet-begeleide minderjarige vreemdelingen in België*.

22 Art. 61/14 2° Aliens Act.

23 See Helena De Vylder, 'Niet-begeleide minderjarige vreemdelingen: wat na achttien jaar?' in Desmet, Verhellen and Bouckaert (eds.), Rechten van niet-begeleide minderjarige vreemdelingen in België (n. 21 above).

24 Full judicial review appeal: '*minderjarige*' (in Dutch) or '*mineur*' (in French); annulment appeal: '*bevel tot terugbrenging*' and '*voogd*' (in Dutch); '*ordre de reconduire*' and '*tuteur*'/'*ordre de reconduire*' and '*tutrice*' (in French).

25 http://www.rvv-cce.be/nl/arr.

26 Full judicial review appeal: judgments delivered between 1 January and 30 November 2016, which at the time of the research was the most recent available case law; annulment appeal: judgments delivered between 1 January 2015 and June 2017, at the time of the research also the most recent available case law. The time frame for the annulment appeal procedure was extended backwards to have a sufficient critical mass of relevant judgments.

27 This indicates that asylum cases involving minors are far more common than durable solutions cases of unaccompanied minors.

whether or not represented by his/her guardian, or as an accompanied minor. In the latter group, the minor may also be the applicant, or be the child of a parent or guardian who challenges a decision of the CGRS, without being a party to the proceedings ('child of the applicant'). Judgments concerning minors in a different situation than applicant or child of the applicant (for example, minor brothers or sisters of the applicant, minor spouses, and 'left behind' children in the country of origin) were therefore excluded. In addition, the focus was on foreign nationals who were minors at the time of the procedure before the CALL. Judgments about persons who claimed to be minors, but of which the Guardianship Service had ruled that they were of age, or about persons who were minors at the time of certain facts or during an earlier asylum procedure, but who were in the meantime of age, were not included in the analysis.

For the annulment appeal, relevant judgments were judgments on the merits relating to appeals against an order to be brought to the border, delivered to the guardian of an unaccompanied minor in the framework of the durable solution procedure. The following judgments were thus excluded: rejections of an appeal because the applicant has not appeared and is not represented;[28] judgments that found a lack of interest because the minor turned 18;[29] and cases where none of the parties asked to be heard within 15 days of sending a decision rejecting the appeal, so that they were deemed to agree with the decision ground.[30]

On the basis of these criteria, the sample was reduced to 253 relevant judgments in full judicial review appeal. The main countries of origin were Afghanistan, Albania, Guinea, Iran and Russia. At the time of the research, the majority of the asylum cases was handled by one Dutch-speaking Chamber and two French-speaking Chambers.[31] The country of origin often determines the language of the proceedings: 100% of the Afghan and 93% of the Iraq cases were handled by a Dutch-speaking Chamber, whereas 95% of the Guinean and 74% of the Albanian cases came before a French-speaking Chamber. Within the annulment appeal, 48 relevant judgments were identified, the main countries of origin being the DR Congo (25%), Albania (10%), Morocco (10%) and Guinea (8%). These judgments were then analysed making use of Excel and NVivo.

The methodology used has both limitations and benefits. First of all, this chapter focuses on people younger than 18 years as a result of the search terms used ('minor'). This age limit does not necessarily correspond to the reality in which children and young people find themselves: a young person of

[28] Art. 39/59 §2, al. 2 Aliens Act.
[29] Art. 39/56 Aliens Act.
[30] Art. 39/73 §§2 and 3 Aliens Act.
[31] Since February 2018, another Dutch-speaking Chamber has been handling asylum cases on a more regular basis as well.

17 years and six months can be less vulnerable than a young person of 19 years, for example. This limitation applies not only to this chapter, however, but also more generally to the children's rights framework. Moreover, it is theoretically possible that the search terms did not capture all relevant judgments. In view of the neutral selection criterion, however, it can be assumed that the analysis relates to a representative sample of judgments in the time frames concerned. Nevertheless, compared to the total number of judgments that the CALL has already pronounced, the sample is still limited. Therefore, it cannot be deduced from this research whether and to what extent these findings also apply to the case law in general (in particular judgments in which no minors are involved). Furthermore, this is not a longitudinal analysis, but a 'photo' of the situation during a specific time frame. Finally, since this exploratory study consists of a case law analysis, the perceptions and strategies of the actors involved (minors, their parents or guardians, lawyers, the CGRS or the Immigration Office, and judges) are not included here. This also limits the possibility to make explanatory statements at this point.

4. RELATIONSHIP BETWEEN THE OUTCOME OF THE CASE AND THE LANGUAGE OF THE PROCEEDINGS

In a quantitative analysis, the outcome of the case in relation to the language of the proceedings (French or Dutch) was analysed. In the full judicial review appeal, this concerns the confirmation, reform or annulment of the decision of the CGRS; in the annulment appeal, this relates to the rejection of the appeal or the annulment of the decision of the Immigration Office. One reason for this research were claims about differences between the Dutch-speaking and French-speaking asylum jurisprudence within the CALL. For instance, the 2015 AIDA Report for Belgium stated:

> 'Generally speaking, lawyers and asylum seekers are quite critical about the limited use the [Council for Alien Law Litigation] seems to make of its full jurisdiction, which is reflected in the low reform and annulment rates. It is also important to note that there is *a big difference in jurisprudence between the more liberal Francophone and the stricter Dutch Chambers of the CALL*.'[32]

This difference had not been empirically substantiated, however.

For the asylum case law, the outcome of the case was also analysed in relation to the following variables: the legal position of the minor (accompanied or

32 Emphasis added. Asylum Information Database (AIDA), *Country Report: Belgium*, 2015, 24.

unaccompanied), the role of the minor in the proceedings (applicant or child of applicant), the Chamber, the judge, and the country of origin. These variables could not explain, however, the divergence noted between the Francophone and the Dutch-speaking Chambers. The Dutch case law did show a greater consistency in the relative share of the three types of decisions across the different judges and countries of origin than the French case law.[33]

4.1. FULL JUDICIAL REVIEW APPEAL (ASYLUM CASE LAW)

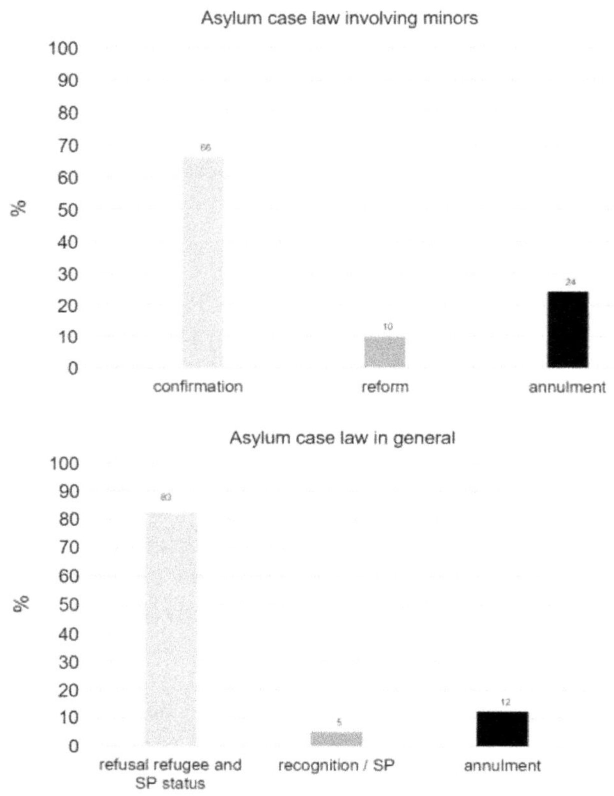

Figure 1. Comparison between asylum case law involving minors and asylum case law in general, per type of decision[34]

[33] See Desmet, 'Minderjarigen in de volle rechtsmachtprocedure van de Raad voor Vreemdelingenbetwistingen' (n. 1 above) 202–205.

[34] The figure 'Asylum case law in general' is based on Figure 16 from Bamps et al., 'Présentation du Conseil du Contentieux des Étrangers' (n. 4 above) 43.

Whereas this chapter distinguishes between 'confirmation', 'reform' and 'annulment' of a decision of the CGRS, the statistics of the CALL differentiate between 'refusal of the refugee and subsidiary protection (SP) status', 'recognition as refugee/subsidiary protection' and 'annulment'. Theoretically speaking, a confirmation of a decision of the CGRS does not necessarily equal a refusal of the refugee status and subsidiary protection status, whereas reforming a decision of the CGRS does not *per se* imply a recognition as refugee or the granting of subsidiary protection. This is so because also the Minister or the Immigration Office can appeal a decision of the CGRS that he or she considers to be in violation of the Aliens Act or the relevant royal decrees.[35] This situation did not occur within the sample of judgments, though, so that the different types of decision can be equated.

A comparison per type of decision between the sample of judgments and the general asylum case law shows that decisions involving minors are twice as often reformed (10% versus 5% overall) and annulled (24% versus 12% overall) (see Figure 1). In judgments in which minors are involved, as applicant or as child of the applicant, the Council thus refuses international protection less often than in general (66% confirmations of the decision of the CGRS versus 83% overall).

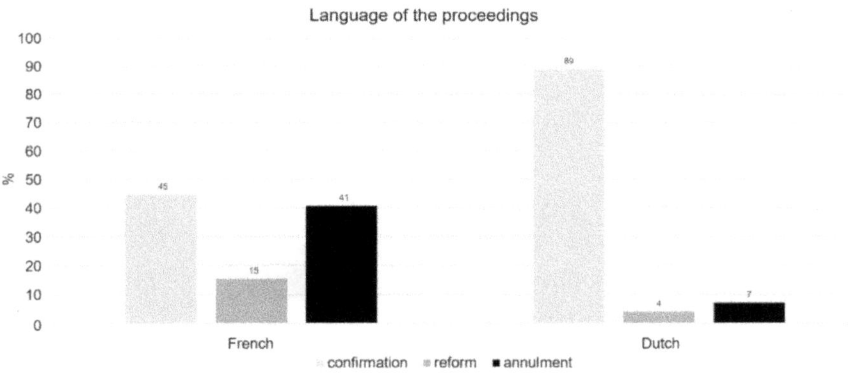

Figure 2. Comparison between French and Dutch asylum case law involving minors, per type of decision

Within the group of judgments analysed, this difference in outcome is entirely attributable to the Francophone case law, where the number of confirmations of decisions of the CGRS is considerably lower (45%) than the global share of confirmations (83%) (see Figure 2). Within the French Chambers, there are more reforms (15%) and especially more annulments (41%) than in the general asylum case law. In Dutch judgments, an – albeit smaller – difference is

35 Art. 39/56, 2nd al. Aliens Act.

noticeable in the opposite direction: recognition as a refugee or the granting of subsidiary protection status is slightly more often refused in the sample of judgments (88%) than in general (83%). In only 4% of the cases, do Dutch Chambers reform a decision of the CGRS and grant international protection; in 7% a decision is annulled.

4.2. ANNULMENT APPEAL (DURABLE SOLUTION PROCEDURE FOR UNACCOMPANIED MINORS)

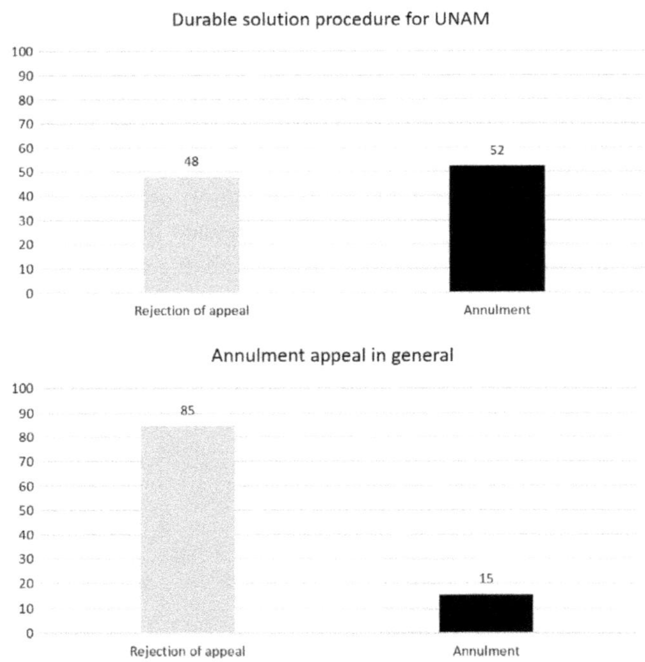

Figure 3. Comparison between case law on family reunification or return as durable solution for UNAM and the annulment appeal in general, per type of decision[36]

Both branches of case law – full judicial review appeal (asylum) and annulment appeal – are in general characterised by a similar share of confirmations of the decisions of the CGRS and the Immigration Office (83%[37] and 85% respectively).

---

36 The figure 'Annulment appeal in general' is based on the numbers of 2016 in Figure 17 in Bamps et al., 'Présentation du Conseil du Contentieux des Étrangers' (n. 4 above) 44. As mentioned above, the sample covers a larger period (January 2015–June 2017). In 2015, 18% of the decisions of the Immigration Office were annulled.

37 See Figure 1.

Comparing the samples of judgments analysed here – asylum cases involving minors and durable solution cases regarding unaccompanied minors – a similar trend can be identified, in that the Council seems to be stricter when (unaccompanied) minors are involved, and thus annuls more judgments. This trend is even more pronounced in the annulment procedure, where more than half of the decisions of the Immigration Office (52%) were annulled and sent back to the Immigration Office for a new decision to be taken (compared to 34% of the decisions being reformed or annulled in the asylum case law involving minors) (see Figure 3). One possible explanation is that in the sample of asylum cases involving minors, also cases were included where minors were children of the applicants, and thus potentially less directly affected by the decision on international protection (or at least considered to be so by the judge).

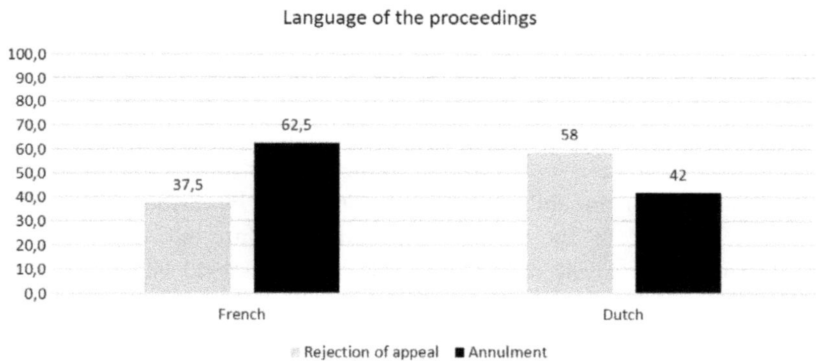

Figure 4. Comparison between French and Dutch judgments relating to family reunification or return as a durable solution for UNAM, per type of decision

Breaking down the type of decisions as to the language in which the proceedings regarding the return of an unaccompanied minor were held, reveals that the French-speaking Chambers rejected the appeal in 37.5% of the cases, whereas the Dutch-speaking Chambers did so in 58% of the cases. Also here, the French-speaking Chambers thus demonstrate a more critical stance towards the first instance decisions than the Dutch-speaking Chambers (annulling more), but the difference is less pronounced than in the asylum case law.

Comparing the French-speaking Chambers in both strands of case law, the share of confirming decisions is rather similar (45% in full judicial review appeal compared to 37.5% in annulment appeal). Between the Dutch Chambers, a more prominent difference emerges between full judicial review appeal (89% confirmations) and annulment appeal (58% confirmations, thus rejections of the appeal). These figures thus corroborate, for the sample of judgments analysed, the finding that Dutch-speaking asylum Chambers are substantively more reluctant to contest first instance decisions, than both the French-speaking asylum Chambers and the Dutch-speaking Chambers in annulment procedures.

5. LEGAL WEIGHT ATTACHED TO THE PRINCIPLE OF THE BEST INTERESTS OF THE CHILD

The principle of the best interests of the child has been incorporated differently in the two legal frameworks under review (international protection, on the one hand, and durable solutions for unaccompanied minors, on the other). For both legal frameworks, there are of course the general sources regarding the best interests of the child at the international (Art. 3(1) UNCRC), European (Art. 24(2) Charter of Fundamental Rights of the European Union) and national (Art. 22bis(4) Constitution) level. Until recently, the best interests of the child was not included in the Aliens Act with regard to international protection. Only a 2013 Royal Decree held that '[t]he best interests of the child is a paramount consideration that shall guide the [CGRS] ... when investigating the application for international protection.'[38] This provision imposes, however, a greater legal weight ('paramount') to be attached to the best interests of the child than the UNCRC ('primary'). In November 2017 (thus after the sample was taken), the same provision has been included in the Aliens Act.[39] In contrast to this relative absence of the best interests of the child principle in Belgian asylum legislation, the best interests of the child has been incorporated in various national legal provisions relevant to the durable solution procedure for unaccompanied minors. The best interests of the child must be considered before taking any return decision.[40] This is explicitly repeated when a return decision concerns an unaccompanied minor.[41] Moreover, when investigating the possibility of return to the country of origin or a country where the unaccompanied minor has a legal residence right, the state authorities must ensure that it is in the best interest of the child to be placed in the reception structure.[42] Finally, the Belgian Constitutional Court has confirmed that these provisions of the Aliens Act only permit 'the return of the minor ... or family reunification as durable solution ... in so far as that return or reunification is compatible with the best interests of the child.'[43]

---

38 Art. 14 §4 Royal Decree of 11 July 2003 determining the procedure and functioning of the Office of the Commissioner General for Refugees and Stateless persons.

39 Art. 57/1 §4 Aliens Act, inserted by Art. 37 of the Law of 21 November 2017. It is regrettable that this provision was included in an article that, at least for the remainder, focuses on accompanied minors.

40 Art. 74/13 Aliens Act: 'When taking a decision to expel, the Minister or his authorized representative shall take into account the best interests of the child, family life and the state of health of the third-country national concerned.' This is a transposition of Directive 2008/115/EC of the European Parliament and of the Council on common standards and procedures in Member States for returning illegally staying third-country nationals [2008] OJ L348/98, Art. 5.

41 Art. 74/16 §1 Aliens Act: 'Before taking a decision to expel an illegally staying unaccompanied foreign minor, the Minister or his representative shall consider every proposal for a durable solution of his/her guardian and take into account the best interests of the child.'

42 Art. 74/16 §2, 2nd para., 3° Aliens Act.

43 Constitutional Court 18 July 2013, No. 106/201, B.6.6. The Court also held that the competences of the Minister or his representative regarding the enforcement of migration

The CALL thus has a legal obligation to take the best interests of the child into account, both in asylum cases involving minors (full judicial review appeal) and regarding the durable solution procedure for unaccompanied minors (annulment appeal). The legal sources upon which this obligation is based are different, however, with a 'light' incorporation of the best interests of the child principle in Belgian asylum legislation (at least until recently), versus a strong entrenchment of the best interests of the child in the national legal framework regarding durable resolutions and return of unaccompanied minors. This seems to be reflected in the extent to which the applicant invokes the best interests of the child before the CALL (rarely in asylum case law,[44] versus frequently in relation to the durable solution procedure), as well as in the extent to which the best interests of the child principle is invoked by the CALL itself (again, rarely in asylum cases,[45] versus frequently in appeals against orders to be brought to the border, issued to the guardian of an unaccompanied minor). Moreover, the legal weight attached to the principle of the best interests of the child differs in both strands, as is elaborated on in the next sections.

5.1. FULL JUDICIAL REVIEW APPEAL (ASYLUM CASE LAW)

The asylum case law demonstrates a remarkable diversity in approaches to the legal weight of the principle of the best interests of the child. These approaches are hereinafter analytically disentangled, but various of these often concur together in one judgment. They can be situated on a continuum, ranging from the rejection of any impact of the best interests principle, to a procedural and (exceptionally) a substantive approach.

A first approach is that Article 3(1) UNCRC[46] and Article 22bis(4) of the Constitution,[47] are denied direct effect, whereby the CALL refers to established case law of the Council of State and the Court of Cassation.[48] In asylum cases, however, the debate about the direct effect of Article 3 UNCRC has lost

policies 'are restricted by the obligation to determine a durable solution that is adapted to the situation of each minor'. Ibid., B.9.2.

44 See also J.-F. Hayez, 'Les mineurs dans la procédure devant le Conseil du Contentieux des Étrangers' in Adam et al. (eds.), *10 jaar Raad voor Vreemdelingenbetwistingen: daadwerkelijke rechtsbescherming – 10 ans du Conseil du Contentieux des Étrangers: la protection jurisdictionnelle effective* (n. 4 above) 373.

45 Reference is rather made to the 'young age' of the applicant.

46 CALL 19 February 2016, No. 162420; CALL 4 March 2016, No. 163488; CALL 4 July 2016, No. 171191.

47 CALL 3 February 2016, No. 161305.

48 See e.g. references in CALL 4 March 2016, No. 163488 to: Council of State 7 February 1996, No. 58032; Council of State 11 June 1996, No. 60097; Council of State 26 September 1996, No. 61990; Council of State 1 April 1997, No. 65754; Court of Cassation 4 November 1999, AR C.99.0048.N; Court of Cassation 4 November 1999, AR C.99.0111N.

importance because of the applicability of Article 24(2) of the Charter. Given that the legal framework on applications for international protection in the Aliens Act is based on the transposition of the recast Qualification Directive,[49] the best interests of the child must be taken into account in asylum cases.

A second reasoning concerns matters in which children are not applicants themselves, but in which the applicants ask to consider the best interests of their child or children. The CALL then has held that the principle of the best interests of the child is not applicable, because the applicants did not submit their appeal on behalf of their child as well,[50] or because no decision is being taken about the children.[51] However, the principle of the best interests of the child does not only apply to decisions that have a *direct* impact on children (for example, when they themselves are applicants for international protection), but also to decisions that have an *indirect* impact on children.[52]

In a third line of argumentation, the Council refers to its limited competence within the full judicial review procedure (i.e. assessing whether the applicant is a refugee or is entitled to subsidiary protection), and considers that the best interests of the child would only be affected by another decision (for example, a removal measure or the granting of a residence right) for which the CALL is not competent.[53] Such an approach is clearly at odds with the fact that the best interests of the child must be considered in '*all* actions concerning children',[54] including the assessment of their application for international protection, or that of their parents.

Fourthly, the CALL often states that:

> 'the general consideration that the best interests of the child is the primary consideration in any decision affecting the child, does not affect the particularity of asylum law, where Articles 48/3 and 48/4 of the Aliens Act in implementation of European legislation and of the Geneva Convention of 28 July 1951 provide clearly defined conditions for recognition as a refugee or the granting of subsidiary protection status.[55]

---

49 Directive 2011/95/EU of the European Parliament and of the Council on standards for the qualification of third-country nationals or stateless persons as beneficiaries of international protection, for a uniform status for refugees or for persons eligible for subsidiary protection, and for the content of the protection granted [2011] OJ L337/9.

50 CALL 3 February 2016, No. 161305 (using the wording of Council of State 29 May 2013, No. 223630, note W. Vandenhole [2014] Tijdschrift voor Vreemdelingenrecht 322).

51 CALL 29 November 2016, No. 178619.

52 UN Committee on the Rights of the Child, 'General Comment No. 14 (2013) on the right of the child to have his or her best interests taken as a primary consideration (art. 3, para 1)' (2013) UN Doc. CRC/C/GC/14, §19.

53 CALL 3 February 2016, No. 161278, see also CALL 13 May 2016, No. 167645 (family reunification) and CALL 23 September 2016, No. 175274 (granting of residence right).

54 Art. 3(1) UNCRC, emphasis added; see also Art. 24(2) Charter ('in all actions relating to children').

55 CALL 23 November 2016, No. 178246.

This paragraph is taken from a judgment of the Council of State of 29 May 2013.[56] Within the Dutch-speaking Chambers of the CALL, this approach seems to be established case law,[57] whereby it is usually, but not always[58] combined with other arguments concerning the non-applicability or non-relevance of the best interests principle. No reference was found to this phrase within the Francophone case law analysed.

Vandenhole proposes three possible interpretations of this wording: as an expression of the principle that the specific provisions of asylum law have priority over the general provision concerning the best interests of the child (*lex specialis derogat legi generali*), as an expression of the priority of the Regulations and Directives of the Common European Asylum System and of the Refugee Convention on Article 22bis of the Constitution, or as an expression of the view that the best interests of the child should not affect the recognition as a refugee or the granting of subsidiary protection status. Referring to the case law of the Belgian Constitutional Court[59] and the European Court of Human Rights,[60] Vandenhole rightly argues that the view that the best interests of the child should not be considered in asylum case law cannot be maintained.

An argumentation that is closely linked to the former one, states – in various wordings – that the best interests of the child are not 'sufficient', nor for a parent to make a well-founded fear of persecution or a real risk of serious harm plausible, nor for minor asylum seekers themselves to obtain international protection.[61] However, taking into account the best interests of the child does not mean that these interests systematically prevail in the weighing against other interests, of, for instance, other children, of parents or other caretakers, and of the state (e.g. in migration control). According to the UN Committee on the Rights of the Child (CRC Committee), 'the right of the child to have his or her best interests taken as a primary consideration means that the child's interests have *high priority*', which does not imply that the best interests of the child should always prevail.[62] The UNHCR Guidelines on asylum claims of children also explicitly state that a child-sensitive interpretation of the Refugee Convention does not imply that minor asylum seekers should automatically

56 Council of State 29 May 2013, No. 223630, note W. Vandenhole [2014] Tijdschrift voor Vreemdelingenrecht 322.

57 CALL 26 January 2016, No. 160786; CALL 26 January 2016, No. 160793; CALL 3 February 2016, No. 161305; CALL 15 March 2016, No. 164120; CALL 4 November 2016, No. 177356; CALL 23 November 2016, No. 178246; CALL 24 November 2016, No. 178391.

58 In judgment No. 177356, the reasoning regarding the particularity of asylum law is the only justification for not considering the best interests of the child. CALL 4 November 2016, No. 177356.

59 Constitutional Court 18 July 2013, No. 106/2013, B.12.5.

60 *Nunez v. Norway* App No. 55597/09 (ECHR, 28 June 2011) §84.

61 CALL 12 January 2016, No. 159721; CALL 26 January 2016, No. 160793; CALL 15 March 2016, No. 164120; CALL 4 July 2016, No. 171191; CALL 23 November 2016, No. 178248.

62 UN Committee on the Rights of the Child (n. 52 above) §§37–39.

be recognised.[63] The principle of the best interests of the child requires, however, that the claim be examined from the child's perspective, both when the child is the applicant him- or herself and when the parents request international protection.[64] Moreover, the Belgian legislator requires that the best interests of the child are 'a paramount consideration' that shall guide the CGRS during the investigation of the application for international protection.[65] Through the above argumentation, however, the Council refrains from a substantive assessment of the best interests of the child.

In two judgments, the principle of the best interests of the child was discussed in the context of the obligation to state reasons and the burden of proof respectively. A decision by the CGRS was annulled because it had not responded to the applicant's arguments regarding the child's best interests.[66] In another judgment, the CALL held that the applicant had to provide concrete elements to show that her minor child feared persecution or that she would run a real risk of serious harm, in order to become eligible for refugee status or for subsidiary protection status.[67]

The CALL also regularly checks whether the CGRS has provided sufficient procedural safeguards when handling an application for international protection of an unaccompanied minor, such as being heard by a specialised protection officer in the presence of a guardian and a lawyer.[68] Here, the Council supervises the (procedural) determination of best interests (BID), but not the (substantive) best interests assessment (BIA).[69] This test often occurs as well without explicit reference to the best interests principle. On the other hand, it is not clear why this procedural check sometimes is, and sometimes is not carried out in the judgments.

Subsequently, there are a number of judgments in which the best interests of the child are considered, but are given a negative interpretation. For example, the Council has held that the recognition of an incorrect or hypothetical nationality cannot be in the interest of the applicant's daughter.[70]

---

63 UNHCR, *Guidelines on International Protection: Child Asylum Claims under Articles 1(A)2 and 1(F) of the 1951 Convention and/or 1967 Protocol relating to the Status of Refugees* (2009) UN Doc. HRC/GIP/09/08, §4.

64 Ibid., §9. See also §10: 'The principle of the best interests of the child requires that the harm be assessed from the child's perspective. This may include an analysis as to how the child's rights or interests are, or will be, affected by the harm. Ill-treatment which may not rise to the level of persecution in the case of an adult may do so in the case of a child.'

65 Art. 14 §4 Royal Decree of 11 July 2003 determining the procedure and functioning of the Office of the Commissioner General for Refugees and Stateless persons; since November 2017 also included in the Aliens Act, see n. 39 above.

66 CALL 13 October 2016, No. 176236.

67 CALL 26 July 2016, No. 172398.

68 CALL 24 November 2016, No. 178391; CALL 11 April 2016, No. 165452, see also CALL 19 February 2016, No. 162420.

69 UN Committee on the Rights of the Child (n. 52 above) §§48–99.

70 CALL 26 January 2016, No. 160793; CALL 15 March 2016, No. 164120. See also CALL 23 November 2016, No. 178248.

In one judgment from the sample of 253 rulings, the CALL makes a more substantive assessment of the best interests of the child.[71] The applicant was a Sunni Arab woman with a son with a serious mental disability (who was not a party to the proceedings himself). Whereas the argument of the applicant was based on the Aliens Act, the Royal Decree of 11 July 2003, Article 24(2) of the Charter, and the UNHCR Guidelines on child asylum claims, the judge referred of his own accord to Recital 18 of the recast Qualification Directive as the only legal source to respect the best interests of the child – which is not the strongest legal basis. The Council considered that, in view of the situation in Baghdad (and, by extension, Iraq), the applicant's son, being a Sunni with a serious mental disability, had a well-founded fear of persecution. Because the son always needed the attention and assistance of his mother, the Council also established a well-founded fear of persecution on the part of the applicant 'because of the serious medical problems of her son since she, as a Sunni, because of his behavior will also attract the negative attention from the (Shiite) people and militias without having the protection of the Iraqi authorities against this'. In this case, both mother and son were recognised as refugees, among other things on the basis of the dependency relationship of the son with regard to the mother, and despite the fact that the son himself was not a party to the proceedings. This judgment stands therefore in contrast with the argumentation in other judgments discussed above, that the principle of the best interests of the child is not applicable because the child is not an applicant himself.[72]

Even within a limited group of judgments, there thus appears to be within the full judicial review procedure a great diversity in approaches to the legal significance of the principle of the best interests of the child. A negative attitude seems to prevail. In the majority of cases the best interests principle is considered to be inapplicable or irrelevant, only a procedural review – although it is a full judicial review procedure – is carried out, and/or the principle is interpreted in a negative way. Such approaches are not in line with international and European regulations and case law, which explicitly require that the best interests of the child is given a high priority, also in asylum cases. The 2013 Royal Decree even assigns a decisive significance to the best interests of the child when assessing applications for international protection. It is therefore high time for the CALL to proceed to a substantive assessment of the best interests of the child in its full judicial review procedure, in compliance with the guidelines of the CRC Committee. For legal protection and legal certainty, it is essential that legal questions are answered in the same way, in accordance with the European and

---

71 CALL 29 June 2016, No. 170819.

72 In other judgments as well, the fact that a minor was not a party to the proceedings (but the applicant's child) has not prevented the Council from considering the situation of the minor. See CALL 14 January 2016, No. 159980; CALL 11 February 2016, No. 161927.

international human rights framework. In this respect, the recent 'upgrading' of the requirement that the best interests of the child guide the CGRS as a paramount consideration from the 2013 Royal Decree to the Aliens Act may induce lawyers to invoke the best interests principle more frequently, and thus oblige judges to respond to this argument.

5.2. ANNULMENT APPEAL (DURABLE SOLUTION PROCEDURE FOR UNACCOMPANIED MINORS)

In the judgments concerning family reunification or return as a durable solution for an unaccompanied minor, the range of approaches taken towards the legal weight of the principle of the best interests of the child is less diverse. Some judgments also deny the direct effect of Article 3(1) UNCRC[73] and/or Article 22bis(4) of the Constitution.[74] This does not necessarily imply that these judgments do not consider the best interests of the child, given that in relation to the durable solution procedure for unaccompanied minors and return, the obligation to consider the best interests of the child has also been explicitly enshrined in the Aliens Act.[75]

On the other hand, various judges refer to the best interests of the child in their grounds for annulment. These grounds may relate to a violation of general principles of good governance, such as the principle of due diligence or the formal obligation to state reasons and/or to a violation of specific provisions in the Aliens Act that include the obligation to consider the best interests of the child. The Court observes then, for instance, that the Immigration Office has not carried out a diligent investigation, but has only based itself on assumptions without offering the necessary guarantees as to appropriate reception and care in the country of origin. The Council concluded that the contested decision had not considered the best interests of the child, and annulled the decision on the basis of a violation of the principle of due diligence.[76] The judgment of the Constitutional Court of 18 July 2013, that explicitly stated that return or

[73] CALL 14 September 2015, No. 152423; CALL 26 October 2015, No. 155331; CALL 29 April 2016, No. 167002.

[74] CALL 9 February 2017, No. 182033.

[75] E.g. in judgment No. 185728, the CALL annuls the judgment on the basis of a lack of verification by the Immigration Office of the guarantees of reception and care by the parents or family members of the minor, without even responding to the arguments of the applicant about Arts. 3 UNCRC and 22bis Constitution. CALL 21 April 2017, No. 185278.

[76] CALL 14 January 2015, No. 136183. See also CALL 2 February 2015, No. 137706, where the Council observes that it is 'particularly undiligent not to carry out an investigation regarding the best interests of the child', and also decides that the principle of due diligence has been violated. For a similar reasoning leading to a violation of the obligation to state reasons, see e.g. CALL 29 April 2016, No. 167002.

reunification can only be a durable solution when in the best interests of the unaccompanied minor, is also frequently referred to by the CALL.[77]

In an interesting judgment, the best interests of the child did not only concern the unaccompanied minor herself, but also the child she had with a refugee recognised in Belgium.[78] The Council referred to the fact that Article 74/13 of the Aliens Act – which requires that in any expulsion decision, the best interests of the child are considered – concerns a transposition of Article 5 of the Returns Directive, which renders the Charter of Fundamental Rights of the European Union applicable. Given that the Explanations relating to the Charter indicate that Article 24 of the Charter is based on Article 3 UNCRC,[79] the latter provision is relevant for a more appropriate understanding of Article 24 of the Charter. Referring to the fact that Article 3(1) UNCRC is not only applicable to measures that have a direct impact on children, but also to those that impact children indirectly,[80] the Council noted that, although the contested decision mentions that the unaccompanied minor has a child with a refugee recognised in Belgium, the best interests of the child of the unaccompanied minor, and specifically the family life in Belgium, were not taken into account. Only the best interests of the party concerned, namely the unaccompanied minor, had been considered. If the durable solution consisted in a reunification with the parents in the country of origin (Serbia), this would imply that either the unaccompanied minor had to leave her child, and the child would thus be separated from the mother, or that she had to take the child with her, in which case the child would be separated from his father because of his refugee status. Information from UNHCR indicated that Roma from Kosovo, like the partner of the unaccompanied minor, are very vulnerable in Serbia, and that it cannot be expected that the family would settle there. The Council concluded that Article 74/13 of the Aliens Act had been violated.

Compared to asylum cases involving minors, the legal weight given to the principle of the best interests of the child in judgments concerning the durable solution procedure for unaccompanied minors seems to be more coherent. Here, the predominant approach is not a dismissive one, but an assessment of whether the best interests of the child have been considered, as required by the national legal provisions at stake. This seems to point in the direction of

77 CALL 14 January 2015, No. 136183.

78 CALL 15 January 2015, No. 136353.

79 Explanations Relating to the Charter of Fundamental Rights [2007] OJ C303/25.

80 Judges of the Council report that also in the annulment appeal procedure in general, the best interests of the child is considered when the decision has an indirect impact on the child. See M. Ryckaseys and S. Kegels, 'Het hoger belang van het kind in het annulatiecontentieux' in C. Adam et al. (eds.), *10 jaar Raad voor Vreemdelingenbetwistingen: daadwerkelijke rechtsbescherming – 10 ans du Conseil du Contentieux des Étrangers: la protection jurisdictionnelle effective* (n. 4 above) 295.

a practical relevance of incorporating best interests of the child provisions in national legislation – even though from a strictly legal point of view the added value thereof is mostly limited, given that Article 24 of the Charter is applicable in most asylum and migration law cases.[81] This lends support to the call of the Federal Migration Centre – Myria – to include a transversal provision in the Aliens Act that obliges the administrative and judicial authorities to consider first and foremost the best interests of children in all procedures that concern them. This would overcome the currently fragmented approach in the Aliens Act, where the best interests of the child is referred to in some provisions (relating to, for instance, unaccompanied minors, return, family reunification, and human trafficking and smuggling) but not in others.[82]

6. FINAL REMARKS

This chapter provided a quantitative and a qualitative analysis of two strands of case law within the full judicial review procedure and the annulment procedure of the Belgian Council for Alien Law Litigation. Within the full judicial review procedure, asylum cases of 2016 in which minors were involved as applicant or child of the applicant, were scrutinised. Within the annulment appeal, the sample concerned cases on the durable solution procedure for unaccompanied minors between January 2015 and June 2017.

The quantitative analysis revealed that, in case law involving (unaccompanied) minors, the Council adopts a more stringent stance towards first instance decisions. In the asylum case law, judgments in which minors are involved are twice as much reformed and annulled than the 'general' case law. This difference is entirely due, however, to the Francophone case law, which is therefore more critical of the decisions of the CGRS than the Dutch-speaking Chambers. In the durable solutions cases, the difference with the overall figures on annulment cases is even more pronounced, as more than three times as many judgments are annulled in the sample than in general. Also here, the French-speaking Chambers tend to annul more, but the difference from the Dutch-speaking Chambers is less pronounced than in the asylum case law.

The quantitative analysis therefore confirms at least in part the hypothesis of a difference between the Dutch-speaking and French-speaking jurisprudence,

81 Except those migration cases that are exclusively based on national legal provisions, such as those relating to humanitarian regularisation (Art. 9bis Aliens Act) and medical regularisation (Art. 9ter Aliens Act).

82 Myria, 'Migratie in cijfers en in rechten' (2015) 11. See also Myria, Unia and Steunpunt tot bestrijding van armoede, bestaansonzekerheid en sociale uitsluiting, 'Parallel report for the Committee on the Rights of the Child' (February 2018) 4.

namely in the relative share of each type of decision, and this especially in the asylum case law. On the basis of this research it cannot be determined whether/to what extent this difference is related to the fact that it concerns judgments about (unaccompanied) minors, or whether this phenomenon manifests itself as well in the other case law of the CALL.[83] In some recent press statements, the CALL acknowledges the divergence within its asylum case law. According to its press magistrate:

> '[t]here is a difference in approach and methodology, which has historically grown. This can partly be explained by a division between Northern European, more administrative thinking, and Southern European, more principled thinking, because of which similar cases lead to different conclusions.'[84]

In the view of the First President of the CALL, 'it concerns differences between Chambers, or between judges, differences that can be linked to the file and do not coincide with the linguistic frontier.'[85] He warns against analysing the case law through the prism of language: 'Next to those who find the Flemish judges too strict, there are all those who would like to prove that the Francophone judges are too lax.'[86]

The qualitative analysis showed major differences in the way in which the Chambers in the full judicial review procedure of the CALL legally approach the principle of the best interests of the child. In the few judgments that mention the best interests of the child, the principle is often rejected as inapplicable or irrelevant. In some judgments, only a procedural assessment takes place, or the concept is interpreted in a negative way. Such approaches go against international and European legislation and case law, in particular Article 3 UNCRC and Article 24 (2) of the Charter. They also do not comply with the legal obligation of the CGRS to consider the child's best interests as a paramount consideration when investigating the application for international protection – which the CALL must supervise. The guidelines of the CRC Committee must substantiate both the substantive determination of the best interests of the child and the procedural safeguards during this process.

---

83 More recently, the news magazine *Alter Échos* reviewed 303 appeal cases of Iraqi asylum seekers between July and December 2018, arriving at similar findings. The Francophone judges confirmed the negative decision of the CGRS in 49% of the cases, whereas the Dutch-speaking judges did so in 88.5% of their judgments. Cédric Vallet, 'Conseil du contentieux des étrangers: deux poids, deux mesures' *Alter Échos* no. 471 (Brussels, 4 March 2019).

84 Bruno Struys, 'Juridische beslissingen over asiel verschillen sterk in twee taalgebieden. Migrant maakt minder kans bij Vlaamse rechter' *De Morgen* (Asse-Kobegem, 6 March 2019) 1.

85 Vallet, 'Conseil du contentieux des étrangers: deux poids, deux mesures' (n. 83 above).

86 Ibid.

In the annulment procedure, the legal approach towards the best interests of the child principle is less divergent than in the asylum case law. Even though some judgments also deny the direct effect of Article 3(1) UNCRC and/or Article 22bis(4) of the Constitution, most judgments do consider the best interests of the child on the basis of the national legal provisions requiring them to do so. This indicates at least the practical – even though not always legal – relevance of incorporating the best interests of the child principle in the domestic legal framework. Finally, there is also the paradoxical outcome that in the annulment procedure, where the Council is limited to a legality control, the best interests of the child turns out to play a greater role than in its full judicial review procedure. This is probably at least partly related to a larger reluctance to consider the best interests of the child in asylum cases, given the claimed 'particularity' of asylum case law. Nevertheless, in order to ensure legal certainty, rights protection and unity of jurisprudence, it is fundamental that legal questions receive the same answer in different judgments, in accordance with the European and international human rights framework.

CHILD ASYLUM SEEKERS IN BOTSWANA

A Critique of the *Ngezi* and *Iragi* Decisions

Elizabeth MACHARIA-MOKOBI*

1. INTRODUCTION

The purpose of this chapter is to assess the role of children's rights in decision-making with special focus on asylum-seeking children in Botswana. This topic is significant because in 2017, the Court of Appeal considered two applications brought by men and women, who had been detained along with their minor children, following failed applications for asylum. The first of these decisions was *Marie Iragi and 2 others v. The Attorney General.*[1] This case concerned two women who sought asylum in Botswana accompanied by three minor children.

* Senior lecturer at the University of Botswana Department of Law.

[1] UAHFT 000017-17 (unreported).

The second case was *Egama Ngezi and 165 others v. The Attorney General.*[2] This case concerned 166 adult asylum seekers and 195 children[3] who were also under detention pending status determination or removal following rejection of their claims for asylum.[4]

In each case, the asylum seekers brought an application for *habeas corpus*. They alleged that they had been subjected to lengthy and indefinite detention, with their children, following their failed applications for asylum. The particular focus of this chapter is the Court's approach to protecting the rights of the child asylum seekers who were detained along with their parents.

The chapter begins with a discussion of the rights of child asylum seekers in light of the Convention on the Rights of the Child which Botswana has ratified and domesticated followed by a discussion on Botswana's children's rights framework in the context of refugees and asylum-seeking children. The chapter then considers the Court of Appeal decision in the consolidated appeal in the *Iragi* and *Ngezi* cases with particular focus on the Court's posture towards asylum-seeking children. The chapter ends with a discussion of the salient points that the Court should have considered in deciding the cases and some recommendations on law and policy reform.

2. THE OPERATION OF THE CONVENTION ON THE RIGHTS OF THE CHILD IN BOTSWANA

Botswana acceded to the Convention on the Rights of the Child (UNCRC)[5] in 1995 and the African Charter on the Rights and Welfare of the Child (ACRWC)[6] in 2001. A further 14 years would pass before the UNCRC was incorporated into Botswana law. In 2009, Botswana amended the Children's Act 1981 and promulgated the new Children's Act 2009 (the Act) ostensibly to implement the UNCRC.[7]

The reasons for the delay in incorporating the UNCRC into Botswana law are twofold. First, there was a need to develop the enabling legislation. Botswana is a dualist state. Treaties concluded by the executive arm of government are not

2 UAHFT 000026-17 (unreported).
3 M. Moseki, 'It has not been an easy journey' in *Prisoners of Injustice*, Ink Centre for Investigative Journalism and the Botswana Gazette Special Report, 20 December 2017, at 2.
4 The judgment noted that the larger part of this group had received rejection decisions from the Refugee Advisory Committee (RAC) which is charged with status determination in Botswana. There was a small minority that was still awaiting status determination decisions.
5 United Nations, Treaty Series, vol. 1577, at 3.
6 Organisation of African Unity (OAU), *African Charter on the Rights and Welfare of the Child*, 11 July 1990, CAB/LEG/24.9/49 (1990), available at: https://www.refworld.org/docid/3ae6b38c18.html.
7 Act No. 8 of 2009.

self-executing.[8] Treaties concluded by the executive generally must go through the process of domestication. This requires the drafting of implementing or enabling legislation by the Attorney General's Office and promulgation of such legislation by Botswana's parliament. Typically, this may take several years.

Unimplemented treaties do have some limited application in Botswana. It is important to note that in terms of section 24 of Botswana's Interpretations Act, the court may use conventions as an aid to construction of existing legislation.[9] This essentially means that undomesticated treaties may be used as a guide to interpretation of existing legislation. Section 24 of the Interpretations Act has the effect of ensuring that Botswana acts in accordance with its international obligations even as it goes through the period of drafting implementing legislation in respect of any conventions it has ratified or acceded to.

The second reason for delay in implementing the UNCRC is that there was a need to engage in public consultation on several UNCRC clauses that would change the legal landscape with regard to children upon domestication of the Convention. For instance, the new legislation was to introduce a bill of rights for children. Traditionally, children are not viewed as rights holders. This is particularly true in the African context.[10] There was a need to educate and sensitise the public to this new approach of viewing children as rights bearers.

There was also need for public consultation on the question of corporal punishment in homes. The UNCRC prohibits corporal punishment in all settings;[11] however, cultural norms existing in Botswana meant that corporal punishment was seen and continues to be seen as a reasonable tool for the disciplining of children.[12] In the end, the consultation on corporal punishment was not successful. There was little support for abolition and corporal punishment remains lawful in all settings in Botswana, subject to the 'reasonable chastisement' exception.[13]

Another example of significant change to be ushered in by implementation of the UNCRC is the possibility of imprisonment for child offenders. The repealed Children's Act 1981 did not have any provisions regarding imprisonment of children. However, the new Children's Act 2009 provided for imprisonment for repeat offenders under section 88.

---

8 O.B. Tshosa, 'The Status and Role of International Law in Botswana' in *Essays on the Law of Botswana*, Juta 2007, at 229–246.

9 Laws of Botswana, ch. 01:04.

10 Africa Committee of Experts on the Rights and Welfare of the Child, 'Africa's Agenda for Children: Fostering an Africa fit for Children', at 2.

11 See Art.19(1), 28(2) and 37 UNCRC.

12 With regard to corporal punishment, it should be noted that Botswana's Children's Act 2009 broke ranks with the CRC by retaining the legality of reasonable corporal chastisement in all settings.

13 *R. v. Janke & Janke* 1913 T.P.D. 382; Kgalaeng v. Attorney-General 1988 BLR 21 (HC).

The objective of the new Children's Act was stated in the preceding Children's Bill of 2008[14] as follows:

> 'The object of the Bill is not only to give effect to Botswana's obligations in terms of the United Nations Convention on the Rights of the Child, and the African Charter on the Rights and Welfare of the Child regarding the well-being of children, but to also promote the well-being of families and communities in Botswana.'[15]

The Children's Act 2009 was therefore intended to give full force and effect to Botswana's obligations in international law with regard to the protection of the rights and welfare of children.[16]

The provisions of the Children's Act 2009 have been accorded primacy over all legislation affecting children in Botswana. This bold statement is found in section 3 of the Act, which provides that in the event of any inconsistency, the provisions of the Act shall take precedence over any other legislation. This statement is subject to a proviso which allows for departure from the provisions of the Children's Act where applying them would harm the child, prejudice the rights and freedoms of others, the national interest, public safety, public order, public morality or health.[17] Although section 3 places the interests of children at the forefront of the application of any law, the competing interests of national security, public safety, public order, public morality or health can tip the balance away from protection of vulnerable migrant children. This is illustrated to good effect in the *Iragi* and *Ngezi* cases discussed below.

The Botswana Children's Act 2009 has adopted three guiding principles from the UNCRC which are pivotal to the protection of child rights. These principles are known as the triangle of child rights.[18] They are the best interests of the child principle, the principle of non-discrimination, and the right to participation in decisions affecting the child. Each of these principles, and its implementation in Botswana law, is discussed below together with key children's rights relevant to this decision.

2.1. THE BEST INTERESTS OF THE CHILD PRINCIPLE

Under Article 3 UNCRC, the state is obliged to uphold the best interests of the child principle.[19] The best interests of the child principle has been interpreted

---

14 Children's Bill 2008, available at: http://www.gov.bw/globalassets/mlg/bills/childrensbills2008.pdf.

15 Memorandum to the Botswana Children's Bill of 2008, at 1.

16 See 'Child Rights' UNICEF Botswana, available at: https://www.unicef.org/botswana/children.html.

17 See also *Ntshekisang v. Ntshekisang* [2011] 2 BLR 894 (HC) at 897–898.

18 See G. Van Bueren, *International Documents on Children*, 2nd edition, Martinus Nijhoff 1998, at 451.

19 See also Art. 4 ACRWC.

to mean that the state should, in taking any decision affecting children, give paramount consideration to what would be in the best interests of the child. This requires 'balancing all the elements necessary to make a decision in a specific situation affecting a specific individual child or group of children'.[20]

The best interests of the child principle is implemented in sections 5 and 6 of Botswana's Children's Act. Section 5 provides that any person or court performing a function or exercising a power under the Act shall regard the best interests of the child as the paramount consideration. Section 6 outlines factors that should be considered in determining what is in the best interests of the child. These factors include the need to protect the child from harm, the child's physical emotional and educational needs, the effect of change on the child's circumstances, the importance of stability in the child's living arrangements, and any other factors that will ensure the general well-being of the child.

There is a fair amount of case law on the best interests of the child principle in Botswana. A few decisions illustrate the application of the principle. In *Ntshekisang v. Ntshekisang*,[21] Justice Moroka noted that the domestication of the UNCRC in the Children's Act 2009 had resulted in a seismic shift in the protection of children in Botswana. In the same case, the judge lamented that the courts did not seem to appreciate the significance of the new Children's Act, observing as follows:

> 'Botswana signed and acceded to the UNCRC on 14 March 1995. As a consequence of this, the convention became legally binding on Botswana. In fulfilment of its obligations under the convention, Botswana amended its Children's Act (Cap 28:04) so as to domesticate the values and principles of the Convention on the Rights of the Child. As a result, the new Children's Act was by Act 8 of 2009 passed by Parliament. It commenced on 19 June 2009. The promulgation of the new Children's Act marked a seismic shift in the law in the handling children's issues in Botswana. The significance of this shift has unfortunately largely gone unnoticed ... In its amended form, the new Children's Act serves as a modern progressive human rights instrument embodying the bill of rights for children in Botswana. It is complementary to the bill of rights enshrined in the Constitution. The coming into force of the new Children's Act changed the legal landscape in the handling of children's issues which courts must acknowledge and make use of. Now the concept of the *best interest of the child* [my emphasis] is no longer a matter for common law or case law acknowledgment. It is a matter of statutory reality. It is thus significant, that courts dealing with matters affecting the lives, welfare and destiny of children be aware of and, make use of the provisions of the Children's Act ...'[22]

[20] Committee on the Rights of the Child, General Comment No. 14 (2013) para. 47.

[21] [2011] 2 BLR 894 (HC) at 897.

[22] See also *Ndlovu v. Macheme* [2008] 3 BLR 230 (HC), where the Court states that the best interests of the child standard has clearly gained supremacy. See also *Mazile v. Mazile* [2001] 1 BLR 175 in a similar vein.

The best interests of the child principle is applied often in divorce and child custody cases. The principle needs to be relied on more in other types of cases that affect children and their general well-being.

2.2. THE RIGHT TO NON-DISCRIMINATION

Under Article 2 UNCRC, a state has the duty to protect the rights of every child within its jurisdiction without discrimination.[23] The principle of non-discrimination under the UNCRC means that each child in the jurisdiction of a state party is entitled to all Convention rights 'without regard to citizenship, immigration status or any other status'.[24] This means that refugee children, asylum-seeking children and even children who are failed asylum seekers should not be excluded from the framework of rights guaranteed to children under the UNCRC, and consequently in national legislation.

The principle of equal protection under the law is found in section 3 of Botswana's Constitution. Section 3 is complemented by section 15 of the Constitution, which provides that no person shall be subjected to discriminatory treatment.[25] The principle of non-discrimination is also enshrined under section 7(a) of Botswana's Children's Act 2009. Section 7(a) of the Act states that no decision or action shall be taken with respect to any child which has the result or likelihood of discrimination against any child on the basis of sex, family, colour, race, ethnicity, place of origin, language, religion, economic status, parents, physical or mental status, or any other status.

The prohibition of discrimination on the basis of place of origin or any other status, means that all laws must be applied in favour of similar treatment for all children, including refugee children, asylum-seeking children and failed asylum-seeking children awaiting removal from Botswana. It is submitted that the language of the statute is broad and inclusive.

However, one must also consider the provisions of section 15(4)(b) of the Constitution, which contains a caveat to the non-discrimination clause. Section 15(4)(b) provides that it is possible for the legislature to promulgate laws that are discriminatory with respect to non-citizens. This caveat would presumably preserve as legal laws that allow for unequal treatment between citizens and non-citizen children. A similar caveat exists under section 3 of the Children's Act, which provides that exercise of the law under the Act is subject to national security, public interest, public safety and public order considerations.

---

23 See also Art. 3 ACRWC.

24 Van Bueren, *International Documents on Children* (n. 18 above), at 452.

25 Botswana Constitution, available at: https://www.parliament.gov.bw/images/constitution.pdf.

The migration control argument that propounds that an influx of refugees would pose a national security risk for Botswana was used to justify the continued detention of asylum seekers and their children in the *Ngezi* and *Iragi* appeal discussed below. It would be hoped that the courts' approach to determining the rights of children, whatever their status, whether immigrant or citizen, should be to protect and preserve their rights. However, the fine balance between children's rights and migration control has yet to be considered fully by any Botswana court.

2.3. THE RIGHT TO PARTICIPATION

The right to participation is enshrined under Article 12 UNCRC, which provides that children capable of forming their own views shall have the right to express their views freely in all matters concerning them, and that their views shall be given due weight in accordance with the age and maturity of the child. Article 12 UNCRC then requires that the views of children subject to judicial or administrative proceedings shall be solicited directly or through a representative or appropriate body.

The right to participation is domesticated in Botswana's Children's Act under section 8, which *preserves* the right of a child with the age, maturity and requisite understanding to participate in the making of any decision that will have a significant impact on their life.

It is noted that the solicitation of the views of children is routine in child custody cases in Botswana. However, in the *Iragi* and *Ngezi* cases discussed below, there was no indication of the children in immigration detention being given an opportunity to participate in decisions being taken regarding their continued detention directly or through a representative. This gap in soliciting the view of minor detainees is significant given the fact that the views of children are regularly solicited in custody cases.

2.4. DETENTION OF CHILDREN

In addition to the triangle of children's rights discussed above, the question of detention of failed child asylum seekers is of particular relevance in the *Iragi* and *Ngezi* cases. The fact that minors formed part of the group of failed asylum seekers detained in the *Iragi* and *Ngezi* cases means that the government was under an obligation to ensure that the special and particular needs of children were placed at the forefront.

Article 22 UNCRC requires that state parties to the Convention ensure that asylum-seeking children, whether accompanied or not, receive appropriate protection and assistance. Further, Article 37 UNCRC requires states to ensure that detention of minors is used as a measure of last resort, and for the shortest possible time. The Children's Act 2009 domesticates these provisions, although not fully or comprehensively. Section 64 of the Children's Act prohibits the detention of children with their primary caregivers. Where the caregiver has been convicted of an offence, the law provides that the child is to be removed into alternative care. The Children's Act also provides that children in conflict with the law may only be imprisoned for repeat offences.[26] This provision is drafted specifically for children in conflict with the law and makes no mention of children in detention for other reasons like child asylum seekers and rejected child asylum seekers.

There is a single provision in the Children's Act 2009 dealing with refugee and displaced children. Section 53 of the Children's Act provides that 'the Minister shall provide or cause to be provided, for refugee and displaced children, such basic social services as are necessary for their survival or sustenance'. Again, there is no provision regarding children seeking asylum. It is apparent that Articles 22 and 37 UNCRC were not fully domesticated in the Children's Act 2009. In dualist systems, the executive always takes the risk, when ratifying or acceding to a convention, that the legislature may not fully domesticate the convention.

2.5. THE RIGHT TO EDUCATION AND FAMILY LIFE

The UNCRC provides that children have a right to education.[27] In the context of child asylum seekers, the UNHCR Guidelines on the Applicable Criteria and Standards relating to the Detention of Asylum Seekers and Alternatives to Detention (UNHCR Guidelines)[28] provide that during detention children should have access to education which should optimally be provided outside the detention premises. There should also be opportunity for recreation and play, which is vital for children's development.[29]

Children also have a right to family unity under Articles 5, 8 and 16 UNCRC. The Convention also confers upon children the right not to be separated from their parents without their consent.[30] Further, in terms of Article 20 UNCRC, children temporarily or permanently deprived of their family environment are entitled to special protection and assistance from the state, which includes alterative care.

---

26 See s. 85(e) as read with s. 88 Children's Act 2009.

27 Art. 28 UNCRC.

28 UNCHR 2012, available at: https://www.unhcr.org/publications/legal/505b10ee9/unhcr-detention-guidelines.html.

29 Guideline 9.2 of the UNHCR Guidelines.

30 Art. 9 UNCRC.

The right to family life and the right to basic education are domesticated and implemented in Botswana's Children's Act 2009 under section 13 and section 18 respectively. Separation of parents from their children, save where it is in the best interests of the child, is prohibited under section 13(4) of the Children's Act. Lastly section 19 provides that every child has a right to leisure, play and recreation.

The next section shall outline the facts and findings of the Court of Appeal in the consolidated appeal in the *Iragi* and *Ngezi* cases.

3. *IRAGI* AND *NGEZI* AT THE COURT OF APPEAL

3.1. THE FACTS

The *Iragi* decision concerned three foreign women who entered Botswana from Zambia at the Kazungula border post, a gazetted entry point, sometime in 2015. Marie Iragi was accompanied by two children Sohia and Aganze, aged 3 and 2 respectively. Sophia Laheri was accompanied by a 1year-old child, Tuizo. Theresa Butoyi was accompanied by two minors, Helena (5) and Rosina (3). They had no travel documents.

The three petitioners presented themselves and their children to immigration officials at the border and declared their intention to apply for asylum in Botswana. The mothers and their children were immediately detained at the Francistown Centre for Illegal Immigrants (the Centre) pending their status determination. The Refugee Advisory Committee (RAC)[31] considered the applications for asylum brought by the women. The applications were refused and these refusals were communicated individually to the three women by letter dated 31 August 2015. In the rejection letter, they were advised to 'approach the nearest immigration office for the purpose of normalising their stay in Botswana'.

The *Ngezi* matter concerned 166 adult asylum seekers and their dependants who consisted of 195 children of various ages.[32] The status of the members of this group of petitioners was varied. A portion of them were failed asylum seekers. Other among them still awaited their status determination hearings. All of the asylum seekers had been detained at the Francistown Centre for Illegal Immigrants for periods varying from six months to about two years without any recourse to the law. The relief they sought was similar to that in *Iragi*, which was an immediate end to their indefinite detention. Those who had received

[31] This is a committee created under the Refugee (Recognition and Control) Act and whose primary duty is status determination.

[32] Moseki, 'It has not been an easy journey' (n. 3 above), at 2.

rejection decisions had also been advised to approach the nearest immigration office to regularise their stay.

The conditions at the Centre were difficult. The Centre also housed hardened criminals who were supposed to be serving prison terms at the Francistown Prison. Since the Francistown Prison was under renovation, the prisoners were transferred to the Centre and they lived side-by-side with failed asylum seekers. Families were separated upon arrival. Men and older, male children were separated from women who remained in custody of the younger children.[33] Anecdotal reports state that families saw each other for a few minutes once a week.[34] The petitioners could not leave the Centre. Some spoke of harsh treatment by guards. The children did not attend school, some for as long as two years. The process that the asylum seekers were expected to follow to normalise their stay in Botswana was not discussed in the judgment. Botswana immigration law allows visitors to enter the country for a maximum of 90 days following which they would have to obtain a residence permit to extend their stay. In order to enter Botswana lawfully, the visitor would also have to bear a valid travel document or risk deportation. A visitor may also remain in Botswana if he or she secures employment. Such a visitor would have to apply for a work permit. These options were not available to the petitioners who had no travel documents and therefore no means of regularising their stay.[35]

Unable to regularise their stay, because they had entered the country without documentation and lacking any other valid reason to remain in Botswana, the petitioners and their children remained at the Centre for Illegal Immigrants for almost two years with no further information regarding their fate following the failed asylum applications.

On 3 April 2017, Marie Iragi and her companions brought an application to the Francistown High Court in urgency for a writ of *habeas corpus*. They alleged that they were unlawfully detained at the Centre. They described the Centre as a prison. They sought declaratory relief that their detention beyond 28 days was unlawful and that the government be ordered to release them forthwith from custody and facilitate their return to their countries of origin.

Attorneys for the government argued that the Centre was not a prison and that even if it was, the petitioners were lawfully detained under the Immigration Act of 2011. No specific arguments regarding the lawfulness of the detention of children for almost two years appear in the judgments. The High Court ordered that the petitioners and their children in both cases be moved to the Dukwi Refugee Camp in order to bring an end to their indefinite detention. The petitioners in the *Ngezi* case then filed a similar application. They too received

33 Moseki, 'It has not been an easy journey' (n. 3 above) at 2.
34 Ibid.
35 See ss. 8 and 18–27 Botswana Immigration Act No. 3 of 2011.

a favourable decision at the High Court which ordered their removal to Dukwi Refugee Camp to end their indefinite detention. All petitioners were moved into the refugee camp which offered reprieve from the Centre. The matter was taken on appeal by the government. The *Iragi* and *Ngezi* cases were consolidated into a single appeal. The object of the appeal was to overturn the decision of the High Court freeing the petitioners for the Centre.

3.2. THE DECISION OF THE COURT OF APPEAL

According to the Court of Appeal, following the rejection of their applications for protection as refugees, the petitioners in *Ngezi* and *Iragi* were irregular migrants who had to be removed from Botswana under the Immigration Act. Consequently, the detention was necessary for their removal because entering Botswana without a travel document, or at a non-gazetted point of entry, or without a permit, rendered one liable to be removed from the territory of Botswana under the Immigration Act.[36]

The Court of Appeal supported this finding by arguing that the Refugee (Recognition and Control) Act of 1967 (the Refugee Act) merely suspended the operation of the rules for removal of undocumented migrants who entered Botswana without travel documents. The Court pointed out that the relevant provisions authorising removal was section 8(2) of the Refugee Act which provided that any person not given recognition as a refugee shall be removed under provisions of the Immigration Act. During the process of status determination, the detention of an asylum seeker was allowable for up to 28 days.[37] Any person whose application for asylum was unsuccessful would immediately be liable for removal under the Immigration Act unless he or she could obtain a work or residence permit to remain under the Immigration Act as a lawful immigrant.[38]

Citing *Mohammed Amend Mire and Ano v. Attorney General*[39] with approval the Court of Appeal adopted the following statement of Justice Makhwade:

> 'Following the rejecting of their asylum applications ... There was no further role for the Minister in terms of the [Refugee] Act to deal with the Petitioners. They are simply immigrants who needed to be dealt with under the Immigration Act and not under the law dealing with political refugees.'

36 See s. 18 Immigration Act.
37 Section 6 Refugee Act.
38 Section 18 Immigration Act.
39 UAHFT 000003-17 (Unreported).

The Court also emphasised that no formal declaration was required to remove undocumented migrants. The position of the Court of Appeal was that migrants could be detained and removed by immigration authorities, with the assistance of the police, and without intervention of the courts. This could be achieved under the provisions of the Prisons (Centres for Illegal Immigrants) Regulations (Prisons Regulations).[40]

Under the Prisons Regulations, the warrant of detention for an undocumented migrant could be issued by an immigration officer or a prisons officer. There was no requirement for intervention by a court of law. The Court of Appeal took the view that the detention of such migrants was justified under section 45(1) of the Immigration Act, which provided that a person liable to be removed from Botswana could be detained at the nearest convenient prison by an immigration officer for such period as may be necessary for the completion of his or her removal.

The Court of Appeal accepted that the failed asylum seekers could not be held indefinitely but stated that no limit was set on the period for which the failed asylum seeker could be detained. The Court of Appeal was disapproving of the fact that that authorities had not informed the petitioners of the progress in efforts to repatriate them.

With respect to the detained children, the Court remarked that one of the consequences of adults claiming asylum accompanied by their children is that the children would be subject to detention with their parents. The Court stated that asylum seekers should be aware of this when they cross the border.

In the end, the Court of Appeal ruled that the petitioners were to return to the Centre. The Court left it to the government to decide the time frame for the transfer of the migrants back to the Centre. The Court also ordered the government to address the petitioners on efforts to repatriate them every 60 days.

Following the Court of Appeal judgment, all but one of the petitioners had left Dukwi Camp. The camp is porous and though permission is required to leave the camp, it is possible to leave through other routes. The migrants left because they were fearful of having to return to the more restrictive environment of the Centre. It is reported that some reapplied for asylum in Zimbabwe, Namibia and South Africa.[41]

No further mention was made of the children in detention. Nor was mention made of the UNCRC or the protective provisions of the Children's Act in the Court of Appeal judgment. It is not clear if any representations were made to the Court from the children's rights perspective by government attorneys or

40 SI 90/2004.

41 Moseki, 'It has not been an easy journey' (n. 3 above) at 2.

attorneys for the petitioners. What is clear is that no arguments on children's rights appeared in the judgment.

4. RECOMMENDATIONS FOR REFORM

Migration control is a question that all states must grapple with. However, populations are increasingly mobile, fleeing all manner of difficulties. Not every person on the move qualifies for protection as a refugee. People migrate for many different reasons and states are understandably wary of weak or porous immigration control mechanisms.[42]

The challenge that Botswana faces is how to tackle the return of failed asylum seekers without criminalisation of their attempts to secure protection under international law and national law. In the *Iragi* and *Ngezi* cases discussed above, the Court of Appeal judgment leaned a long way in favour of migration control arguments to the detriment of a rights-based approach to immigration detention, particularly of children. The Court's statement that child asylum seekers would be detained with their parents was devoid of any recognition of the special position of migrant children and their rights under international and national law. There is also a need for more detailed legislation and policy for the protection of protection for child asylum seekers, mindful of their particular vulnerability, from the moment of application for asylum to the moment of rejection and consequent removal processes.

The argument put forward in this chapter is that Botswana's Court of Appeal missed an opportunity to adopt a rights-based approach to the treatment of detained asylum-seeking children. In future, Botswana should explore under-utilised provisions of its own laws and perhaps also seek to learn lessons from solutions developed across the globe. Proposals on how to harmonise discordant legislation and adopt a more child-centred approach when dealing with asylum-seeking children are considered below.

4.1. THE BEST INTERESTS OF THE CHILD PRINCIPLE

This overarching principle was not mentioned by the Court of Appeal in the *Iragi* and *Ngezi* cases. This is in spite of the fact that a great number of the individuals affected by the decision of the Court were children. It is argued that the principle, which is found in sections 5 and 6 of the Children's Act 2009, ought to have been considered. In particular, the requirement under section 6(a)

---

42 International Organisation for Migration, 'World Migration Report', available at: https://publications.iom.int/system/files/pdf/wmr_2018_en.pdf, at 1.

to ensure that children are protected from harm. It is submitted that harm was occasioned to the detained children though arbitrary detention, discrimination and lack of participation in decisions affecting them. It is recommended that all cases affecting children adopt the best interests of the child principle as the paramount consideration. This was not the approach of the Court of Appeal in *Iragi* and *Ngezi*. Unfortunately, this was patently evident in a decision that ignored children's rights whilst taking decisions that would affect the lives of many.

4.2. ARBITRARY DETENTION OF CHILDREN

The minor children detained in the *Iragi* case were held for almost two years at the Francistown Centre for Illegal Immigrants. It is submitted that the detention was not in the best interests of the children.

As mentioned above, Article 22 UNCRC requires that asylum-seeking children receive appropriate protection and assistance. This provision has not been implemented in Botswana's laws nor were the particular needs of the detained children a consideration in the judgment of the Court of Appeal.

Article 37 UNCRC requires states to ensure that detention of minors is used as a measure of last resort, and for the shortest possible time. The detention experienced by the children in *Iragi* was lengthy. Section 64 of the Children's Act prohibits the detention of children with their primary caregivers; however, no steps were taken to remove the children from the prison-like environment of the Centre to an alternative care setting despite the possibility of doing that under the Children's Act, until the High Court ordered a removal of the failed asylum seekers to the Dukwi Refugee Camp.

According to the UNHCR Guidelines[43] detention is defined as 'the deprivation of liberty or confinement in a closed place which an asylum-seeker is not permitted to leave at will, including, though not limited to, prisons or purpose-built detention, closed reception or holding centres or facilities'. The experience of the petitioners in the *Iragi* and *Ngezi* cases was therefore detention. The detention of the petitioners along with their children can also be described as arbitrary because there was no maximum limit set on the length of the detention and no minimum standards for oversight of the decisions to detain.[44]

Had the detaining authority complied with the relevant prisons regulations that governed the administration of the Francistown Centre for Illegal Immigrants

43 Available at: https://www.refworld.org/docid/503489533b8.html.

44 See Guideline 6, UNHCR Guidelines on Applicable Criteria and Standards Relating to the Detention of Asylum Seekers, 2012.

(the Prison Regulations),[45] it is unlikely that the petitioners would have brought an application for *habeas corpus*. In terms of regulations 16(3) and (4) Prisons Regulations, the officer in charge of the deporting section is required to inform the immigrants of the appointed or likely date of deportation. This was never done. The Court of Appeal noted the government's failure to informing the asylum seekers of the date of their deportation and required that the Government provide updates information on deportations every six months.

It is proposed that a more robust system of reviewing detention of failed asylum seekers is required. It is submitted that a system of judicial oversight is an important and essential safeguard particularly where children are detained. This is because children may only be detained as a last resort. There is a need to assess the reasons for the initial detention and the reasons for the continuing detention of a minor through the courts so that arbitrary detention can be avoided. This can be achieved through periodic appearance before a magistrate in the district where child is detained. The detaining authority would have to inform the court what steps it has taken to ensure prompt and speedy removal. The court will also be able to take steps to end detention that may become arbitrary where it has proved impossible to remove the child concerned safely. It is submitted that the absence of judicial oversight, through the periodic appearance of the undocumented migrants before an independent judicial officer, may result in similar circumstances of lengthy detentions arising again.

4.3. THE RIGHT TO EDUCATION AND FAMILY LIFE

The Children's Act affords children in Botswana the right to free basic education[46] and the right to family life.[47] These rights are afforded to every child in Botswana. It is argued that the children detained for long periods pending their removal in the *Iragi* and *Ngezi* cases from Botswana were entitled to free basic education. With respect to the right to family life, the Children's Act provides that no one may separate a child from his or her parents unless it is in the best interests of the child.[48] Where a child is of an appropriate age to be consulted such child must consent to the separation.[49]

No doubt, Botswana may reserve the right to withhold the enjoyment of the right to education and family life. This may be for reasons of national security, public interest, public safety and public order.[50] However, the Court of Appeal

45 Prisons (Centres for Illegal Immigrants) Regulations, SI 90/2004.
46 Section 18 Children's Act 2009
47 Section 13 Children's Act 2009.
48 Section 13 (4) Children's Act 2009.
49 Section 13(5) Children's Act 2009.
50 Section 3 Children's Act 2009.

did not comment on the fact that many of the detained children were of school-going age and were unable to attend school for up to two years.

Had the state advanced the argument that allowing the detained children to attend school outside the Centre was against public order because there was a risk that some children would abscond, the possibility of providing education inside the Centre could have been pursued. An argument could also be advanced that the detained children were non-citizens and could therefore not expect similar treatment to citizen children. However, it is difficult to see how this argument could overcome the best interests of the child principle. The children were detained by the state; therefore, the state had a duty to act in the best interests of the children. The provision of some education for the children in the Centre would have been more in keeping with Botswana's obligations under the Children's Act and the UNCRC.

With respect to separation of families the UNCRC and the Children's Act provide that children are entitled to family unity and that they should not be separated from their parents without their consent.

Recommendations for law and policy reform regarding education and family life are that Botswana should consider providing education as well as opportunities for play and recreation for school-age asylum-seeking children where detention pending status determination or detention pending removal exceeds a fixed amount of time. Government should also consider ending family separation because this is not in the best interests of the children.

5. CONCLUSION

It is the argument of this chapter that the *Iragi* and *Ngezi* case presented an opportunity to explore the extent to which migrant children can enjoy children's rights guaranteed under the Constitution and the Children's Act. The Constitution promises non-discrimination, subject to certain exceptions. The Children's Act offers all children in Botswana a raft of rights. This chapter sought to explore the extent to which the Court of Appeal recognised and enforce the constitutional right to non-discrimination and Botswana's obligations under the Children's Act and the UNCRC when dealing with asylum-seeking children.

The opportunity was missed when the migration control argument dominated the thinking of the Court of Appeal to the exclusion of children's rights. The migration control argument couches refugee and asylum issues as national security matters. And when dealing with matters of security, derogation from constitutional and other rights is deemed acceptable. It is conceded that Botswana has a legitimate interest in managing an influx of asylum seekers. As the Court argued, Botswana has a small population and a limited capacity to handle large numbers of refugees and asylum seekers. What was missing from the Court of Appeal judgment however was recognition of the particular rights of children who were a large, but virtually silent, group affected by the judgment. A balancing act between national security concerns and the rights of Children under the Constitution and the Children's Act was necessary. It is submitted that there may have been some concessions by the Court particularly concerning indefinite detention of children and the lack of education for the children over several months of detention.

There are several notable discussions on non-discrimination in Botswana.[51] The cases considering the rights of migrant children would have been a sterling opportunity to examine and develop Botswana law on the rights of children and in particular migrant children. What is clear is that the judgment of the Court of Appeal was glaringly silent on the question of child rights. In light of Botswana's obligations under the Convention on the Rights of the Child, which is domesticated in Botswana's Children's Act 2009, it is submitted that the Court of Appeal judgment fell short of Botswana's obligations under its own domestic laws and under international law. It is hoped that judges and lawyers alike will focus more on developing jurisprudence on child rights in Botswana by defending the rights of children whatever their immigration status.

51 *Attorney General v. Dow* [1992] BLR 119 (CA); *Mmusi v. Ramantele* CACGB 104–12; *Attorney General and Others v. Dickson Thapela and Others* CACGB 096–14.

THE IMPACT OF BREXIT ON MIGRANT CHILDREN'S RIGHTS

Taking Responsibility without Solidarity

Alice THORNTON* and Adriana TIDONA**

1. INTRODUCTION

In July 2016 – one month after the decision by the people of the UK to leave the European Union – the House of Lords European Union Committee published a report about problems facing unaccompanied migrant children in the EU.[1] The Committee criticised the actions of the UK government on two fronts: for its reluctance to demonstrate solidarity and its failure to take responsibility for migrant children in its care.

More than three years later, the concerns raised have fallen on deaf ears, as the Brexit negotiations continue to be predominantly dominated by issues relating to the Customs Union and security. The apparent complacency among

* Family paralegal at TV Edwards Solicitors LLP, United Kingdom.
** Migration researcher at Amnesty International, European Regional Office, United Kingdom.
1 European Union Committee, *Children in Crisis: Unaccompanied migrant children in the EU* (HL 2016–17, 34-I).

UK government ministers as to the need to protect children's rights post-Brexit is encapsulated by Dominic Raab's, former Brexit Secretary, comment that:

> 'the UK's commitment to children's rights and the UN convention on the rights of the child is and will remain unwavering. Our ability to support and safeguard children's rights will not be affected by UK withdrawal from the EU.'[2]

This chapter will address the two concerns raised by the EU Committee, considering the UK's approach towards solidarity and its growing self-referential attitude in the application of legal standards for the protection of migrant children. Firstly, this tendency will be examined by comparing the UK's retraction from its commitments towards migrant children under the 'Dubs amendment', a short-lived scheme introduced in 2016 to receive unaccompanied refugee children from Greece and Italy, and the EU's parallel relocation scheme. Building on the shortcomings of these two experiences, the chapter will move on to assess how Brexit may negatively impact the UK's willingness and ability to adequately cater for migrant children's needs in the future, providing an overview of the areas where the dismantling of EU protection standards will be most felt. Equally, the issue of Brexit will finally be approached from the perspective of the value of the UK's contribution to child protection in certain fields where it leads by example at the EU level, such as the cooperation in police and cross-border justice or its innovative approach to the support of child victims of trafficking (VoTs). The chapter will conclude that, despite the uncertainty surrounding Brexit, there are already a number of worrying tendencies emerging towards isolationism and avoidance of supranational accountability.

2. THE THREAT OF LEGAL ISOLATIONISM IN THE UK PRE-BREXIT

Even prior to Brexit negotiations, the UK's inclination towards greater autonomy from the EU was denoted by the government's decision not to take part in the Commission's proposal for an emergency relocation scheme to tackle the refugee crisis and ease the migratory pressure on frontline member states (MS).[3]

---

2 EU (Withdrawal) Bill Deb 15 November 2016, vol. 631, col. 504.

3 Lizzie Dearden, 'EU plan to relocate 160,000 refugees from Italy and Greece by September failing despite record deaths at sea', *The Independent* (16 May 2017), https://www.independent.co.uk/news/world/europe/eu-refugee-quotas-160000-italy-greece-failing-european-commissioner-legal-cases-obligations-a7739396.html.

The failure to opt-in to the scheme was followed by an independent attempt to contribute to the relocation efforts, with a pledge to relocate as many as 3,000 children from Italy and Greece under the so-called 'Dubs amendment'.[4] The House of Lords Committee was highly critical of the UK's reluctance to show solidarity with Europe in helping to relocate unaccompanied migrant children.[5]

In its original formulation, the 'Dubs Amendment' reformed section 67 of the Immigration Act 2016 to reflect the UK's commitment towards unaccompanied refugee children. The relevant provision reads as follows:

> 1. The Sectary of State must, as soon as possible after the passing of this Act, make arrangements to relocate to the United Kingdom and support a specified number of unaccompanied refugee children from other countries in Europe.
> 2. The number of children to be resettled under subsection (1) shall be determined by the Government in consultation with local authorities.
> 3. The relocation of children under subsection (1) shall be in addition to the resettlement of children under the Vulnerable Persons Relocation Scheme.

The intention was to relocate children, defined as anyone under the age of 18, from migrant camps in France, Greece and Italy. The eligibility criteria required children to be present in Europe prior to 18 January 2018 and that it was in the child's best interests to be transferred to the UK. This involved consideration of whether best interests would instead be served by the child remaining in the host country, being transferred to a different Member State or being reunited with family outside of the EU. Further, host countries were asked to prioritise those children likely to be granted refugee status in the UK and/or the most vulnerable, including those at risk of trafficking or sexual abuse, survivors of violence or torture and children with mental or physical disabilities. As will be explained below, while the premises of the scheme were laudable, the plan was affected by a series of shortcomings that eventually contributed to its failure. Before delving into the outcome of the Dubs scheme, it is however useful to see what the parallel proposal of the EU was in terms of migrants' relocation and how it differed from Dubs.

---

4 Home Office, 'Policy Statement: Section 67 of the Immigration Act 2016' (December 2018), https://assets.publishing.service.gov.uk/government/uploads/system/uploads/attachment_data/file/767057/Dubs_policy_statement_-_UPDATED_December_2018_SG__004___002_.pdf; 'Dubs amendment: End of child migrant scheme "shameful"', *BBC News* (9 February 2017), https://www.bbc.co.uk/news/uk-politics-38918317.

5 European Union Committee, *Children in Crisis: Unaccompanied migrant children in the EU* (n. 1 above) [92].

3. THE DUBS AMENDMENT AND THE EU RELOCATION SCHEME

While more limited in its personal scope, the aim of the Dubs scheme was not too far removed from the EU 'Relocation Scheme', albeit with some notable differences.[6] As per its establishing acts,[7] the EU Scheme was designed as a 'corrective' solidarity measure, to provisionally grant support to frontline countries that had been under a heavy inflow of third country nationals. Greece and Italy, particularly, were deemed to have experienced 'unprecedented' migratory flows[8] and were hence the primary beneficiaries of the scheme, much like in the UK's initiative. Unlike Dubs, however, the EU scheme extended beyond children, to include all 'persons in clear need of international protection'.[9]

Another crucial difference between the two schemes is their normative basis. The EU relocation scheme relies on the EU principle of solidarity and shared management of migration under Article 78(3) TFEU.[10] Therefore, it operates on the assumption that the distribution of refugees in the EU 'cannot be sufficiently achieved by the [MS] but can rather, by reason of the scale and effects of the action, be better achieved at Union level'.[11] These overarching principles, reaffirmed in Article 80 TFEU, are explicitly recalled at Recital 17 and Article 9 of the 2015 Decision.[12] This is perhaps the primary element distinguishing the EU Scheme from Dubs: while the former falls within an – albeit relatively underperforming – attempt to tackle migration as an issue that affects all, the

6 Council Decision (EU) 2015/1523 of 14 September 2015 establishing provisional measures in the area of international protection for the benefit of Italy and Greece [2015] OJ L239/146, Recital 39. For an analysis of the UK's position on this aspect, see Steve Peers, 'Can the UK opt-out of mandatory EU refugee quotas?' (*EU Law Analysis*, 11 May 2015), http://eulawanalysis.blogspot.com/2015/05/can-uk-opt-out-of-mandatory-eu-refugee.html.

7 Council Decision (EU) 2015/1523 of 14 September 2015 (n. 6 above); Council Decision (EU) 2015/1601 of 22 September 2015 establishing provisional measures in the area of international protection for the benefit of Italy and Greece [2015] OJ L248/80.

8 Council Decision 2015/1601 (n. 7 above) Recital 10.

9 Ibid., Recital 7.

10 Council Decision 2015/1601 (n. 7 above) Recitals 21, 22 and Art. 9. Consolidated versions of the Treaty on European Union and the Treaty on the Functioning of the European Union (OJ C 202, 7.6.2016), Art. 78(3): 'In the event of one or more [MS] being confronted by an emergency situation characterised by a sudden inflow of nationals of third countries, the Council, on a proposal from the Commission, may adopt provisional measures for the benefit of the Member State(s) concerned.'

11 Council Decision (EU) 2015/1601 (n. 7 above) Recital 44.

12 See Steve Peers, 'Relocation of Asylum-Seekers in the EU: Law and Policy' (*EU Law Analysis*, 25 September 2015), http://eulawanalysis.blogspot.com/2015/09/relocation-of-asylum-seekers-in-eu-law.html; European Council on Refugees and Exiles (ECRE), 'Relocation: a test of European solidarity we cannot afford to fail' (ECRE, 8 September 2017), https://www.ecre.org/relocation-a-test-of-european-solidarity-we-cannot-afford-fail/.

Dubs scheme is an attempt by the UK to emancipate itself from shared efforts at the expense of children's protection.

In its agreed layout, the relocation scheme committed to achieve 'the temporary and exceptional relocation, over two years, from Italy and from Greece to other [MS] of 40 000 persons in clear need of international protection'.[13] Among other things, the criteria employed for an applicant to be considered in 'clear' need of protection were based on the rate of recognition associated to his/her nationality, with priority being given to nationalities associated to 'a threshold of 75%, based on the latest available updated Eurostat quarterly data for first instance decisions'.[14]

A second Decision intervened on the issue of relocation, adding an overly optimistic commitment to increase the original relocation target by 120,000 more pledges.[15] The Decision also intervened on the number of refugees to be relocated from Greece, so as to meet the rise in arrivals in the country at the time, and replaces the voluntary commitment on which the previous relocation scheme was based, with defined quotas.[16]

The distribution of applicants was, at least on paper, informed by three strands of considerations, including: the 'specific qualifications and characteristics of the applicants concerned', the MS' concrete ability to provide adequate support when those relocated are 'particularly vulnerable applicants' and the necessity to ensure that the allocation of relocated applicants between MS was 'fair'. The scheme was designed to benefit only those who lodged an asylum application in Italy or Greece in the identified time frame and who would fall under the responsibility of those countries under Dublin.[17] As such, the scheme aimed to operate without prejudice to situations where the responsibility for asylum seekers reaching Europe through Greece or Italy is attributed to a different MS on the basis of the other Dublin criteria, such as family or humanitarian considerations.[18]

As a centralised, EU-led initiative, the relocation scheme benefited from inbuilt formal and informal oversight elements, consisting of the Commission's and CJEU's review mechanisms and of the equally relevant pressure exerted by the EU MS community. While it is evident that that the EU relocation scheme has by and large failed to meet its original target,[19] it is equally undeniable that

---

13 Council Decision 2015/1601 (n. 7 above) Recitals 7 and 11.

14 Council Decision 2015/1523 (n. 6 above) Art. 3 and Recital 20.

15 Council Decision 2015/1601 (n. 7 above) Art. 4.

16 Peers, 'Relocation of Asylum-Seekers in the EU' (n. 12 above); Steve Peers, 'A Pyrrhic victory? The ECJ upholds the EU law on relocation of asylum-seekers' (*EU Law Analysis*, 8 September 2017), http://www.statewatch.org/analyses/no-320-relocations.pdf.

17 Council Decision 2015/1523 (n. 6 above) recital 28 and Art. 3.

18 See Peers, 'Relocation of Asylum-Seekers in the EU' (n. 12 above); Council Decision 2015/1523 (n. 6 above) Recital 19.

19 European Commission, 'European Agenda on Migration: Continuous efforts needed to sustain progress' (Brussels, 14 March 2018); Amnesty International, 'EU: Countries have fulfilled less

it has contributed to identifying and taking measures against MS failures to abide by their legal obligations. Notably, the Czech Republic, Hungary and Poland, have come under the reprimand of the EU, which launched infringement proceedings against these countries for their refusal to implement their relocation quota.[20] Not being externally accountable for its failures under Dubs, the UK scheme presented weakness in terms of supranational accountability.

Returning to the relocation scheme's eligibility criteria, within the group of applicants considered to be 'in clear need of protection', the scheme explicitly prioritised 'vulnerable applicants' as defined by the Reception Conditions Directive.[21] This explicitly includes accompanied and unaccompanied minors,[22] with their best interests always being a primary consideration.[23] Furthermore, by making direct reference to the Directive,[24] it can be assumed that the scheme operated under the same legal framework set out in that piece of legislation and with the understanding that the rights and safeguards applying in the context of relocations should be equivalent to those granted in other asylum situations. As proof of this, the scheme also expressly extends the procedural guarantees under Dublin III[25] to relocation procedures.[26]

---

than a third of their asylum relocation promises' (Amnesty International, 25 September 2017); Tony Bunyan, 'End of the infamous EU refugee "relocation" scheme' (*Statewatch*, 27 February 2018), http://www.statewatch.org/news/2018/feb/eu-council-end-relocations.htm.

20 European Commission, 'Relocation: Commission refers the Czech Republic, Hungary and Poland to the Court of Justice' (Brussels, 7 December 2017), http://europa.eu/rapid/press-release_IP-17-5002_en.pdf: 'On 15 June 2017, the Commission launched infringement procedures against the Czech Republic, Hungary and Poland. The replies provided by the three Member States were not found satisfactory and the Commission decided to move to the next stage of the infringement procedure by sending reasoned opinions on 26 July 2017.'

21 Directive 2013/33/EU of the European Parliament and of the Council of 26 June 2013 laying down standards for the reception of applicants for international protection (recast) (2013) OJ L180/96 (Reception Conditions Directive), Recital 27 and Art. 6 and 11. For a critical perspective as to the effectiveness of this provision, see: Peers, 'Relocation of Asylum-Seekers in the EU' (n. 12 above).

22 Ibid., Arts. 21, 23 and 24. The Directive imposes a positive obligation on MS to assess the special needs of vulnerable persons, even at 'a later stage' (Art. 22).

23 Council Decision (EU) 2015/1601 (n. 7 above) Recital 33.

24 Ibid., Art. 5(3) and Recital 36, also referring to the rights and guarantees under Directive 2013/32/EU of the European Parliament and of the Council of 26 June 2013 on common procedures for granting and withdrawing international protection [2013] OJ L180/60 (Asylum Procedures Directive).

25 Regulation (EU) No 604/2013 of the European Parliament and of the Council of 26 June 2013 establishing the criteria and mechanisms for determining the Member State responsible for examining an application for international protection lodged in one of the Member States by a third-country national or a stateless person (recast) [2013] OJ L180/31 (Dublin III Regulation).

26 Council Decision 2015/1601 (n. 7 above) Recital 35, whereby: 'applicants should be informed of the relocation procedure … and be notified with the relocation decision which constitutes a transfer decision within the meaning of Article 26 of Regulation (EU) No 604/2013' and that they should 'have the right to an effective remedy against the relocation decision'.

This is particularly important when it comes to examining the different level of protection granted under Dubs and under the EU scheme. By referring to the Common European Asylum System (CEAS) legal standards, the EU relocation scheme operated under the assumption that the children subjected to transfer procedures were treated in compliance with the UN Convention on the Rights of the Child (UNCRC) standards, which is referred to in all instruments.[27] The applicability of the CEAS – and indirectly the UNCRC – standards to relocation procedures attempts to achieve a harmonised approach between MS, removing any ambiguity as to how to assess vulnerabilities and how to apply the principle of the best interests of the child, which constituted a critical point for Dubs.[28]

While overall the ideal premises of the relocation scheme were praised, the uneven engagement shown by MS – who in most cases failed to meet their target of pledges or, as in the case of Czech Republic, Hungary and Poland, refused to abide by the scheme – and some structural limitations affecting the scheme as a whole, critically undermined the effectiveness or sustainability of this solution. In November 2017, as the operational period of the scheme came to an end, the number of relocations came to 31,503.[29]

4. DUBS AMENDMENT AND THE *HELP REFUGEES* CASE

Shortly after its introduction, the UK government sought to justify ending the Dubs Scheme by arguing that it would act as a pull factor for children to come to the UK and as 'a magnet for the traffickers'.[30] Not only does this appear to minimise the strong push factors that act on children to make perilous journeys across Europe, it fails to recognise that the lack of safe, legal mechanisms leaves children in an extremely precarious situation. However, the Dubs registration scheme was imperfect; indeed the Human Trafficking Foundation found that there was:

> '... no common understanding of who is responsible for conducting registration assessments of Dubs children up to the standard that would be required for child

---

[27] Reception Conditions Directive (n. 21 above) Recital 9; Dublin III Regulation (n. 25 above) Recital 13.

[28] See section 4 of this chapter.

[29] EU Commission, 'Relocation: EU Solidarity Between Member States' (November 2017), https://ec.europa.eu/home-affairs/sites/homeaffairs/files/what-we-do/policies/european-agenda-migration/20170927_factsheet_relocation_sharing_responsibility_en.pdf.

[30] HC Deb 9 February 2017, vol. 621.

safeguarding in the UK and virtually no co-ordination between the Home Office, local authorities and with the NGOs on the ground which hold data on children.'[31]

Without suitable information, facilities and support from the authorities, children will look to others and this will only serve to increase their risk of being smuggled or becoming a VoT. However, entirely removing a safe route for unaccompanied minors – some of the most vulnerable individuals – almost guarantees it. One UNHCR study found that the closure of the 'Calais jungle' resulted in almost all of the 90 Afghan children known to the authorities ending up back in the hands of smugglers, as the children attempted to continue their journey.[32]

The criticisms levied against the Dubs registration scheme were further compounded when, after consultation with the local authorities, it was announced that the UK could only reasonably accommodate 480 children, nowhere near the initial figures suggested at approximately 3,000 children.[33]

As such, Help Refugees, a UK-based non-government organisation, brought a judicial review against the Secretary of State for the Home Department. Its arguments were twofold: that the Secretary of State had failed to discharge her duty to carry out a consultation process with the local authorities and that the inadequate reasons given to rejected children constituted a breach of the common law duty of procedural fairness. In October 2018, the Court of Appeal only upheld the appeal on the second ground.

The appellants, firstly, argued that the Secretary of State was making decisions with incomplete or incorrect information, as the consultation process had not be adequately carried out. The Court held, however, that the legislation gave the Secretary of State wide discretion as to how to conduct the consultation. The Secretary of State's duty was to determine the 'reasonably highest figure', which was the highest number of children that could be accommodated in the UK, balanced against the social and financial policy considerations.[34] As reasonableness was a matter of judgement for the Secretary of State, the Court held that the consultation process and eventual figure of 480 children settled upon was entirely proper.

---

31 Christine Beddoe, 'An independent inquiry into the situation of separated and unaccompanied minors in parts of Europe' (Human Trafficking Foundation, July 2017), https://www.antislaverycommissioner.co.uk/media/1262/nobody-deserves-to-live-this-way.pdf, 36.

32 Christine Mougne, 'Trees only move in the wind: A study of unaccompanied Afghan children in Europe' (UN High Commissioner for Refugees Policy Development and Evaluation Service, PDES/2010/05, June 2010), [143].

33 Beddoe, 'An independent inquiry into the situation of separated and unaccompanied minors in parts of Europe' (n. 31 above) 9.

34 *R. (Help Refugees Ltd) v. Secretary of State for the Home Department* [2018] EWCA Civ 2098, [2018] 4 WLR 168 [96].

In the second ground of appeal it was argued that informing 1,400 out of the 1,800 children assessed that they simply did not meet the relevant criteria amounted to inadequate reasons. Despite very clear criteria, the vast majority of children were not told of the exact ground they failed to satisfy. As highlighted by the Court, telling children 'criteria not met' 'is barely a reason at all' and prevents them from being able to challenge the decision.[35] Therefore, the Court held that this practice was unlawful.

While one may be grateful for the small victories, on closer inspection the language and reasoning of the Court seemingly fails to grasp some of the nuances of international children rights law. Lord Justice Hinkinbottom held that he did 'not consider that a detailed consideration of the role played by article 3(1) [of the UNCRC] in our domestic jurisprudence is required or warranted'.[36] The reason he gives for this conclusion is that section 67 already has best interests considerations built into it and that this is a case that focuses on procedural requirements and fairness.[37] For this reason, Article 3 'reinforces' but did not 'substantively add to' the Secretary of State's obligations already inherent in section 67.[38]

While the UNCRC has not been explicitly incorporated into the legal system through an Act of Parliament, the domestic courts ought to apply a canon of construction which assumes that domestic legislation is intended to conform to relevant international law obligations.[39] Further, key provisions of the UNCRC, including Article 3, are found in Article 24 of the EU Charter of Fundamental Rights (the CFR). The CFR is placed on the same footing as EU Treaties via Article 6 of the TEU, so will apply in all situations governed by EU law. Therefore, children's UNCRC rights are more concretely protected via EU law, but post-Brexit the UNCRC ought to still have a persuasive influence over the jurisprudence of the domestic courts.[40]

Yet, Lord Justice Hickinbottom's remarks fail to fully appreciate Article 3 UNCRC and UN Committee General Comment No. 14 (GC No. 14). Article 3 explicitly relates to 'all actions concerning children': there is no caveat or restriction. Further, GC No. 14 states that best interests is a threefold concept: (i) a substantive right; (ii) a fundamental, interpretative legal principle, and (iii) a rule of procedure.[41] While substantively best interests are explicitly

---

35 Ibid., [132].

36 Ibid., [83].

37 Ibid., [84]–[85].

38 Ibid., [84].

39 *R. v. Secretary of State for the Home Department, ex parte Brind* [1991] UKHL 4, [1991] 1 AC 747.

40 See further at section 5 below.

41 UN Committee on the Rights of the Child, General Comment No. 14 (2013) on the right of the child to have his or her best interests taken as a primary consideration (Art. 3, para. 1), CRC/C/GC/14, [6].

required to be considered under section 67, states' obligations do not end there. The judge should also have considered thoroughly the process by which the Secretary of State ought to have ensured that the best interests of children were protected. GC No. 14 outlines that the procedural element of the best interests principle requires parties to:

> 'explain how the right has been respected in the decision, that is, what has been considered to be in the child's best interest; what criteria it is based on; and how the child's interests have been weighed against other considerations, be they broad issues of policy or individual cases'.[42]

It is not apparent from the judgment whether any of these additional safeguards were satisfied, but at the very least it was not open to the judge to disregard Article 3 and fail to engage with the protections that it guarantees for children.

Instead, the Court reaches the same conclusion via the application of the duty of procedural fairness at common law.[43] While it may have made no difference in the outcome, the failure of the Court of Appeal to approach this from an international law perspective is worrying, if not entirely unsurprising.

This appears to reflect a recent trend in the case law of England and Wales, whereby judges are increasingly seeking to rely on common law principles rather than European or international standards. This is most apparent in case law relating to the domestic implementation of rights found under the ECHR. For instance, in *Osborne v. Parole Board* the Court similarly preferred to draw on the common law duty of fairness rather than the ECtHR jurisprudence.[44] To some extent, this was understandable given the judicial concerns at the time that the UK government may seek to withdraw from the ECHR. As such, it made sense for the judges to develop the common law to prevent it from being an 'ossuary',[45] if the UK ever were to leave the ECHR. The same excuses cannot be given in this circumstance, as – if we are to believe Dominic Raab – the UK's commitment to the UNCRC is 'unwavering'.[46] Yet if *Help Refugees* is indicative of anything, it is that Brexit may be a catalyst for a greater trend towards isolationism and reliance on historic common law principles, even in relation to such widely agreed international principles as those found under the UNCRC.

The next section will look in detail at some of the areas where the UK's tendency towards legal isolationism has been more marked and will consider the potential risks that this attitude carries with it.

---

42 Ibid.

43 See *R. (Citizens UK) v. Secretary of State for the Home Department* [2018] EWCA Civ 1812, [2018] 4 WLR 123.

44 *Osborne v. Parole Board* [2013] UKSC 61, [2014] AC 1115 [62].

45 *Kennedy v. The Charity Commission* [2014] UKSC 20, [2015] AC 455, [133].

46 HC Deb 15 November 2016, vol. 631, col. 504.

5. THE FUTURE OF CHILDREN'S RIGHTS IN A POST-BREXIT SCENARIO

The EU Justice Select Committee noted on the part of the UK government 'a worrying level of complacency … that other international arrangements will fill the void left by this important EU legislation'.[47] The Chairperson of the Committee, Baroness Kennedy, went further to state that 'the uncertainty ultimately leaves vulnerable children as the victims'.[48]

The UK government has clearly stated that it will not be transposing the CFR into domestic legislation.[49] Importantly for our purposes, this means losing Article 24 of the CFR on 'the rights of the child'. Currently, the CFR will apply in all situations governed by EU law.[50] Article 24 was explicitly based on the UNCRC.[51] Without the direct incorporation of the UNCRC into domestic legislation, Article 24 is the only foothold that children and legal practitioners have for the enforcement of the rights found within the CFR. While the UK has strong protection of the best interests of children under section 1(1) of the Children Act 1989, this only relates to family law proceedings. Not only does the best interests principle under the UNCRC apply to all proceedings relating to children, there are a greater range of rights protected by the UNCRC, including but not limited to the incredibly strong protection of the right to be heard under Article 12.

What is becoming increasingly apparent is the sense that the UK is able to achieve all this and more on its own and has turned its back on the international community's standards. This tendency is only accentuated by the prospect of the CJEU decision-making and jurisprudence no longer being binding on

47 Lord Boswell of Aynho, 'Follow-Up to the Committee's Report: Brexit: Justice for Families, Individuals and Businesses?' (EU Justice Select Committee, 16 October 2018), https://www.parliament.uk/documents/lords-committees/eu-justice-subcommittee/JusticeforFamilies/LBtoDG-Follow-uptoCtteeRpt-CivilJusticeCooperation-161018.pdf.

48 '"Vulnerable children will be victims" of Government's failure to provide clarity – Lords warn Government over family justice system after Brexit' (House of Lords Media Notices, 17 October 2018), https://www.parliament.uk/business/lords/media-centre/house-of-lords-media-notices/house-of-lords-media-notices---2018/october-2018/vulnerable-children-will-be-victims-of-governments-failure-to-provide-clarity-lords-warn-government-over-family-justice-system-after-brexit/?fbclid=IwAR0lu8vqyg9Hli2_dYPj__JhmrFcx0M5xLLoVgsPYHI8tQEWXSexhtt6UUQhttps://bit.ly/2FpOICq.

49 Mirja Gutheil and others, 'The future relationship between the UK and the EU in the field of international protection following the UK's withdrawal from the EU' (EU Parliament, Study Requested by the LIBE Committee, Policy Department for Citizens' Rights and Constitutional Affairs, Directorate General for Internal Policies of the Union, October 2018), http://www.europarl.europa.eu/RegData/etudes/STUD/2018/608836/IPOL_STU(2018)608836_EN.pdf, 51 and 53.

50 C-617/10 *Åklagaren v. Hans Åkerberg Fransson* ECLI:EU:C:2013:105.

51 Explanations relating to the Charter of Fundamental Rights (2007/C 303/02) of 14 December 2007.

the UK.[52] As things stand, the UK post-Brexit will not be obliged to adhere to the Luxembourg's Court rulings nor will MS 'be able to start infringement proceedings against the UK Government for failing to comply with EU law'.[53] While by remaining a member of the ECtHR the country will continue to participate in the elaboration of European standards in the field of asylum and migration, where the Strasbourg judge has even shown a more proactive attitude, the CJEU dictates maintain a stronger and more direct influence on MS' domestic law and practice.[54]

In a recent study by the EU Parliament Policy Department for Citizens' Rights and Constitutional Affairs,[55] they note the key role played by the CFR as a channel for the direct incorporation and interpretation of international standards, observing how 'although human rights provided by the ECHR are more binding, as they were incorporated into domestic law through the 1998 Human Rights Act, the Act does not include some of the rights from other UN legal standards, which are reflected in the EU Charter'.[56] While the ECtHR has arguably made progress in embracing the UNCRC standards in its own jurisprudence,[57] there is no shortage of criticism as to whether the Strasbourg judge is yet able (or willing) to take a stronger stance in cases concerning the assessment of children's best interest by domestic courts.[58]

---

52 European Union (Withdrawal) Act 2018, s 6: 'Interpretation of retained EU law (1) A court or tribunal – (a) is not bound by any principles laid down, or any decisions made, on or after exit day by the European Court, and (b) cannot refer any matter to the European Court on or after exit day. (2) Subject to this and subsections (3) to (6), a court or tribunal may have regard to anything done on or after exit day by the European Court, another EU entity or the EU so far as it is relevant to any matter before the court or tribunal.' See also Department for Exiting the European Union, *The Future Relationship Between the United Kingdom and The European Union* (White Paper, Cm 9593, 2018) s 4.1, and ILPA, 'ILPA submission to the Joint Committee on Human Rights on the human rights implications of Brexit' (17 October 2016) https://bit.ly/2QI3K7F, among other commentaries.

53 Gutheil and others, 'The future relationship between the UK and the EU in the field of international protection following the UK's withdrawal from the EU' (n. 49 above) 54.

54 Ibid.: it is noted that 'the ECtHR has been more influential in matters of asylum rights when compared to the CJEU … On the other hand, CJEU rulings, according to CJEU case law, are binding more generally unless the CJEU indicates otherwise'.

55 Ibid., 52.

56 Ibid.

57 For a detailed study on the rights of the child in the ECtHR jurisprudence, see Anette Faye Jacobsen, 'Children's Rights in the European Court of Human Rights – An Emerging Power Structure' (2016) 24 The International Journal of Children's Rights 548, among others.

58 *Fröhlich v. Germany*, App no. 16112/15 (ECHR, 26 July 2018) and Evelyn Merckx, 'Fröhlich v. Germany: (Ab)using The Child's Best Interests To Safeguard Those Of Others' (*Strasbourg Observers*, 20 November 2018) https://bit.ly/2FPn6Wt. For other perspectives on the ECtHR's approach to the assessment of the best interest of the child, see Lydia Bracken, 'Assessing the best interests of the child in cases of cross-border surrogacy: inconsistency in the Strasbourg approach?' (2017) 39 Journal of Social Welfare and Family Law 368; Gabriel Füglistaler, 'The Principle of Subsidiarity and the Margin of Appreciation Doctrine in the European Court of

The analysis of the case of *Fröhlich v. Germany* by Evelyn Merckx, offers insights on the ECtHR's role and attitude in such cases and valuable observations on the inherent limitations in the action of domestic authorities. Noting the Court's cautious attitude in cases involving a best interests assessment by the domestic authorities and the inadequate implementation of children's rights to be heard and informed, Merckx notes:

> 'It is understandable that the ECtHR is hesitant to find a violation in cases where the domestic authorities made a "best interests" analysis. However, given the fact that the outcome of such a case depends largely on the interpretation of that vague concept by the domestic judge, the child's right to be heard should be correctly enforced as a guarantee that it will not be invoked to safeguard other interests'.[59]

Having touched upon some of the issues that the UK is likely to encounter insofar as the protection of fundamental rights is concerned, this chapter will move to examine the effects of Brexit on specific areas of high strategic importance for the protection of migrant children in the UK. It will focus on third-country nationals – with the rights of EEA children and their families beyond the scope of this chapter – examining how their position will be affected as a result of the UK's discontinued participation in EU efforts in the fields of asylum, trafficking and large IT data systems.

6. THE UK'S POSITION IN RELATION TO THE EU CEAS

Historically, the UK's participation in EU migration law and policy has been based on a 'selective' approach,[60] allowing the country to opt-in to certain pieces of legislation, as a result of its special status in the Area of Freedom, Security and Justice (AFSJ).[61] The UK opted to take part in the first phase of the CEAS instruments but not in their recast, with the exception of the Dublin III Regulation and the Eurodac Regulation, among others.[62] It should, however, be

Human Rights Post-2011 Jurisprudence' (2016) 295 IDHEAP 46; ECtHR, 'Guide on Article 8 of the European Convention on Human Rights: Right to Respect for private and family life' (Council of Europe and ECtHR, 2017), https://www.refworld.org/pdfid/5a016ebe4.pdf [179].

59 Merckx, 'Fröhlich v. Germany' (n. 58 above).

60 Cathryn Costello and Emily Hancox 'The UK, the Common European Asylum System and EU Immigration Law' (Migration Observatory policy primer, 2 May 2014), https://migrationobservatory.ox.ac.uk/wp-content/uploads/2016/04/PolicyPrimer-UK_EU_Asylum_Law.pdf; See also Consolidated version of the Treaty on the Functioning of the European Union – Protocol (No 21) on the Position of the UK and Ireland in respect of the Area of Freedom, Security and Justice.

61 Ibid., Protocol No. 21. See also Gutheil and others, 'The future relationship between the UK and the EU in the field of international protection following the UK's withdrawal from the EU' (n. 49 above) 13.

62 Gutheil and others, (n. 49 above) 35–36.

noted that insofar as the guarantees applying to procedures under Dublin III are concerned, the Regulation makes reference to standards of the other recast instruments to which the UK does not subscribe: the asylum reception and procedures Directives.[63] These instruments grant higher procedural and substantive guarantees to vulnerable asylum seekers, including accompanied and unaccompanied minors.[64] Yet, by not entirely participating in the second phase of the CEAS,[65] the UK's position does not reflect the interrelation between these instruments and Dublin and therefore may not fully guarantee the same level of protection required by other MS.

The discretion afforded to the UK in the definition of its participation in the CEAS has received criticism for its impact on fundamental rights. A study of 2017 tackles the flexibility afforded to the country in the area of asylum, arguing that the sensitive interests underlying this field, and hence the implications on individual rights, are too serious to justify such discrepancies in MS' position. Specifically, it is argued that:

> 'even if the UK's treatment of asylum seekers is of a standard high enough ... its refusal to sign up to the legally enforceable safeguards that underlie the Dublin system raise questions as to whether the EU should in principle tolerate such cherry-picking in respect of a sensitive area of law that directly affects the lives of vulnerable individuals.'[66]

Irrespective of the UK's opt-outs in terms of procedures or reception standards, transfers of asylum seekers under Dublin are explicitly informed by UNCRC standards[67] and therefore currently oblige the UK to abide by the principle of the best interests of the child in transfer proceedings. After Brexit, the UK will be faced with the choice of directly incorporating the UNCRC in its domestic asylum legislation – an unlikely hypothesis given the UK's tendency to fold in on itself in terms of legislative standards – or downgrade the Convention to a more distant benchmark. This would be particularly concerning given that in 2017 the UN Committee on the rights of the child took crucial steps in the field of the protection of migrant children, clarifying the scope and applicability

---

63 Dublin III Regulation (n. 25 above) Recitals 11 and 12; Gutheil and others, (n. 50 above) 37–38.

64 Reception Conditions Directive (n. 21 above) Arts. 11, 21 and 22; Asylum Procedures Directive (n. 24 above) Arts. 11 and 31(7)(b). See also ECRE, 'The concept of vulnerability in European asylum procedures' (31 August 2017), available at: https://bit.ly/2f9gOmN.

65 The UK is required to abide by its obligations under the non-recast version of the Reception Conditions Directive. See ECRE, 'Information Note on Directive 2013/33/EU of the European Parliament and of the Council of 26 June 2013 laying down standards for the reception of applicants for international protection (recast)' (July 2015), https://bit.ly/2tZYyms, 5.

66 Nadine El-Enany, 'The Perils of Differentiated Integration in the Field of Asylum' in Bruno De Witte, Andrea Ott and Ellen Vos (eds.), *Between flexibility and disintegration: the trajectory of differentiation in EU law* (Edward Elgar Publishing, 2017) 2 and 5.

67 Dublin III Regulation (n. 25 above) Recital 13.

of the UNCRC to the different stages of children's migration experience and interpreting it in light of the particular needs of this group.[68]

The withdrawal of the UK from the Dublin system has been extensively discussed elsewhere.[69] For the purposes of this analysis, it must be recalled that by no longer being part of the system, and in the absence (at present) of plans for an arrangement to continue the UK's participation 'the protective provisions of the Regulation, in particular those making provision for family reunion, especially in the cases of unaccompanied minors, would be lost'.[70]

As observed by commentators, the withdrawal from Dublin may do the UK more harm than good, considering that the country has been largely privileged by its geographical position in the application of Dublin rules and in fact received considerably fewer arrivals than its neighbours.[71] With Dublin rules being lifted, the UK may become a very appealing destination for asylum seekers wishing to circumvent the arguably defective mechanism of the system, as the country would no longer be able to rely on 'take-back' requests to transfer them to the country of first irregular entry, which have so far largely favoured it.[72] The UK's disproportionate and repressive response to the resumed channel crossings from France, with 428 people reaching the UK between January 2018 and February 2019,[73] may be a preview of what is to come.[74]

---

68 UN Committee on the Protection of the Rights of All Migrant Workers and Members of their Families (CMW), Joint General Comment No. 4 (2017) of the Committee on the Protection of the Rights of All Migrant Workers and Members of their Families and No. 23 (2017) of the Committee on the Rights of the Child on State obligations regarding the human rights of children in the context of international migration in countries of origin, transit, destination and return, 16 November 2017, CMW/C/GC/4-CRC/C/GC/23 and UN Committee on the Protection of the Rights of All Migrant Workers and Members of their Families (CMW), Joint General Comment No. 3 (2017) of the Committee on the Protection of the Rights of All Migrant Workers and Members of their Families and No. 22 (2017) of the Committee on the Rights of the Child on the general principles regarding the human rights of children in the context of international migration, 16 November 2017, CMW/C/GC/3-CRC/C/GC/22.

69 Nikolaj Nielsen, 'Brexit would prevent UK from returning asylum seekers' (*EU Observer*, 20 June 16), https://bit.ly/2RM5YHN.

70 ILPA, 'ILPA submission to the Joint Committee on Human Rights' (n. 52 above) [35].

71 Ibid, [35]. See also Victoria Roeck, 'Reuniting Unaccompanied Minor Asylum Seekers Post Brexit: Challenges and Alternatives' (*Yale Journal of International Law*, 2016), http://www.yjil.yale.edu/reuniting-unaccompanied-minor-asylum-seekers-post-brexit-challenges-and-alternatives/.

72 Gutheil and others, 'The future relationship between the UK and the EU in the field of international protection following the UK's withdrawal from the EU' (n. 49 above) 70; Nielsen, 'Brexit would prevent UK from returning asylum seekers'(n 70). See also Markella Papadouli, 'Brexit: What's in Pandora's Box for asylum seekers and victims of human trafficking?' (30 July 2017), http://www.ccarht.org/site/brexit-whats-in-pandoras-box-for-asylum-seekers-and-victims-of-human-trafficking/.

73 Mattha Busby, 'Channel crossings: two arrested as suspected people smugglers' *The Guardian* (3 January 2019), https://bit.ly/2TGwVKi.

74 Statistics at: https://commonslibrary.parliament.uk/home-affairs/immigration/migrants-crossing-the-english-channel/. See also Steve Peers, 'Manufacturing Discontent: Q and A on the legal

The advantages of the CEAS-style system, with its shared migration management, are likely behind the UK's declared intention to remain part of Eurodac and Dublin.[75] In this vein, the 'White Paper' published by the UK government in July 2018 introduces the country's proposal for a 'whole of route' approach to migration management, specifying its desire for 'ongoing operational cooperation' with Frontex and Europol, and hinting at its interest in continuing a 'Dublin-like' cooperation,[76] including keeping its access to Eurodac 'or an equivalent system'.[77]

While, as the UK Immigration Law Practitioners' Association (ILPA) observes, '[t]here is nothing to prevent its continuing to operate a system resembling the [CEAS] within the UK',[78] it is to be hoped that any agreement to enable such an arrangement on the side of the EU operates on the understanding that the UK will fully conform with the procedural and substantive guarantees enshrined in the CEAS.[79]

An argument in favour of this outcome can be found in a study commissioned by the EU LIBE Committee in 2018, according to which: 'the divergence of standards of refugee recognition, protection and rights is unlikely to be helpful to the UK ... in order to both regain sovereignty while retaining cooperation with the EU, the UK may want to replicate EU legal standards in its domestic law.'[80]

However, ILPA further notes that even in the event of the formal alignment of UK domestic law to EU standards in this field, 'the supervisory role of the [CJEU] in interpreting refugee law', inevitably prevents the current state of things being retained.[81]

---

issues of asylum-seekers crossing the Channel' (*EU Law Analysis*, 3 January 2019), http://eulawanalysis.blogspot.com/.

75 Gutheil and others, 'The future relationship between the UK and the EU in the field of international protection following the UK's withdrawal from the EU' (n. 49 above) 70.

76 See Department for Exiting the European, *The Future Relationship* (n. 52 above), 2.5.1 [100(b)] and Gutheil and others, 'The future relationship between the UK and the EU in the field of international protection following the UK's withdrawal from the EU' (n. 49 above) 70–73.

77 Department for Exiting the European Union, *The Future Relationship* (n. 52 above) 2.5.1 [100].

78 ILPA, 'ILPA submission to the Joint Committee on Human Rights' (n. 52 above) 33.

79 See Gutheil and others, 'The future relationship between the UK and the EU in the field of international protection following the UK's withdrawal from the EU' (n. 49 above) 53.

80 Ibid., 53.

81 ILPA, 'ILPA submission to the Joint Committee on Human Rights' (n. 52 above) [34]. See also Gutheil and others, 'The future relationship between the UK and the EU in the field of international protection following the UK's withdrawal from the EU' (n. 49 above) 55: 'the UK will want to continue to participate in some of the EU measures, it might be required to abide by the jurisdiction of the CJEU, although there are countries that are applying EU law but are not within the CJEU's jurisdiction', offering the example of 'all non-EU Schengen/Dublin associated countries, which have access to databases of EU data without the jurisdiction of the CJEU ... the EU has agreements with these countries which stipulate that if any substantial difference between the CJEU and their courts arises on the interpretation of their agreement which cannot be settled by discussion in the Mixed Committee, the agreement will be terminated'.

While the unaltered participation in these arrangements post-Brexit may be wishful thinking for the UK – and it is unlikely that such wishes will be granted without the UK being required to agree to parallel commitments – the country's pledge for the creation of 'new arrangements that enable unaccompanied asylum-seeking children in the EU to join close family members in the UK',[82] may be a sign of opening to the above effect.[83] Such declaration, however, has so far not been accompanied by any concrete terms and therefore currently lacks practical value. Furthermore, the unpredictability that characterised the transfer of migrant children under the Dubs scheme does not augur well for the outcome of such commitment.

7. THE PROTECTION OF CHILD VoT IN THE UK

While one could see the potential advantages of leaving the CEAS, from the rather vague viewpoint of regaining autonomy in the management of asylum matters, when it comes to the protection of child VoTs the UK has nothing to gain and a substantial amount to lose post-Brexit.

Currently, in addition to the relatively 'soft' commitments in terms of international law,[84] the UK's obligations in this area come from its obligations under the Council of Europe (CoE) Convention on action against trafficking in human beings,[85] the ECHR[86] and the EU Anti-trafficking Directive.[87]

---

82 Department for Exiting the European Union, *The Future Relationship* (n. 52 above) [100(c)].

83 See also Gutheil and others, 'The future relationship between the UK and the EU in the field of international protection following the UK's withdrawal from the EU' (n. 49 above) 56 and 58.

84 At the international level, the UK obligations in terms of anti-trafficking can be traced back to the Universal Declaration of Human Rights (UDHR) of 1948. See on this United Nations Human Rights, Office of the High Commissioner, 'Human Rights and Human Trafficking: Fact Sheet No. 36' (United Nations, 2014), http://www.ohchr.org/Documents/Publications/FS36_en.pdf, 4 and 51; European Court of Human Rights, 'Factsheet – Trafficking in human beings' (December 2018), https://www.echr.coe.int/Documents/FS_Trafficking_ENG.pdf; OSCE Office of the Special Representative and Co-ordinator for Combating Trafficking in Human Beings and others, *Trafficking in Human Beings Amounting to Torture and other Forms of Ill-treatment* (Occasional Paper Series no. 5, June 2013). See also Mogos O. Brhane, 'Trafficking in Persons for Ransom and the Need to Expand the Interpretation of Article 3 of the UN Trafficking Protocol' (2015) 4 Anti-Trafficking Review 120.

85 Council of Europe, 'Council of Europe Convention on Action against Trafficking in Human Beings'(Warsaw, 16.V.2005, CETS 197), https://rm.coe.int/168008371d.

86 Art. 4 ECHR prohibits slavery and forced labour and has been explicitly interpreted by the ECtHR as prohibiting human trafficking. This was first established in *Rantsev v. Cyprus and Russia* App no. 25965/04 (ECHR, 7 January 2010), as a result of which states that are signatories to the ECHR are considered to be under an obligation to establish a 'legal and regulatory framework' to tackle trafficking ([284]). The provisions under Arts. 2 and 3 also play a prominent role in tackling trafficking.

87 Directive 2011/36/EU of the European Parliament and of the Council of 5 April 2011 on preventing and combating trafficking in human beings and protecting its victims, and replacing Council Framework Decision 2002/629/JHA [2011] OJ L 101/1.

Domestically, since 2015 the UK's obligations for combating trafficking in human beings have been regulated by the Modern Slavery Act 2015 (MSA). The Act, which was an overall well-received legislative innovation,[88] regulates trafficking and other forms of exploitation: on the one side providing for the support and assistance measures for victims and on the other trying to tackle these issues by means of new and experimental arrangements.

The Independent Child Trafficking Advocates (ICTAs)[89] are an example of this. The recast Reception Conditions Directive emphasises continuity in representation to 'ensure the minor's well-being and social development'.[90] This is exactly what ICTAs intended to ensure by providing specialist, independent support for trafficked children. A one-year trial was conducted beginning on 8 September 2014. Researchers found that one of the most unique features of ICTAs was their adoption of a 'hub and spoke' model.[91] It represents guardians being at the centre of the child's care, working with multiple agencies to ensure that specific risks relating to trafficking were at the forefront of all decision-makers' minds. ICTAs therefore acted as 'anchors' for both children and organisations, with their expertise in trafficking and knowledge of the child's specific needs.[92] The EU Agency for Fundamental Rights stresses that without specialist knowledge children are exposed to further risks, especially when they are particularly vulnerable.[93] It is hoped that Brexit and its tendency towards isolationism does not dissuade the UK from looking across its borders at how standards for the care of migrant children could be further improved.

Further, while the UK's continued membership of the CoE will mean that its obligations under the Trafficking Convention and ECHR will remain unaltered post-Brexit, the disapplication of the EU anti-trafficking standards will cause a great loss in procedural and substantive safeguards, especially insofar as children are concerned.

The additions brought by the UK's opt-in to the Directive have been clearly visible in the UK legal framework.[94] Most importantly, on top of a wide array of

88 'Campaigners celebrate Modern Slavery Act success' (ECPAT UK, March 2015), https://www.ecpat.org.uk/news/campaigners-celebrate-modern-slavery-act-success.

89 See Modern Slavery Act 2015, s 48.

90 Reception Conditions Directive (n. 21 above) Art. 24(1).

91 Ravi K.S. Kohli and others, 'Evaluation of Independent Child Trafficking Advocates trial: Final Report' (Home Office December, 2015).

92 Ibid., 25.

93 EU Agency for Fundamental Rights, 'Guardianship for children deprived of parental care: With a particular focus on their role in responding to child trafficking' (Publications Office of the European Union, 2015) 32.

94 As noted by ILPA, 'ILPA submission to the Joint Committee on Human Rights' (n. 52 above) [47] '[w]hen the UK decided to opt in, the Commission identified that it would need to amend existing trafficking offences to ... make mandatory appointing special representatives to support child witnesses during police investigations and criminal trials and to set out the rights of trafficked persons to assistance and support'.

safeguards for victims, ranging from social support to the possibility of obtaining a residence permit,[95] the Directive places a strong focus on the position of trafficked children, which is not currently reflected in full in the MSA. Key provisions to this effect – such as Preamble 2 or Article 16 – have not been transposed in domestic law.[96] Further complications have been raised in relation to the discrepancies in the transposition of the provision by UK nations.[97]

Significant discrepancies exist between the texts – and hence the substantive guarantees – provided by EU and UK instruments, creating serious risks for the level of protection afforded to trafficked children after Brexit. Reference must be made, for instance, to the issue of consent to acts forming part of the trafficking experience under UK and EU law. Article 2(5) of the Directive provides that when trafficking 'involves a child it shall be a punishable offence of trafficking in human beings even if none of the means set forth in paragraph 1 have been used'.[98] Recital 11 similarly provides that 'when a child is concerned, no possible consent should ever be considered valid'.

Conversely, section 1(5) of the MSA states that:

> '[t]he consent of a person (whether an adult or a child) to any of the [prohibited acts] does not preclude a determination that the person is being held in slavery or servitude, or required to perform forced or compulsory labour.'

This formulation marks an inevitable fracture in the level of protection granted in the two instruments, as the MSA would seem to give the same consideration to the element of consent irrespective of the person's age, thereby indirectly implying that there might be situations where the child's consent may be relevant for the purposes of determining whether there has been a prohibited behaviour.[99]

---

95 Ibid., [48]–[49].

96 Nuala Mole, 'Some Thoughts on the Impact of Brexit on the Rights of Children' (2017) 6 European Human Rights Law Review 529, 529.

97 Chloe Setter and Catherine Baker, *Child trafficking in the UK 2018: A snapshot* (ECPAT UK, June 2018)12.

98 Directive 2011/36/EU of the European Parliament and of the Council of 5 April 2011 on preventing and combating trafficking in human beings and protecting its victims, and replacing Council Framework Decision 2002/629/JHA (2011) OJ L 101 (Anti-trafficking Directive), Art. 2(1): 'Member States shall take the necessary measures to ensure that the following intentional acts are punishable: The recruitment, transportation, transfer, harbouring or reception of persons, including the exchange or transfer of control over those persons, by means of the threat or use of force or other forms of coercion, of abduction, of fraud, of deception, of the abuse of power or of a position of vulnerability or of the giving or receiving of payments or benefits to achieve the consent of a person having control over another person, for the purpose of exploitation.'

99 For an analysis of the effects of Brexit on trafficking victims, including the discrepancies in terms of protection, see Papadouli, 'Brexit: What's in Pandora's Box for asylum seekers and victims of human trafficking?' (n. 72 above): 'Unless mirroring provisions are incorporated into UK law soon, dealing with the host of issues above and further issues such as guardian

An argument could be made that the introduction at the domestic level of standards equivalent to those provided under the EU instruments may compensate for this loss.[100] However, as with asylum, the marked supranational character of trafficking as a phenomenon sensibly benefits from solutions that are also supranational in their nature. Further, the harm caused by trafficking is of such seriousness that a regulatory approach that allows a margin of discretion to those responsible for implementation is also deeply concerning. In the UK, this phenomenon is directly observed by the civil society organisation ECPAT UK (Every Child Protected Against Trafficking UK) in the context of the appointment of guardians for child VoTs.[101] Owing to the structural tendency towards legal harmonisation that is inherent in EU law, there is a constant attempt to minimise this margin of discretion by establishing common standards. With the UK leaving the EU, however, the divergences between the practices and standards upheld locally risk expanding uncontrollably, no longer hindered by the CJEU scrutiny or MS pressure.[102]

In spite of the legislative innovation brought by the MSA and some encouraging steps in terms of the overall response to the phenomenon, reports from specialist organisations on the ground insist that more needs to be done, especially with a view to upholding child protection standards in the UK's future management of asylum and migration.[103]

8. COOPERATION IN EU INFORMATION SYSTEMS AND THE AREA OF FREEDOM, SECURITY AND JUSTICE (AFSJ)

Another great loss caused by Brexit will be the end of cross-border cooperation with EU MS as well as IT networks in the area of security, crime prevention and migration management, resulting from the UK's withdrawal from: Europol,

appointment, unaccompanied children victims of human trafficking may suffer a great loss due to Brexit.'

100 ILPA, 'ILPA submission to the Joint Committee on Human Rights' (n. 52 above) [44].

101 Setter and Baker, *Child trafficking in the UK 2018* (n. 97 above) note that guardians 'must have the legal capacity to instruct solicitors on the child's behalf and to hold authorities to account effectively' but that 'the picture with regard to guardianship in the UK is mixed, with each administration adopting a conflicting approach. This worryingly means children receive different standards of protection in each area'.

102 Brexit and Children's Coalition, 'Making Brexit work for children: The impact of Brexit on young people' (November 2017), https://bit.ly/2RNy9WL 24 and 26.

103 Setter and Baker, *Child trafficking in the UK 2018* (n. 97 above): 'despite progress made in reporting of such cases and the advent of dedicated legislation across the UK. The ever-increasing statistics remind us that much more needs to be done to tackle child exploitation, both at home and overseas, and to protect its victims'.

Eurojust, the European Arrest Warrant, the European Criminal Records Information System (ECRIS), Schengen Information System (SIS, second generation) and the European Protection Order.[104] These systems play a key role in the conduct of investigations of crimes with a cross-border element, such as trafficking, and bring an added value to the tracing of missing persons.[105] This should be considered on top of the specialised instruments and agencies in the field of EU migration, to which the UK also subscribes: Eurodac, the European Asylum Support Office (EASO) and Frontex, among others. During its membership, the UK has been a keen member of EU security bodies and its general interest in continuing its participation in this framework has been reaffirmed during Brexit negotiations.[106]

In 2018, the EU took steps to reform and expand the mandate of its IT systems to achieve a greater interoperability and overcome 'a number of key shortcomings in the EU's information'.[107] To this end, the EU is working to establish a European integrated border management (EIBM), to 'prevent and detect cross-border crime, such as migrant smuggling, trafficking in human beings [and] referring persons who are in need of, or wish to apply for, international protection to the appropriate authorities'.[108]

While there are implications in terms of data protection and human rights,[109] a greater integration of IT systems can significantly contribute to tackling transnational crime. Europol, Eurodac, Eurojust and the Schengen Information System (SIS), particularly, have key powers in terms of data and information storage and a direct impact in combatting human trafficking or tracing missing persons, 'including children and vulnerable adults in need of protection'.[110] Perhaps as a reaction to Europol's report that 10,000 migrant

---

104 Brexit and Children's Coalition, 'Making Brexit work for children' (n. 102 above) 16–17.

105 Ibid., 16: 'the second generation Schengen Information System (SIS II) is an extensive database of (approximately 70 million) real time alerts about individuals and objects (such as vehicles) of interest to EU law enforcement agencies. It includes information on people wanted under a European Arrest Warrant for alleged crimes against children and on missing children.'

106 Department for Exiting the European Union, *The Future Relationship* (n. 52 above) 2.3.2 [55]–[56] and 2.5.1 [100]. See also Brexit and Children's Coalition, 'Making Brexit work for children' (n. 102 above) 15–18.

107 See Anja Radjenovic and Alina Dobreva, 'Protection of EU external borders' (European Parliament, January 2019), http://www.europarl.europa.eu/RegData/etudes/BRIE/2018/630316/EPRS_BRI(2018)630316_EN.pdf 1 and 8: to this effect 'in December 2017, the Commission put forward two specific proposals on interoperability: one for a regulation establishing a framework for interoperability between EU information systems on borders and visas and another for a regulation establishing a framework for interoperability between EU information systems on police and judicial cooperation, asylum and migration.'

108 Ibid., 4.

109 EU FRA, Opinion: 'Interoperability and fundamental rights implications' (April 2018), available at: https://bit.ly/2RO8GfY.

110 See Radjenovic and Dobreva, 'Protection of EU external borders' (n. 107 above) 3.

children went missing after arriving in Europe in 2016,[111] the reform proposal mentions the value of interoperability for the protection of children[112] and the issue is further pushed for in the report on the situation of fundamental rights in 2017, which calls on MS to 'introduce specific safeguards to guarantee that the interoperability of large-scale IT systems respects the fundamental rights of all citizens, with special attention being paid to the rights of children and vulnerable persons' and 'ensure that [its implementation] also fulfils child protection objectives, such as identifying missing children and assisting family reunification'.[113]

The UK's position vis-à-vis the Schengen system would remain relative unchanged by Brexit, as its participation in the SIS is inherently limited by not being part of the Schengen area, meaning that 'the UK cannot issue or access Schengen-wide alerts for refusing entry or stay into the Schengen area'.[114]

ECPAT and others expressed concern in this respect, warning against the risks associated with the country's isolation from systems of critical value for cross-border investigation and prosecution, and called for 'a strategy ... to negotiate on-going membership of the EU-level data, intelligence-sharing, training, research and security infrastructure with a view to protecting children'.[115] The largest losses would arguably come from the discontinuance of the UK's participation in Eurojust (particularly relevant for international trafficking), Europol, the European Arrest Warrant (EAW), the ECRIS and the European Protection Order for victims of crime.[116] The importance of these instruments is only enhanced when one considers that the UK faces particular issues when it comes to the rate of identification of victims and that the incidence of child trafficking has been observed to have grown considerably in recent times.[117]

---

111 Mark Townsend, '10,000 refugee children are missing, says Europol' *The Guardian* (30 January 2016), https://bit.ly/2bJXtHq.

112 European Commission Proposal (of June 2018) for a Regulation on establishing a framework for interoperability between EU information systems (police and judicial cooperation, asylum and migration) (12 December 2017), p.18, at: https://bit.ly/2Bk4Qmm.

113 Report on the situation of fundamental rights in the European Union in 2017 (2018/2103(INI)), available at: https://bit.ly/2D8RU2V, at para. 17.

114 European Commission, Migration and Home Affairs, the Schengen Information System, available at: https://ec.europa.eu/home-affairs/what-we-do/policies/borders-and-visas/schengen-information-system_en. See also Gutheil and others, 'The future relationship between the UK and the EU in the field of international protection following the UK's withdrawal from the EU' (n 49 above) 64, 74–75 and 83–84.

115 Brexit and Children's Coalition, 'Making Brexit work for children' (n. 102 above) 18.

116 Ibid., 17.

117 Setter and Baker, *Child trafficking in the UK 2018* (n. 97 above), state that based on 'Government estimates that there are 13,000 victims of modern slavery nationally, of which around a third (more than 4,000) are believed to be children. The head of the National Crime Agency (NCA) has stated more recently that the actual number of adult and child victims could be in the tens of thousands. In 2017, there were 2,118 children referred into the National

For example, Eurojust helps to enable cross-border cooperation in criminal investigations through the use of Joint Investigation Teams (JITs), consisting of judicial and police authorities from at least two MS. In 2016, 40% of JITs were related to human trafficking and the UK received the most funding of all EU MS, establishing 32 JITs in total.[118] In 2017, in spite of the announcement of Brexit, the UK remained the most active country in this area, taking part in 24 new JITs for a total of 65 cases.[119] The overall number of registered trafficking cases went from 93 to 132. Further, the contribution of the UK continued to be of great relevance, featuring as one of the most active MS for Europol cooperation.[120]

The UK's participation in Eurodac and Dublinet, which are designed to assist MS in the application of Dublin rules by storing asylum seekers' data and information, both in terms of fingerprints (Eurodac)[121] or international protection applications (Dublinet),[122] would also be undermined by Brexit. While not being part of all CEAS instruments, the UK participates in Eurodac and also opted in to reform proposals of 5 December 2016,[123] which expands the categories and types of data stored as well as the conditions of storage. Without disregarding the serious risks in terms of refugees' data protection carried by the reform proposal, which among other things aims to lower the age for fingerprinting from 14 to 6 years old,[124] the EU Fundamental

Referral Mechanism (NRM)' and 'Children comprised nearly half (41%) of the total number of suspected trafficking victims in 2017, and the number of children suspected of trafficking rose by a staggering 66% compared to the previous year', cross-referencing National Crime Agency (2018) and National Referral Mechanism statistics.

118 Anti-Trafficking Monitoring Group, 'Brexit & the UK's fight against modern slavery' (July 2017), https://www.antislavery.org/wp-content/uploads/2017/07/ATMG-Brexit-paper.pdf, 8–9. See also Susie Alegre and others, 'The Implications of the United Kingdom's Withdrawal From the European Union for the Area of Freedom, Security and Justice' (EU Policy Department for Citizens' Rights and Constitutional Affairs, December 2017), https://bit.ly/2BYxOc8, 16 and 32–33.

119 Eurojust, *Eurojust Annual Report 2017* (Eurojust, 2017) 15, 17 and 21.

120 Anti-Trafficking Monitoring Group, 'Brexit & the UK's fight against modern slavery' (July 2017), https://www.antislavery.org/wp-content/uploads/2017/07/ATMG-Brexit-paper.pdf, 7–8.

121 See Gutheil and others, 'The future relationship between the UK and the EU in the field of international protection following the UK's withdrawal from the EU' (n. 49 above) 58.

122 Ibid., 22.

123 Robert Goodwill, 'UK Parliament, European Union opt-in decision: EURODAC Regulation: Written statement – HCWS364' (15 December 2016), https://bit.ly/2AJE713.

124 Commission, 'Proposal for a Regulation of the European Parliament and of the Council on the establishment of "Eurodac" for the comparison of fingerprints for the effective application of [Regulation (EU) No 604/2013 establishing the criteria and mechanisms for determining the Member State responsible for examining an application for international protection lodged in one of the Member States by a third-country national or a stateless person], for identifying an illegally staying third-country national or stateless person and on requests for the comparison with Eurodac data by Member States' law enforcement authorities and Europol for law enforcement purposes (recast)' COM (2016) 272 final.

Rights Agency (FRA) noted the potential advantages of such reform to enhance child protection. This is provided that implementation is carried out in both a child-friendly and gender-sensitive manner, with due regard for fundamental rights.[125] As with Dublin, the continued access to Eurodac forms part of the UK's proposed plan after Brexit.[126]

9. CONCLUSION

Above all else the EU migrant crisis is a cross-border problem, requiring a cross-border solution. This chapter has examined how Brexit is likely to undermine the protection of fundamental rights of migrant and refugee children in the UK in a variety of areas, as well as what steps the UK has taken in an attempt to tackle the problem. While recognising the problems that persist when trying to cooperate at the supranational level, it would be naïve to think that meaningful change can occur in the context of dealing with the EU migrant crisis at a domestic level. This was all too painfully highlighted by the Dubs registration scheme enacted by the UK. After the UK had already been criticised by the EU Select Committee for its failure to take responsibility, it is difficult to see how the UK will improve its measures while outside of the EU.

However, the impact of Brexit is likely to be more pervasive in that all branches of the UK government may lean towards introspection and isolationism. For example, the decision not to incorporate the CFR into domestic legislation post-Brexit or the failure of the judges in *Help Refugees* to accord adequate weight and significance to the international framework governing children's rights is concerning. There is a growing complacency that the UK is able to implement the gold standard of human rights protection, without learning from or working with its European counterparts. This chapter suggests that there may in fact be a lot that the UK stands to lose through its decision to leave the EU, particularly affecting vulnerable, migrant children.

Overall, the impact of Brexit on migrant children's rights is hard to quantify, as the exact shape that Brexit will take is constantly evolving and almost impossible to predict. Yet, we may legitimately be concerned by what the outcome will be if it continues in its current direction. This chapter has sought to discuss just some of the implications that Brexit may have on migrant children, but the full extent of Brexit's consequences will only be known after January 2020 and beyond.

---

125 EU Agency for Fundamental Rights, 'The impact of the proposal for a revised Eurodac Regulation on fundamental rights' (FRA Opinion 6/2016, Vienna, 22 December 2016), 23. In particular, it was noted that: 'storing younger children's biometric data … would bring child protection advantages, particularly if accompanied by other measures. It could help detect and protect child victims of trafficking as well as trace and protect unaccompanied children who go missing, abscond or otherwise disappear.'

126 Department for Exiting the European Union, *The Future Relationship* (n. 52 above) 2.5.1. [100].

INDEX

ABOUT THE EDITORS

MARK KLAASSEN is Assistant Professor at the Institute of Immigration Law, Leiden University. His research focusses on the role of human rights and children's rights in international, European and Dutch immigration law. He regularly coordinates and lectures in various courses related to immigration law at Leiden Law School. He is a member on the Advisory Committee on Migration Affairs, an advisory body for the Dutch government and parliament on immigration law and policy, and a board member of the Dutch Association for Migration Research.

STEPHANIE RAP is Assistant Professor in children's rights at the Department of Child Law, Leiden University. Her academic interest lies in the field of the effective participation of children in diverse (judicial) procedures and settings, such as in asylum procedures, child justice, child care and protection and in schools. She teaches in the LL.M. programme entitled *Advanced Studies in International Children's Rights* at Leiden University on topics related to child justice, child victims and child protection. She is a member of the editorial board of the Flemish Journal on Youth and Children's Rights.

PETER RODRIGUES is Professor of Immigration Law at Leiden University and Chair of the Institute of Immigration Law. Between 2001–2010 he was head of the department of Research and Documentation at the Anne Frank House, Amsterdam. He has published widely on migration, statelessness, discrimination on the grounds of race and nationality, equal treatment and group actions. He has a special research interest in minors and migration and teaches the course on children's rights and migration in the LL.M. programme entitled *Advanced Studies in International Children's Rights* at Leiden University.

TON LIEFAARD is Vice-Dean of Leiden Law School and holds the UNICEF Chair in Children's Rights at Leiden University. He is the Director of the LL.M. programme entitled *Advanced Studies in International Children's Rights.* He teaches and publishes widely on issues related to international children's rights, child justice, children deprived of liberty, child-friendly justice and access to justice for children. He serves as a member of the Advisory Group of the UN Global Study on Children Deprived of their Liberty and is a member of the editorial boards of the International Journal of Children's Rights, Youth Justice and the Flemish Journal on Youth and Children's Rights.

www.ingramcontent.com/pod-product-compliance
Ingram Content Group UK Ltd.
Pitfield, Milton Keynes, MK11 3LW, UK
UKHW051921100926
8556IPUK00021B/1303

9 781780 689494